Retracing the Past

Readings in the History of the American People

VOLUME TWO • SINCE 1865

Third Edition

EDITORS

Gary B. Nash

University of California, Los Angeles

Ronald Schultz

University of Wyoming

 HarperCollinsCollegePublishers

Acquisitions Editor: Bruce Borland
Developmental Editor: Carol Einhorn
Project Coordination, Text and Cover Design: Proof Positive/
    Farrowlyne Associates, Inc.
Cover Illustration: San Francisco Art Commission/Don Beatty
Photo Researcher: Leslie Coopersmith
Production Manager: Kewal Sharma
Compositor: Proof Positive/Farrowlyne Associates, Inc.
Printer and Binder: Malloy Lithographing, Inc.
Cover Printer: Malloy Lithographing, Inc.

For permission to use copyrighted material, grateful acknowledgment is made to
the copyright holders on the first page of each reading, which are hereby made part
of this copyright page.

Retracing the Past: Readings in the History of the American People, Volume Two,
Since 1865, Third Edition

Library of Congress Cataloging-in-Publication Data

Retracing the past : readings in the history of the American people /
    editors, Gary B. Nash, Ronald Schultz. — 3rd ed.
        p. cm.
        Contents: v. 1. To 1877 — v. 2. Since 1865.
        ISBN 0-06-501060-4 (v. 1). — ISBN 0-06-501061-2 (v. 2)
        1. United States—History. I. Nash, Gary B. II. Schultz,
    Ronald, 1946– .
    E178.6.R45 1993
    973—dc20   93-27282
                                                             CIP

93 94 95 96 9 8 7 6 5 4 3 2 1

CONTENTS

Preface **v**

PART ONE
AN INDUSTRIALIZING PEOPLE 2

PART TWO
A MODERNIZING PEOPLE 76

PART THREE
A RESILIENT PEOPLE 180

PREFACE

This two-volume reader has been constructed to accompany the third edition of *The American People: Creating a Nation and a Society* (New York: HarperCollins, 1993), but we hope it will also prove a useful supplement to other books in American history. The essays have been selected with three goals in mind: first, to blend political and social history; second, to lead students to a consideration of the roles of women, ethnic groups, and laboring Americans in the weaving of the nation's social fabric; and third, to explore life at the individual and community levels. The book is also intended to introduce students to the individuals and groups that made a critical difference in the shaping of American history or whose experience reflected key changes in society.

A few of the individuals highlighted are famous—Benjamin Franklin, Abraham Lincoln, and Jackie Robinson, for example. A number of others are historically visible but are not quite household names—Squanto, Anne Hutchinson, Tecumseh, and John Muir. Some will be totally unknown to students, such as George Robert Twelves Hewes, a Boston shoemaker who witnessed some of the most important events of the American Revolution, and Absalom Jones, who bought his way out of slavery and became a leader of Philadelphia's free African-American community after the Revolution. Often the focus is on groups whose role in history has not been adequately treated—the Chinese in the building of the transcontinental railroad, the grassroots black leaders during Reconstruction, and the Hispanic agricultural workers of this century.

Some of these essays take us inside American homes, farms, and factories, such as the essays on working women in New York City before the Civil War and the families of Butte, Montana, who welcomed the radio into their lives during the 1920s and 1930s. Such essays, it is hoped, convey an understanding of the daily lives of ordinary Americans, who collectively helped shape their society. Other essays deal with the vital social and political movements that transformed American society: the debate over the Constitution in the 1780s; reform in the antebellum period; populism and progressivism in the late nineteenth and early twentieth centuries; and the rise of political conservatism in our own time.

Readability has been an important criterion in the selection of these essays. An important indicator of readability, in turn, is how vividly and concretely the authors have brought the past to life. The main objective of these readers is a palpable presentation of the past—one that allows students to sense and feel the forces of historical change and hence to understand them.

Gary B. Nash
Ronald Schultz

ACKNOWLEDGMENTS

In developing this volume of readings, the editors have been well advised by the following academic colleagues, who reviewed the previous edition and read preliminary tables of contents:

Rosemary Abend
El Camino College

Gregg Andrews
Southwest Texas State University

Ron Aquila
Ball State University

Sidney Bland
James Madison University

James D. Bolton
Coastline Community College

Catherine C. Catalfano
St. Vincent College

Gene Clanton
Washington State University

David Edmunds
Indiana University

James Fell
Metropolitan State College

Gretchen Harvey
North Dakota State University

Frances S. Hensley
Marshall University

Jerrold Hirsch
Northeast Missouri State University

M. Paul Holsinger
Illinois State University

Thomas B. Jones
Metropolitan State University

Tim Lehman
Rocky Mountain College

Sylvia W. McGrath
Stephen F. Austin State University

David Moore
Loyola University

Ian Mylchreest
University of Nevada

W. R. Swagerty
University of Idaho

In addition, Ronald D. Schultz of the University of Wyoming played a major role in preparing the introductory notes and in readying the manuscript for publication.

GBN

Retracing
the
Past

PART ONE

AN INDUSTRIALIZING PEOPLE

The post–Civil War decades witnessed the rapid expansion of heavy industry, large-scale immigration and urbanization, the effective completion of western settlement, and the continued subordination of African Americans not only in the South but in northern and western cities as well. But while the economic success of the late nineteenth century meant prosperity for some, it also meant wrenching changes in the lives of ordinary people, many of whom became disenchanted with the nation's new urban-industrial order.

The end of the Civil War posed one of the most critical questions in American social relations. The Thirteenth, Fourteenth, and Fifteenth Amendments to the Constitution had promised ex-slaves citizenship and civil rights and guaranteed freedmen the right to vote. But constitutional doctrine was one thing and social practice another. In "Black Reconstruction Leaders at the Grassroots," Eric Foner reveals the vital role of African-American leaders in shaping social and political relations in the postwar South. Much of the local character of southern politics before 1877, he argues, derived from the active participation of ex-slaves in the formal political process.

By the end of the nineteenth century, however, American race relations belied the promise of the Reconstruction era. In the North, informal discrimination kept African Americans outside the political process and confined them to menial, low-paying jobs. In the South, individual states passed "Jim Crow" laws that effectively disenfranchised African-American men, while the sharecropping system kept black families tied to the land through permanent indebtedness. When the federal government refused to enforce the Fourteenth and Fifteenth Amendments, it was left to reform organizations to provide an avenue for racial reform. In "Populist Dreams and Negro Rights," Lawrence C. Goodwyn analyzes the attempt by Texas Populists to achieve a semblance of racial parity during the 1890s. In the process, he also reveals the depth of the forces set against racial equality at the close of the century.

In 1865, the United States spanned some 3000 miles between its Atlantic and Pacific coasts, yet the cheapest and most effective form of transportation between East and West remained the arduous ocean route around the southern tip of South America. In 1863, the Civil War Congress sought to bind the nation together more effectively by authorizing the construction of a transcontinental railroad. Working feverishly from bases in California and Nebraska, Chinese and Irish immigrants forged a rail link that made rapid settlement of the western territories a practical possibility. In "The Chinese Link a Continent and a Nation," Jack Chen takes us into the world of Chinese workers who, using an unsurpassed knowledge of explosives learned in their native land, risked life and limb to blast a path for the Central Pacific Railroad through the granite mountains of the Sierra Nevada range. Christine Stansell, on the other hand, reconstructs the lives of "Women on the Great Plains" of Kansas, Nebraska, and the Dakotas. She finds that while some women welcomed resettlement as an adventure and a chance for a better life, most found western life something to be endured in the hope that the trappings of "civilization" would quickly follow along the rails stretching from the East.

The rapidly changing world of the industrial Northeast created both unparalleled opportunities for wealth and unprecedented examples of poverty and social dislocation. In this fluid world, the promise of upward mobility held a special appeal, as evidenced by the enormous popular success of Horatio Alger's rags-to-riches tales. In over a hundred short novels, Alger portrayed fictional characters who started low in life but rose to the heights of wealth. In "Of Factories and Failures," Carol Nackenoff reexamines the Alger stories in light of the growing importance of large factories in American working life. Alger, she argues, portrayed factory labor as a sure path to failure and warned his readers about the snares of dependent wage work. For Alger, respectable work was the key to success.

The rise of heavy industry also meant the rise of a wage-dependent industrial working class. But as David Brundage argues in "The Producing Classes and the Saloon," dependence on wage labor rubbed hard against the grain of working-class culture, with its emphasis on personal and political independence. Brundage contends that workers in Denver joined the Knights of Labor during the 1880s as much to assert their independent culture as to defend their position in the workplace.

The growing division between the very wealthy and the very poor challenged the social ethic of ordinary Americans, for whom a comfortable sufficiency remained the national ideal. As Milton Goldin shows in his study of "The Gospel of Andrew Carnegie," even this captain of industry felt the effects of the popular ethic. By donating millions of dollars to libraries and museums, Goldin argues, Carnegie sought to make wealth not a stigma but a means to improve American society.

1

BLACK RECONSTRUCTION LEADERS AT THE GRASSROOTS

ERIC FONER

The end of the Civil War in 1865 raised the question of the position of freedpeople in American society. Now that they were no longer slaves, would black Americans be allowed the same rights as white citizens? Should black males be allowed to vote? To serve on juries? To hold office? To own property? The Fourteenth and Fifteenth Amendments to the Constitution provided one answer to these questions: they gave to freedmen all of the rights of American citizenship, including the right to vote.

But constitutional principle was one thing and southern practice another. Through intimidation and violence, southern whites sought to maintain the old system of racial domination and white supremacy that had prevailed in the prewar South. Throughout the region, blacks were beaten for attempting to vote, black political leaders were assassinated, and the Ku Klux Klan was organized with the object of keeping blacks "in their place." By the late 1860s it was clear that white southerners were determined to prevent any change in their system of racial privilege and power.

However, the history of Reconstruction was not only a story of black suppression and white domination. Wherever they could, freedpeople reestablished the family and kinship ties they had lost during slavery. Meanwhile, thousands of ex-slaves flocked to urban areas in search of employment, and others purchased land and livestock in order to establish their economic independence. Most important, with citizenship rights guaranteed by the Constitution and the Union Army, southern blacks eagerly embraced politics as a means to gain an equal place for themselves in American society. From a series of black political conventions held in the early years of Reconstruction emerged a group of local black leaders who spoke for the rights of freedmen to not only economic opportunity and political and legal equity, but also the possession of confiscated Confederate land. In this essay, Eric Foner tells the story of these grassroots leaders and in the process reveals the hopes and dreams of freedpeople as well as the limits of black Reconstruction.

In November 1869, in Greene County, Georgia, disguised Klansmen forced Abram Colby into the woods "and there stripped and beat him in the most cruel manner, for nearly three hours." Born a slave and freed in 1851, Colby earned his living as a minister and barber. Since the end of the Civil War he had taken an active part in black political life, organizing "one of the largest and most enthusiastic" branches of Georgia's Equal Rights Association in 1866 and winning election to the state legislature two years later. According to the local agent of the American Missionary Association, Colby was whipped because he had recently appealed to Governor Rufus Bullock to protect the county's black population, and his assailants "had besides, as they said, many old scores against him, as a leader of his people in the county." Eighteen months later South Carolina Klansmen whipped Samuel Bonner, an unassuming black sharecropper, along with his mother and sister. Before the assault Bonner was asked if he were a Republican. "I told them," he later recalled, "I was that, and I thought it was right."

Minor episodes in the history of Reconstruction, these incidents nonetheless illuminate larger themes of its political culture and the nature of grassroots black leadership. Colby exemplifies the humble social status of local black leaders; although free before the Civil War, he was illiterate and, according to the 1870 census, owned no property. His experience in the legislature reveals the fragility of the black–white cooperation in Reconstruction politics, for white Republicans were among those who voted to expel Colby and other blacks. Bonner's willingness to assert his convictions in the face of violence epitomizes the depth of commitment that animated the Reconstruction black community. These small dramas guide us into the world of local black politics, its organization, ideology, and leadership during Reconstruction.

Southern black politics, of course, did not begin with the Reconstruction Act of 1867, as Abram Colby's career illustrates. Before the end of the Civil War, black political organizations had appeared in such Union-occupied areas as New Orleans. And in 1865 and 1866, in black conven-

tions throughout the southern states, future Reconstruction leaders like James T. Rapier and William H. Grey first came into prominence. By and large, however, the tone of these early conventions was moderate. Throughout the South, 1865 was a year of labor conflict, with freedpeople refusing to sign contracts and some seizing plantations and staking a claim to the soil. But the free-born mulattoes, ministers, and northern blacks who dominated the conventions all but ignored the land question.

Whatever the accomplishments of these conventions (and one delegate told the 1866 gathering in Tennessee that his constituents believed "we do nothing but meet, pass resolutions, publish pamphlets, and incur expenses"), the process of selecting delegates politicized black communities. Some delegates were elected by local mass meetings; others were sent by churches, clubs, and black army units stationed in the South. In the fall of 1866, two black men held "a regular canvass" in Greene County, North Carolina; an organized election followed to choose a delegate to the state's second black convention. The local chapters of the Georgia Educational Association, established at the state's January 1866 black convention, became "schools in which the colored citizens learn their rights." Nonetheless, this first phase of political organization was spotty and uneven—large areas of the black belt remained untouched by organized political activity.

It was in 1867, the *annus mirabilis* of Reconstruction, that a wave of political activism swept across the black belt. Itinerant lecturers, black and white, brought their message into the heart of the rural South. A black Baptist minister calling himself Professor J. W. Toer toured parts of Georgia and Florida "with a magic lantern to exhibit what he calls the progress of reconstruction. . . . He has a scene, which he calls 'before the proclamation,' another 'after the proclamation' and then '22nd Regt. U.S.C.T. Duncan's Brigade.'" Voting registrars held public meetings to instruct blacks on the nature of American government and "the individual benefits of citizenship in the nation and in the state." In Monroe County, Alabama, where no black political meetings had occurred before 1867, freedpeople crowded around the registrar shouting "God bless you," "Bless God for this." Throughout the South there were complaints of blacks neglecting plantation labor: "they stop at any time and go off to Greensboro or any other place to attend a political meeting" complained a white Alabamian. So great was the enthusiasm for politics that, as one former slave minister later wrote, "politics got in our midst and our revival or religious work for a while began to wane." Although suffrage was restricted to men, black women and even children often played a vocal part in political gatherings. One plantation manager summed up the situation: "You never saw a people more excited on the subject of politics than are the negroes of the south. They are perfectly wild."

The meteoric rise of black political activity was reflected in the growth of the Union League. Few developments of this period are more tinged with irony than the metamorphosis of a loyalist club, developed among the respectable middle classes of the Civil War North, into the political expression of impoverished freedpeople. An earlier generation of historians tended to dismiss the Union League by portraying it as a vehicle through which carpetbaggers manipulated the votes of gullible blacks, who were attracted to its meetings by secret passwords and colorful initiation rites. In fact, its purposes were far more complex: the league served simultaneously as "a political school for the people," as a North Carolina teacher described it, a vehicle for the emergence of a greatly expanded class of black political leaders, and an institutional structure blacks could utilize for their own purposes and through which they could articulate their own aspirations.

Even before 1867, local Union League branches had sprung up among blacks in some parts of the South, and the order had spread rapidly among Unionist whites in the Alabama, Georgia, and Tennessee hill country. In 1867, as blacks poured into the league, many white members either withdrew or formed segregated local chapters. Many local leagues were all-black or all-white, but integrated leagues also existed, in which black and white Republicans achieved a remarkable degree of interracial harmony. In Union County, North Carolina, a racially mixed league met "in old fields, or in some out of the way house, and elect[ed] candidates to be received into their body."

By the end of 1867 it seemed that virtually every black voter in the South had enrolled in the Union League, the Loyal League, or some equivalent local political organization. Meetings were generally held in a black church or school, or at the home of some prominent black individual, or if necessary, secretly in woods or fields. In Paulding, Mississippi, a hundred or more blacks, along with a few whites, met monthly at the home of Jim Cruise, a black house carpenter. Usually, a Bible and a copy of the Declaration of Independence and the Constitution lay on a table, a minister opened the meeting with a prayer, new members took an initiation oath, and there were pledges to support the Republican party and uphold the principle of equal rights.

The main function of these meetings, however, was political education. "We just went there," related Henry Holt, an illiterate black league member from North Carolina, "and we talked a little; made speeches on one question and another." Republican newspapers were read aloud, candidates were nominated for office, and political issues were debated. One racially mixed league discussed at various meetings the organization of a July 4 celebration, cooperation between the league and the Heroes of America (a secret white Unionist organization dating from the Civil War), and issues like disenfranchisement, debt relief, and public education which were likely to arise at the forthcoming constitutional conventions. In Maryville, Tennessee, the Union League held weekly discussions on the issues of the day—the impeachment of President Johnson, the national debt, and such broader questions as, Is the education of the female as important as that of the male? Should students pay corporation tax? Should East Tennessee be a separate state? Although mostly white in membership in a county only one-tenth black, this league called for Tennessee to send at least one black to Congress. In 1868 its members elected a black justice of the peace and four blacks to the seven-member city commission.

It would be an error, however, to assume that the Union leagues were "political" only in the sense of electoral politics. Their multifaceted activities reflected what might be called the politicization of everyday life during Reconstruction. Colleton County, South Carolina, league members (led by a freedman with the venerable Palmetto State name Wade Hampton) marched in a body to the local magistrate demanding the arrest of a white man who had injured a black with a slingshot. A local North Carolina league official—a minister describing himself as "a poor Colord man"—proposed to Governor Holden that the league "stand as gardians" for blacks who "don't know how to make a bargain . . . and see that they get the money." In Alabama's black belt, league organizer George W. Cox was besieged by freedpeople requesting information about suing their employers, avoiding fines for attending political meetings, and ensuring a fair division of crops at harvest time. Two of the most militant collective actions by blacks during Georgia Reconstruction, the Ogeechee uprising of 1869 and Cudjo Fye's "rebellion" of 1870, were sparked by the arrest of league members by white authorities.

In 1867 and 1868 Union League activity reached its zenith. By 1869 it had begun to decline in many parts of the South, disrupted by Klan violence or absorbed into the burgeoning apparatus of the Republican party. "It is all broke up," said one black member from Graham, North Carolina, an area of rampant Klan activity. In Texas, Republican chieftain James Tracy moved to assimilate the leagues into a more disciplined party structure, evoking strong protests from militant black leaders like the legislator Matthew Gaines. But in wide areas of the black belt, the tradition of local political organization embodied in the leagues persisted throughout Reconstruction. Sometimes the names changed, but the structure and purposes remained the same. In Abbeville County, South Carolina, the Union League was succeeded by The Brotherhood, the United Brethren, and finally, in 1865, the Laboring Union; as former slave A. J. Titus explained, "they was all laboring men, you see." In the Vicksburg region a successor to the Union

League, called the "council" by blacks, met until 1874 to discuss self-protection and Republican politics. Its members, armed with pistols and shotguns, unsuccessfully resisted white efforts to oust black sheriff Peter Crosby in the Vicksburg crisis of December 1874.

In this hothouse atmosphere of political mobilization, the Union leagues generated a new class of local black political leaders. Local leaders in the black belt, where few free blacks had lived before the Civil War, and especially outside Lousiana and South Carolina, with their large and politically active freeborn communities, tended to be former slaves of very modest circumstances. Many were teachers and preachers or other individuals who possessed a skill of use to the community. Former slave Thomas Allen, a Union League organizer elected to the Georgia legislature, was a propertyless Baptist preacher, shoemaker, and farmer. But what established him as a leader was literacy: "In my county the colored people came to me for instructions, and I gave them the best instructions I could. I took the New York Tribune and other papers, and in that way I found out a great deal, and I told them whatever I thought was right." In occupation, the largest number of local black leaders appear to have been artisans, men whose skill and independence marked them as leaders but who were still deeply embedded in the life of the black community. There were others, apparently lacking in distinctive attributes of status, respected for personal qualities—oratorical ability, a reputation for moral standing, or simply good sense, honesty, or a concern for the welfare of their neighbors. Calvin Rogers, a black constable murdered by the Florida Klan, was described by another freedman as "a thorough-going man; he was a stump speaker, and tried to excite the colored people to do the right thing. . . . He would work for a man and make him pay him." Others were men who had achieved prominence as slaves before emancipation, like Louisiana justice of the peace Hamilton Gibson, a "conjurer."

In his study of social and political organizations among Memphis blacks, Armstead Robinson has identified a fairly sharp distinction between political leaders, who tended to be prosperous and light of skin, and religious/benevolent leaders, who were generally unskilled former slaves. In the less-stratified rural black belt, however, lines of occupation and social function frequently overlapped; preachers and teachers earned their living in part as artisans or laborers, politicians helped establish churches, meetings of fraternal organizations discussed political events, and Union leagues raised money for black schools. This was a world suffused with politics, in which local leaders gave articulate expression to the multiplicity of grievances and the timeless aspirations of their humble constituents.

In Union leagues, Republican gatherings, and impromptu local meetings, black and white Republicans in these years debated the basic question of the polity—What was the meaning of freedom and citizenship in a republican America? Black leaders drew upon a broad range of experiences and ideas, some derived from slavery itself and others grounded in the traditions of the larger society, in defining the bounds of black politics. The language of American republicanism suffused black political culture. As Rev. J. M. Hood put it at the North Carolina Constitutional Convention of 1868, "the colored people had read . . . the Declaration [of Independence] until it had become part of their natures." A petition of eleven Alabama blacks complaining in 1865 of contract frauds, injustice before the courts, the refusal of whites to rent land to freedpeople, and other abuses, concluded with a revealing masterpiece of understatement: "this is not the pursuit of happiness." And ten years later, a group of Louisiana freedpeople felt it appropriate to open their petition for the removal of a hostile local official with these well-known words: "We the people of Louisiana in order to establish justice, insure domestic tranquility, promote the general welfare . . . do ordain and establish this Constitution."

There was much more here than simply accustomed language; blacks, freeborn and slave, were staking their claim to equal citizenship in the American republic. To them the republican inheritance implied the rights to vote and to education, the free exercise of religion, access to the courts, and equal opportunity in all the avenues of economic enterprise—every right already enjoyed by whites. As one black delegate to the Virginia Constitutional Convention put it, no civil right "ever enjoyed by citizens prior to the year 1861" could now justifiably be denied to blacks. Anything less would be a violation of the principles upon which the nation had been founded. As Louisiana's Oscar J. Dunn insisted, "it is the boast and glory of the American republic that there is no discrimination among men, no privileges founded upon birth-right. There are no hereditary distinctions." Continued proscription of blacks, Dunn warned, would undermine the republic and "open the door for the institution of aristocracy, nobility, and even monarchy."

At their most utopian, blacks in Reconstruction envisioned a society purged of all racial distinctions. This did not mean the abandonment of race consciousness—there is abundant evidence that blacks preferred black teachers for their children as well as black churches and ministers. But in the polity, blacks, who had so long been proscribed because of their color, defined equal citizenship as color-blind. Thomas Bayne told the Virginia Constitutional Convention that his constituents expected him to help draft a constitution "that should not have the word black or white anywhere in it." Politicians seeking to arouse a sense of racial self-consciousness sometimes found black audiences unreceptive to their message. Martin Delany, the "father of black nationalism," discovered in South Carolina that it was "dangerous to go into the country and speak of color in any manner whatever, without the angry rejoinder, 'we don't want to hear that; we are all one color now.'" He was astonished to find that the freedpeople did not share his belief in the necessity of electing blacks (particularly Martin Delany) to office. Rather, they believed "that the Constitution had been purged of color by a Radical Congress."

The black claim to equal citizenship was grounded in more than a restatement of republican principles, however. Repeatedly in Reconstruction it was linked as well to black participation in the Civil War. Indeed, while blacks revered Lincoln as the Great Emancipator, it was also an article of faith that they had helped emancipate themselves. "They say," an Alabama planter reported in 1867, "the Yankees could never have whipped the south without the aid of the negroes." At the same time, the secular claim to citizenship was underpinned by a religious messianism deeply rooted in the black experience. As slaves, blacks had come to think of themselves as analogous to the Jews in Egypt, an oppressed people whom God, in the fullness of time, would deliver from bondage. They viewed the Civil War as God's instrument of deliverance, and Reconstruction as another step in a divinely ordained process. Black religion reinforced black republicanism, for, as Rev. J. M. P. Williams, a Mississippi legislator, put it in an address to his constituents in 1871, "my dear friends, remember this, of one blood God did make all men to dwell upon the face of the whole earth . . . hence, their common origin, destiny and equal rights." Even among nonclerics, secular and religious modes of political discourse were virtually interchangeable. One example is a speech by North Carolina black Edwin Jones, as reported by a justice of the peace in 1867: "He said it was not now like it used to be, that . . . the negro was about to get his equal rights. . . . That the negroes owed their freedom to the courage of the negro soldiers and to God. . . . He made frequent references to the II and IV chapters of Joshua for a full accomplishment of the principles and destiny of the race. It was concluded that the race have a destiny in view similar to the Children of Israel."

Republicanism, religious messianism, and historical experience combined to produce in black political Reconstruction culture a profound sense of identification with the American polity. The very abundance of letters and petitions addressed by ordinary freedpeople to officials of the army, the Freedmen's Bureau, and state and federal authorities revealed a belief that the political order was open to black participation and persuasion. Blacks enthusiastically embraced that hallmark of the Civil War era, the rise of an activist state. With wealth, political experience, and tradition all mobilized against them in the South, blacks saw in political authority a countervailing power. On the local and state level, black officials pressed for the expansion of such public institu-

tions as schools and hospitals. And in proposing measures (generally not enacted) for free medical care and legal assistance for the poor, government regulation of private markets, restrictions on the sale of liquor, and the outlawing of fairs and hunting on Sunday, they revealed a vision of the democratic state actively promoting the social and moral well-being of its citizenry.

It was the national government, however, that blacks ultimately viewed as the guarantor of their rights. Those whose freedom had come through the unprecedented exercise of federal authority were utterly hostile to theories of state rights and local autonomy. As Frederick Douglass put it, until Americans abandoned the idea of "the right of each State to control its own local affairs, . . . no general assertion of human rights can be of any practical value." Blacks did not share fears of "centralism" common even in the Republican party; like white Radical Republicans, black leaders found in the guarantee of republican government—the "most pregnant clause" of the Constitution, Robert B. Elliott called it—a grant of federal power ample enough to promote the welfare and protect the rights of individual citizens. Throughout Reconstruction, black political leaders supported proposals for such vast expansions of federal authority as James T. Rapier's plan for a national educational system, complete with federally mandated textbooks.

The course of events during Reconstruction reinforced this tendency to look to the national government for protection. The inability of state and local authorities to control violence prompted demands for federal intervention. "We are more slave today in the hand of the wicked than we were before," read a desperate plea from five Alabama blacks. "We need protection . . . only a standing army in this place can give us our right and life." Blacks enthusiastically supported the Enforcement Acts of 1870 and 1871 and the expansion of the powers of the federal judiciary. One black convention went so far as to insist that virtually all civil and criminal cases involving blacks be removable from state to federal courts, a mind-boggling enhancement of federal judicial authority. To constitutional objections, most blacks would agree with Congressman Joseph

Rainey: "Tell me nothing of a constitution which fails to shelter beneath its rightful power the people of a country."

Republican citizenship implied more than political equality overseen by an active state, however. It helped legitimize the desire for land so pervasive among the freedpeople, for a society based upon a landed aristocracy and a large propertyless lower class could not be considered truly republican. "Small estates are the real element of democracy," wrote the *New Orleans Tribune*. "Let the land go into the hands of the actual laborers."

In 1865 and 1866 the claim to land found little expression at statewide black conventions. In 1867, however, the situation was very different. At the grassroots, demands for land among blacks and, in some areas, poor whites animated early Republican politics. The advent of suffrage and Thaddeus Stevens's introduction of a confiscation bill in the House rekindled expectations that had, in most areas, subsided after January 1866. A northern correspondent reported that "Thad Stevens' speech has been circulated among those of them who can read and fully expounded to those of them who cannot." As southern Republican parties were organized in the spring of 1867, virtually every convention found itself divided between "confiscation radicals" and more moderate elements. In Mississippi, a black delegate proposed that the party commit itself to the confiscation of Confederate estates and their distribution to freedpeople. At a black mass meeting in Richmond, a freedman announced that large holdings belonging to rebels should be confiscated for the benefit of poor, loyal blacks. The issue was most divisive in North Carolina, where local demands for land were voiced by both black Union leagues and loyalist whites in the Heroes of America. One delegate told the state Republican convention, "the people of this State have a hope in confiscation, and if that is taken away the Republican party [will] give away the power they have gained."

The outcome of the confiscation debate reveals a great deal about the limits within which black politics could operate during Reconstruction. No state convention endorsed the idea,

although a few called for planters voluntarily to sell land to impoverished freedmen. The obstacles to confiscation were indeed immense. National Republican leaders, including long-time radicals like Henry Wilson, publicly condemned Stevens's initiative. "Let confiscation be, as it should be, an unspoken word in your state," Wilson advised North Carolina black leader James H. Harris. Democratic victories in the 1867 northern elections reinforced the conviction that Reconstruction had gone far enough; more radical policies would jeopardize Republican electoral chances in 1868 and beyond.

Even among southern Republicans there was strong opposition to the confiscation idea. Most white Republican leaders were committed to what Mark Summers calls the "Gospel of Prosperity," believing that their party's prospects hinged on a program of regional economic development and diversification. While envisioning the eventual demise of the plantation system, this "gospel" called for respect for individual enterprise and desired to encourage northern investment in the South, both seemingly incompatible with confiscation. Then, too, most white Republicans fully embraced the free labor ideology, insisting that while possession of land was unquestionably desirable, the freedpeople, like all Americans, would have to acquire it through hard work. Alabama carpetbagger C. W. Dustan solemnly announced that lands "cannot be owned without being earned, they cannot be earned without labor. . . ." (Dustan did not exactly follow this free labor prescription in his own life: he acquired a sizable holding by marrying the daughter of a Demopolis planter.)

Of course, as Thomas Holt has demonstrated, the black community itself was divided on the land question. The free labor ideology, with its respect for private property and individual initiative, was most fully embraced by two sets of black leaders—those from the North and the better-off southern free Negroes. Prominent northern blacks like Jonathan Gibbs and James Lynch would insist during Reconstruction that the interests of labor and capital were identical. Among "black carpetbaggers" only Aaron A.

Bradley became actively involved in the land struggles of the freedpeople. So, too, the free black leadership of Charleston and New Orleans rejected confiscation. At Louisiana's Republican state convention, "all the freedmen, *save one*, were in favor of confiscation, and the measure would have been adopted . . . had it not been for the energetic exertions of the white and free born colored members." Their own experience convinced successful free blacks that freedpeople required not government largesse but only an equal chance.

I have dwelt at length on the years 1867 and 1868, not only because of the remarkable political mobilization of the black community, but because many of the dilemmas that would confront black political leaders were by then already fully evident. In utopian aspirations for a New South with a reconstructed racial and economic order, these years revealed the radical potential inherent in Reconstruction. But the fate of the confiscation debate presaged the rapid waning of the radical impulse, both nationally and in the South. Increasingly, black politics took on a defensive cast; in place of demands for a fundamental restructuring of southern society, politics came to revolve around preserving what gains had been achieved and making the existing order operate fairly (a difficult task at best in a plantation society).

Comprising the vast majority of Republican voters, blacks would remain junior partners within the party. Even in Louisiana they would be barred from the most important positions; as one prominent black there complained in 1874, "we share, neither . . . in the control of the government which we have created, nor participate in the patronage resulting from political victories we have won." Only in Mississippi and South Carolina would blacks come to play a dominant role in shaping Reconstruction policy. But even there, politics never escaped a "colonial" pattern—the interests of the national Republican party always took precedence over the needs of the localities. Unable to establish their own legitimacy in the eyes of their powerful opponents, the survival of the new southern governments ultimately rested on federal support. Thus, the

boundaries of Reconstruction were determined in Washington. As Albert T. Morgan observed of Mississippi, "three-fourths of the republican members of the Legislature regard themselves as still under the control and dominion of *Congress* as the supreme government. They can hardly settle our per diem without the feeling of *subserviency to Congress.*"

As Reconstruction wore on, black political leaders were caught in a web of seemingly insoluble dilemmas. The few black congressmen had to choose between supporting national economic policies like a deflationary monetary program, arguably detrimental to the interests of their constituents, and joining Democrats in opposition, which would further alienate northern Republican support. Their broad conception of federal authority was increasingly out of step with a national party described by U.S. Attorney General Amos T. Akerman as "anxious for an end of Southern troubles" and convinced that "Southern Republicans must cease to look for special support to Congressional action." By the mid-1870s it was well understood in the South that the remaining Republican states could expect no help from federal authorities. Former slave Jerry Thornton Moore, president of a local Republican club in Aiken County, South Carolina, was told by his white landlord that Democrats planned to carry the 1876 elections "if we have to wade in blood knee-deep." "Mind what you are doing," Moore responded; "the United States is mighty strong." Replied the white man, "but, Thornton, . . . the northern people is on our side."

Increasingly abandoned by the national party, black politicians had nowhere to turn. Democrats offered even less than Republicans, and at any rate, black voters refused to countenance independent politics. When Alabama legislator C. S. Smith proposed to the 1876 national black convention that blacks declare their political autonomy, he won hearty applause inside the hall, but "colored men on street corners" spoke of cutting his throat.

Blanche K. Bruce earned a grassroots reputation as a "conservative negro" for a Senate speech condemning Republican indifference to the plight of southern freedpeople. When Edward Shaw, a prominent Memphis black leader, ran for Congress in 1870 against the white Republican incumbent, he received only 165 votes. The 1870s did witness a rise in black political assertiveness and an increase (where Reconstruction survived) in the number of blacks holding office, but this could only take place within the context of the Republican party.

At the local level, numerous enclaves of genuine black political power existed during Reconstruction. Reporter Edward King, traveling across the South in 1873 and 1874, encountered many examples of black officeholding—black aldermen and city councilmen in Petersburg, Houston, and Little Rock; parish jury members in Louisiana; black magistrates in the South Carolina low country. Hundreds, perhaps thousands of blacks held positions ranging from constable to school board official, tax assessor, and sheriff. Their numbers were fewest in states like Georgia and Florida, where conservative Republicans had drafted constitutions centralizing appointive power in the hands of the governor, and most extensive in South Carolina and Mississippi. About a third of Mississippi's black population lived in one of the thirteen counties that elected a black sheriff, the official who collected taxes appointed registrars, and controlled selection of juries.

The existence of black and sympathetic white local officials often made a real difference in the day-to-day lives of the freedpeople, ensuring that those accused of crimes would be tried before juries of their peers (who, whites complained, often refused to convict in cases of vagrancy or theft) and enforcing fairness in such prosaic aspects of local government as road repair, public employment, and poor relief. In Louisiana, blacks, whites, and Chinese were employed to repair the levees, and, in a startling departure from traditional practice, all received the same wages. As the chief engineer reported, "our 'Cadian friends were a little disgusted at not being allowed double (colored) wages, and the Chinamen were astonished at being allowed as much and the American citizens of African descent were delighted at being '*par*.'" Any

doubt as to the importance of sympathetic local officials is quickly dispelled by a glance at the conduct of local government in counties remaining under Democratic control (as well as some localities dominated by conservative white Republicans). In such areas blacks persistently complained of exclusion from juries, discrimination in tax assessment and collection, and an inability to obtain justice before the courts. In one Democratic Alabama county in 1870, a black woman brutally beaten by a group of white men was forced to raise $16.45 for court costs before the judge released the offenders and instructed the injured woman to drop the matter or face a jail sentence. This state of affairs harked back to the mockery of justice practiced in southern courts during Presidential Reconstruction and looked ahead to the situation that would obtain under the Redeemers.

For some black politicos, as for many whites in nineteenth-century America, official positions became a means of social advancement. Politics was one of the few areas of dignified work open to black men of talent and ambition, and compared with other employment opportunities, the rewards of even minor office could seem dazzlingly high. The thirteen dollars per diem earned by members of the Louisiana Constitutional Convention, or the seven dollars per day plus mileage paid to North Carolina legislators, far outstripped the wages most blacks could ordinarily command. More important offices garnered far higher rewards—sheriffs could earn thousands of dollars in commissions and fees, and state officeholders were handsomely paid during Reconstruction. Blacks consistently opposed attempts to reduce the pay of officials. As one black put it at the Virginia Constitutional Convention, "the salary is none too great. Many of us have no incomes." And, at any rate, as another black delegate observed, "all our troubles have arisen from not paying people for their services."

Some black politicians translated official positions into significant personal gain. Josiah Walls, a Florida congressman, was able to acquire a large estate formerly owned by Confederate general James H. Harrison, and Senator Blanche K.

Bruce accumulated a fortune in real estate. Louisiana lieutenant governor C. C. Antoine owned an expensive racehorse whose earnings were considerable. On a less-exalted level, about one-third of the forty-six blacks who served in the Virginia legislature used their salaries to purchase land. Like white politicos, some black officials were less than scrupulous in the pursuit of wealth. P. B. S. Pinchback, who lived in luxury in New Orleans, told a reporter that his wealth derived from "speculation upon warrants, bonds and stocks." Pinchback forthrightly admitted that inside information enabled his speculations to succeed: "I belonged to the General Assembly, and knew about what it would do. . . . My investments were made accordingly."

For most black leaders, however, politics brought little personal wealth. Even the most prominent found it difficult to translate political standing into a real share in the economic resources of their states. A Charleston streetcar company formed by leading black politicians and chartered by the state failed, as did the Mississippi River Packet Company organized by Pinchback, Antoine, and others. The black community was too poor to subscribe capital to such endeavors, and whites shunned them entirely.

Far from being a vehicle for social mobility, politics in many cases entailed devastating financial loss. Former slave Henry Johnson, a South Carolina Union League and militia leader, was a bricklayer and plasterer by trade. "I always had plenty of work before I went into politics," he remarked, "but I have never got a job since. I suppose they do it merely because they think they will break me down and keep me from interfering with politics." Jefferson Long, a Macon tailor, had commanded "much of the fine custom of the city" before embarking on a career that would take him briefly to Congress. However, "his stand in politics ruined his business with the whites who had been his patrons chiefly." Robert Reed, a black Alabama legislator, was told by local whites "that there is not a white man in the State that can beat me farming, and if I kept out of politics I would be the richest man in the State." Reed did not stop political organizing, but the costs of such commitment could be

high. When North Carolina black leader A. H. Galloway, a former soldier, brick mason, and state legislator, passed away in 1870, a black newspaper commented, "He died poor, very poor."

Loss of livelihood was not the most serious danger black political leaders had to face. Political violence, so pervasive in large portions of the Reconstruction South, was often directed precisely at local leaders—black officeholders, Union League organizers, and militia captains. As Emanuel Fortune, himself driven from Jackson County, Florida, by the Klan, explained, "the object of it is to kill out the leading men of the republican party. . . . They have never attacked any one but those who have been somewhat prominent in the party, men who have taken prominent stands." At least 10 percent of the black delegates to the 1867–68 constitutional conventions were victims of violence, including six actually murdered. Other assassination victims included men like Richard Burke, an Alabama preacher, schoolteacher, legislator, and Union League officer, and Wyatt Outlaw, Republican organizer in Alamance county, North Carolina. During the mid-1870s Redemption campaigns, political violence claimed the lives of black constables and justices of the peace in Issaquena County, Mississippi, and black militiamen and local officials in Hamburg, South Carolina, among many others. For every leader murdered, many more were driven from their homes. To remain politically active in such circumstances required a rare degree of personal courage and the kind of integrity epitomized by former slave David Graham, a deputy U.S. marshal in South Carolina, who told a congressional committee: "The white people liked me very well until I got into politics, and they have hated me ever since. . . . I heap rather farm than be in politics; politics is the most disgusting thing I was ever in in my life. I can't sleep in my house only part of the time. I want to get out of politics, but here I is; these other leading fellows can't get along without me."

Violence devastated the Republican party in many a local community. After a series of outrages in Union County, South Carolina, one black commented, "the Republican party, I may say, is scattered and beaten and run out. . . . They have no leaders up there—no leaders." The reign of terror in Yazoo County, Mississippi, in 1875, according to one black official, "got the republicans so demoralized that we did not know what to do. We had no leaders. Every leader had been run out of the town and out of the county. They did not know what to do, so they just 'hung up.'"

Indeed, it might be argued that the black community was more dependent on its political leadership, more vulnerable to the destruction of its political infrastructure by violence, than the white community. Local black leaders played such a variety of roles in schools, churches, and fraternal organizations, as well as politics, that the killing or exiling of one man affected a multiplicity of areas. For a largely illiterate constituency, local leaders were bridges to the larger world of politics, indispensable sources of political information and guidance. They were also looked to for assistance in contract disputes, advice about the marketing of crops, and all sorts of other issues. John R. Lynch later recalled how, when he served as a Mississippi justice of the peace, free blacks "magnified" his office "far beyond its importance," bringing him complaints ranging from disputes with their employers to family squabbles. Black officials epitomized the revolution that seemed to have put the bottom rail on top, the openness of the new political order to black influence. Their murder or exile inevitably had a demoralizing impact on their communities.

Alone among the nations that abolished slavery in this hemisphere, the United States accorded its former slaves legal and political equality within a few years after emancipation. The unprecedented character of this development, the sense among blacks that their newly won

rights were constantly at risk, the refusal of large numbers of Democrats to acknowledge freed blacks as part of the "political nation," helps explain the abnormal aspects of Reconstruction politics—the high degree of political mobilization in the black community, the burdens placed upon black leaders by their constituents, and the widespread use of violence and economic coercion as political weapons.

In the spring of 1868 a northern correspondent, reporting on election day in Alabama, captured the sense of hope with which Reconstruction opened, the conviction among the enfranchised black voters that politics could indeed change their lives. "In defiance of fatigue, hardship, hunger, the threats of employers," blacks had flocked to the polls. Not one in fifty wore an "unpatched garment," few possessed a pair of shoes, yet they stood for hours in a "pitiless storm." Why? "The hunger to have the same chances as the white men they feel and comprehend. . . . That is what brings them here" to vote. With the overthrow of Reconstruction, politics could no longer serve as an effective vehicle for expressing such aspirations. The emerging black political class was devastated by Redemption—murdered or driven from their communities by violence or deprived of the opportunity to hold office, except in a few exceptional areas of the South. Black politicians ceased to exercise real power, apart from a handful of men dependent on federal patronage and on prominent politicos who advised Republican presidents on token appointments for blacks. Men of ambition in the black community now found other outlets for their talents, whether in education, business, the church, or the professions. Nearly a century would pass before the southern black community was again as fully galvanized at the grassroots by political activity.

2

THE CHINESE LINK A CONTINENT AND A NATION

JACK CHEN

It is a historical commonplace that America is a nation of immigrants. From the original settlers of Jamestown in 1607 to the Hispanic and Asian immigrants of the 1990s, new Americans have loomed large in the national experience. But while immigration has always played an important role in American life, its impact was perhaps greatest during America's industrial revolution of the nineteenth century. From the 1820s, when 100,000 men, women, and children entered the United States, to the first decade of the twentieth century, when 8.2 million landed on American shores, more than 33 million immigrants came to the United States and helped build it into the world's premier industrial power.

Among these millions of immigrants, one group has received scant attention—the Chinese peasants, almost entirely males, who came to America as contract laborers to provide agricultural labor for California's central valley and to build railroads and levees in the West. Unlike European immigrants who arrived as free men and women in New York and other eastern cities, the Chinese who landed in San Francisco were bound to the mercantile companies that acted as labor contractors and had advanced them the cost of their fare. Under this contract system, one of the Six Companies in San Francisco negotiated with an employer to provide workers at an agreed-upon rate. The Companies were then responsible for the supply, supervision, and discipline of the contract laborers.

As Jack Chen shows in this essay, these Chinese contract laborers braved the harshest of conditions to fulfill their contract to build America's first transcontinental railroad. Employing skills in excavation and the use of explosives, which they had brought from China, these Chinese workers carved a path through the solid granite of the Sierra Nevada range that opened the West to the remainder of the nation.

The expansion of the railroad system in the United States was astonishingly swift. England had pioneered the building of railways and for a time was the acknowledged leader in the field, but from the moment the first locomotive was imported into the United States in 1829 the far-sighted saw railways as the obvious solution for transport across the vast spaces of the American continent. By 1850, 9,000 miles of rails had been laid in the eastern states and up to the Mississippi. The California Gold Rush and the opening of the American West made talk about a transcontinental line more urgent. As too often happens, war spurred the realization of this project.

The West was won. California was a rich and influential state, but a wide unsettled belt of desert, plain, and mountains separated it and Oregon from the rest of the states. As the economic separation of North and South showed, this situation was fraught with danger. It could lead to a political rift. In 1860, it was cheaper and quicker to reach San Francisco from Canton in China—a sixty-day voyage by sea—than from the Missouri River, six months away by wagon train. The urgent need was to link California firmly with the industrialized eastern states and their 30,000 miles of railways. A railway would cut the journey to a week. The threat of civil war loomed larger between North and South over the slavery issue. Abraham Lincoln's Republican administration saw a northern transcontinental railway as a means to outflank the South by drawing the western states closer to the North. In 1862, Congress voted funds to build the 2,500-mile-long railway. It required enormous resourcefulness and determination to get this giant project off the drawing boards. Not much imagination was required to see its necessity, but the actual building presented daunting difficulties. It was calculated that its cost would mount to $100 million, double the federal budget of 1861.

It was Theodore Judah, described by his contemporaries as "Pacific Railroad Crazy," who began to give substance to the dream. An eastern engineer who had come west to build the short Sacramento Valley Railroad, he undertook a pre-liminary survey and reported that he had found a feasible route crossing the Sierra by way of Dutch Flat. But the mainly small investors who supported his efforts could not carry through the whole immense undertaking. With rumors of civil war between North and South, San Francisco capitalists, mostly Southerners, boycotted the scheme as a northern plot, and pressed for a southern route. Then the Big Four, Sacramento merchants, took up the challenge: Leland Stanford as president, C. P. Huntington as vice-president, Mark Hopkins as treasurer, and Charles Crocker, in charge of construction, formed the Central Pacific Railway Company. Judah was elbowed out.

The Big Four came as gold seekers in 1849 or soon after but found that there was more money to be made in storekeeping than in scrabbling in the rocks in the mountains. As Republicans, they held the state for the Union against the secessionists. Leland Stanford, the first president of the Central Pacific, was also the first Republican governor of California.

The beginnings were not auspicious. The Union Pacific was building from Omaha in the East over the plains to the Rockies, but supplies had to come in by water or wagon because the railways had not yet reached Omaha. The Civil War now raged and manpower, materials, and funds were hard to get. The Indians were still contesting invasion of their lands. By 1864, however, with the Civil War ending, these problems were solved. The UP hired Civil War veterans, Irish immigrants fleeing famine, and even Indian women, and the line began to move westward.

The Central Pacific, building eastward from Sacramento, had broken ground on January 8, 1863, but in 1864, beset by money and labor problems, it had built only thirty-one miles of track. It had an even more intractable manpower problem than the UP. California was sparsely populated, and the gold mines, homesteading, and other lucrative employments offered stiff competition for labor. Brought to the railhead, three out of every five men quit immediately and took off for the better prospects of the new Nevada silver strikes. Even Charles Crocker, boss of construction and raging like a mad bull in the railway camps, could not control them. In the winter of 1864, the company had only 600 men working on the line when it had advertised for 5,000. Up to then, only white labor had been recruited, and California white labor was still motivated by the Gold Rush syndrome. They wanted quick wealth, not hard, regimented railway work. After two years only fifty miles of track had been laid.

James Strobridge, superintendent of construction, testified to the 1876 Joint Congressional Committee on Chinese Immigration: "[These] were unsteady men, unreliable. Some would not go to work at all. . . . Some would stay until pay day, get a little money, get drunk and clear out." Something drastic had to be done.

In 1858, fifty Chinese had helped to build the California Central Railroad from Sacramento to Marysville. In 1860, Chinese were working on the San Jose Railway and giving a good account of themselves, so it is surprising that there was so much hesitation about employing them on the Central Pacific's western end of the first transcontinental railway. Faced with a growing crisis of no work done and mounting costs, Crocker suggested hiring Chinese. Strobridge strongly objected: "I will not boss Chinese. I don't think they could build a railroad." Leland Stanford was also reluctant. He had advocated exclusion on the Chinese from California and was embarrassed to reverse himself. Crocker, Huntington, Hopkins, and Stanford, the "Big Four" of the Central Pacific, were all merchants in hardware, dried goods, and groceries in the little town of Sacramento. Originally, they knew nothing about railroad building, but they were astute and hard-headed businessmen. Crocker was insistent. Wasted time was wasted money. The CP's need for labor was critical. The men they already had were threatening a strike. Finally fifty Chinese were hired for a trial.

BUILDING THE TRANSCONTINENTAL RAILROAD

In February 1865, they marched up in self-formed gangs of twelve to twenty men with their own supplies and cooks for each mess. They ate a meal of rice and dried cuttlefish, washed and slept, and early next morning were ready for work filling dump carts. Their discipline and grading—preparing the ground for track laying—delighted Strobridge. Soon fifty more were hired, and finally some 15,000 had been put on the payroll. Crocker was enthusiastic: "They prove nearly equal to white men in the amount of labor they perform, and are much more reliable. No danger of strikes among them. We are training them to all kinds of labor: blasting, driving horses, handling rock as well as pick and shovel." Countering Strobridge's argument that the Chinese were "not masons," Crocker pointed out that the race that built the Great Wall could certainly build a railroad culvert. Up on the Donner Pass today the fine stonework embankments built by the Chinese are serving well after a hundred years.

Charles Nordhoff, an acute observer, reports Strobridge telling him, "[The Chinese] learn all parts of the work easily." Nordhoff says he saw them "employed on every kind of work. . . . They do not drink, fight or strike; they do gamble, if it is not prevented; and it is always said of them that they are very cleanly in their habits. It is the custom, among them, after they have had their suppers every evening, to bathe with the help of small tubs. I doubt if the white laborers do as much." As well he might. Well-run boarding-houses in California in those days proudly advertised that they provided guests with a weekly bath.

Their wages at the start were $28 a month (twenty-six working days), and they furnished all their own food, cooking utensils, and tents. The headman of each gang, or sometimes an American employed as clerk by them, received all the wages and handed them out to the members of the work gang according to what had been earned. "Competent and wonderfully effective because tireless and unremitting in their industry," they worked from sun-up to sun-down.

All observers remarked on the frugality of the Chinese. This was not surprising in view of the fact that, with a strong sense of filial duty, they came to America in order to save money and return as soon as possible to their homes and families in China. So they usually dressed poorly, and their dwellings were of the simplest. However, they ate well; rice and vermicelli (noodles) garnished with meats and vegetables; fish, dried oysters, cuttlefish, bacon and pork, and chicken on holidays, abalone meat, five kinds of dried vegetables, bamboo shoots, seaweed, salted cabbage, and mushroom, four kinds of dried fruit, and peanut oil and tea. This diet shows a considerable degree of sophistication and balance compared to the beef, beans, potatoes, bread, and butter of the white laborers. Other supplies were purchased from the shop maintained by a Chinese merchant contractor in one of the railway cars that followed them as they carried the railway line forward. Here they could buy pipes, tobacco, bowls, chopsticks, lamps, Chinese-style shoes of cotton with soft cotton soles, and ready-made clothing imported from China.

On Sundays, they rested, did their washing, and gambled. They were prone to argue noisily, but did not become besotted with whiskey and make themselves unfit for work on Monday. Their sobriety was much appreciated by their employers.

Curtis, the engineer in charge, described them as "the best roadbuilders in the world." The once skeptical Strobridge, a smart, pushing Irishman, also now pronounced them "the best in the world." Leland Stanford described them in a report on October 10, 1865, to Andrew Johnson:

> As a class, they are quiet, peaceable, patient, industrious, and economical. More prudent and economical [than white laborers] they are contented with less wages. We find them organized for mutual aid and assistance. Without them, it would be impossible to complete the western portion of this great national enterprise within the time required by the Act of Congress.

Crocker testified before the congressional committee that "if we found that we were in a hurry for a job of work, it was better to put on Chinese at once." All these men had originally resisted the employment of Chinese on the railway.

Four-fifths of the grading labor from Sacramento to Ogden was done by Chinese. In a couple of years more, of 13,500 workers on the payroll 12,000 were Chinese. They were nicknamed "Crocker's Pets."

APPRECIATING CHINESE SKILLS

The Chinese crews won their reputation the hard way. They outperformed Cornish men brought in at extra wages to cut rock. Crocker testified,

> They would cut more rock in a week than the Cornish miners, and it was hard work, bone labor. [They] were skilled in using the hammer and drill, and they proved themselves equal to the very best Cornish miners in that work. They were very trusty, they were intelligent, and they lived up to their contracts.

Stanford held the Chinese workers in such high esteem that he provided in his will for the permanent employment of a large number on his estates. In the 1930s, some of their descendants were still living and working lands now owned by Stanford University.

The Chinese saved the day for Crocker and his colleagues. The terms of agreement with the government were that the railway companies would be paid from $16,000 to $48,000 for each mile of track laid. But there were only so many miles between the two terminal points of the projected line. The Union Pacific Company, working with 10,000 mainly Irish immigrants and Civil War veterans, had the advantage of building the line through Nebraska over the plains and made steady progress. The Central Pacific, after the first easy twenty-three miles between Newcastle and Colfax, had to conquer the granite mountains and gorges of the Sierra Nevada and Rockies before it could emerge onto the Nevada-Utah plains and make real speed and money. The line had to rise 7,000 feet in 100 miles over daunting terrain. Crocker and the Chinese proved up to the challenge. After reaching Cisco, there was no easy going. The line had to be literally carved out of the Sierra granite, through tunnels and on rock ledges cut on the side of precipices.

Using techniques from China, they attacked one of the most difficult parts of the work: carrying the line over Cape Horn, with its sheer granite buttresses and steep shale embankments, 2,000 feet above the American River canyon. There was no foothold on its flanks. The indomitable Chinese, using age-old ways, were lowered from above in rope-held baskets, and there, suspended between earth and sky, they began to chip away with hammer and crowbar to form the narrow ledge that was later laboriously deepened to a shelf wide enough for the railway roadbed, 1,400 feet above the river.

Behind the advancing crews of Chinese builders came the money and supplies to keep the work going. This was an awesome exercise in logistics. The Big Four, unscrupulous, dishonest, and ruthless on a grand scale, were the geniuses of this effort. The marvel of engineering skill being created by Strobridge and his Chinese and Irish workers up in the Sierra was fed by a stream of iron rails, spikes, tools, blasting powder, locomotives, cars, and machinery. These materials arrived after an expensive and hazardous eight-month, 15,000-mile voyage from East Coast ports around Cape Horn to San Francisco, thence by river boat to Sacramento, and so to the railhead by road.

The weather, as well as the terrain, was harsh. The winter of 1865–1866 was one of the severest on record. Snow fell early, and storm after storm blanketed the Sierra Nevada. The ground froze solid. Sixty-foot drifts of snow had to be shoveled away before the graders could even reach the roadbed. Nearly half the work force of 9,000 men were set to clearing snow.

In these conditions, construction crews tackled the most formidable obstacle in their path: building the ten Summit Tunnels on the twenty-mile stretch between Cisco, ninety-two miles from Sacramento and Lake Ridge just west of Cold Stream Valley on the eastern slope of the summit. Work went on at all the tunnels simultaneously. Three shifts of eight hours each worked day and night.

The builders lived an eerie existence. In *The Big Four,* Oscar Lewis writes,

Tunnels were dug beneath forty-foot drifts and for months, 3,000 workmen lived curious molelike lives, passing from work to living quarters in dim passages far beneath the snow's surface. . . . [There] was constant danger, for as snows accumulated on the upper ridges, avalanches grew frequent, their approach heralded only by a brief thunderous roar. A second later, a work crew, a bunkhouse, an entire camp would go hurtling at a dizzy speed down miles of frozen canyon. Not until months later were the bodies recovered; sometimes groups were found with shovels or picks still clutched in their frozen hands.

On Christmas Day, 1866, the papers reported that "a gang of Chinamen employed by the railroad were covered up by a snow slide and four or five [note the imprecision] died before they could be exhumed." A whole camp of Chinese railway workers was enveloped during one night and had to be rescued by shovelers the next day.

No one has recorded the names of those who gave their lives in this stupendous undertaking. It is known that the bones of 1,200 men were shipped back to China to be buried in the land of their forefathers, but that was by no means the total score. The engineer John Gills recalled that "at Tunnel No. 10, some 15–20 Chinese [again, note the imprecision] were killed by a slide that winter. The year before, in the winter of 1864–65, two wagon road repairers had been buried and killed by a slide at the same location."

A. P. Partridge, who worked on the line, describes how 3,000 Chinese builders were driven out of the mountains by the early snow. "Most . . . came to Truckee and filled up all the old buildings and sheds. An old barn collapsed and killed four Chinese. A good many were frozen to death." One is astonished at the fortitude, discipline, and dedication of the Chinese railroad workers.

Many years later, looking at the Union Pacific section of the line, an old railwayman remarked, "There's an Irishman buried under every tie of that road." Brawling, drink, cholera, and malaria took a heavy toll. The construction crew towns on the Union Pacific part of the track, with their saloons, gambling dens, and bordellos, were nick-named "hells on wheels." Jack Casement, in charge of construction there, had been a general in the Civil War and prided himself on the discipline of his fighting forces. His work crews worked with military precision, but off the job they let themselves go. One day, after gambling in the streets on payday (instigated by professional gamblers) had gotten too much out of hand, a visitor, finding the street suddenly very quiet, asked him where the gamblers had gone. Casement pointed at a nearby cemetery and replied, "They all died with their boots on." It was still the Wild West.

It is characteristic that only one single case of violent brawling was reported among the Chinese from the time they started work until they completed the job.

The Central Pacific's Chinese became expert at all kinds of work: grading, drilling, masonry, and demolition. Using black powder, they could average 1.18 feet daily through granite so hard that an incautiously placed charge could blow out backward. The Summit Tunnel work force was entirely composed of Chinese, with mainly Irish foremen. Thirty to forty worked on each face, with twelve to fifteen on the heading and the rest on the bottom removing material.

The Donner tunnels, totaling 1,695 feet, had to be bored through solid rock, and 9,000 Chinese worked on them. To speed the work, a new and untried explosive, nitroglycerin, was used. The tunnels were completed in November 1867, after thirteen months. But winter began before the way could be opened and the tracks laid. That winter was worse than the preceding one, but to save time it was necessary to send crews ahead to continue building the line even while the tunnels were being cut. Therefore, 3,000 men were sent with 400 carts and horses to Palisade Canyon, 300 miles in advance of the railhead. "Hay, grain and all supplies for men and horses had to be hauled by teams over the deserts for that great distance," writes Strobridge. "Water for men and animals was hauled at times 40 miles." Trees were felled and the logs laid side by side to form a "corduroy"

roadway. On log sleds greased with lard, hundreds of Chinese manhandled three locomotives and forty wagons over the mountains. Strobridge later testified that it "cost nearly three times what it would have cost to have done it in the summertime when it should have been done. But we shortened the time seven years from what Congress expected when the act was passed."

Between 10,000 and 11,000 men were kept working on the line from 1866 to 1869. The Sison and Wallace Company (in which Crocker's brother was a leading member) and the Dutch merchant Cornelius Koopmanschap of San Francisco procured these men for the line. Through the summer of 1866, Crocker's Pets—6,000 strong—swarmed over the upper canyons of the Sierra, methodically slicing cuttings and pouring rock and debris to make landfills and strengthen the foundations of trestle bridges. Unlike the Caucasian laborers, who drank unboiled stream water, the Chinese slaked their thirst with weak tea and boiled water kept in old whiskey kegs filled by their mess cooks. They kept themselves clean and healthy by daily sponge baths in tubs of hot water prepared by their cooks, and the work went steadily forward.

Crocker has been described as a "hulking, relentless driver of men." But his Chinese crews responded to his leadership and drive and were caught up in the spirit of the epic work on which they were engaged. They cheered and waved their cartwheel hats as the first through train swept down the eastern slopes of the Sierra to the meeting of the lines. They worked with devotion and self-sacrifice to lay that twenty-odd miles of track fro the Central Pacific Company in 1866 over the most difficult terrain. The cost of those miles was enormous—$280,000 a mile—but it brought the builders in sight of the easier terrain beyond the Sierra and the Rockies. Here costs of construction by veteran crews were only half the estimated amount of federal pay.

By summer 1868, an army of 14,000 railway builders was passing over the mountains into the great interior plain. Nine-tenths of that work force was Chinese. More than a quarter of all Chinese in the country were building the railway.

When every available Chinese in California had been recruited for the work, the Central Pacific arranged with Chinese labor contractors in San Francisco to get men direct from China and send them up to the railhead. It was evidently some of these newcomers who fell for the Piute Indian's tall tales of snakes in the desert "big enough to swallow a man easily." Thereupon "four or five hundred Chinese took their belongings and struck out to return directly to Sacramento," reports the *Alta California*. "Crocker and Company had spent quite a little money to secure them and they sent men on horseback after them. Most of them came back again kind of quieted down, and after nothing happened and they never saw any of the snakes, they forgot about them." At least one Chinese quit the job for a similar reason. His daughter, married to a professor of Chinese art, told me that her father had worked on the railway but quit because "he was scared of the bears." He later went into domestic service.

By September 1868, the track was completed for 307 miles from Sacramento, and the crews were laying rails across the plain east of the Sierra. Parallel with the track layers went the telegraph installers, stringing their wires on the poles and keeping the planners back at headquarters precisely apprised of where the end of the track was.

THE GREAT RAILWAY COMPETITION

On the plains, the Chinese worked in tandem with all the Indians Crocker could entice to work on the iron rails. They began to hear of the exploits of the Union Pacific's "Irish terriers" building from the east. One day, the Irish laid six miles of track. The Chinese topped this with seven. "No Chinaman is going to beat us," growled the Irish, and the next day, they laid seven and half miles of track. They swore that they would outperform the competition no matter what it did.

Crocker taunted the Union Pacific that his men could lay ten miles of track a day. Durant,

president of the rival line, laid a $10,000 wager that it could not be done. Crocker took no chances. He waited until the day before the last sixteen miles of track could be laid and brought up all needed supplies for instant use. Then he unleashed his crews. On April 28, 1869, while Union Pacific checkers and newspaper reporters looked on, a combined gang of Chinese and eight picked Irish rail handlers laid ten miles and 1,800 feet more of track in twelve hours. This record was never surpassed until the advent of mechanized track laying. Each Irishman that day walked a total distance of ten miles, and their combined muscle handled sixty tons of rail.

So keen was the competition that when the two lines approached each other, instead of changing direction to link up, their builders careered on and on for 100 miles, building lines that would never meet. Finally, the government prescribed that the linkage point should be Promontory, Utah.

Competition was keen, but there seems to be no truth in the story that the Chinese and Irish in this phase of work were trying to blow each other up with explosives. It is a fact, however, that when the two lines were very near each other, the Union Pacific blasters did not give the Central Pacific men timely warning when setting off a charge, and several Chinese were hurt. Then a Central Pacific charge went off unannounced and several Irishmen found themselves buried in dirt. This forced the foremen to take up the matter and an amicable settlement was arranged. There was no further trouble.

On May 10, 1869, the two lines were officially joined at Promontory, north of Ogden in Utah. A great crowd gathered. A band played. An Irish crew and a Chinese crew were chosen to lay the last two rails side by side. The last tie was made of polished California laurel with a silver plate in its center proclaiming it "The last tie laid on the completion of the Pacific Railroad, May 10, 1869." But when the time came it was nowhere to be found. As consternation mounted, four Chinese approached with it on their shoulders and they laid it beneath the rails. A photographer stepped up and someone shouted to him

"Shoot!" The Chinese only knew one meaning for that word. They fled. But order was restored and the famous ceremony began; Stanford drove a golden spike into the last tie with a silver hammer. The news flashed by telegraph to a waiting nation. But no Chinese appears in that famous picture of the toast celebrating the joining of the rails.

Crocker was one of the few who paid tribute to the Chinese that day: "I wish to call to your minds that the early completion of this railroad we have built has been in large measure due to that poor, despised class of laborers called the Chinese, to the fidelity and industry they have shown." No one even mentioned the name of Judah.

The building of the first transcontinental railway stands as a monument to the union of Yankee and Chinese-Irish drive and know-how. This was a formidable combination. They all complemented each other. Together they did in seven years what was expected to take at least fourteen.

In his book on the building of the railway, John Galloway, the noted transportation engineer, described this as "without doubt the greatest engineering feat of the nineteenth century," and that has never been disputed. David D. Colton, then vice-president of the Southern Pacific, was similarly generous in his praise of the Chinese contribution. He was asked, while giving evidence before the 1876 congressional committee, "Could you have constructed that road without Chinese labor?" He replied, "I do not think it could have been constructed so quickly, and with anything like the same amount of certainty as to what we were going to accomplish in the same length of time."

And, in answer to the question, "Do you think the Chinese have been a benefit to the State?" West Evans, a railway contractor, testified, "I do not see how we could do the work we have done, here, without them; at least I have done work that would not have been done if it had not been for the Chinamen, work that could not have been done without them."

It was heroic work. The Central Pacific crews had carried their railway 1,800 miles through the Sierra and Rocky mountains, over sagebrush desert and plain. The Union Pacific built only 689 miles, over much easier terrain. It had 500 miles in which to carry its part of the line to a height of 5,000 feet, with another fifty more miles in which to reach the high passes of the Black Hills. With newly recruited crews, the Central Pacific had to gain an altitude of 7,000 feet from the plain in just over 100 miles and make a climb of 2,000 feet in just 20 miles.

All this monumental work was done before the age of mechanization. It was pick and shovel, hammer and crowbar work, with baskets for earth carried slung from shoulder poles and put on one-horse carts.

For their heroic work, the Chinese workmen began with a wage of $28 a month, providing their own food and shelter. This was gradually raised to $30 to $35 a month. Caucasians were paid the same amount of money, but their food and shelter were provided. Because it cost $0.75 to $1.00 a day to feed a white unskilled worker, each Chinese saved the Central Pacific, at a minimum, two-thirds the price of a white laborer (1865 rates). Chinese worked as masons, dynamiters, and blacksmiths and at other skilled jobs that paid white workers from $3 to $5 a day. So, at a minimum, the company saved about $5 million by hiring Chinese workers.

Did this really "deprive white workers of jobs" as anti-Chinese agitators claimed. Certainly not. In the first place, experience had proved that white workers simply did not want the jobs the Chinese took on the railroad. In fact, the Chinese created jobs for white workers as straw bosses, foremen, railhandlers, teamsters, and supervisors.

The wages paid to the Chinese were, in fact, comparable to those paid unskilled or semiskilled labor in the East (where labor was relatively plentiful), and the Chinese were at first satisfied. Charles Nordhoff estimated that the frugal Chinese could save about $13 a month out of those wages. The *Alta California* estimated their savings at $20 a month and later, perhaps, as wages increased, they could lay aside even more. With a bit of luck, a year and a half to two years of work would enable them to return to China with $400 to buy a bit of land and be well-to-do farmers.

But the Chinese began to learn the American way of life. On one occasion in June 1867, 2,000 tunnelers went on strike, asking for $40 a month, an eight-hour day in the tunnels, and an end to beating by foremen. "Eight hours a day good for white man, all same good for Chinese," said their spokesman in the pidgin English common in the construction camps. But solidarity with the other workers was lacking, and after a week the strike was called off when the Chinese heard that Crocker was recruiting strikebreakers from the eastern states.

When the task was done, most of the Chinese railwaymen were paid off. Some returned to China with their hard-earned savings, and the epic story of building the Iron Horse's pathway across the continent must have regaled many a family gathering there. Some returned with souvenirs of the great work, chips of one of the last ties, which had been dug up and split up among them. Some settled in the little towns that had grown up along the line of the railway. Others took the railway to seek adventure further east and south. Most made their way back to California and took what jobs they could find in that state's growing industries, trades, and other occupations. Many used their traditional and newly acquired skills on the other transcontinental lines and railways that were being swiftly built in the West and Midwest. This was the start of the diaspora of the Chinese immigrants in America.

The Union and Central Pacific tycoons had done well out of the building of the line. Congressional investigation committees later calculated that, of $73 million poured into the Union Pacific coffers, no more than $50 million could be justified as true costs. The Big Four and their associates in the Central Pacific had done even better. They had made at least $63 million and owned most of the CP stock worth around $100 million and 9 million acres of land grants to boot.

Ironically, the great railway soon had disastrous results for the Chinese themselves. It now cost only $40 for an immigrant to cross the conti-

nent by rail and a flood of immigrants took advantage of the ease and cheapness of travel on the line the Chinese had helped to build. The labor shortage (and resulting high wages) in California turned into a glut. When the tangled affairs of the Northern Pacific line led to the stock market crash of Black Friday, September 19, 1873, and to financial panic, California experienced its first real economic depression. There was devastating unemployment, and the Chinese were made the scapegoats.

BUILDING OTHER LINES

The expansion of the railroads was even faster in the following decade. In 1850, the United States had 9,000 miles of track. In 1860, it had 30,000. In 1890, it had over 70,000 miles. Three years later, it had five transcontinental lines.

The first transcontinental railway was soon followed by four more links: (1) the Southern Pacific–Texas and Pacific, completed in 1883 from San Francisco to Texas by way of Yuma, Tucson, and El Paso; (2) the Atchinson, Topeka, and Santa Fe, completed in 1885 from Kansas City to Los Angeles via Santa Fe and Albuquerque; (3) the Northern Pacific, completed in 1883 from Duluth, Minnesota, to Portland, Oregon; and (4) the Great Northern (1893). The skill of the Chinese as railroad builders was much sought after, and Chinese worked on all these lines. Some 15,000 worked on the Northern Pacific, laying tracks in Washington, Idaho, and Montana; 250 on the Houston and Texas line; 600 on the Alabama and Chattanooga line; 70 on the New Orleans line. Nearly 500 Chinese were recruited for the Union Pacific even after the lines were joined. Many worked in the Wyoming coal mines and during the summer months doubled as track laborers. They carried the Southern Pacific line over the burning Mojave Desert. They helped link San Francisco with Portland in 1887.

The Canadian Pacific seized the chance to enlist veteran Chinese railwaymen from the Southern Pacific and Northern Pacific railroads and also brought Chinese workers direct from China. In 1880, some 1,500 were working on that line, increasing to 6,500 two years later. Casualties were heavy on this line. Hundreds lost their lives while working on it.

Chinese railwaymen helped on the Central and Southern Pacific's main line down the San Joaquin Valley in 1870 and 1871. They worked on the hookup to Los Angeles and the loop with seventeen tunnels over the Tehachapi Pass completed in 1876. On this line, 1,000 Chinese worked on the 6,975-foot San Fernando Tunnel, the longest in the West. This rail link between San Francisco and Los Angeles, tapping the rich Central Valley, played a major role in the development of California's agriculture, later its biggest industry. They worked on the line north from Sacramento along the Shasta route to Portland, which was reached in 1887. In 1869, the Virginia and Truckee line employed 450 Chinese, veterans of the Central Pacific, to grade its track. When the Virginia and Truckee's Carson and Colorado branch line was planned from Mound House to Benton, its tough manager Yerington arranged with the Unions for the grading to be done by white labor to Dayton and by Chinese from Dayton on south. "If the entire line had to be graded by white labor, I would not think of driving a pick into the ground, but would abandon the undertaking entirely," he said.

Chinese laborers worked on the trans-Panamanian railway, which linked the Pacific and the Atlantic before the Panama Canal was completed. This railway played a major role in speeding up the economic development of the United States, but it was not built without sacrifice: hundreds of the Chinese builders died of fever and other causes during its construction.

This by no means completes the list of contributions of the Chinese railway workers. The transcontinental lines on which they worked "more than any other factor helped make the United States a united nation," writes the *Encyclopaedia Britannica* ["Railways"]. They played a major role in building the communications network of iron roads that was the transport base of American industrial might in the twentieth century.

Speaking eloquently in favor of the Chinese immigrants, Oswald Garrison Villard said,

> I want to remind you of the things that Chinese labor did in opening up the Western portion of this country. . . . [They] stormed the forest fastness, endured cold and heat and the risk of death at hands of hostile Indians to aid in the opening up of our northwestern empire. I have a dispatch from the chief engineer of the Northwestern Pacific telling how Chinese laborers went out into eight feet of snow with the temperature far below zero to carry on the work when no American dared face the conditions.

And these men were from China's sun-drenched south, where it never snows.

In certain circles, there has been a conspiracy of silence about the Chinese railroadmen and what they did. When U.S. Secretary of Transportation John Volpe spoke at the "Golden Spike" centenary, not a single Chinese American was invited, and he made no mention in his speech of the Chinese railroad builders.

3

THE PRODUCING CLASSES AND THE SALOON: DENVER IN THE 1880s

DAVID BRUNDAGE

Spurred by war contracts and the rapid expansion of railroads after the Civil War, the United States experienced a prolonged period of heavy industrialization in the final decades of the nineteenth century. In rapid succession the small prewar steel, railroad, and mining industries became giant enterprises, employing thousands of workers and spreading their influence throughout the nation. After 1865, thousands of rural Americans and foreign immigrants flocked to the nation's industrial centers and to the mining regions of the Rocky Mountain West, finding new kinds of work and novel rhythms of labor wherever they went.

As these new workers quickly learned, their new jobs required more concentration, discipline, and unremitting labor than they had experienced before. Gone were the human and seasonal rhythms of the farm or the artisan's shop, and in their place workers found themselves with little control over the pace of work, the tasks they performed, or the hours they worked. To many, servile dependence seemed to be the essence of the new industrial order.

Not all workers accepted this new industrial order, however. Beginning in the 1870s, workers formed national unions to defend themselves and fought long and hard to regain a degree of control over their working lives. One of the most innovative of these labor organizations was the Knights of Labor. Formed by Uriah Stephens in 1869, the Knights of Labor attempted to bring together all workers—skilled and unskilled, black and white, women as well as men—to claim an equitable place for themselves in American industrial society.

In this essay, David Brundage follows the fortunes of the Knights of Labor in Denver, the hub of a rapidly growing mining and manufacturing region. As he reveals, wage rates and workplace rules were important to the Knights of Labor, and they engaged in many struggles over these basic issues. But the Knights also fought to defend aspects of working-class social and cultural life that were threatened by the new industrial order. Among these hard-drinking men—for whom the saloon was a center of recreation, political discussion, and working-class mutuality—attempts by reformers to control drinking were seen as concerted assaults on their independence, their manliness, and their distinctive way of life. As much a social movement as a trade union, the Knights of Labor defended the traditional culture of Denver workers and in the process made itself an integral part of working-class life.

This essay reminds us that labor history has expanded dramatically in scope beyond the institutional and bread-and-butter issues that defined its subject matter in the past. In the hands of a new generation of labor historians, such as David Brundage, the story of American workers now includes the close study of their private lives, their political aspirations, their culture, and their distinctive view of the world.

"The Producing Classes and the Saloon: Denver in the 1880s." Labor History, *26 (1985), pp. 29–52. Reprinted by permission of B. P. Ink.*

The autumn of 1886 witnessed a political upheaval in the ranks of the American labor movement. Spearheaded by the Henry George campaign in New York City and drawing on the increasing strength of the Order of the Knights of Labor, independent labor parties sprang up in towns and cities across the nation, raising a working-class challenge to the political stability of the Gilded Age. The rapidly growing western city of Denver, Colorado, experienced this political upheaval but with a significant difference. Here a group of local labor leaders mounted their movement not through a United Labor Party, but rather through Colorado's two-year-old Prohibition Party. Joseph R. Buchanan, a key Denver labor leader and a national figure in the Knights of Labor, gave unqualified support to the Prohibitionists and Joseph Murray, a pioneer organizer of the working-class movement in Colorado, stood as the party's candidate for Congress. "I am a Socialist myself," Murray declared during the campaign, "and think more of my standing as a Knight of Labor than anything else." But for Murray prohibition was essential because "it was necessary to get men sober before he could awaken them to the greatness of the labor and industrial question."

The existence of temperance sentiments among groups of 19th century workers, and within the Knights of Labor in particular, is now familiar to historians. Such sentiments, however, are usually seen as derived from a conservative middle-class ideology revolving around self-help and self-discipline. Although these ideas may have played some role in the support which Buchanan and Murray gave to the Prohibition Party, other quite distinct concerns were predominant. Above all, they were seeking to undermine the influence of the urban saloon, an institution which they believed hindered the development of a unified labor movement and served as an important social base for a corrupt and anti-labor political machine. A study of their perspectives on the saloon and of the labor movement's efforts to build alternative social institutions to it demonstrates the wide gulf which separated labor's project from that of middle-class temperance reformers. The 1886 campaign was a failure. Murray and the Prohibition ticket went down to defeat and, more importantly, the campaign exacerbated internal conflicts within the city's labor movement. Nevertheless, as the following will show, opposition to the saloon within the Denver labor movement represented primarily an effort to strengthen working-class consciousness and build a working-class political presence.

When Buchanan and Murray took on the saloon they were challenging an institution with deep roots in the fabric of urban working-class life. "The saloon exists . . . because it serves a want—a need," wrote a workingman to the Denver-based *Miner's Magazine* in the early 20th century. "It offers a common meeting place. It dispenses good cheer. It ministers to the craving for fellowship. To the exhausted, worn out body, to the strained nerves—the relaxation brings rest." As this statement indicates, the functions of the urban saloon went far beyond the provision of alcohol. The saloon in Denver provided at least three distinct services to working-class customers: it offered food and lodging at reasonable prices, served as a meeting hall for various organizations, and was a principal setting for male working-class recreation.

Food and lodging assumed particular importance in Denver in the late 1870s and early 1880s, when the Leadville mining boom and the rapid growth of Colorado railroad construction turned the city into "the temporary abiding place of multitudes of strangers and immigrants" bound for Rocky Mountain mines and grading camps. Every month from the fall of 1879 to the spring of 1881, for example, an average of perhaps 500 railroad workers passed through Denver en route to the Denver and Rio Grande's grading camps alone. This floating population, overwhelmingly male, came to rely on the cluster of boarding-house saloons and small hotels located near the city's Union Station. Providing inexpensive lodgings, these establishments also offered companionship and frequently a meal for the price of a nickel beer.

Over the course of the 1880s, however, the

character of Denver's working class changed dramatically. The construction of smelters and railroad shops and the expansion of firms producing mining equipment created a powerful demand for industrial labor within the city itself. From 1880 to 1890, Denver's population nearly tripled, climbing from 35,629 to 106,713, while distinct working-class neighborhoods took shape to the north and west of the central business district. By the latter date, moreover, over 46% of the city's labor force was composed of first- or second-generation immigrants, with Irish, English, and Germans representing the largest contingents. As immigrant workers attempted to preserve a sense of cultural identity in a new environment, Denver experienced a proliferation of ethnic social clubs and benefit societies. Societies and clubs, however, required meeting space and, as in other American cities, Denver saloons often provided that space.

Within the Irish and German communities of Denver, the saloon was a particularly important meeting hall. The Irish-American Progressive Association, the Irish Fellowship Association, and the Ancient Order of Hibernians all held their meetings in the city's drinking establishments. For the German community, Turner Hall emerged as a major cultural center: in addition to a saloon, it housed exercise rooms, equipped through financial assistance from the Coors and Zang breweries, and the largest lecture hall in the city. Not only benevolent and fraternal organizations, but also trade unions which drew their members from particular immigrant groups, gravitated to the ethnic saloon. German bakers, for example, who attempted to organize a union in the early 1880s, held their meetings at Turner Hall. The Amalgamated Society of Carpenters, composed for the most part of English craftsmen, held their weekly meetings at the Little Emma.

The requirements of space naturally provided a major consideration in the choice of the saloon as a meeting hall. The typical working-class family in Denver during this period resided in a small one-story house, containing from three to six rooms—hardly adequate for holding large meetings. Yet space was not the only consideration, for the real strength of the saloon lay in its ability to provide a meeting hall and to meet the needs of recreation simultaneously. The significance of this third function of the urban saloon should not be underestimated. While fraternal societies did provide a focus for recreation, Denver workers also sought less demanding forms of leisure. And, as even city boosters admitted, Denver was "sadly deficient in places of legitimate amusement" at the opening of the 1880s. Although increasingly excluded by ordinance from the new middle-class suburbs, and generally off-limits to women, the corner saloon in Denver's working-class neighborhoods served as a primary locus of male sociability.

The last two decades of the 19th century, of course, saw the rapid development of new forms of recreation which constituted at least potential alternatives to the saloon. In 1883 the first professional baseball game was played in Denver, and the popularity of the sport grew rapidly over the next twenty years. Also in 1883 the intra-urban Denver Circle Railroad constructed Jewell Park at the end of its line in an effort to attract Sunday fare-payers, thus initiating a process which would culminate in Denver's two large "streetcar amusement parks" of the 1890s. Their development was particularly important for it represented the movement of women and children into the world of urban recreation.

The saloon, however, was not yet ready to give up its place in urban life. During the 1880s, a new type of drinking establishment grew up alongside the neighborhood tavern and ethnic saloon. Concentrated in the tenderloin district near the city center, a group of larger saloons began to attract considerable numbers of both working-class and middle-class customers. In part their appeal stemmed from sheer display: Ed Chase's "Palace Saloon" was famous for the rows of silver dollars embedded in its floor and for its elaborately crafted bar. Equally important, however, was the provision of musical and dramatic entertainment. The "concert halls" and "variety theatres" of Denver's tenderloin added a new dimension to the patterns of urban leisure.

It is not surprising, then, that the Denver saloon increased in importance over the course of the 1880s. At the opening of the decade, there were 363 Denver residents for each saloon; at its close, the figure had dropped to 334.

The saloon, of course, generated opposition, particularly within Denver's middle class. The "Blue Ribbon" campaign of the late 1870s and the activities of the Women's Christian Temperance Union and the Anti-Saloon league in the 1880s and 1890s represented major efforts on the part of the middle-class reformers to alter the habits of working-class drinkers. Some of Denver's large employers, hoping to strengthen industrial discipline among their workers, gave important support to these efforts. The Union Pacific Railroad, which operated repair shops in the city, provided an example: from the late 1860s on, the UP had aided the Young Men's Christian Association by establishing boarding houses and reading rooms as alternatives to the saloon for railroad workers along its lines. In the last two decades of the 19th century, both the Denver Tramway Company and the Denver and Rio Grande Railroad provided reading rooms at their Denver shops for workers whose punctuality and productivity were undermined by nearby saloons. In light of the labor militancy which all three firms experienced in the 1880s, a second function of the reading room might be suggested, that of securing workers' loyalty to the firm. "By a careful selection of books," the historian of the Denver and Rio Grande has noted, the company "had the opportunity to indoctrinate readers with knowledge that bespoke management's problems, if not its high ideals."

Even when not directly hostile to labor organizing, middle-class temperance activists made few efforts to enlist the Denver labor movement in their work. Disturbed by the growing social heterogeneity of urban life and increasingly drawn to programs for controlling the poor, organizations like the Colorado Women's Christian Temperance Union seemed to find the labor movement as threatening as the immigrant saloon. Thus, although the WCTU established a department to consider "the relation of temperance to labor" in the late 1880s, the question remained a low priority. In 1890, the department superintendent called for a joint WCTU–Knights of Labor meeting in Denver but complained afterwards that "it was very poorly attended by the temperance people." Her exhortation to the WCTU that "we need to understand the labor question just as much as they do the temperance question" seems to have fallen upon deaf ears.

Leading figures in the Denver labor movement, however, already understood the importance of the temperance question. Like the middle-class temperance reformers, they had been attempting to construct substitutes for the saloon since the early 1880s. The underlying dynamic which gave force to the middle-class anti-saloon crusade—that is, the drive for industrial discipline and social control—was noticeably absent from labor's temperance project. A very different dynamic was at work here. In their establishment of reading rooms, workers' meeting halls, and recreational forms outside of the saloon, temperance advocates in Denver's labor organizations were attempting to build the foundations of a "movement culture" which would challenge, not uphold, existing patterns of social inequality.

By the autumn of 1886, a labor movement of impressive dimensions had emerged in the Colorado city. The Order of the Knights of Labor had grown rapidly, climbing from one local assembly in 1881 to thirteen in 1886 and embracing a wide spectrum of working-class occupations. Trade unions had experienced equally rapid growth, increasing in number from five to thirteen over these years and establishing a central voice in the Denver Trades and Labor Assembly. Moreover, the jurisdictional disputes which marred the relations between Knights and trade unions in many cities were largely absent in Denver. The second local assembly of the Knights to be organized in the city had been dubbed the "Union Assembly," all of its charter members being trade unionists, and by 1886 a number of Knights assemblies were affiliated with the Trades Assembly. As late as 1888, a "most friendly feeling" was said to exist between Knights and trade unionists in Denver.

Joseph R. Buchanan, a resident of Denver from 1878 to 1887, was a central figure in the forging of this alliance. While a member of the General Executive Board of the Knights of Labor, Buchanan was also an active member of the International Typographical Union. He had helped to organize the Denver Trades' Assembly in 1882 and the weekly newspaper which he began editing that year, the *Labor Enquirer,* served as the official organ of both the Trades' Assembly and the Denver Knights. At the 1886 General Assembly of the Order, Buchanan attempted to mediate the differences between the Knights and the trade unions, calling for "a complete coalition" between them based on the establishment of national trade districts.

The problem of working-class unity, however, extended far beyond the relationship between various labor organizations. As Buchanan recognized, ethnic divisions and conflicts within the 19th century American working class constituted a major obstacle to the growth of a unified labor movement. "We are all very clannish," he complained, "and each clan must have its own club or society to keep us from identifying with the people among whom we have come to live." The problem of ethnic diversity, moreover, was exacerbated by the fact that middle-class leaders of Denver's ethnic organizations often took strong anti-labor positions. Buchanan noted, for example, that C.E. McSheehy, an important figure in several Irish-American organizations, was famous for his "long and prevaricating tirades upon trades unionists."

Denver's labor movement made impressive strides in the face of these obstacles. In May and August of 1884, workers at the Union Pacific railroad shops in the city staged short and successful strikes in response to wage cuts. These strikes, which united Irish, German, and Yankee shop workers under the banner of the Knights of Labor, provided a powerful example of working-class unity across ethnic lines. Nevertheless, Buchanan and other Denver labor leaders believed that the Order of the Knights of Labor, "embracing as it does, all classes of producers," required more than solidarity among workers on the shop floor; it also required a set of social institutions which could carry that solidarity throughout the wider community. It was this project which led the Denver labor movement towards an attack on the saloon and towards an effort to replace it with institutions generated by the labor movement itself.

The struggle to establish a workers' meeting hall was central to this project. Ethnic clubs and societies might rely on the meeting space provided by the immigrant saloon, but organizations which embraced all of the producing classes would need meeting places which were free from divisive cultural influences. In 1883, Joseph Buchanan lamented the absence of suitable meeting halls for workers' organizations in Denver but offered the offices of the *Labor Enquirer* as a possibility. "The room is small," he admitted, "but fifteen or twenty can be comfortably accommodated and writing material, copies of various trades and labor constitutions, and other little conveniences will be freely tendered." The Knights of Labor in Denver, however, were unable to establish a permanent meeting hall in this period. Although city directories include listings for a "Knights of Labor Hall" in 1884, 1885, and 1886, these were actually three separate halls at different addresses, indicating a certain lack of success in establishing a central meeting place for the working-class community. In May 1884, a meeting of the Denver Typographical Union began in the Knights of Labor Hall, but after a few minutes adjourned to the liquor-serving Turner Hall. The Knights' hall had been "deemed unsafe."

Denver labor activists met with more success in building alternative forms of recreation, focusing their efforts on three vehicles designed to carry workingmen out of the saloon: the "sociable," the day excursion, and the reading room. The first sociable, or ball, was given by the Union Assembly of the Knights of Labor in August 1883. Music and other entertainment was offered and non-alcoholic refreshments were served "by the ladies," wives and daughters of Union Assembly members. Thereafter, the Union Assembly attempted to give sociables on the schedule of "one every two weeks." While on occasion these balls would be geared toward fund-raising (in April 1886, for example, a Knights of Labor ball was held "for the benefit of strikers on the Southwest system"), most were purely recreational in function.

Nevertheless, the importance of the sociables in the movement culture which Denver Knights of Labor were building should not be minimized. The ethnic character of saloon life was not the only issue involved here: the culture built around the saloon was primarily a male culture which excluded women and threatened the stability of the working-class family. Yet, as the female work force of Denver climbed from 1,681 to 8,143 over the course of the 1880s, working-class women played an increasingly important role in the city's labor movement. In July 1884, thirty-seven Denver women organized the "Hope Assembly" of the Knights of Labor and over the next few years the assembly established a boarding house and an employment agency for the city's single "female wage-slaves." More importantly perhaps, in their co-operative laundry and co-operative store, Denver Knights of Labor created institutions which spoke directly to the needs of housewives, the overwhelming majority of working-class women. The Knights' sociables carried this concern for working-class wives into the realm of recreational life.

This concern should not be confused with an interest in women's equality. Indeed, the fact that in Denver's 1885 labor parade, Hope Assembly members rode in twenty-four carriages provided by the city's male labor organizations suggests a firm belief in the notion of a "weaker sex." Nevertheless, in a period in which Denver's middle-class recreational life was marked by a clear pattern of "separate spheres" for men and women, the Knights of Labor sought to create patterns of leisure which would bring men and women together—thus strengthening both the working-class family and the Order itself. These concerns, as much as a concern with the effects of alcohol abuse on family life, led to the Knights' emphasis on the sociable as an alternative to the saloon.

The day excursion was another such alternative. In July 1883, the Denver Knights of Labor held the first of a series of annual picnics at Argo, "one of the nicest resorts in the state." For fifty cents, an individual could purchase a ticket which included round-trip rail fare and admission to the park. Unlike the saloon, the day excursion involved the entire family while simultaneously providing respite from an increasingly oppressive urban environment. Family-oriented recreation, of course, did not need to be organized by the labor movement. "I find, working eight hours," a Denver workingman reported to the Colorado Bureau of Labor Statistics in 1888, "that I can get time to become acquainted with my family, and plan things that will interest them, which I never could before." But the Knights of Labor railroad excursions, like their sociables, brought the family together within the context of the wider working-class movement. For all their talk of "hearth and home," the Knights of Labor conceived of the family, not as an isolated haven from the world, but rather as the cornerstone of the working-class community.

But of all the alternatives to the saloon, the reading room was perhaps the most important. "An imperative want of the working people in Denver is that of a reading room," noted Joseph Buchanan in 1883, "where the different trades and occupations can meet for social converse, to read such books and periodicals as may prove of interest to them." But reading rooms were hardly new to Denver. Indeed, the institution had played an important role in the efforts of employers and middle-class temperance activists to instill self-discipline and loyalty among workers in the city. When the Knights of Labor finally established their central reading room in Denver in May 1885, the local press instinctively compared it to these earlier efforts, especially those of the YMCA.

Upon closer examination, however, the differences appear far more salient. A statement by Buchanan, who set up a reading room in his editorial office in 1883, illustrates the character of these differences. "We extend to every workingman in the city *who believes in fair pay for fair work* an invitation to make himself at home in the *Enquirer* office. Plenty of *the right kind* of reading matter always on the table." Buchanan's notion of "the right kind of reading matter" can be gauged by the writings recommended in the columns of the *Labor Enquirer.* These included Laurence Gronlund's *The Cooperative Commonwealth,* various works by Marx (who was compared to Newton and Galileo in scientific importance), and, of course, Henry George's *Progress and Poverty.* Thus for Buchanan and other labor activists in Denver, liberating workingmen from the influence of the saloon was only the first step in the development of leisuretime activities which would stress self-education in political economy and strategies for social change.

The Knights of Labor's vision of social change was far-reaching. "The great objects of the Order is a complete change in our social and economic environment," wrote one Denver Knight to the *Journal of United Labor.* "The Order . . . proposes to abolish the competitive system under which we now live and in its place substitute the co-operative system." There can be no doubt that education, and self-improvement generally, were seen as essential preconditions for the building of the co-operative system; hence the importance of reading rooms in the Knights' activities. But self-improvement for the co-operative commonwealth bore little resemblance to self-improvement as conceptualized by the YMCA and its business supporters. The 1887 attack which the Denver *Labor Enquirer* launched upon the Young Men's "Capitalist" Association for its connections with Jay Gould and the Union Pacific Railroad should make this clear.

Perhaps the best indicator of the gulf between middle-class temperance and that of the labor movement, however, is the strong support which organized socialists in Denver gave to the crusade against the saloon. In 1883 Joseph Buchanan became a socialist and the Rocky Mountain organizer for Burnette G. Haskell's International Workingmen's Association. Although the IWA, shrouded in the secrecy and ritual of conspiratorial revolutionism, failed to attract supporters in Denver, Buchanan continued to give socialist ideas a presence in the city through the mid-1880s. His tireless propaganda efforts bore fruit in December 1885 when "thirty to forty socialists" in Denver organized the Rocky Mountain Social League for the purpose of "propagating their doctrines."

The membership of the League was drawn from the broad social groupings which the Knights of Labor called "the producing classes." Its charter members included a printer, a house painter, a dentist, a tailor, and an undertaker. Primarily a discussion group, the League held meetings every Sunday evening over the next two years. Although prominent ministers and politicians occasionally addressed these meetings, more typical were speeches like that given by a Denver iron molder on "Why I am a Socialist." Buchanan maintained that League members were "intelligent propagandists of the doctrines of modern socialism" and that they constituted "a strong socialist element in the [Knights of Labor] assemblies and the unions."

The Rocky Mountain Social League played a major role in shaping the Denver labor movement's attack on the saloon. Like the Knights of Labor, in which they apparently often held membership, activists in the League believed that working-class consciousness required sobriety and self-improvement. "Socialism is a science," Buchanan argued, "and science does not attract the ignorant, groveling herd who can comprehend nothing but that which ministers to their gross animal appetites." Thus the Rocky Mountain Social League took a strong position against the saloon and the broader culture of which it was part. In April 1886, "Comrade Ann Bartlett delivered a sermon which she said was intended for a temperance meeting, but that it could be applied to the League." Opposition to the saloon extended to kindred vices and in February 1886 the League voiced "extreme dissatisfaction with the action of the mayor and city council in granting licenses to the gambling halls, as contrary to the good morals of his city."

The Rocky Mountain Social League, however, not only took formal positions against the saloon;

its weekly meetings also provided a practical alternative to the saloon. These meetings involved not just men but entire families and attempted to combine political agitation, self-improvement, and recreation in a single institution. The flavor of a League meeting is best conveyed by an entry in the diary of Anna Haskell, who came to Denver in 1887 with her husband, the West Coast socialist leader Burnette Haskell:

> I said Victor Hugo's "To the Rich and Poor" at the meeting tonight, and I think I said it very well. The audience seemed to think so. The meeting was very interesting. Some children sung, and others had a dialogue which was very interesting and they have good singing. They have adapted appropriate words to well known music—and there are a number of good singers among them. The baby was awful funny. In the meeting he went and sat himself down on a big black dog and while Burnette was speaking he went and stood directly in front of him and had everyone in the room laughing.

It was this mixture of politics and poetry, of education and family-oriented recreation, that gave the Rocky Mountain Social League its appeal to Denver's working people. Institutions such as the League were at the core of the movement culture being constructed by the city's labor activists.

Thus the opposition of leaders in the Denver labor movement to the saloon derived not only from their abiding belief in the importance of temperance. It also emerged from their perception of the manner in which the saloon functioned to divide the city's working class along lines of ethnicity and gender and to encourage a passive and non-intellectual approach to leisure. The latter point became the basis for the labor movement's uneasiness in the face of new forms of urban leisure (particularly professional sports), the new popular press, and the variety theatre.

Associated with the rise of professional sports in late 19th century America was the growth of a number of widely-read popular publications devoted to the coverage of sporting events. The most important of these was probably the New York–based *Police Gazette,* which combined sporting news with a sensationalized coverage of major crimes and scandals. Denver labor activists watched the growth of such publications with considerable anxiety for they seemed to threaten the cultivation of a working-class consciousness rooted in self-improvement and education. J.N. Corbin, for example, a leader of the 1884 strikes at the Union Pacific shops who emerged as a major figure in the Denver Knights of Labor, argued that the Order was essentially "a school room." His *Union Pacific Employes' Magazine,* a monthly journal giving attention to political economy, religion, current events, and science—as well as to conditions in the railroad industry—represented an attempt to put this vision into practice. Not surprisingly, Corbin denounced the *Police Gazette* and other examples of the "debasement of the popular press."

More problematic for the labor movement was the growing popularity of baseball. When Knights of Labor organized competitive teams at the major railroad shops in Denver, they were using the popularity of baseball to cultivate workers' loyalty to the labor movement. On the other hand, as a spectator sport, baseball tended to draw workingmen out of the orbit of the labor movement and could, on occasion, even hinder its efficient working. In 1888, for example, the Denver Typographical Union levied a fine on its delegates to the city Trades' Assembly when it discovered that despite "a knowing that there was important business in the interest of the Union to be transacted," the delegates "did not remain in the hall over half an hour, but attended a baseball game in the Athletic Park."

Finally, the variety theatre seemed threatening to the labor movement. Even if some theatres admitted women, they destroyed the delicate balance between family and community which the Knights of Labor sought to establish and encouraged an approach to leisure which put little emphasis on education. The saloon, in sum, was only one part of a larger complex of urban recreational patterns which seemed to undermine the approach of Denver's labor activists to the building of working-class consciousness. "The whiskey drinker and variety theatre-attending workman who reads the *Police Gazette* is also the one who says he has no use for socialism," complained Joseph Buchanan. "Let us give thanks for that—thanks that [socialism] attracts only men whose minds are raised above the rumhole and the haunts of vice."

However, the saloon remained a central target of attack within the Denver labor movement—in part, because its very character seemed to reflect the process by which the rise of monopoly undermined community life. In the years between the Civil War and the opening of the 20th century, the United States witnessed a major alteration in drinking habits, with the consumption of fermented liquor, beer especially, supplanting that of distilled sprits. This trend was reflected in Colorado, where the production of beer increased tenfold between 1878 and 1893. Here, as elsewhere, the increase in production was associated with a trend towards concentration in fewer establishments. Although twenty-three breweries were operating in the state in 1880, only eleven were in existence ten years later. Small local breweries were increasingly displaced by emerging Denver-area breweries like Zang, Tivoli, and Coors, which came to dominate the market. Thus Colorado brewing was undergoing the same processes of consolidation and concentration as that affecting many other American industries in this period.

This process of transformation affected not only the production of beer but retailing as well. In the early 1880s, larger breweries began the practice of paying for the licenses of saloons in Denver and requiring that only their product be sold. This practice, along with the outright ownership of saloons by breweries, dramatically altered the position of the saloon within the urban environment. For many Denver residents, as historian Elliott West has noted, "the neighborhood tavern became an extension of impersonal corporations," its bartender "no longer a longtime friend and familiar merchant but a person hired by unknown owners." Thus, the anti-monopoly rhetoric which was so characteristic of the American labor movement in the Gilded Age

found a clear target in the brewing industry and the urban saloon.

Joseph Murray, the socialist and Knights of Labor organizer who ran for Congress on the Colorado Prohibition Party ticket in 1886, brought many of these themes together during the course of his campaign. Murray frequently pointed to the importance of the movement culture which working people could build as an alternative to the saloon, noting that "we are building [co-operative] mills, a public hall and reading room in Stout [Colorado]; in short, doing what all people can do by remaining sober and industrious." More to the point, he argued that the growth of the working-class movement in general would be furthered by the destruction of the saloon. Murray told his audiences that "as soon as the people are educated up to sobriety . . . then all the working men will be Knights of Labor." Finally he argued from the vantage point of the Prohibition hustings that those who controlled the large breweries were "the idle rich." Murray brought the language of anti-monopoly and class struggle into the movement for prohibition.

But the Denver saloon was not only an example of the trend towards monopoly in economic life. As in many other American cities during the late 19th century, it was also a political institution of some importance. Specifically, the Denver saloon provided a major social base for the Republican Party's political machine in the city. This point is central in explaining the move of Murray and Buchanan from the advocacy of temperance to the call for total prohibition. Their attack on the saloon was also an attack on its closest ally, the Colorado Republican Party.

From 1878 to 1893, in the words of an early Denver historian, the Republican Party "was the actual government of both Denver and Colorado," generally holding the governorship and majorities in the Denver city council and state legislature. While the labor movement's charge that the party was simply a tool of large corporate mining and railroad interests may have been exaggerated, it is true that the Colorado GOP defined its central mission as that of providing a suitable environment for the accumulation of capital. This led it to oppose virtually all of labor's political demands—the prohibition of child and convict labor, the eight-hour day on state and municipal work, effective lien laws—as "class legislation." The Republican stance towards the labor movement was perhaps best expressed by Governor Frederick Pitkin when he called out troops to crush the Leadville miners strike in 1880.

Colorado Democrats attempted to use the anti-labor positions of the GOP to their own advantage, putting forward their own party as the "true friend of the laboring classes." After a bitter fight, for example, the Democratic convention of 1880 did pass a resolution condemning Pitkin's use of the militia at Leadville. Nevertheless, the party generally opposed strikes and claimed that "the worst enemies" of the workingmen were not capitalists but "the leeches, styled professional workingmen"—that is, labor leaders like Buchanan. Not surprisingly, then, Joseph Murray could argue that "there was no distinctive difference between the two parties . . ."

Yet working-class third-party activity had shown few results in Denver. In the municipal elections of 1883, the Trades' Assembly put forward a Workingmen's Ticket which included a stone cutter and a tailor as city council candidates. In the following year, support was generated within the city's labor movement for the Greenback-Labor Party and an officer of the Trades' Assembly was represented on the party's ticket for state office. Neither effort was able to alter the loyalty of Denver's voters of the Republican Party, however.

A number of factors account for these third-party failures. The Republicans' emphasis on accumulation, while running against specific programs put forward by the Denver labor movement, gave them a basis for claiming Colorado's "prosperity" as their own creation—although the claim must have sounded increasingly hollow in the depressed years of the 1880s. Secondly, the fact that a large proportion of Denver's native-born working people had migrated from the free soil states of the Midwest gave the GOP an edge

in a period in which "the bloody shirt" of the Civil War had not yet lost its powers. Finally, the city's labor movement—despite its rapid growth—lacked the financial resources to effectively contest for political power.

Yet, by the mid-1880s, labor activists were beginning to argue that there was another key to Republican strength at the Denver polls: the saloon. Indeed, saloon keepers and brewery owners had good reason to take interest in Denver's political life. Continuously threatened by higher licensing fees and stricter closing ordinances, if not by outright prohibition, brewers and saloon keepers attempted to maintain close connections with both of the major political parties. Philip Zang, the city's largest brewer, had served one term as a Democrat on the city council and throughout the 1880s there was always at least one saloon keeper on the governing body. Standing at the center of Republican politics in Denver, however, was Ed Chase, the proprietor of the Palace Saloon.

If the Palace was representative of the new, large-scale drinking establishments which were re-orienting urban leisure patterns during the late 19th century, its owner was an almost archetypal saloon politician. Although Chase had been a member of the Denver city council during the 1870s, he gave up his position to work for the Republican Party behind the scenes. Political influence was of great importance for Chase; his business activities included gambling and prostitution, activities for which cooperation from city authorities was essential. In exchange for such cooperation, Chase provided two important sources of Republican strength in Denver. First, he coordinated financial contributions from saloon keepers to the party, reaching a peak with a $25,000 party fund for the close election of 1889. Secondly, Chase coordinated the mobilization of Republican voters. On election days throughout the 1880s, the Palace Saloon became a center of intense activity as the poor and often transient residents of Denver's First Ward were rounded up, provided with free beers, and directed to the polls. Chase, of course, was an unusual political figure and his influence may well have been overstated. Nevertheless, the publicity which his activities received undoubtedly encouraged support within the labor movement for total prohibition. Thus the move towards prohibition represented not only an attack on the saloon, but an attempt to dismantle a power base of the Republican Party.

Colorado's Prohibition Party shared the labor movement's hostility to the Republicans. Although Prohibitionists frequently compared their efforts with those of the original "free soil party," they argued that the GOP was now bankrupt of "high moral ideas." Moreover, the Prohibition Party in Colorado from its founding in 1884 had advanced a broad program of reform extending far beyond the liquor question. It advocated state ownership of irrigation ditches, free coinage of silver, and an end of railroad pools and rebates. In 1884, the Prohibitionists had not run a slate at all, but rather had endorsed the entire Greenback-Labor ticket. But the real key to the party's labor base was its nomination of Joseph Murray as its candidate for Congress in 1886. Murray's biography reads like a history of the Denver labor movement: he had been a founder of the Greenback-Labor Party, the organizer of the first Knights of Labor local assembly in the state, a leader in the Trades' Assembly's Workingmen's Ticket campaign, and a charter member of the Rocky Mountain Social League. His candidacy gave the "Prohibition-Labor Party," as it was styled in 1886, an enormous amount of prestige within the Denver labor movement.

The Democratic party had been making appeals to Colorado workingmen since the 1870s, generally without much success. In 1886, however, the Democrats put forward a genuinely pro-labor candidate. Myron Reed, a well-known Congregational minister in Denver, was a member of the Knights of Labor and had been closely identified with the city's labor movement for nearly two years. His congressional candidacy, moreover, appeared to have a real chance of success. Despite Joseph Murray's tremendous popularity, then, a number of leaders in the Denver labor movement began to feel that "a vote for

Murray is a vote wasted—a vote in the air." The individual most responsible for shifting labor's support from the Prohibitionists to the Democrats was the president of the city's Journeymen Taylor's Union, John B. Lennon. Indeed, the final weeks of the 1886 campaign were dominated by a bitter struggle between Lennon and Joseph Buchanan over how labor should vote.

Lennon was a strong supporter of temperance throughout his life. As the Treasurer of the American Federation of Labor in the early 20th century, Lennon would become one of the foremost advocates of a conservative "business unionism" which avoided entanglements with third-party reform movements. It is tempting to interpret the conflict between Buchanan and Lennon, then, as emblematic of a general struggle between "reform" and "pure-and-simple" visions of the American labor movement. This interpretation, however, will not suffice: to read Lennon's later positions back into the 1880s precludes an understanding of the fundamental issues in dispute.

In the early 1880s, Lennon maintained a close personal relationship with Buchanan, was instrumental in building trade union support for the Order of the Knights of Labor, and took an active role in a number of third-party movements. In January 1886, he proclaimed himself a socialist and helped to organize the Rocky Mountain Social League in Denver, serving as the chair of its meetings on several occasions over the next few months. Denver's "socialism," however, could embrace a wide spectrum of viewpoints in the early months of 1886; the events of May of that year forced it towards greater clarity. The Haymarket bombing, the arrest of the Chicago anarchists, and the "red scare" which these events foreshadowed generated an intense debate within Denver's labor movement and within the ranks of the socialist movement itself.

At the May 16th meeting of the Rocky Mountain Social League, Lennon introduced a resolution which condemned the Chicago anarchists for their alleged resort to violence. After considerable debate, the resolution was tabled;

the following week, it was rejected, replaced by a resolution which condemned the Chicago police. Lennon withdrew from the League following his defeat and in the late summer of 1886 began making public appearances on behalf of the Colorado Democratic Party. Although Lennon's motives remain unclear, Buchanan's charge that he was simply "a political prostitute" seems inaccurate, and Buchanan himself retracted the charge early in 1887. A more persuasive explanation for Lennon's turn to the Democrats would focus on his understanding of the altered conditions after May 1886. Lennon may have understood the anti-labor reaction which Haymarket would set off and, in an effort to preserve the tenuous working-class gains of the previous five years, may have sought to provide the labor movement with a modicum of "respectability" in the eyes of middle-class society. This would have necessitated retreating from labor radicalism and seeking out political allies within the middle class. The Democrats' cultivation of the labor vote through their nomination of Myron Reed for Congress dovetailed perfectly with this line of thought.

Although the increasingly bitter conflict between the Knights of Labor and the trade unions in 1886 provided a backdrop to the struggles within the Denver labor movement, the latter did not fall neatly along a Knights of Labor–trade union axis. Indeed, John Lennon's first step in building labor support for the Democrats was to call a meeting of "the Knights of Labor of Denver, in joint session." The meeting voiced support for the entire Democratic ticket and called on Joseph Murray to withdraw from the race for Congress. The meeting had no official status, however, and in the next few weeks a number of Knights of Labor assemblies in the city disassociated their organizations from the actions of the joint session and reiterated their support for Murray and the Prohibitionists.

Although Reed carried Denver's Arapahoe County by five hundred votes, both of labor's Congressional candidates lost the election to the Republican incumbent. But the most important result of the 1886 election did not lie in the returns. Its real impact was that of exacerbating tensions within Denver's labor movement. These tensions came to a head on October 10, when the city's Trades' Assembly severed its connection with the *Labor Enquirer* and passed a resolution of censure against its editor, Joseph Buchanan. While the Trades' Assembly conceded Buchanan's right "to advocate or oppose any political party or candidate, and indulge in the organization of new departures," it nonetheless felt obliged to protect "against any attempted deception on the part of any one in conveying the impression that the organized workingman of Colorado will cast his ballot as directed by any alleged labor leader."

We must still face one important question: to what extent was Prohibitionism in particular, rather than third-party politics in general, the key to divisions within the Denver labor movement? While no definitive answer can be offered here, it is important to note that the project of building a movement culture wholly outside the realm of the saloon had its limitations. These limitations appear clearly in the records of the Denver Typographical Union. Despite their image as "respectable" aristocrats of labor, rank-and-file printers demonstrated a deep commitment to the social and cultural life of the saloon. On a number of occasions during the 1880s, for example, the union was forced to withhold benefits from members who were injured while under the influence of alcohol. The union's leaders complained of important business being discussed "in beerhalls and alleys." And at least one plan for a union picnic, the classic recreational substitute for the saloon, had to be dropped for lack of interest among the members. Implacably hostile to middle-class temperance movements, Denver's organized workers may have been equally hostile to the efforts of a Buchanan or a Murray.

The deep roots of the saloon in working-class life may have given the Democratic Party another basis of strength in the city's labor movement. Leaders of the party recognized the role played by brewers and saloon keepers in the Republican machine and in the election of 1889 even endorsed prohibition as a weapon against the GOP. On the other hand, the Democrats had attempted to build political support among Denver's workers by defending the integrity of working-class cultural patterns—which included the saloon. Thus, prior to the 1885 Denver labor parade, when some middle-class temperance supporters called for a closing of the saloons, the Democratic press reacted with outrage. To close the saloons during the parade, it argued, would be "an insult" to "the intelligence and self-respect" of Denver's workingmen. The defense of working-class life, of course, played a major role in the election of 1886. Although most of the Democrats' publicity around the candidacy of Myron Reed stressed his progressive position on labor issues, they also constantly reminded voters of "the very liberal views he entertains" on the liquor question. Reed was adamantly opposed to legislation against the saloon.

The 1886 election ended the Denver labor movement's experiment with political prohibitionism. Although efforts were made to unite the Prohibition Party with the new Colorado Union Labor Party in 1888, these proved to be unsuccessful, Reverend Gilbert DeLaMatyr, a member of the Knights of Labor who had been active in the Prohibition campaign of 1886, became the Union Labor Party's gubernatorial candidate in 1888, reflecting the movement of many "prohibition-laborites" into the broader political organization. Prohibitionism seemed to them an exceedingly unrealistic form of labor politics.

The disenchantment with the Prohibition Party as a vehicle of working-class political action, however, should not obscure an accurate analysis of the causes underlying the opposition of important elements of the labor movement to the urban saloon. In Denver at any rate, this opposition cannot be seen as a "filtering down" of middle-class temperance ideology. Rather it was the product of a major effort to build working-class consciousness and to destroy the social base of a political party system which upheld the status quo.

4

POPULIST DREAMS AND NEGRO RIGHTS: EAST TEXAS AS A CASE STUDY

LAWRENCE C. GOODWYN

The last decade of the nineteenth century was a time of upheaval in a century marked by unprecedented change. In the Northeast, mammoth factories and the immigrants who labored in them dominated the cities of America's industrial heartland. Throughout the country, an ever-growing network of railroads connected even out-lying regions to the burgeoning metropolises of the nation. And in these metropolises, financial and industrial cartels, monopolies, and holding companies exercised an economic and political influence unparalleled in American life.

Facing these changes were workers and farmers. American workers responded to the growing power of industrial capitalism with the collective power of their numbers and struggled with their employers over control of the workplace and the process of production itself. For their part, the small farmers of the South and Midwest responded by forming organizations to fight discriminatory railroad freight rates and to challenge the power of eastern banks to yoke them to a cycle of unending indebtedness.

In the South, the farmer's protest was embodied in the Southern Farmers Alliance and its successor, the Populist or People's party, which sought to forge an alliance between black and white small farmers that would reinstate the power of the small producer in American society. As Lawrence C. Goodwyn shows in this essay, this Populist ideal followed a path fraught with danger. Faced with a resurgent white supremacist movement and mounting southern terrorism directed against its black members, the Populist movement found itself unable to protect its unique interracial coalition. Racism had again triumphed in America. Yet the idea of an interracial radical movement did not die with the decline of Populism; it took root after 1910 in the southern and western branches of the Socialist Party, which elected local and state officials to represent the interests of small farmers and rural workers much as the Populists had done before them.

Nearly a century later the Populist decade lingers in historical memory as an increasingly dim abstraction. The very word "Populism" no longer carries specific popular meaning. It is now invoked to explain George Wallace, as it was used to explain Lyndon Johnson in the sixties, Joe McCarthy in the fifties, and Claude Pepper in the forties. Though afflicting principally the popular mind, this confusion is at least partly traceable to those historians who have insisted on concentrating on Populism as exhortation, so that Ignatius Donnelly's utopian novels or Mary Lease's pronouncements on the respective uses of corn and hell become the explanatory keys to agrarian radicalism. For scholars who mine political movements with a view to extracting cultural nuggets, the focus has been chiefly upon the word, not the deed; in the process the agrarian crusade has become increasingly obscure.

Much of the difficulty centers on the subject of race. There is essential agreement that, on economic issues, Populists were men of the Left, primitive to some, prophetic to others, but leftists to all. But did their banner indicate a highly selective nativist radicalism for whites only, or did they grapple with the inherited legacies of the caste system as part of an effort to create what they considered a more rational social and economic order? The analysis of Populist rhetoric has left us with contradictory answers.

While party platforms can be useful tools in determining professed attitudes, the gap between asserted ideals and performance is sufficiently large to defeat any analysis resting on the implicit assumption that political manifestos have an intrinsic value apart from the milieu in which they existed. In America the distance between assertion and performance is especially evident in matters of race; as a result, on this issue above all, the context of public assertions is central to the task of their political evaluation. An inquiry into the murkiest corner of Populism, interracial politics, should begin not merely with what Populists said but what they did in the course of bidding for power at the local level. What was the stuff of daily life under Populist rule in the rural enclaves where the third party came to exercise all the authority of public office, including police authority? What can we learn not only about Populist insurgency but also about the orthodoxy the third party opposed?

Grimes County, Texas, was one of many counties scattered across the South and West where the People's party achieved a continuing political presence in the latter part of the nineteenth century. Located some sixty miles north of Houston in the heart of what the natives call the Old South part of Texas, Grimes County displayed the cotton-centered economy typical of rural East Texas in 1880. Its largest town, Navasota, contained 1,800 persons in 1890 and its second largest town, Anderson, the county seat, only 574 persons as late as 1900. Farms in Grimes County ranged from plantation size in the rich bottomland country of the Brazos River on the county's western border to small, single-family agricultural units on the poorer land of the northern part of the county. The 1890 census revealed a county population of 21,312, of which 11,664 were black.

Populism in Grimes County is the story of a black–white coalition that had its genesis in Reconstruction and endured for more than a generation. In time this coalition came to be symbolized by its most enduring elected public official, Garrett Scott. The Scotts had roots in Grimes County dating back before the Civil War. Their sons fought for the Confederacy and returned to face a postwar reality by no means unique in the South; possessing moderately large holdings of land but lacking necessary capital to make it productive, the Scotts did not achieve great affluence. During the hard times that continued to afflict undercapitalized Southern agriculture through the 1870s Garrett Scott became soft-money agrarian radical. His stance was significant in the political climate of Grimes County in the early 1880s. During Reconstruction Negroes in the county had achieved a remarkably stable local Republican organization, headed by a number of resourceful black leaders. When Reconstruction ended and white Democrats regained control of the state governmental machinery in Texas, Grimes County blacks retained local power and sent a succession of black legislators to Austin for the next decade. The local effort to end this Republican rule took the usual postwar Southern form of a political movement of white solidarity under the label of the Democratic party. In supporting the Greenback party Garrett Scott not only was dis-associating himself from the politics of white racial solidarity, he was undermining it.

In 1882 a mass meeting of various non-Democratic elements in Grimes County nominated a variegated slate for county offices. Among the candidates were black Republicans, "lily-white" Republicans, and Independent Greenbackers. Garrett Scott was on the ticket as the Independent Greenback candidate for sheriff. Not much is known about the racial climate in Grimes County in 1882, but it must not have been wholly serene, because the "lily-white" nominee for county judge, Lock McDaniel, withdrew from the ticket rather than publicly associate with black candidates. Garrett Scott did not withdraw, and in November he was elected. Also elected, as district clerk, was a black man who became a lifelong political ally of Scott, Jim Kennard. Thus began an interracial coalition that endured through the years of propagandizing in Texas by the increasingly radical Farmers Alliance and through the ensuing period of the People's party. The success of the coalition varied with the degree of white participation. After the collapse of the Greenback party in the mid-eighties visible white opposition to the Democratic party declined for several years before Grimes County farmers, organized by the Alliance, broke with the Democracy to form the nucleus of the local People's party in 1892. Scott and Kennard were the most visible symbols of the revitalized coalition, but there were others as well. Among them were Morris Carrington, a Negro school principal, and Jack Haynes, both staunch advocates of Populism in the black community, as well as J. W. H. Davis and J. H. Teague, white Populist leaders. These men led the People's party to victory in the county elections of 1896 and again in 1898.

A subtle duality creeps into the narrative of events at this point. To the world outside Grimes County in the 1890s, to both Populists and Democrats, Garrett Scott was simply another Populist officeholder, distinguished for his anti-monopoly vies and his generally radical approach to monetary policy. To his white supporters within Grimes County he was doubtless respected for the same reasons. But to the Democrats of Grimes County the sheriff symbolized all that was un-Southern and unpatriotic about the third party. Under Populist rule, it was charged, Negro school teachers were paid too much money; furthermore, in Scott's hands the sheriff's office hired Negro deputies. The two Democratic newspapers in Navasota were fond of equating Populist rule with Negro rule and of attributing both evils to Scott. The Navasota *Daily Examiner* asserted that "the Negro has been looking too much to political agitation and legislative enactment. . . . So long as he looks to political agitation for relief, so long will he be simply the means of other men's ambition." To the Navasota *Tablet* Scott was simply "the originator of all the political trouble in Grimes County for years." Both these explanations oversimplify Grimes County politics. The political presence and goals of blacks were definite elements of local Populism, as was, presumably, the personal ambition of Garrett Scott. But the Populists' proposed economic remedies had gained a significant following among the county's white farmers, and this was of crucial importance in inducing white Populists to break with Democrats and ally themselves with blacks. Garrett Scott was a living embodiment of white radicalism; he did not cause it. Beyond this political cohesion of blacks was a local phenomenon that had preceded Scott's entry into Grimes County politics and had remained relatively stable since the end of the war. The ease with which Democratic partisans saw the fine hand of Garrett Scott in Negro voting was more a reflection of their own racial presumptions than an accurate description of the political dynamics at work in the county.

Through the election of 1898 Democrats in

Grimes County had labored in vain to cope with the disease of Populism among the county's white farmers. Finally, in the spring of 1899, the Democrats moved in a new direction. The defeated Democratic candidate for county judge, J. G. McDonald, organized a clandestine meeting with other prominent local citizens and defeated Democratic office seekers. At this meeting a new and—for the time being—covert political institution was created: the White Man's Union. A charter was drawn providing machinery through which the Union could nominate candidates for county offices in elections in which only White Man's Union members could nominate candidates for county offices in elections in which only White Man's Union members could vote. No person could be nominated who was not a member; no person could be a member who did not subscribe to these exclusionary bylaws; in effect, to participate in the organization's activities, so adequately expressed in its formal title, one had to support, as a policy matter, black disenfranchisement. Throughout the summer and fall of 1899 the White Man's Union quietly organized.

Writing years later McDonald explained that care was taken not to launch the organization publicly "until the public attitude could be sounded." By January 1900 the covert organizing had been deemed sufficiently successful to permit the public unveiling of the White Man's Union through a long story in the *Examiner*. During the spring the *Examiner*'s political reporting began to reflect a significant change of tone. In April, for example, the *Examiner*'s report of a "quiet election" in nearby Bryan noted that friends of the two mayoral candidates "made a display of force and permitted no Negroes to vote. All white citizens went to the polls, quietly deposited their ballots for whom they pleased and went on about their business." The *Examiner* had progressed from vague suggestions for disenfranchisement to approval of its forcible imposition without cover of law.

The first public meetings of the White Man's Union, duly announced in the local press, occupied the spring months of 1900 and were soon augmented by some not-quite-so-public night riding. The chronology of these events may be traced through the denials in the local Democratic press of their occurrence. In July the *Examiner* angrily defended the county's honor against charges by the Negro Baptist State Sunday School Conference that the county had become unsafe for Negroes. The Austin *Herald* reported from the state capital that the Sunday School Board, "after mature thought and philosophical deliberation," had decided to cancel its annual meeting scheduled for Navasota. The *Examiner* cited as "irresponsible slush" the charge that Negroes were being threatened and told to leave the county, but within weeks reports of just such events began cropping up in the *Examiner* itself. One example of terrorism left no one in doubt, for it occurred in broad daylight on the main street of the county seat: in July Jim Kennard was shot and killed within one hundred yards of the courthouse. His assailant was alleged to be J. G. McDonald.

Intimidation and murder constituted an even more decisive assault on the People's party than had the ominous bylaws of the White Man's Union. The Populist leadership recognized this clearly enough, and Scott went so far as to attempt to persuade Southern white farmers to shoulder arms in defense of the right of Negroes to vote. Beyond this we know little of the measures attempted by the local Populist constabulary to contain the spreading terrorism. A well-informed member of the Scott family wrote a detailed account of these turbulent months, but the manuscript was subsequently destroyed. In the early autumn of 1900 members of the White Man's Union felt sufficiently strong to initiate visits to white farmers with a known allegiance to the People's party. Under such duress some of these farmers joined the White Man's Union.

In August the Union, aided by a not inconsiderable amount of free publicity in the local press, announced "the Grandest Barbecue of the Year," at which "the workings of the White Man's Union" would be explained to all. The leadership of the People's party objected to announced plans to include the local state guard unit, the Shaw Rifles, in the program. After some discussion the Texas adjutant general, Thomas Scurry, placed at the discretion of the local commander the question of the attendance of the Shaw Rifles in a body. The commander, Captain Hammond Norwood, a leading Navasota Democrat and a member of the White Man's Union, exercised his option, and the Shaw Rifles appeared en masse at the function. Populist objections were brushed aside.

Shortly after this well-attended barbecue had revealed the growing prestige of the White Man's Union as well as the inability of the People's party to cope with the changing power relationships within the county, a black exodus began. People left by train, by horse and cart, by day and by night. The *Examiner,* with obvious respect for the new political climate its own columns had helped engender, suggested elliptically that the exodus could produce complications. Some citizens, said the *Examiner,* "are beginning to feel a little nervous as the thing progresses, and lean to the idea that the action will bring on detrimental complications in the labor market."

The next day however the paper printed a public address that it said had been "ordered published by the executive committee of the White Man's Union in order to combat the many reports that are calculated to injure the Union." After reaffirming the Union's intent to end "Negro rule" in the county, the report concluded with a message "to the Negroes":

> Being the weaker race, it is our desire to protect you from the schemes of those men who are now seeking to place you before them. . . . Therefore, the White Man's Union kindly and earnestly requests you to keep hands off in the coming struggle. Do not let impudent men influence you in that pathway which certainly leads to trouble. . . . In the future, permit us to show you, and convince you by our action, that we are truly your best friends.

Fourteen days later a black Populist leader, Jack Haynes, was riddled with a shotgun blast by unknown assailants. He died instantly in the fields of his cotton farm.

The White Man's Union held a rally in Navasota two nights later that featured a reading of original poetry by one of the Union's candidates, L. M. Bragg. The verse concluded:

> *Twas nature's laws that drew the lines*
> *Between the Anglo-Saxon and African races,*
> *And we, the Anglo-Saxons of Grand Old*
>   *Grimes,*
> *Must force the African to keep his place.*

Another White Man's Union rally held in Plantersville the same week displayed other Union candidates whose conduct won the *Examiner*'s editorial approval: "They are a solid looking body of men and mean business straight from the shoulder." Apparently this characterization of the Plantersville speakers was not restricted to approving Democrats; Populists, too, responded to events initiated by the men who "meant business." In October the Plantersville school superintendent reported that only five white families remained in his school district and that all the Negroes were gone. The superintendent stated that twelve white families had left that week, and "the end is not in sight."

Amid this wave of mounting terror the People's party attempted to go about its business, announcing its nominating conventions in the local press and moving forward with the business of naming election judges and poll watchers. But there were already signs of a fatal crack in Populist morale. The People's party nominee for county commissioner suddenly withdrew from the race. His withdrawal was announced in the *Examiner,* and no explanation was offered.

Throughout the late summer and autumn of 1900 the demonstrated power of the White Man's Union had protected McDonald from prosecution in the Kennard slaying. Nothing short of a war between the Populist police authority and the White Man's Union could break that extralegal shield. An exasperated and perhaps desperate Garrett Scott angrily challenged a White Man's Union official in October to "go and get your Union force, every damn one of them, put them behind rock fences and trees and I'll fight the whole damn set of cowards." That Scott had to use the first person singular to describe the visible opposition to the Union underscores the extent to which terror had triumphed over the institutions of law in Grimes County. By election eve it was clear that the Populist ticket faced certain defeat. The third party had failed to protect its constituency. White Populists as well as black were intimidated. Many would not vote; indeed, many were no longer in the county.

Over 4,500 votes had been cast in Grimes in 1898. On November 6, 1900, only 1,800 persons ventured to the polls. The People's party received exactly 366 votes. The Populist vote in Plantersville fell from 256 in 1898 to 5 in 1900. In the racially mixed, lower-income precinct of south Navasota the Populist vote declined from 636 to 23. The sole exception to this pattern came in a geographically isolated, lower-income precinct in the extreme northern part of the county that contained few Negroes and thus, presumably, fewer acts of terrorism. The Populist vote in this precinct actually increased from 108 to 122 and accounted for one-third of the county-wide vote of 366. In north Navasota, also almost all white but not geographically isolated from the terror, the Populist vote declined from 120 to 3. An additional element, nonstatistical in nature, stamped the election as unusual. The underlying philosophy of the South's dominant political institution, the Democratic party, has perhaps never been expressed more nakedly than it was in Grimes County in 1900 when "the party of white supremacy," as C. Vann Woodward has called the Southern Democracy, appeared on the official ballot as the White Man's Union.

On the way to its landslide victory the Union had grown more self-confident in its willingness to carry out acts of intimidation and terrorism in defiance of the local Populist police authority. Now that that authority had been deposed and a sheriff friendly to the White Man's Union had

been elected, would terrorism become even more public?

On November 7, 1900, the morning after the election, a strange tableau unfolded on the streets of Anderson, the tiny county seat. Horsemen began arriving in town from every section of the county, tied their horses all along the main street, and occupied the second floor of the courthouse. In a nearby house Garrett Scott's sister, Cornelia, and her husband, John Kelly, watched the buildup of Union supporters on the courthouse square, not fifty yards from the sheriff's official residence on the second floor of the county jail. They decided the situation was too dangerous to permit an adult Populist to venture forth, so the Kellys sent their nine-year-old son with a note to warn Scott not to appear on the street.

At about the same time that this mission was carried out Garrett Scott's younger brother, Emmett Scott, came into town from the family farm, rode past the growing clusters of armed men, and reined up in front of the store belonging to John Bradley, his closest friend in town. Bradley was a Populist, but, as befitting a man of trade, a quiet one. His store was adjacent to the courthouse.

Cornelia Kelly's son found the sheriff at Abercrombie's store across the street from the jail and delivered the warning note. As Scott read it an outbreak of gunfire sounded from the direction of Bradley's store. Scott stepped to the street and peered in the direction of the fusillade. Rifle fire from the second floor of the courthouse immediately cut him down. Upon hearing the gunfire Cornelia Kelly ran out of her house and down the long street toward the courthouse. The gunsights of scores of men tracked her progress. Seeing her brother's body in the street she turned and confronted his attackers. "Why don't you shoot me, too," she yelled, "I'm a Scott." She ran to her brother and, with the assistance of her son, dragged him across the street to the county jail. He was, she found, not dead, though he did have an ugly wound in his hip. Inside Bradley's store, however, three men were dead—Emmett

Scott, Bradley, and Will McDonald, the son of a Presbyterian minister and a prominent member of the White Man's Union. McDonald had shot Scott shortly after the latter had entered the store; the two men grappled for the gun, and the fatally wounded Scott fired one shot, killing McDonald. Bradley was killed either by a shot fired from outside the store where Union forces had gathered near the courthouse or by a stray bullet during the struggle inside.

The siege of Anderson continued for five days, with the wounded sheriff and his deputies—black and white—in the jail and the White Man's Union forces in the courthouse. Shots crossed the fifty yards between the two buildings intermittently over the next several days. On the evening of the fatal shooting another member of the Scott clan, Mrs. W. T. Neblett, had left Navasota for Austin to plead with the governor, Joseph D. Sayers, for troops. On Friday she returned, accompanied by the adjutant general of the State of Texas, Thomas Scurry—the same official who had earlier acquiesced in the participation of the statue guard in the White Man's Union barbecue. After conferring with the contending forces Scurry pondered various methods to get the wounded Scott out of town and into a hospital; gangrene had set in. For protection, Scurry suggested that he be authorized to select a group of twenty prominent citizens of Navasota to escort the sheriff from the jail to the railroad station. Since most of the "prominent citizens" of Navasota were members of the White Man's Union, it is perhaps understandable that Scott declined this offer. The adjutant general then suggested that the Shaw Rifles be employed as an escort. This idea was respectfully declined for the same reason. Asked what he would consider a trustworthy escort, the wounded sheriff suggested a state guard from outside the county.

On Saturday, four days after the shooting, a company of Houston light infantry of the Texas Volunteer to State Guard detrained at Navasota and marched the eleven miles to Anderson. On Sunday morning Garrett Scott was placed on a mattress, the mattress put in a wagon, and the procession began. In the wagon train were most of the members of the large Scott clan—Emmett Scott's widow and children, the Kelly family, and the Nebletts, all with their household belongings piled in wagons. A file of infantrymen marched on either side as the procession formed in front of the jail, moved past hundreds of armed men at the courthouse and onto the highway to Navasota, and then boarded a special train bound for Houston.

Thus did Populism leave Grimes County. From that day in 1900 until well after mid-century Negroes were not a factor in Grimes County politics. J. G. McDonald regained his judgeship and served for many years. The White Man's Union continued into the 1950s as the dominant political institution in the county. None of its nominees, selected in advance of the Democratic primary, was ever defeated. The census of 1910 revealed the extent of the Negro exodus. It showed that Grimes County's Negro population had declined by almost thirty per cent from the 1900 total. School census figures for 1901 suggest an even greater exodus.

To this day the White Man's Union, as a memory if no longer as an institution, enjoys an uncontested reputation among Grimes County whites as a civic enterprise for governmental reform. In this white oral tradition the general events of 1900 are vividly recounted. Specific events are, however, remembered selectively. The exodus of Negroes from the county is not part of this oral tradition, nor is the night riding of the White Man's Union or the assassination of the Negro Populist leaders.

As for Garrett Scott, he endured a long convalescence in a San Antonio hospital, regained his health, married his nurse, and moved to a farm near Houston. He retired from politics and died in his bed. He is remembered in the oral tradition of the black community as "the best sheriff the county ever had." Kennard and Haynes were killed because they "vouched" for Scott among Negroes. In this black oral tradition the Negro exodus plays a central role. It is perhaps an accurate measure of the distance between the races in Grimes County today that two such contradictory versions of famous events could exist side by side without cross-influence.

To these two oral traditions a third must be added—the Scott tradition. The Scotts were, and are, a proud family. One by one, as they died, they were brought home to be buried in the family plot in the Anderson cemetery, little more than a mile from the site of the bloody events of 1900. Tombstones of female members of the clan bear the Scott middle name, defiantly emblazoned in marble. Edith Hamilton of Richards, Grimes County, was ten years old in November 1900 and remembers vividly the day her nine-year-old brother carried her mother's message to Garrett Scott. She remembers the defiance of her mother, the political commitment of her father, the acts of intimidation by the White Man's Union, the Negro exodus, and what she calls the "intelligence of Uncle Garrett." "They said that Uncle Garrett was a nigger-lover," recalls Mrs. Hamilton. "He wasn't a nigger-lover, or a white-lover, he just believed in being fair to all, in justice."

The Scott oral tradition—similar to the black oral tradition and at odds with the white tradition—is virtually the only legacy of the long years of interracial cooperation in Grimes County. Beyond this the substance of political life that came to an end in Grimes County in 1900 cannot be measured precisely from the available evidence. Very little survives to provide insight into the nature of the personal relationship that existed between Garrett Scott and Jim Kennard, between any of the other Populist leaders of both races, or between their respective constituencies. Scott and his third-party colleagues may have been motivated solely by personal ambition, as the White Man's Union charged; on the other hand, the impulses that made them Populists in the first place may have led them toward public coalition with blacks. It is clear that such stridently white supremacist voices as the Navasota *Tablet* were unable to project any reason other than personal ambition to explain the phenomenon of white men willingly associating themselves politically with black men. To what extent this attitude reflected Populist presumptions is

another question. White Populists and black Republicans shared an animosity toward the Southern Democracy that grew in intensity during the bitter election campaigns of the 1890s. Democratic persistence in raising the cry of "Negro domination" to lure Populist-leaning voters back to the "party of the fathers" was effective enough to keep white Populists on the defensive about the race issue throughout the agrarian revolt in the South. The circumstance of a common political foe nevertheless provided Populists and Republicans with a basis for political coalition that was consummated in a bewildering variety of ways—and sometimes not consummated at all. The stability of local black organizations and their demonstrated capacity to withstand Democratic blandishments or acts of intimidation were only two of the factors governing the complex equation of post-Reconstruction interracial politics. A stable, local black political institution existed in Grimes County, and its enduring qualities obviously simplified the organizational task confronting Garrett Scott. What might be regarded as "normal" Bourbon efforts to split blacks from the Populist coalition—mild intimidation, petty bribery, campaign assertions that the Democrats were the Negroes' "best friends," or a combination of all three—failed to achieve the desired results in Grimes County in the 1890s. The precise reasons are not easily specified. The Navasota *Tablet*, seeing the world through lenses tinted with its own racial presumptions, ascribed the credit for Negro political cohesion solely to the white sheriff. In the face of all Democratic stratagems, the third party's continuing appeal to Negroes was, in the *Tablet*'s view, a thing of "magic." A white supremacist view does not automatically exclude its holder from rendering correct political analyses on occasion, and it is possible that the *Tablet*'s assessment of the cause of Negro political solidarity was correct; however, such an analysis does not explain how the Negro Republican organization was able to send a succession of black legislators to Austin in the 1870s and 1880s, before Garrett Scott became politically active. It seems relevant that when Grimes County Democrats decided upon an overt campaign of terrorism, the men they went after first were the leading black spokesmen of Populism in the county rather than the third party's white leadership. To this extent the actions of Democratic leaders contradicted their public analysis of the causal relationships inherent in the continuing Populist majorities.

Before they indulged in terrorism the Democrats already possessed another method of splitting the Populist coalition: regaining the loyalty of white Populists. Against the historic Democratic campaign cry of white supremacy, the People's party had as its most effective defense the economic appeal of its own platform. The persuasiveness of Populism to white farmers in Grimes County was confirmed by newspaper accounts of the public reaction to the Populist–Democratic debates that occurred during the years of the agrarian uprising. While the reports in the *Examiner* were uniformly partisan and invariably concluded that Democratic spokesmen "won" such debates hands down, the papers conceded that Populist speakers also drew enthusiastic responses from white residents. The absence of reliable racial data by precincts renders a statistical analysis of the Populist vote in Grimes County impossible; however, the fragmentary available evidence suggests that the People's party was generally able to hold a minimum of approximately thirty per cent of the county's white voters in the four elections from 1892 to 1898 while at the same time polling approximately eighty to ninety per cent of the Negro electorate. The inability of the Democratic party to "bloc vote" the county's white citizenry, coupled with the party's failure to win black voters by various means or, alternatively, to diminish the size of the Negro electorate, combined to ensure Democratic defeat at the polls. The fact merits emphasis: both the cohesion of black support for the People's party and the maintenance of substantial white support were essential to the local ascendancy of Populism.

This largely deductive analysis, however, reveals little about the internal environment within the third-party coalition during the bitter struggle for power that characterized the decade of Populist–Democratic rivalry. However scrutinized, the bare bones of voting totals do not flesh out the human relationships through which black and white men came together politically in this rural Southern county. In the absence of such crucial evidence, it seems prudent to measure the meaning of 1900 in the most conservative possible terms. Even by this standard, however, a simple recitation of those elements of Grimes County politics that are beyond dispute isolates significant and lasting ramifications.

An indigenous black political structure persisted in Grimes County for thirty-five years following the Civil War. Out of his own needs as a political insurgent against the dominant Southern Democratic party, Garrett Scott decided in 1882 to identify his Greenback cause with the existing local Republican constituency. Once in office as sheriff he found, among other possible motives, that it was in his own self-interest to preserve the coalition that elected him. It is clear that the style of law enforcement in Grimes County under Scott became a persuasive ingredient in the preservation of black support for the People's party. The presence of black deputy sheriffs and Scott's reputation within the black community seem adequate confirmation of both the existence of this style and its practical effect. The salaries paid Negro school teachers constituted another element of third-party appeal. Comparisons with white salaries are not available, but whatever black teachers received, partisans of the White Man's Union publicly denounced it as "too much." It is evident that Grimes County Negroes supported the People's party for reasons that were grounded in legitimate self-interest—an incontestable basis for political conduct. The point is not so much that the county's Negroes had certain needs, but that they possessed the political means to address at least a part of those needs.

From this perspective the decisive political event of 1900 in Grimes County was not the overwhelming defeat of the local People's party but the political elimination of that part of its constituency that was black. Scott was valuable to Negroes in short-run terms because he helped to translate a minority black vote into a majority coalition that possessed the administrative authority to improve the way black people lived in Grimes County. In the long run, however, it was the presence of this black constituency—not the conduct of a single white sheriff nor even the professed principles of his political party—that provided the Negroes of the county with what protection they had from a resurgent caste system. As long as Negroes retained the right to cast ballots in proportion to their numbers they possessed bargaining power that became particularly meaningful on all occasions when whites divided their votes over economic issues. Disfranchisement destroyed the bargaining power essential to this elementary level of protection. Arrayed against these overriding imperatives for Negroes such questions as the sincerity of Garrett Scott's motives fade in importance. Whatever the sheriff's motives, both the political realities that undergirded the majority coalition and Scott's ability to respond to those realities shaped a course of government conduct under the People's party that was demonstrably of more benefit to Negroes than was the conduct of other administrations before or since. The permanent alteration of those realities through black disfranchisement ensured that no other white administration, whether radical, moderate, or opportunistic, would be able to achieve the patterns in education and law enforcement that had come to exist in the county under Populism. Stated as starkly as possible, after 1900 it was no longer in the interest of white politicians to provide minimal guarantees for people who could not help elect them.

Beyond this crucial significance for the county's black people, disfranchisement also institutionalized a fundamental change in the political environment of whites. More than a third party passed from Grimes County in 1900; in real political terms an idea died. Though a new political idea invariably materializes in democratic societies as an expression of the self-interest of a portion of the electorate, the party that adopts the idea in the course of appealing for the votes of that sector of the electorate inevitably is placed in the position of having to rationalize, defend, explain, and eventually promote the idea. If the concept has substance, this process eventually results in the insinuation of the idea into the culture itself. In this sense it is not necessary to know the precise depth of the commitment to Negro rights of the Grimes County People's party to know that the *idea* of Negro rights had a potential constituency among white people in the county as long as black people were able to project its presence through their votes. Given the endurance of this real and potential constituency, one could reasonably intuit that twentieth-century politics in Grimes County would have contained one, or a dozen, or a thousand Garrett Scotts—each more, or less, "sincere" or "ambitious" than the Populist sheriff. Disfranchisement destroyed the political base of this probability. A political party can survive an electoral defeat, even continuing defeat, and remain a conveyor of ideas from one generation to the next. But it cannot survive the destruction of its constituency, for the party itself then dies, taking with it the possibility of transmitting its political concepts to those as yet unborn. It is therefore no long possible to speak of two white political traditions in Grimes County, for the White Man's Union succeeded in establishing a most effective philosophical suzerainty. Seventy years after disfranchisement Mrs. Hamilton can recall the racial unorthodoxy of Uncle Garrett; she cannot participate in such activity herself. "The Negro people don't want this school integration any more than the whites do," she now says. "They're not ready for it. They don't feel comfortable in the school with white children. I've talked to my maid. I know."

While Garrett Scott's memory has been preserved, the local presence of the creed of his political party died with the destruction of that party. There has been literally no political place to go for subsequent generations of Scotts and Teagues, or Kennards and Carringtons. This absence of an alternative political institution to the Democratic party, the party of white supremacy, has been a continuing and unique factor in Southern politics. The circumstance is based on the race issue, but in its long-term political and social implications it actually transcends that issue.

The Populist era raises a number of questions about the interaction of the two races in the South, both within the third party and in the larger society. It is widely believed, by no means merely by laymen, that after the failure of Reconstruction meaningful experiments with the social order were finished in the South and that the aspirations of blacks were decisively thwarted. The example of Grimes County suggests, however, the existence of a period of time—a decade perhaps, or a generation—when nascent forms of indigenous interracial activity struggled for life in at least parts of the old Confederacy. Was some opportunity missed and, if so, how? How widespread through the South, and the nation, was this opportunity?

The White Man's Union was organized and led by men who considered themselves the "best people" of the South. If this attitude was typical, major adjustments must be made in our understanding of precisely how, and for what reasons, the antebellum caste system, in altered form, was reinstitutionalized in Southern society a generation after the formal ending of slavery. Was the "red-neck" the source of atrocity, or was he swept along by other stronger currents? And what of the Populist role? To what extent was agrarian racial liberalism in Texas traceable to an overall philosophy within the third-party leadership? Through what intuition of self-interest did the radical organizers of the Farmers Alliance, the parent institution of the People's party, accept the political risks of public coalition with blacks? What were their hopes and fears, and where did they falter? And, finally, what does the substance of their effort tell us about the Democrats in the South and Republicans in the North who opposed them?

Answers to these questions rest, in part, on detailed knowledge of such events as those in Grimes County, but they require more than compilations of local histories, just as they assuredly require more than cultural assessments based on novels, speeches, and party manifestoes considered apart from their organic milieu. These answers will not provide much of a synthesis—Populism was too diverse, too congregational, and too ideologically thin—but they should tell us more about the larger society that, along with the Populists, failed to erect the foundations for a multiracial society in the nineteenth century. As the inquiry proceeds, it should be remembered that Populism perished before developing a mature philosophy—on race, on money, or on socialism. One must generalize, therefore, not only from contradictory evidence but, more important, from incomplete evidence. An analogy, doubtless unfair, could be made with the plight that would face modern historians of Marxism had that movement been abruptly truncated at the time, say, of the Brussels Conference in 1903. Who could have predicted on the evidence available to that date the Stalinist reign of terror that evolved from the mature, victorious revolutionary party of 1917? By the same token sweeping generalizations about what Populist radicalism could have become are not only romantic but historically unsound.

It should be sufficient to observe that in the long post-Reconstruction period—a period not yet ended—during which the social order has been organized hierarchically along racial lines, Populism intruded as a brief, flickering light in parts of the South. For a time some white Southerners threw off the romanticism that has historically been a cover for the region's pessimism and ventured a larger, more hopeful view about the possibilities of man in a free society. Under duress and intimidation this public hope failed of persuasion at the ballot box; under terrorism it vanished completely.

The Grimes County story dramatically illustrates this failure, but in the insight it provides into the underlying politics of black disfranchisement and the achievement of a monolithic one-party political environment in the American South it is not unique. Other Populists in East Texas and across the South—white as well as black—died during the terrorism that preceded formal disfranchisement. In Texas the extra-parliamentary institutions formed by white Democrats to help create the political climate for disfranchisement bore a variety of local names: the Citizens White Primary of Marion County; the Tax-Payers Union of Brazoria County; the Jaybird Democratic Association of Fort Bend County; and the White Man's Union of Wharton, Washington, Austin, Matagorda, Grimes, and other counties. The available historical material concerning each of these organizations comes largely from the founders themselves, or their descendants, reflecting an incipient or a mature oral tradition—one oral tradition. The secondary literature based on these accounts, including scholarly works used in graduate schools as well as primary and secondary textbooks, is correspondingly inadequate.

A surprising amount of uninterpreted material from violently partisan white supremacist sources has found its way into scholarly literature. One example from the Grimes experience pertains directly to the scholarly characterization of Negro political meetings during the Populist era. It is worth attention as an illustration of the impact of white supremacist modes of thought on modern scholarship. The sunup-to-sundown work routine of Southern farm labor obviously precluded daytime political meetings. Accordingly, Kennard, Haynes, and Carrington campaigned among their black constituents by holding political meetings in each of the towns and hamlets of the country at night. Democratic partisans termed these rallies "Owl Meetings" and characterized black Populist leaders as "'fluence men." Drawing upon their own party's time-honored campaign technique with Negroes, Democrats further asserted that owl meetings were more concerned with sumptuous banquets and whisky than with politics. If partisans of white supremacy had difficulty finding reasons for white acceptance of political coalition with blacks, they were culturally incapable of ascribing reasons for Negro support of the third party to causes other than short-run benefits in terms of money and alcohol. The point is not that Democrats were always insincere in their descriptions (as white supremacists they were quite sincere), but that scholars have

subsequently accepted such violently partisan accounts at face value. The darkly sinister picture of "'fluence men" corrupting innocent blacks with whisky at surreptitious owl meetings served to justify, at least to outsiders, the use of terrorism as the ultimate campaign technique of Democratic interracial politics. This sequential recording of events has found its way into scholarly monographs that otherwise demonstrate no inherent hostility to the Populistic inclinations of Southern farmers, black or white. In *The People's Party in Texas* Roscoe Martin precedes his brief allusion to the White Man's Union with a résumé of owl meetings and "'fluence men" that reflects in detail the bias of white supremacist sources. Other scholars writing broadly about Gilded Age politics have routinely drawn upon such monographs as Martin's, and by this process "'fluence men" have materialized as an explanation of Negro political insurgency in the nineties. In the heat of local political combat, however, Democratic leaders often were able to face a wholly different set of facts in the course of persuading their followers, and the citizenry as a whole, to adjust to the necessity of terrorism. As the time approached for actual precinct campaigning in Grimes County in the autumn of 1900, the executive board of the White Man's Union published a notice of the Union's intentions, climaxed by a "fair distinct warning" to the county's Negro leadership. The statement is revealing—not only of the transformation visited upon normal campaign practices when they were viewed through the cultural presumptions of white supremacy but also of the dangers of uncritical acceptance of such perspectives by scholars relying upon monoracial sources. The notice read in part:

> The Union is largely composed of the best citizens of the county. . . . They are the tax payers, representing the worth, the patriotism, the intelligence, and the virtues of the county. . . . We are not fighting any political party or individuals, but only those who band together under any name who seek to perpetuate negro rule in Grimes County. [Good citizens] are astounded at the

manner in which the children's money has been expended. Colored teachers with fat salaries and totally incompetent have been appointed for political "fluence." Our white teachers, male and female, enjoy no such fat salaries as these colored politicians or these sweet colored girls. . . . One of the most corrupting practices in the past has been the system of Owl Meetings which has been in vogue for years. . . . This is the school and hot bed where the negro politician received his inspiration, and riding from one end of the county to the other as an apostle of his race, corrupting his own people who may be in the honest pathway of duty. We give fair warning that any effort to continue these Owl Meetings—by the appointment of special deputies sheriffs to organize and carry them on—will be prevented. No threat of shotguns will deter us from the discharge of this duty.

Even without recourse to other perspectives this view of the existing political situation in Grimes County contains serious internal contradictions. Black Populist leaders were "incompetent" but as "apostles of their race" they had been so effective that their efforts needed to be stopped. Black teachers were paid "fat salaries" solely for political reasons, but among those receiving such gross patronage were "sweet colored girls," who obviously were not conducting owl meetings. The assertion that black teachers were actually paid more than white teachers must be rejected out of hand. In addition to the compelling fact that such an arrangement would have constituted poor political behavior on the part of a third party strenuously endeavoring to hold a substantial portion of the white vote and the further reality that such expenditures were unnecessary since parity for blacks in itself would have represented a notable accomplishment in the eyes of Negro leaders, Democrats had access to the records of all county expenditures and no such charge was ever leveled, much less documented, at any other time during the Populist decade. Whites complained that Negro teachers received "too much," not that they received more than white teachers. In any case, it seems necessary only to observe that American political parties have routinely utilized night gatherings with-

out having their opponents characterize them as owl meetings and that persons who benefited from incumbency were not presumed to be acting in sinister ways when they campaigned for their party's re-election. The only thing "special" about Garrett Scott's deputies was that some of them were black. Viewed as some sort of black abstraction Jim Kennard might appear convincing as a shadowy "'fluence man," but as an intelligent and determined voice of the aspirations of Negro people he merits scholarly attention from perspectives not bounded by the horizons of those who murdered him. To an extent that is perhaps not fully appreciated, decades of monoracial scholarship in the South have left a number of Jim Kennards buried under stereotypes of one kind or another. They sometimes intrude anonymously as "'fluence men," but they simply do not appear as people in books on Southern politics.

This circumstance suggests that not only the broad topic of interracial life and tension but the entire Southern experience culminated by disfranchisement needs to be tested by a methodology that brings both black and white sources to bear on the admittedly intricate problem of interpreting a free society that was not free. At all events, evidence continues to mount that monoracial scholarship, Northern and Southern, has exhausted whatever merit it possessed as an instrument of investigating the variegated past of the American people. The obvious rejoinder—that written black sources do not exist in meaningful quality—cannot, of course, be explained away; at the same time, this condition suggests the utility of fresh attempts to devise investigatory techniques that offer the possibility of extracting usable historical material from oral sources. The example of the erroneous report in the Navasota *Examiner* of Morris Carrington's death illustrates, perhaps as well as any single piece of evidence, not only the dangers inherent in relying on such "primary sources" for details of interracial tension in the post-Reconstruction South but also the value of received oral traditions in correcting contemporary accounts. Nevertheless, the problem of evaluating such source material remains; white and black versions of the details of racial conflicts are wildly contradictory. When they are measured against other contemporary evidence, however, the interpretive problem becomes considerably less formidable; indeed, the task of penetrating the substance behind partisan contemporary accounts may be lessened through recourse to available oral sources, as I have attempted to demonstrate.

Since much of the *Realpolitik* of the South, from Reconstruction through the modern civil rights movement, rests on legal institutions that, in turn, rest on extralegal methods of intimidation, the sources of political reality may be found less in public debate than in the various forms of intimidation that matured in the region.

However determined a historian may be to penetrate the legal forms to reach this extralegal underside of the political culture of the South he is, in our contemporary climate, blocked off from part of his sources by his skin color. For black scholars there are limits to the availability both of courthouse records in the rural South and of responsive white oral sources. There are corresponding limits to the information white scholars can gain from interviews in black communities. Here, then, is fertile ground for scholarly cooperation. Methods of achieving this cooperation need to be explored. In its fullest utilization the subject is not black history or Southern history but American history.

5

WOMEN ON THE GREAT PLAINS, 1865–1890

CHRISTINE STANSELL

In the generation after the Civil War, tens of thousands of families left the familiar surroundings of their eastern homes, kin, and friends to settle west of the Mississippi River. Although long considered the "Great American Desert," the midwestern prairies in fact contained some of the most fertile land in North America. But what drew these droves of settlers to the Dakotas, Kansas, and Nebraska was less a matter of high soil fertility than one of changes in federal land policy during the Civil War. With the issue of free soil versus slavery no longer inhibiting congressional debate, the Civil War Congress passed the Homestead Act in 1862. This act permitted any adult citizen or permanent resident to claim 160 acres of western federal land for a $10 filing fee and granted title to such persons after five years of successful residence. It was this prospect of free land that created a veritable land rush in the postwar era.

While the burdens of migration and resettlement fell on every homesteader, they fell especially hard on pioneer wives and mothers. Removal to the trans-Mississippi West meant severing connections with an intimate network of female friends and relatives who had provided not only companionship but assistance in childbirth, ill-health, and times of stress. Isolated within the family group, homesteading women had only their own resources and the labor of their husbands and children to rely on as they engaged in the arduous task of farmmaking on the trackless prairies. As Christine Stansell reveals in this essay, resettlement on the Great Plains brought other problems as well, not the least of which was how to maintain familiar notions of womanliness while living in sod huts and working on the windswept prairies. While some wives welcomed the challenge, Stansell suggests that most simply endured, hoping life would be easier and more "womanly" for their daughters. This essay affords the opportunity to evaluate how much traditional values held by eastern women were changed by the frontier experience.

"Women on the Great Plains, 1865–1890." Women's Studies, *4 (1976),*
pp. 87–98. Reprinted by permission of the author.

In 1841, Catharine Beecher proudly attested to the power of her sex by quoting some of Tocqueville's observations on the position of American women. On his tour of 1831, Tocqueville had found Americans to be remarkably egalitarian in dividing social power between the sexes. In his opinion, their ability to institute democratic equality stemmed from a clearcut division of work and responsibilities: "in no country has such constant care been taken . . . to trace two clearly distinct lines of action for the two sexes, and to make them keep pace with the other, but in two pathways which are always different." In theory, men and women controlled separate "spheres" of life: women held sway in the home, while men attended to economic and political matters. Women were not unaware of the inequities in a trade-off between ascendancy in the domestic sphere and participation in society as a whole. Attached to the metaphorical bargain struck between the sexes was a clause ensuring that women, through "home influence," could also affect the course of nation-building. For Miss Beecher, domesticity was also imperial power: "to American women, more than to any others on earth, is committed the exalted privilege of extending over the world those blessed influences, which are to renovate degraded man, and 'clothe all climes with beauty.'"

Yet despite Beecher's assertions to the contrary, by 1841 one masculine "line of action" was diverging dangerously from female influences. Increasing numbers of men were following a pathway which led them across the Mississippi to a land devoid of American women and American homes. In the twenty-odd years since the Santa Fe trade opened the Far West to American businessmen, only men, seeking profits in furs or trading, had gone beyond the western farmlands of the Mississippi Valley; no women participated in the first stages of American expansion. Consequently, by 1841 the West was in one sense a geographical incarnation of the masculine sphere, altogether untouched by "home influence." Although in theory American development preserved a heterosexually balanced democracy, in actuality, the West, new arena of political and economic growth, had become a man's world.

In 1841, the first Americans intending to settle in the trans-Mississippi region rather than only trap or trade began to migrate over the great overland road to the coast. For the first time, women were present in the caravans, and in the next decades, thousands of women in families followed. Their wagon trains generally carried about one-half men, one-half women and children: a population with the capacity to reinstate a heterosexual culture. Only during the Gold Rush years, 1849–1852, were most of the emigrants once again male. Many of the forty-niners, however, chose to return East rather than to settle. In the aftermath of the Rush, the numerical balance of men and women was restored. By 1860, the sex ratio in frontier counties, including those settled on the Great Plains, was no different from the average sex ratio in the East.

Despite the heterosexual demography, however, the West in the years after 1840 still appeared to be masculine terrain. Everywhere, emigrants and travellers saw "such lots of men, but very few ladies and children." In mining camps, "representatives of the gentler sex were so conspicuous by their absence that in one camp a lady's bonnet and boots were exhibited for one dollar a look." Similarly, "the Great Plains in the early period was strictly a man's country." Even later, historians agree that "the Far West had a great preponderance of men over women," and that the absence of "mothers and wives to provide moral anchorage to the large male population" was a primary cause of its social ills. What accounts for the disparity between these observations and the bare facts of demography? In many frontier regions, women failed to reinstitute their own sphere. Without a cultural base of their own, they disappeared behind the masculine preoccupations and social structure which dominated the West. Despite their numbers, women were often invisible, not only in the first two decades of family settlement but in successive phases as well.

In this essay, I try to sketch out some ways of understanding how the fact of this masculine imperium affected women's experiences in the great trans-Mississippi migrations. The following pages are in no way a monograph but rather a collection of suggestions which I have developed through reading and teaching about the West, and which I hope will encourage others to begin investigating this neglected area. Western migration constituted a critical rite of passage in nineteenth-century culture; its impact still reverbates a century later in our own "Western" novels, movies, and television serials. Women's relationship to this key area of the "American experience" has remained submerged and unquestioned. There are only a few secondary books on women in the West, and the two best-known works are simplistic and sentimental. Few writers or scholars have attempted to look at frontier women in the light of the newer interpretations of women's history which have evolved over the last four years. There are a wealth of questions to investigate and a wealth of sources to use. To demonstrate how new analyses can illuminate conventional teaching and lecture material, I have chosen one clearly defined area of "pioneer experience," settlers on the Great Plains from 1865–1890. The half-dozen books I use here are nearly all published and readily available.

Until after the Civil War, emigrants usually travelled over the Great Plains without a thought of stopping. Explorers, farmers, and travellers agreed that the dry grasslands of the "Great American Desert"—the Dakotas, western Kansas, and western Nebraska—were not suitable for lucrative cultivation. In the late 60's, however, western land-grant railroads attempting to boost profits from passenger fares and land sales by promoting settlement in the region launched an advertising campaign in America and Europe which portrayed the Plains as a new Eden of verdant grasslands, rich soil, and plenteous streams. The railroad propaganda influenced a shift in public opinion, but technological advances in wheat-growing and steadily expanding urban markets for crops were far more significant in attracting settlers from Europe and the Mississippi Valley to the region. Emigrants came to take advantage of opportunities for more land, more crops, and more profits.

Who decided to move to the new lands? In the prevailing American notions of family relations, decisions about breadwinning and family finances were more or less in the hands of the male. Of course, removal to the Plains was a significant matter, and it is doubtful that many husbands and fathers made a unilateral decision to pull up stakes. Unfortunately, no large body of evidence about the choice to migrate to the Plains has been found or, at least, utilized in scholarly studies. I have sampled, however, some of the more than seven hundred diaries of men and women traveling to California and Oregon twenty years earlier. These indicate that the man usually initiated a plan to emigrate, made the final decision, and to a greater or lesser degree imposed it on his family. Men's involvement with self-advancement in the working world provided them with a logical and obvious rationale for going West.

The everyday concerns of "woman's sphere," however, did not provide women with many reasons to move. In the system that Tocqueville praised and Beecher vaunted, women's work, social responsibilities, and very identities were based almost entirely in the home. Domesticity involved professionalized housekeeping, solicitous child-rearing, and an assiduous maintenance of a proper moral and religious character in the family. Clearly, women could keep house better, literally and metaphorically, in "civilized" parts, where churches, kinfolk, and women friends supported them. The West held no promise of a happier family life or a more salutary moral atmosphere. On the contrary, it was notoriously destructive to those institutions and values which women held dear.

The Plains region was an especially arid prospect for the transplantation of womanly values. Lonely and crude frontier conditions prevailed into the 90's; in some areas, the sparse population actually declined with time: "following the great boom of the 80's, when the tide of migration began to recede, central Dakota and western Nebraska and Kansas presented anything but a land of occupied farms." The loneliness which women endured "must have been such as to crush the soul," according to one historian of the region. Another asserts that "without a doubt" the burden of the adverse conditions of Plains life—the aridity, treelessness, heat, perpetual wind, and deadening cold—fell upon the women. Almost without exception, others concur: "although the life of the frontier farmer was difficult special sympathy should go to his wife" . . . "it is certain that many stayed until the prairie broke them in spirit or body while others fled from the monotonous terror of it." An observer who visited the Plains in the 50's found life there to be "peculiarly severe upon women and oxen." The duration as well as the severity of cultural disruption which Plains women experienced was perhaps without parallel in the history of nineteenth-century frontiers.

First of all, emigrant women did not move into homes like the ones they had left behind, but into sod huts, tarpaper shacks, and dugouts. Seldom as temporary as they planned to be, these crude structures still existed as late as the nineties. Most settlers lived in one room "soddies" for six or seven years: if luck left a little cash, they might move into a wooden shack. Thus a farmer's wife often spent years trying to keep clean a house made of dirt. The effort became especially disheartening in rainstorms, when leaking walls splattered mud over bedclothes and dishes: "in those trying times the mud floors were too swampy to walk upon and wives could cook only with an umbrella held over the stove; after they were over every stitch of clothing must be hung out to dry." Dry weather gave no respite from dirt, since dust and straw incessantly sifted down from the walls. Housekeeping as a profession in the sense that Catharine Beecher promulgated it was impossible under such circumstances. Soddies were so badly insulated that during the winter, water froze away from the stove. In summer, the paucity of light and air could be stifling.

Often there was simply no money available to build a decent house. Drought, grasshoppers, or unseasonable rains destroyed many of the harvests of the 80's and 90's. Even good crops did not necessarily change a family's living condi-

tions, since debts and mortgages which had accrued during hard times could swallow up any profits. But in any case, home improvements were a low priority, and families often remained in soddies or shacks even when there was cash or credit to finance a frame house. The farmer usually earmarked his profits for reinvestment into the money-making outlay of better seeds, new stock, machinery, and tools. Farm machinery came first, labor-saving devices for women last: "there was a tendency for the new homesteader to buy new machinery to till broad acres and build new barns to house more stock and grain, while his wife went about the drudgery of household life in the old way in a little drab dwelling overshadowed by the splendour of machine farming." Washers and sewing machines graced some farms in the 80's, but "for the most part . . . the machine age did not greatly help woman. She continued to operate the churn, carry water, and run the washing machine—if she were fortunate enough to have one—and do her other work without the aid of horse power which her more fortunate husband began to apply in his harvesting, threshing, and planting."

Against such odds, women were unable to recreate the kinds of houses they had left. Nor could they reinstate the home as a venerated institution. A sod house was only a makeshift shelter; no effort of the will or imagination could fashion it into what one of its greatest defenders eulogized as "the fairest garden in the wide field of endeavour and achievement." There were other losses as well. Many feminine social activities in more settled farm communities revolved around the church, but with the exception of the European immigrant enclaves, churches were scarce on the Plains. At best, religious observance was makeshift; at worst, it was non-existent. Although "it is not to be supposed that only the ungodly came west," one historian noted, "there seemed to exist in some parts of the new settlements a spirit of apathy if not actual hostility toward religion." Circuit-riders and evangelical freelancers drew crowds during droughts and depressions, but during normal times, everyday piety was rare. Few families read the Bible, sang hymns, or prayed together: "when people heard that a family was religious, it was thought that the head of the household must be a minister."

Women were also unable to reconstitute the network of female friendships which had been an accustomed and sustaining part of daily life "back home." Long prairie winters kept everyone housebound for much of the year. During summers and warmer weather, however, men travelled to town to buy supplies and negotiate loans, and rode to nearby claims to deliver mail, borrow tools, or share news. "As soon as the storms let up," the men could get away from the isolation," wrote Mari Sandoz, Nebraska writer and daughter of a homesteader: "But not their women. They had only the wind and the cold and the problems of clothing, shelter, food, and fuel." On ordinary days men could escape, at least temporarily, "into the fields, the woods, or perhaps to the nearest saloon where there was warmth and companionship," but women had almost no excuses to leave. Neighbors lived too far apart to make casual visiting practicable; besides, a farmer could seldom spare a wagon team from field work to take a woman calling. Hamlin Garland, who moved to the Plains as a young boy, remembered that women visited less than in Wisconsin, his former home, since "the work on the new farms was never-ending": "I doubt if the women—any of them—got out into the fields or meadows long enough to enjoy the birds and the breezes."

In most respects, the patterns of life rarely accommodated women's needs. Plains society paid little mind to women, yet women were essential, not incidental, to its functioning. Without female labor, cash-crop agriculture could never have developed. A man could not farm alone, and hired help was almost impossible to come by. Ordinarily, a farmer could count only on his wife and children as extra hands. On the homestead, women's responsibilities as a farmhand, not as a homemaker or a mother, were of first priority. Women still cooked, sewed, and washed, but they also herded livestock and toted water for irrigation.

The ambitious farmer's need for the labor power of women and children often lent a utilitarian quality to relations between men and women. For this single settler, marriage was, at least in part, a matter of efficiency. Courtships were typically brief and frank. Molly Dorsey Sanford, a young unmarried homesteader in Nebraska territory, recorded in her diary over half a dozen proposals in a few years. Most of her suitors were strangers. One transient liked her cooking, another heard about a "hull lot of girls" at the Dorsey farm and came to try his luck, and an old man on the steamboat going to Nebraska proposed after an hour's acquaintance. Jules Sandoz, father of Mari Sandoz, married four times. Three wives fled before he found a woman who resigned herself to the emotionless regimen of his farm. Stolid and resilient, the fourth, Mari's mother, lived to a taciturn old age, but her daughter could not forget others of her mother's generation who had not survived their hasty marriages: "after his arrival the wife found that her husband seldom mentioned her in his letters or manuscripts save in connection with calamity. She sickened and left her work undone . . . so the pioneer could not plow or build or hunt. If his luck was exceedingly bad, she died and left him his home without a housekeeper until she could be replaced." With characteristic ambivalence, Sandoz added, "at first this seems a calloused, even a brutal attitude, but it was not so intended."

Instrumentality could also characterize other family relations. Jules Sandoz "never spoke well of anyone who might make his words an excuse for less prompt jumping when he commanded. This included his wife and children." Garland described himself and his fellows as "a Spartan lot. We did not believe in letting our wives and children know they were an important part of our contentment." Jules' wife "considered praise of her children as suspect as self praise would be." Preoccupied by her chores, she maintained only minimal relationships with her family and assigned the care of the younger children to Mari, the oldest daughter.

In the domestic ideology of the family, careful and attentive child-rearing was especially important. Unlike the stoic Mrs. Sandoz, the American women who emigrated were often openly disturbed and troubled by a situation in which mothering was only peripheral to a day's work, and keenly felt the absence of cultural support for correct child-rearing. Mrs. Dorsey, the mother of diarist Molly Sanford, continually worried that her children, exiled from civilization, would turn into barbarians. In towns like Indianapolis, the family's home, schools, churches, and mothers worked in concert. In Nebraska, a mother could count on few aids. The day the Dorseys reached their claim, Molly wrote, "Mother hardly enters into ecstasies . . . she no doubt realizes what it is to bring a young rising family away from the world . . . if the country would only fill up, if there were only schools or churches or even some society. We do not see women at all. All men, single, or bachelors, and one gets tired of them." Molly occasionally responded to her mother's anxiety by searching herself and her siblings for signs of mental degeneration, but Mrs. Dorsey's fears were never warranted. The children grew up healthy and dutiful: in Molly's words, "the wild outdoor life strengthens our physical faculties, and the privations, our powers of endurance." To her confident appraisal, however, she appended a cautionary note in her mother's mode: "so that we do not degenerate mentally, it is all right; Heaven help us." Mrs. Dorsey, however, could seldom be reassured. When a snake bit one of the children, "Poor Mother was perfectly prostrated . . . she sometimes feels wicked to think she is so far away from all help with her family." On her mother's fortieth birthday, Molly wrote, "I fear she is a little blue today. I do try so hard to keep cheerful. I don't know as it is hard work to keep myself so, but it is hard with her. She knows now that the children ought to be in school. We will have to do the teaching ourselves." Without help from the old networks of kin and institutions, a mother could not be assured of success in fending off such dangers.

As Mrs. Dorsey saw her ideas of child-rearing atrophy, she also witnessed a general attenuation of the womanliness which had been central to her own identity and sense of importance in the world. Her daughters particularly taxed her investment in an outmoded conception of womanhood. Molly, for instance, was pleased with her facility in learning traditionally male skills. "So it seems I can put my hand to almost anything," she wrote with pride after helping her father roof the house. Mrs. Dorsey regarded her daughter's expanding capacities in a different light. When Molly disguised herself as a man to do some chores, "it was very funny to all but Mother, who fears I am losing all the dignity I ever possessed." Molly was repentant but defensive: "I know I am getting demoralized, but I should be more so, to mope around and have no fun."

Mrs. Dorsey's partial failure to transmit her own values of womanhood to her daughter is emblematic of many difficulties of the first generation of woman settlers. Women could not keep their daughters out of men's clothes, their children in shoes, their family Bibles in use, or their houses clean; at every step, they failed to make manifest their traditions, values, and collective sensibility. It was perhaps the resistance of the Plains to the slightest feminine modification rather than the land itself which contributed to the legend of woman's fear of the empty prairies: "literature is filled with women's fear and distrust of the Plains . . . if one may judge by fiction, one must conclude that the Plains exerted a peculiarly appalling effect on women." The heroine of Rolvaag's *Giants in the Earth* echoed the experience of real women in her question to herself: "how will human beings be able to endure this place? . . . Why, there isn't even a thing that one can *hide behind!*" The desolation even affected women who passed through on their way to the coast. Sarah Royce remembered shrinking from the "chilling prospect" of her first night on the Plains on the Overland Trail: "surely there would be a few trees or a sheltering hillside. . . . No, only the level prairie. . . . Nothing indicated a place for us—a cozy nook, in which for the night we might be guarded."

Fright was not a rarity on the Plains. Both men and women knew the fear of droughts, blizzards, and accidental death. Yet the reported frequency of madness and suicide among women is one indication that Dick may have been right in his contention that "the real burden . . . fell upon the wife and mother." Men's responsibilities required them to act upon their fears. If a blizzard hung in the air, they brought the cattle in; if crops failed, they renegotiated the mortgages and planned for the next season. In contrast, women could often do nothing in the face of calamity. "If hardships came," Sandoz wrote, "the women faced it at home. The results were tersely told by the items in the newspapers of the day. Only sheriff sales seem to have been more numerous than the items telling of trips to the insane asylum."

Men made themselves known in the acres of furrows they ploughed up from the grassland. Women, lacking the opportunities of a home, had few ways to make either the land or their neighbors aware of their presence. The inability of women to leave a mark on their surroundings is a persistent theme in Sandoz's memoirs. When Mari was a child, a woman killed herself and her three children with gopher poison and a filed down case knife. The neighbors agreed that "she had been plodding and silent for a long time," and a woman friend added sorrowfully, "If she could' a had even a geranium, but in that cold shell of a shack. . . ." In Sandoz's memory, the women of her mother's generation are shadows, "silent . . . always there, in the dark corner near the stove."

I have emphasized only one side of woman's experience on the Plains. For many, the years brought better times, better houses, and even neighbors. A second generation came to maturity: some were daughters like the strong farm women of Willa Cather's novels who managed to reclaim the land that had crushed their mothers. Yet the dark side of the lives of the first women on the Plains cannot be denied. Workers in an enterprise often not of their own making, their labor was essential to the farm, their womanhood irrelevant. Hamlin Garland's *Main Travelled Roads*, written in part as a condemnation of "the futility of woman's life on a farm," elicited this response from his mother: "you might have said more but I'm glad you didn't. Farmer's wives have enough to bear as it is."

6

OF FACTORIES AND FAILURES: EXPLORING THE INVISIBLE FACTORY GATES OF HORATIO ALGER, JR.

CAROL NACKENOFF

Books promising to reveal the way to wealth have a long history in American culture, beginning with Benjamin Franklin's pamphlet by that title, which was published in 1747. Appealing to those with few family and social connections and to those with limited access to education, these guidebooks to prosperity held out the promise of lifting "self-made men" out of poverty and poorly paid employment into the world of independent wealth and respectability. While these manuals for success had little actual effect in a society in which social mobility had been sharply limited since the mid-eighteenth century, they nonetheless appealed to a wide readership of citizens who believed passionately in the American myth of success.

Among the most famous and popular of these handbooks for success were the 135 books penned by the late-nineteenth-century writer Horatio Alger, Jr. Following a prescribed formula, his "rags-to-riches" stories featured young boys of unimpeachable character ready to begin their journey through life with confident expectation. Like Christian in John Bunyan's perennially popular religious tract *The Pilgrim's Progress*, Alger's expectant lads confronted many temptations and a host of seedy characters intent on derailing their quest for success, but drawing on hard work and high moral principles, they always reached their final goal.

In this essay, Carol Nackenoff takes a fresh look at Alger's stories. Coupled with Alger's traditional advice to work hard and remain true to mainstream moral principles she finds equally important advice to avoid the sort of factory work that was coming to dominate the age. Alger's message to American youth was clear: Factory work was unrespectable labor, and one could never pass through factory gates and find happiness and success inside.

What happens to the growing young bootblacks, newsboys, and street urchins who surround the hero in Horatio Alger, Jr.'s Gilded Age tales? What lot falls to someone who does *not* succeed? What does success save Alger's heroes *from*? Such questions lead to a rather novel way of thinking about Alger's success formulas.

The Gilded Age characters of Horatio Alger, Jr. have long been treated as symbols of success, but that success is much misunderstood. A few astute readers have seen that, for Alger, the meaning of success is not identical with the acquisition of wealth. The stories stress the importance of morality, the prevalence of middle-class occupations and modest rewards, and the unattractiveness of selfish materialism. What has been less well recognized is Alger's rootedness in the economic transformations of the second half of the Nineteenth Century, and the role these transformations play in the definition of success.

It is my contention that, in Alger's fiction, economic success is measured against common and undesirable outcomes of the Gilded Age. The author of over one hundred juvenile tales arranged to rescue his characters from some of the worst consequences of an industrializing economy. Heroes acquire the ability to distance themselves from hardship, economic marginality, and instability which are ever-present in these novels. Failure is the backdrop against which success is defined in Alger's universe, and factory labor is clearly part of the lot one seeks to escape.

THE MOST VISIBLE FAILURES

With the intervention of benefactors and surrogate parents, Alger heroes and a few of their companions are helped out of poverty and through the dangerous shoals of adolescence. Not all are. "Turning bad" is the most frequent scenario Alger envisioned for those who are not rescued. Youngsters who cannot earn a living wage by their labors and those who develop vices are likely to turn to crime.

Adult criminals are found in virtually all Alger stories, especially those who live off the honest earnings of others—pickpockets, highwaymen, kidnappers, counterfeiters, forgers, confidence men. Many adult failures have fallen prey to drink and gambling. Tramps wander the countryside in the summer or lounge on City Hall Park benches, surviving by begging or stealing. Charles Loring Brace, social worker and author, friend of Alger and provider of some of his source material, included in the "Proletaires of New York" a large class of criminals and paupers, the only saving grace of whom is that this life is not yet "so deeply stamped in the blood" as their English counterparts. The "dangerous classes" of New York ". . . are as ignorant as London flashmen or costermongers. They are far more brutal than the peasantry from whom they descend. . . ."

Female street urchins had little to look forward to. According to Brace, who set up a lodging house for some of these girls which provided instruction in morals and in economic self-sufficiency, many of these girls could be expected to end up in a life of prostitution. Alger rescues heroine Tattered Tom on the brink of adolescence and returns her to the care and moral supervision of her long lost mother. Better yet, a vehicle is provided for the salvation of more girls:

> For her sake, her mother loses no opportunity of succoring those homeless waifs, who, like her own daughter, are exposed to the discomforts and privations of the street, and through her liberality and active benevolence more than one young Arab has been reclaimed and is likely to fill a respectable place in society.

One measure of success, then, is that young people who succeed preserve their morals and good character intact where family and clergy are no longer present as moral influences. For little boys too young to fend for themselves (e.g., Phil, the Fiddler, and Mark, the Match Boy), as well as for female street urchins, triumph means return to real or adoptive parents, upon whom they can depend for economic security and moral influence.

Not all the poor are criminal. Brace observed that there are, in addition to vagrants and criminal elements in New York,

> still other tens of thousands, poor, hard-pressed, and depending for daily bread on the day's earnings, swarming in tenement-houses, who behold the gilded rewards of toil all about them, but are never permitted to touch them.

Alger's homeless men and women are occasionally glimpsed in ten-cent lodging houses, sleeping en masse on straw-covered floors. Others inhabit community poor homes and even asylums. Squalid, crowded tenements sometimes house heroes or acquaintances. Perhaps these places of squalor house the grown-ups in Alger who are not bad but rather apparently lack the right disposition or will to succeed. One is told that some dispirited individuals have simply given up, lacking courage to deal with setbacks.

Despite occasional glimpses of men walking the streets in search of work, most of the poor on display are windows, orphans, invalids, and those who have succumbed to vice. But what of those who have no cushion protecting them from having to accept work on any terms offered? Where are the *working* poor?

Women are not infrequently depicted in Alger as hard-working poor. Females who labor are likely to be shown engaged in the process of manufacture, though they work in their homes as hatmakers and seamstresses. These widows and single women are paid by the piece, and generally cannot achieve self-sufficiency though they work long hours. Women, unlike men, are not geographically mobile in Alger's world; they have fewer opportunities, and are more dependent upon their employers. A kindly character in *Rufus and Rose* was entirely dependent on her earnings as a seamstress; she had to sit and labor from early morning until evening, and barely earned enough to survive. She clearly was losing

her health, and could earn only a third of what the hero did selling newspapers. When asked whether they won't pay her any more, she replies:

> No, they find plenty who are ready to take their work at the price they are willing to pay. If anybody complains, they take away their work and employ somebody else.

A similar experience is described in *Helen Ford*. A character who sews constantly finds her wages decreased twenty percent because shops were giving out less work while more people desired work; "many could not obtain a chance to work at any price." Here, Alger forcefully editorializes:

> Perhaps no employment is more confining and more poorly compensated than that of sewing. The narrow choice allowed to women, who are compelled to labor for their livelihood, leads to an unhealthy and disastrous competition in this department of toil, and enables employers to establish a disgracefully low scale of prices [here Alger refers the readers to an article in the "Atlantic Monthly"].

This grim picture does not allow much hope of success apart from rescue. The best case provides either for marriage or for installation in the home of a hero who has made good.

These are the most visible classes that Alger's boys and girls stand to join if they are not successful. But these are not the only classes—and outcomes—from which the hero must be rescued in Alger. Far less visible, but arguably equally ominous, is the factory.

SAVED FROM THE FACTORY

In an Alger story serialized beginning December, 1892, Ben Bruce determines to leave the home of his mean stepfather. He meets a friend of his who is superintendent of a "factory for the manufacture of leather board." The superintendent asks the boy how he would like to work there.

Ben Bruce, expressing a desire to secure a better education, nonetheless answers: "If the choice lies between working on a farm and working in your factory, I will work for you if I can get the chance." The starting wage is adequate, and the hero inquires whether he would be preparing himself for "higher" work; the superintendent answers in the affirmative. Just when it looks like they are about to strike a bargain, the dam which provides water power for the factory is blown up, apparently by two discharged workmen. Since the factory must be shut down until the dam is rebuilt, this ends the boy's hope of employment there. And so, Alger "blows up" this option rather than forsake Ben there. The boy is saved!

Though Alger frequently set his tales in late antebellum America, the factory was, even at that point, an inescapable presence in the northeastern landscape. Such boosters of industrialism as Edward Everett (for whom Alger would run errands as a Harvard freshman in 1848) could proclaim the factory at Lowell, begun in the second decade of the century, the "fulfillment of the American Revolution and a model of republicanism." But others were not so sanguine. Antebellum travellers to England worried over the poverty and moral debasement that accompanied industrialization and wondered whether they were looking at America's future and the demise of republican virtue. "The machine unmans the user," Emerson would write after his 1847 trip abroad. By the late 1830s, the vision of the American factory as a community was increasingly difficult to maintain in light of labor discontent, worker combinations, and emerging analyses of wage slavery.

The rare brick, furniture, or shoe manufactory in Alger stories still involved pre-industrial skilled craft work; mechanization had not appreciably altered the nature of work. At the outset of *Five Hundred Dollars* (serialized beginning 1889), Bert Barton is thrown out of work as a shoe pegger by the introduction of a machine. Though such effects of mechanization of a craft were hardly rare in the 1880s, this was an extremely rare occurrence in Alger's fiction.

A few Alger heroes begin work life in a factory, but circumstances (e.g., dullness in a trade; malicious intervention by the superintendent's son) quickly conspire to compel them to look for other work. One scholar notes:

> on the rare occasions when he [Alger] did [start a boy in a factory] he could only think to have the lad fired or laid off at the outset, as if desperate for some contrivance to expel him as quickly as possible into the world where a man could make his mark.

Alger's factory work is virtually never described. Often, the reader has no idea what is made, and is not taken into areas of production. The author exhibits little or no curiosity about this place of work. Robert Rushton, for instance, provides the chief support of his family by working in the factory in Millville. Beyond this, one learns only that the brick factory provided about the only avenue of employment to be had in town, that Robert was able to earn six dollars a week, and that tardiness resulted in a twenty-five cent docking.

Alger boys exit the factory; they do not seek to make their way within it. Heroes are not dependent upon factory work as the sole possible employment unless they confine their search to the local community in which they begin life. In Alger's city, there are other things to do.

When seeking work, the central character will often turn down manual labor or the opportunity to learn a craft or trade. The stinginess of the man to whom the hero would be apprenticed is sometimes adduced as the reason for refusal, or the boy might submit that he does not want to live away from his mother (which he inevitably chooses to do when he leaves for the city). Often, he merely asserts that he doesn't believe he is cut out for certain types of work, or doesn't think he would like it. Alger heroes are clearly destined for another fate.

To what length Alger is willing to go to keep the boy afloat and away from the factory gates! The young hero may join a circus, or even whistle and give bird imitations on the stage for a living. When one nearly penniless boy claims to feel foolish playing the harmonica on stage for money, his companion replies: "it would be more ridiculous *not* playing for money. Whatever talents we possess our Creator meant us to exercise for our benefit and the pleasure of the community."

Alger's young boys not infrequently discover positions that do not pay a living wage, but they walk away. Even if they are hard up, they are never put into the position of having to accept anything that is offered. Something or someone intervenes to obviate the necessity of such a choice. Some choices are simply unacceptable. The factory, and working class jobs more broadly, fall into this category.

Once the boy gets to the city—which is most frequently New York—Alger provides quite a bit of detail about city sights, scenes, architecture, and prices. Some of these novels took the reader on a guided tour of Manhattan sights, with perhaps even an expedition by ferry to Brooklyn. More than one Alger enthusiast has claimed that these books were veritable Baedeker's guides. According to one:

> You could find out *what* to do, *where* to go, *how* to begin, and *how* to proceed in the city. . . . A young man from the country could brief himself on transportation around the city, the ways to obtain lodging and employment. . . .

However, when Alger's heroes wander the streets in search of work, factories disappear. P.T. Barnum's is there, but not its surroundings. One does not know who occupies factory positions or why but we know that heroes do not. To remove even the possibility of exchanging one's labor power for a wage in the factory, the factory must become invisible.

One of Alger's Chicago stories, *Luke Walton*, is deposited for copyright the same month and year that Carrie Meeber comes to Chicago in *Sister Carrie* (August, 1889). Luke sees many of the same new downtown sights Carrie does. Yet

Dreiser's Carrie, who trudges the streets in search of work, could not avoid passing and viewing the manufacturing establishments on her long walk from home on the west side of the river to the downtown area. Unable to find a position as a shop girl, she eventually finds a poorly paid, unpleasant position manufacturing shoes. The factory girls she eventually leaves behind have little hope of betterment. Carrie could not help but see men toiling at heavy labor in the streets; poorly clad shop girls who worked so hard and had so little; the pale, ragged creatures in states of mental stupor who walked the streets or held out their hands for change. And yet, when Alger's newsboy walks home to his poor and unfashionable neighborhood, he does not seem to pass any factories or see the ways many people labor. Away from the bustling downtown commercial center, across the Chicago River, there is only the usual Alger drama.

One would hardly realize that Alger inhabited the same universe as Edward Bellamy, who published his extremely popular novel *Looking Backward* in 1888, purporting to solve the most pressing issue of the day—the labor problem. The era was notable for labor organization, strikes, and violence, but Alger allows almost no worker combinations on strikes to cross the pages of even his later novels. When one labor uprising is mentioned in *A Debt of Honor*, it is a passing reference by someone remote from the scene of action; the destruction of property noted above in *Ben Bruce* is extremely unusual.

Once jobs in factories, crafts, and trades drop from sight, career and earning trajectories of Alger characters do not mirror options in the economy. All his boys find employment in the white-collar workforce, though less than 20% of all workers are so employed by 1900. Boys are found earning at the high end of the scale for average weekly adult earnings during the period.

Engels had noted in 1845 that the structure of the city almost conspires to keep the manufacturing establishments and the squalid tenements of the poor out of view of the untroubled bourgeoisie, lining the streets with tidy shops and concealing what lies behind. Alger did see the tenements, and saw those left unemployed by panics and depressions; he even condemned those who did not see poverty or try to assist the worthy among the poor. But he did not see any pattern to poverty and unemployment among males that did not stem from character flaws. It is clear that, at least so far as concerns the factory, Alger's boys share the privileged gaze of the bourgeoisie.

FACTORIES AND FAILURE

This "blindness" is part of a pattern in Alger to go to great lengths to rescue heroes from the prospect of factory labor. Factory labor is something to be avoided or escaped. In part, this reflects the fact that Alger was the product of literary traditions which preceded realism. Though his most popular works tended to feature neglected street urchins of New York, he may well have believed some things were not the fit subject of discussion. William Dean Howells' literary realism had to do battle with an earlier faith; "in the strife-torn, graft-ridden years of the late Nineteenth Century, industrial society had understandably seemed to literary men an enemy, not a subject." The author E.C. Stedman, whom Alger greatly admired, expressed a wish to lift readers above the sordid details of contemporary life. Alger admired Howells, but his own literary work reflected more the views of the *Christian Union:*

> Realism . . . [seemed bent on] crowding the world of fiction with commonplace people whom one could positively avoid coming into contact with in real life; people without native sweetness or strength, without acquired culture or accomplishments, without the touch of the ideal which makes the commonplace significant and worthy of study.

Alger's heroes were always those exceptional boys, regardless of the economic circumstances in which they found themselves. The common place children were there, but not at center stage.

Alger did not think the factory offered a very good route of mobility. It did not nurture aspiration. Alger spent his youth in Marlboro, Massachusetts, which he remembered as engaging in shoe manufacturing. "Though diversified, the local economy was not immune to the cyclical fluctuations which plagued the shoe industry at large." Nearby towns, more dependent upon manufacture than Marlboro, suffered frequent cycles of boom and bust. When forced to shut down temporarily in a glutted market, an Alger shoemaker comments:

> That's the worst of the shoe trade. It isn't steady. When it's good everybody rushes into it, and the market soon gets overstocked. Then there's no work for weeks. If a man manages to save up a little money in good times, he has to spend it then. . . ."

Alger's "experience" with manufacturing was that it did not provide a reliable income. Thus, heroes sought to escape business cycle fluctuations and discover steady work with reliable and rising wages. Boys sought careers at work.

Rosy depictions of factory opportunities were repeated throughout the century by industrialists and their supporters. They were even found in one advice manual Alger recommended to a young friend. Such depictions also provoked this 1889 response:

> If you tell a single concrete workman on the Baltimore and Ohio Railroad that he may yet be president of the company, it is not demonstrable that you have told him what is not true, although it is within bounds to say that he is far more likely to be killed by a stroke of lightning.

Alger seems to realize there is something in this position. He was not as positive as some of his contemporaries and at least a few later historians about opportunities in the nineteenth century factory. "We find that *many of our most conspic-uous public men* have commenced their careers as newsboys," Alger was fond of repeating. He did not say "factory hands."

The bulk of evidence unturned by historians and sociologists would seem to be on his side. Scholars have tended to find that the route from shop hand to supervisor was neither quick nor terribly likely. There might be some upward mobility through positions, but downward mobility was perhaps as likely, and lateral movement from department to department was also common. Patronage was instrumental to advancement. A pioneer among these studies, examining mobility in Newburyport, Massachusetts, argues:

> Most of the social gains registered by laborers and their sons during these years were decidedly modest—a move one notch up the occupational scale, the acquisition of a small amount of property. Yet *in their eyes* these accomplishments must have loomed large.

Aside from the mobility issue, there were other reasons to bypass the factory. A significant element in Alger's elimination of this option lies in his distrust of capitalists. The term itself tends to connote for him selfish men who are unconcerned with the interests of their workers and who would readily exploit their dependence to depress their wages. They tend to worship money and ignore community. Capitalists lack respect for the exchange of equivalents, failing to pay labor at its value (whatever this means—Alger does not much trouble himself with the basis of wages or profits, but he believes workers deserve a living wage). They could choose to behave differently, but they have taken money out of proper perspective. Individuals who put money before people are anything but successes in Alger's universe, and he frequently arranges some sort of economic justice for them.

It is essential to Alger's formula for advancement that character be noticed. Character is the most valuable asset that the hero brings to the marketplace; its recognition becomes the means

by which the boy rises. The factory system was surely not one to illustrate Alger's principle that, by application, hard work, cheerfulness, loyalty to one's employer, and honesty, any boy can hope to be noticed for his endeavors and advance. In the emerging industrial order, there was less opportunity for the individual to engage in personal contact with a boss, impress him, or employ his education or wits in new and different tasks. The factory wage labor system was impersonal, and offered workers limited scope within which to affect their destinies. The equivalents in market exchange were hides, not character.

It was not a world in which community of interest between employer and employee would endure. The boss who notices and rewards the trusted employee and who invites him home to dinner bridges the gap between social classes—in effect, negates the meaning of class. The only class worthy of mention is an aristocracy of character.

Factory labor was not likely to take a street-hardened hero without advantages and uplift him, exposing him to a better class of people who would encourage him to better himself. Without the human contact and example of men of good character, the factory would not nurture character or virtue. Even if indifferent workers might comply with factory discipline in order to keep their jobs, the work environment did not help make them men—it did not improve them, and hardened companions might even lead them astray. Those with power may well stand to affect the identity and morals of those over whom they exercise control. If capitalists and their factory agents do not stand for virtue, what will become of their employees?

Self-improvement was a moral imperative. Certain occupations were less desirable because they did not allow the youth to grow and improve by using his mind:

> Idealess occupations, associates, and books should be avoided, since they are not friendly to intelligent manhood and womanhood. Ideas make the wise man; the want of them the fool.

In the Harvard Unitarian tradition, "Man had both a mind (that is, a spirit) and a body, but his destiny clearly lay in developing the power of the former." Physical labor, while honorable, might not provide the opportunities necessary to development. Even if crafts or trades offered the prospect of steady work, there was perhaps inadequate opportunity for self-improvement; the case is similar to that of the factory.

Distaste for such labor was also linked to issues of power. The laborer tended to be subject to the close control of others and had little discretion. The Alger hero manages to find work in which he retains a great deal of control over his bodily movements and tasks, and in which mental and manual labor are not separated. Often, the employer sends the boy off as his agent in some business matter; the boy is highly independent and may even define the employer's interest in some cases.

Alger's guidance, however unwitting, is largely geared to escaping proletarianization. The successful attain middle class occupations and comforts while *avoiding* manufacturing establishment, crafts, and trades. Alger does not place his faith in opportunity in the growing productive sector, but with sectors engaged in the distribution and exchange of the new wealth of a capitalist economy. Merchandising, the growing trade sector, finance, banking, and real estate tend to provide the routes into middle class comforts for Alger's heroes.

Stories frequently end when the boy escapes economic marginalization. Beyond a "competence" and beyond comfort, money allowed one to help others. Success was measured by preservation and development of character, by escape from privation and insecurity, and by avoidance of the factory.

If a boy cultivates character and remembers duties and obligations, he is likely to improve his lot. Two benevolent merchants in New York who started out poor state the success formula and the nature of the aspirations particularly well:

> Most of the men in this city who have succeeded in business or in the professions started as poor boys. . . . There are the same chances now that there always were. Serve your employer well, learn business as rapidly as possible, don't fall into bad habits, and you'll get on.

CONCLUSION

Failure in Alger is linked with a transition from youth to adulthood without establishing secure, stable employment with opportunities for incremental advancement of one's wage. Failures continue not to know from whence their next meals come. Failures do not establish careers. Failures do not develop the personal relationship with employers that the hero does; they do not merit the attention of benefactors. Unconnected and alone, they are treated impersonally as labor. Those who do not succeed are buffeted about by the vicissitudes of the business cycle—cut adrift in times of depression without the means to fend for themselves. They have nothing to fall back on, and lack skills in high demand. Failures do not have bank accounts, and they do not own property. This certainly appears to describe the fate of those being incorporated into the industrial wage labor force.

It is against twin spectres of economic marginalization and proletarianization that economic success is defined. Both scenarios threaten the moral order. The Alger story takes a boy who has been cut adrift from the traditional economy and thus economically marginalized—and inserts him into the new economic world—bypassing the mines and factories.

The persisting invocation of the Alger story in American popular culture owes something to the continuing presence of outcomes and work environments to be avoided in an industrialized and deindustrializing economy. Employment instability, dead-end jobs, low wages, impersonalized work environments, and routinized activity are still present. A comforting measure of success lies in the fate one has eluded. In a world increasingly economically interdependent, the dream of interdependence and self-reliance—and of desirable, fulfilling work—may be all the more seductive.

7

THE GOSPEL OF ANDREW CARNEGIE

MILTON GOLDIN

At the close of the Civil War in 1865, the United States remained a predominantly agrarian nation, with only a few faint signs of future prominence as an international economic power. But by the end of the nineteenth century the United States was fast becoming the industrial giant of the world, with American steel, machinery, and electrical and consumer goods dominating international markets from Europe to Asia. This growing global economic dominance was due in large part to the nation's rapidly expanding population, its vast size, and its abundant resources.

However, successful economic development requires organizational ability and investment capital well as raw materials and abundant labor. After the Civil War, entrepreneurial genius came from a group of business leaders that an earlier generation of historians labeled "robber barons" because of their single-minded pursuit of profit and lack of social and moral concerns. Working in the fields of transportation, oil, steel, and finance, men such as Jay Gould, John D. Rockefeller, and Leland Stanford built enormous fortunes by forming cartels and monopolies that allowed them to dominate entire industries and—some thought—the American economy itself.

In recent years, historians have moved beyond the robber-baron image of early-twentieth-century "Progressive" writers to develop a more complex picture of the nation's early industrial leaders. In this essay, Milton Goldin looks at the career of Andrew Carnegie, a robber baron at least as well known for his philanthropy as for his organizational vision and wealth. As Goldin reveals, Carnegie thought that men of great wealth made the best use of their money when they employed it to advance the welfare of the nation. True to his beliefs, Carnegie used his wealth to endow libraries universities, and research institutions and, in the process, set a precedent that other turn-of-the-century capitalists such as John D. Rockefeller and his son would follow.

"The Gospel of Andrew Carnegie." History Today, *June 1988. Reprinted by permission of History Today Ltd.*

For thirty-five years after the Civil War, the United States of America sustained the greatest period of economic growth of any country in history. Its wealth quadrupled. Fifth among the world's major powers in 1865, it was first by 1901. Its citizenry came to believe that nothing was impossible and that anything wrong could be made right, provided enough energy was applied to a problem.

One of the great symbols of American wealth and dynamism was a slight, Scottish immigrant with pale, penetrating eyes and a broad nose. Andrew Carnegie rose to fame and fortune in a way that made Horatio Alger look phlegmatic. After retiring from business activity, he donated some $350 million to philanthropic causes and shipped free Scotch whiskey to the White House.

What largely accounted for both the surge in American wealth and Carnegie was a development still imperfectly understood today—the extent to which the North's victory affected the capitalist spirit. Nearly all writers on American history now agree that the conflict actually impeded economic growth, instead of stimulating industry as was thought by earlier scholars. But, after 1865, expansionist outlooks characteristic of the country's early history re-emerged, and wartime profiteers invested in railroads, built factories, and, with notable energy, manipulated stocks and bonds. So monumental was their sheer greed that they were called "robber barons" with justification. By 1890, the United States census bureau estimated that 9 percent of the nation's families owned 71 per cent of its wealth.

Not unnaturally, the rest of the population noticed significant changes in the distribution of wealth and also grasped that businessmen who wanted to control raw materials, markets, workers, and the legal system might also have greater power than ordinary citizens in local, state, and federal governments. Its assumptions were correct. By 1888, the Pennsylvania Railroad had gross receipts of $115 million and employed 100,000 men. In the same year, the entire State of Massachusetts had gross receipts of $7 million and employed 6,000 persons.

On the face of it, robber barons were so far ahead in the race for power as early as 1870 that the rest of the population feared it would never catch up. Revolution became a distinct possibility. The personal fortunes of the rich beggared anything seen before in America. When George Washington died in 1799, he left an estate of only $500,000 and was accounted one of the richest men of the time. Not until 1847 was the word "millionaire" used in a New York newspaper to denote a person of unusual wealth, and before the Civil War there were only a handful of multimillionaires.

Forum magazine estimated 120 men worth over $10 million in 1891, and the following year, the *New York Times* listed 4,047 millionaires. Robert Lincoln, the son of a president whose later life was dedicated to the preservation of the Union, became a corporation lawyer and a millionaire. Apparently because his mother annoyed him, Robert had her committed to an insane asylum.

By the early 1870s, when the unbridled speculation of post-war America reached its first major crisis in a depression, the result was a near-breakdown of society. Hundreds of thousands of people were thrown out of work and off farms. State militias and federal troops mobilised to crush strikes and to put down expected insurrections. In New York, some 70,000 men left their jobs to strike for an eight-hour day at no decrease in pay, as provided for in an 1870 state law. Around them, writes one social historian, "multitudes of the lowest grades of the city poor" begged for food on the streets, and shelters were overwhelmed by the homeless, who had to be lodged in police stations. Yet, among city fathers, the major question was, "How can we get rid of the transients at the least cost and trouble to the community?"

This harsh attitude toward the poor reflected a Calvinist philosophy that had informed Americans since Colonial days. During that period, Americans did not interpret poverty as a personal or communal failing, mainly because the needy were neighbours. Churches took poor relief as their responsibility, stressed that the existing social order was right and reasonable, and bestowed special praise on generous givers for rising above the common herd with donations for families in need. Typically, colonists cared for dependents in their own homes, disrupting lives as little as possible. This was in sharp contrast to practices in the motherland, where the British had a bewildering array of almshouses, workhouses, and other institutions to house and to feed swarms of beggars.

The Colonial period was an age of emerging humanitarianism, and throughout the western world prosperous citizens led the middle classes in providing succour for the less fortunate. On the other hand, destitute strangers were not welcomed anywhere in North America because of the high costs of maintaining them. The purpose of poor-relief legislation was as much to keep non-residents out as it was to help neighbours. When the first Jews in North America arrived in New Amsterdam from Recife in 1654, Governor Peter Stuyvesant, whose intolerance of Quakers was already notorious, wanted the newcomers ousted at once. The refugees wrote to brethren in Amsterdam, who were directors of the Dutch West India Company, and pleaded to be allowed to stay. The Company finally ordered Stuyvesant to permit them to remain—not because of humanitarian considerations, but because the Jews pledged that they would care for their own in cases of need.

Until the Civil War, philanthropic practices remained largely the same as during the Colonial period, with clerics taking major roles in raising and disbursing funds. What changed was the manner in which funds were raised. In addition to taxes and collections in churches, an Assistance Society in New York, organised in December 1808, raised relief funds via printed appeals and house-to-house solicitations. During the war, a great Metropolitan Fair was held in the city for the benefit of sick and wounded Union soldiers, which helped set an example for future fund-raising events.

No previous experience prepared anyone for the 1870s, however, thanks to the staggering dimensions of the economic disaster. The State of Massachusetts dumped 7,000 unwanted homeless on the State of New York. In both states, public welfare agencies were permeated not only by gross inefficiency but by the wholesale corruption that marked government at all levels in the post–Civil War years. The gentry, or more specifically the descendants of men and women who had invented America, abandoned hope for government's ability to deal with any problem, let alone charity.

Yet, impressed by post-war strides in industry made possible through technology, a group of militant reformers thought that philanthropy could become "scientific." They believed that charity could be rationalised and the poor saved from alcoholism, commonly thought to be the basic cause of impoverishment. Scientific philanthropy would eliminate crafty paupers who took advantage of soup kitchens and cast-off clothing provided by givers. Scientific philanthropy would make better men and women of givers and receivers alike and end poverty altogether. Finally, scientific philanthropy would cut mounting public expenditures for the poor.

But who would pay for philanthropy, scientific or otherwise? The people who had the most money were the robber barons, and so far as reformers could see, robber barons were not so much threatening American standards of living as they were threatening American ways of life.

Inevitably, reformers had two questions to answer. Did robber barons care about the poor? And if they did care, on what basis would they give?

With amusing regularity, interpretations of the robber barons' business tactics and generosity have changed from generation to generation, since the early years of the twentieth century. The muckrakers, notably Ida Tarbell and Lincoln Steffens, accounted them despoilers, thieves, and threats to the public welfare whose donations were devices to assuage guilty consciences. A quarter of a century later, President Herbert Hoover acclaimed them industrial statesmen and magnificent benefactors. Then came the Depression of the 1930s and Hoover, himself, fell into disgrace for his economic policies, despite his reputation as a businessman, engineer, and humanitarian organising relief in Europe during and after the First World War. Writers such as Gustavus Myers (whose earlier *History of the Great American Fortunes* was updated) and Matthew Josephson again accounted robber barons despoilers and thieves partly on the basis of Balzac's dictum that behind every great fortune must lie a great crime.

Early in the 1950s, after the Rockefeller family had given away $25 billion since John D. Senior's earliest contributions, former despoilers and thieves received acclaim in the press as business pioneers and model givers. Then came the 1960s, when the doctrines of Social Darwinism and WASP superiority that the rich of the 1900s espoused were in especially bad repute. The robber barons were hauled out to be demolished yet again in Ferdinand Lundberg's *The Rich and the Super Rich.*

Today, in the midst of untrammeled economic growth, Andrew Carnegie, Jay Gould, John D. Rockefeller, Charles Schwab, J.P. Morgan, Leland Stanford, and Henry Frick—the *crème-de-la-crême* of robber barons—are again described as managerial geniuses and outstanding philanthropists, instrumental in moving mankind forward to its present and exalted status.

In many ways, the most puzzling of these men is Carnegie. The first robber baron to accumulate a fortune of nearly $450 million, he is also accounted the model philanthropist for being the first robber baron to give unprecedented amounts to universities, institutes, libraries, to churches for organs, to a foundation that provides pensions for professors, to a fund that honours "heroes," and to innumerable individuals and smaller causes. Admiring contemporaries put his name on hundreds of buildings, avenues, and streets. John D. Rockefeller wrote, "I would that more men of wealth were doing as you are doing with your money but be assured your example will bear fruit."

Like so much else in his extraordinary career, the picture of a warm and generous tycoon,

which Carnegie assiduously cultivated, is deceptive. All his life, he was a mass of contradictions.

During an eighty-four-year lifetime, he had time not only to play the role of self-made man and multi-millionaire, but of intellectual and spokesman for the new entrepreneurial classes. His energy, like his duplicity, was limitless. The same man who courageously assailed American imperialism in the Philippines and sincerely worked for world peace deceitfully sold overpriced and underdone armour plate to the American Navy. Carnegie boasted about his close personal relations with workers and said, "The best workmen do not think about money." To reinforce this claim, he constantly demanded that his subordinates reduce wages so that he could earn higher profits.

In 1892, Carnegie ordered Frick, his junior, to cut overheads at the huge Homestead steel plant, near Pittsburgh. He then left for a vacation in the Scottish Highlands. There followed a bloody strike at Homestead during which an anarchist shot Frick, and Irish immigrants fought gun battles with Pinkerton agents. Carnegie later said publicly that he knew nothing about the disorders until they were over but would have handled matters differently had he known. In private, he praised Frick for breaking the strike.

Ironically, Andrew Carnegie's father, William, by trade a linen weaver in Dunfermline, Scotland, was a local leader of the Chartists. His mother, Margaret, was the daughter of a shoemaker and political and social reformer. After William Carnegie's business failed in 1848, the family, including thirteen-year-old Andrew, emigrated to Allegheny, Pennsylvania (later a suburb of Pittsburgh), where two of Mrs. Carnegie's sisters were living.

William failed for a second time in a hand-loom business and, with his son, sought work in the local cotton mills. Andrew began his labours as a bobbin boy working from 6 a.m. to 6 p.m., earning $1.20 a week. A short time later, his father quit—factory work turned out to be impossible for this small enterpriser—and Andrew got another job dipping newly-made spools in an oil vat. He was paid $3 a week for work in a foul-smelling basement. Thereafter, just a whiff of oil could make him deathly sick.

A game of chequers between his uncle and the manager of the local telegraph office set Carnegie on the road to wealth. The manager mentioned that he was looking for a messenger boy. Andrew got the job and diligently memorised the name of every street in Pittsburgh. He also arrived earlier each day at the telegraph office than any other worker, stayed later, learned the Morse code, and astounded fellow workers by the speed with which he took down words. Among those he impressed was Thomas A. Scott, superintendent of the Pennsylvania Railroad at Pittsburgh. Scott hired him as secretary, telegrapher, and general factotum for $35 a week, a hefty increase over the $800 a year he had been earning.

Carnegie continued to arrive earlier at the office and to leave later than other employees. It is to his hard work and telegraphic skills that biographers ascribe his early successes. But thousands of other young men in hundreds of other places also arrived earlier, stayed later, and learned Morse code but did not become multi-millionaires. The differences between them and Carnegie were that he had business acumen, a willingness to gamble, made salesmanship into an art form, and was a born courtier, adept at outrageous but irresistible flattery. Applying this talent to Scott, he became the superintendent's favourite. Scott passed on tips on investments, including one to buy $500-worth of Adams Express stock. Carnegie, who probably did not have even $50, told his mother about the offer, and she mortgaged the family home to raise the money.

When the first dividend payment arrived, writes Carnegie in his autobiography, "I shall remember that check as long as I live. It gave me the first penny of revenue from capital—something that I had not worked for with the sweat of my brow. 'Eureka!' I cried. 'Here's the goose that lays the golden eggs.'" Thus was Andrew Carnegie introduced to capitalist enterprise.

Some time later, Carnegie was riding on a company train when approached by a rustic named T.T. Woodruff who asked whether he was an employee of the Pennsylvania Railroad. Receiving an answer in the affirmative, Woodruff opened a green bag and produced a model of the first sleeping car. An impressed Carnegie arranged for Woodruff to meet Scott. In appreciation, Woodruff offered the go-getter a one-eighth interest in his sleeping-car company, which Carnegie financed with a bank loan of $217.50. The investment was soon to be worth more than $5,000 a year to the young investor.

In 1859, Carnegie replaced Scott as superintendent, Scott having advanced to a vice-presidency. During the Civil War, much too busy with his career to bother with the armed forces, Carnegie bought himself out of the draft. He helped the North use railroads and the telegraph, however, to win a victory.

By 1873, Carnegie already had extensive interests in bridge building, telegraphy, and in sleeping cars, but it was to be during the depression that he would make the move into the steel industry which was to lift him out of the ranks of the rich into those of the super-rich. On a trip to England, he visited a mill in which the new Bessemer converter was being used to manufacture steel. Overnight, he grasped the implications of the process and became a booster of steel products.

Back in the United States, he displayed that sycophantic skill that was his hallmark. His first steel plant was named for J. Edgar Thomson, president of the Pennsylvania Railroad. The name was chosen not only to indicate that there existed no bad blood between the two men (Carnegie left the Railroad in 1865) but because Thomson was a buyer of steel rails and could also transport steel products to customers.

By 1899, a Carnegie Steel Company was making 695,000 tons more of steel every year than the total output of Great Britain. Carnegie had always refinanced internally, through surpluses of earnings, and consequently, he owed nothing to banks. The practice insulated him from the stock market but left no way to publicly evaluate the worth of his steel company. He rectified the problem by setting his own value on the factories—$157,950,000—which was later artificially inflated to $250 million when John D. Rockefeller indicated interest in buying him out. The price led the oil magnate to drop out of the running.

Charles Schwab, a subordinate, broached the subject of a purchase with J.P. Morgan, who wanted to include Carnegie Steel in a supertrust of steel corporations he was organising. Morgan agreed to a price of $447 million, which was two-thirds more than Carnegie had thought it was worth only months before, and, on January 4th, 1901, the deal was consummated.

Carnegie received $303,450,000 in 5 per cent bonds and stock with a market value of about $144 million. Shrewd to the very end, he also held a mortgage on Morgan's new United States Steel Corporation—a detail that nearly put him back in possession of the whole overpriced monstrosity when it almost went bankrupt a few years later.

In 1868 at the age of thirty-three Carnegie was already earning $50,000 a year, but had given no major gifts to charity. In papers discovered by executors, there was a memorandum that had been written in December of the year. "By this time in two years I can so arrange all my business as to secure at least $50,000 per annum," he wrote. "Beyond this never earn—make no effort to increase fortune, but spend the surplus each year for benevolent purposes. Cast aside business forever, except for others."

Carnegie did not cast aside business in two years, and his philanthropies began with modest gifts for public baths in Dunfermline, during the late 1860s. What he concentrated on, before he had $447 million to give, was writing about the glories of American business and philanthropy in a series of books and articles. The most influential of these on the philanthropic practices of the American rich was "Wealth," an article published in the June 1889 issue of the *North American Review* and republished shortly afterwards in

Great Britain in the *Pall Mall Gazette*, under the title, "The Gospel of Wealth." The American publication of the article was followed six months later in the *North American Review* by "The Best Uses of Philanthropy" and in 1900 by a collection of his essays in book form, *The Gospel of Wealth*.

Carnegie's masterful salesmanship is immediately evident in these writings. A true Dr. Pangloss, he does not even suggest the possibility that his may not be the best of all possible worlds. His basic assumptions in "Wealth" are that the rich deserve their money and know what is best for society. What, then, is there left to discuss? In Carnegie's view, how the rich should spend their fortunes.

Considering the orgies, banquets on horseback, sixty-room mansions, and works of art with which his fellow robber barons happily indulged themselves, this would seem to have been a pressing issue only to Carnegie. But he shifts the argument from the present to the future and from idle frivolities to matters of moral substance. Because no one can take his fortune with him when he dies, Carnegie argues, the man of great wealth (and virtue) actually has only three ways to dispense his fortune: he can leave it to his family; he can bequeath it for public purposes; or he can spend it during his lifetime for public purposes and take an active pleasure in the good that he does.

In Carnegie's view, the first mode is undesirable because its consequences are to make a god of money ("The thoughtful man must shortly say, 'I would as soon leave to my son a curse as the almighty dollar. . .'"), and the second mode will inevitably result in disappointed heirs contesting wills in courts. "There remains, then, only one mode of using great fortunes," he concludes, "and in this we have the true antidote for the temporary unequal distribution of wealth, the reconciliation of the rich and the poor and a reign of harmony. . . ."

The rich man, he believes, should spend his fortune during his lifetime in ways that will benefit mankind and influence society for the better, and:

under its sway we shall have an ideal State, in which the surplus wealth of the few will become, in the best sense, the property of the many, because administered for the common good, and this wealth passing through the hands of the few, can be made a much more potent force for the elevation of our race than if distributed in small sums to the people themselves.

His views did not go unchallenged. In London, the Reverend Hugh Price Hughes agreed that if tensions between haves and have-nots grew in intensity, social disaster threatened. In an article, "Irresponsible Wealth," in the magazine *Nineteenth Century,* Hughes also wrote:

In a really Christian country—that is to say, in a community reconstructed upon a Christian basis—a millionaire would be an economic impossibility. Jesus Christ distinctly prohibited the accumulation of wealth.

In Massachusetts, the Reverend William Jewett Tucker, professor of religion at Andover Seminary and later president of Dartmouth College, acknowledged in the June 1891 issue of the *Andover Review:*

. . . the great benefit to society from the gifts of the rich, from those which have been received and from those which are likely to be received. But I believe that the charity which this gospel enjoins is too costly, if taken at the price which the author puts upon it; namely the acceptance of his doctrine of the relation of private wealth to society.

Tucker concluded:

The assumption . . . that wealth is the inevitable possession of the few, and is best administered by them for the many, begs the whole question of economic justice now before society. . . . But charity, as I have claimed, cannot solve the problems of the modern world.

When Morgan bought him out, Carnegie was sixty-five years old, and generosity was still not

his strong suit. Donations had hardly made a dent in his fortune—except for gifts to libraries in the United States and in Great Britain. He insisted that receiving libraries match his building donations by providing annual operating expenses and purchasing books. He also donated organs to churches, for which the applying church had to prove that it was not in debt.

Carnegie rejected contributions to medical causes, a field in which John D. Rockefeller was specialising, and social reform, for which he thought government should be the prime giver, to concentrate on education. His first great benefaction was for a Carnegie Institute in Pittsburgh. His second was to the Carnegie Trust for the Universities of Scotland, but many Scots were suspicious. *Blackwood's Edinburgh Magazine* flatly thought him nothing but an American money-making machine, adding, "In old days, a rich man enjoyed his wealth—and if he did the community 'no good,' at least he did not insult it with patronage."

As usual ignoring criticism, Carnegie gave the trust a $10 million endowment, half of which was to be used to finance the education of "students of Scottish birth or extraction." But this, too, inspired protest. British upper classes feared that lower orders would forget "their proper station in life," if given free access to education.

When he returned to the United States from his annual trip to Scotland in 1901—from this point on, the British would be just as happy to see him travel west each year as to welcome him back—Carnegie found a host of volunteers, including every college president in the country, ready to help him spend his money. At his new mansion in New York, he thought about creating a national university in Washington DC, an idea that went back to the country's founding fathers. The university took form, however, as the Carnegie Institution of Washington, an establishment without students but with departments of research in evolution, marine biology, history, economics, and sociology.

The Carnegie Institution, which established an outstanding reputation, required large contributions to sustain operations but did not use up the bulk of Carnegie's fortune. One of his philanthropic tenets was to avoid "indiscriminate charity" and Carnegie still faced the problem of where to make a really large gift. In 1905, he endowed a Carnegie Teachers Pension Fund Foundation with $10 million. From this seed grew the Carnegie Foundation for the Advancement of Teaching, which eventually received a national charter by Act of Congress and $125 million from Carnegie himself.

Carnegie demanded that educational institutions that applied to the Foundation, which was originally conceived to provide pensions for underpaid professors, meet certain standards. Among them, no school could have an endowment of less than $200,000, no school could receive a substantial portion of its operating funds from public sources, and no school could accept applicants with less than minimum preparation for college studies. Above all, he prohibited colleges under sectarian control from receiving grants.

By insisting on these criteria, and certainly with no plan beforehand to reform education in America, Carnegie did more to advance standards of higher education in the United States than any contemporary educator or governmental official. As usual, he was roundly attacked for his efforts, this time by heads of institutions who wished to be included but wanted denominational controls maintained. One such was Abram W. Harris, president of Northwestern University, who wrote that his institution was "really nonsectarian in spirit," although a majority of its trustees were Methodists. Carnegie responded:

I [have seen] in my travels around the world what denominationalism really [means]—several sects each claiming to proclaim the truth and by inference condemning the others as imperfect.

Northwestern did not get a grant.

The $125 million he gave to the Foundation was by far the largest single amount that he would give to any of the organisations he founded, or to which he contributed. Thereafter, large-scale philanthropy ceased to be of prime interest to him. Carnegie had discovered that giving away money gave him no special place in the hearts of recipients. For the public, there were two classes of men—those who were rich and had money to give and those who were poor and needed contributions from the rich. Those who wanted money were interested in immediate and direct benefits, not in the philosophy of the giver.

By 1910, Carnegie was increasingly involved in problems of world peace. Benefactions went to the Peace Palace at the Hague (1903) and to the Carnegie Endowment for International Peace (1910). It would come as a shock to him in 1914 that the world's great powers had as little interest in his exertions for peace as the public had had earlier in his philosophy of philanthropy.

On those who had money to give, however, Carnegie's philanthropy had a profound influence. His benefactions offered proof that no single private sector giver or group of givers, no matter how rich, could decide for a whole community the terms of its welfare programmes.

On the other hand, the philanthropic foundation, which Carnegie pioneered, became the standard gift-giving vehicle for the rich. After Carnegie, every self-respecting robber baron had to have at least one foundation. There were only five such entities at the end of the nineteenth century. Six more were created in the first decade of the twentieth century, twenty-two during the second decade, and forty-one in the third. Today, there are over 25,000 foundations in the United States.

The most dedicated students of Carnegie's philanthropy were John D. Rockefeller, his son, John, Jr., and his five grandsons. It would not only be the enormous wealth of this family that made it the core of the American Establishment, but a network of think-tanks, institutes, and experts financed through Rockefeller grants. Andrew Carnegie could indirectly be thanked for these results.

PART TWO

A MODERNIZING PEOPLE

Although the United States entered the twentieth century as one of the world's most advanced industrial nations, many Americans retained their traditional social and religious values and an isolationist view of the world. Between 1900 and 1940, however, intense social change and the worst economic depression in the nation's history forced many ordinary people to question these traditional values and brought others to embrace new, "modern" ways of life and thought. The tension between tradition and modernity thus became an integral part of everyday life in the early-twentieth-century world.

The early twentieth century witnessed the first sustained migration of African Americans from the rural South into the nation's northern and southern cities. Since there were few urban jobs for black men before World War I, the first wave of migrants was composed mostly of African-American women, who moved to the cities in order to find work as domestics and laundresses. As Jacqueline Jones argues, these women formed "A Bridge of Bent Backs and Laboring Muscles" that linked their new urban lives with the lives of family members who remained in the rural South. The result was the creation of migration routes that would lead tens of thousands of African Americans to northern industrial centers in the second and third decades of the century.

The urban centers that attracted these migrants were also the homes of millions of immigrants who had come from Europe and Latin America to work in the nation's new industrial enterprises. Poor, unskilled strangers in an unfamiliar country, most of these immigrants lived close to the margins of subsistence and relied on relatives and ethnic political machines to secure jobs, housing, and relief in hard times. The poverty, poor public health, and political corruption that accompanied immigration, industrialization, and rapid urban growth prompted middle- and upper-class reformers to seek novel solutions to this unprecedented cluster of social problems. Under the banner of Progressivism, these reformers established commissions, to investigate the causes of poverty, founded settlement houses to integrate immigrants into American society, and lobbied legislatures for political reforms. But, as Maureen A. Flanagan argues in "Gender and Urban Political Reform," men and women often differed in their approaches to reform and arrived at conflicting solutions to the nation's mounting social problems.

While cities were the most obvious areas in need of reform during the early decades of the century, numerous problems also existed in rural areas and in the nation's rapidly vanishing wilderness. As the pressure of burgeoning population gradually transformed the natural landscape into farms, ranches, and cities, some reformers wondered about the health of nature itself. Would the heedless destruction of natural resources eventually strip the nation of its scenic resources? And would there be anything left of the country's magnificent wilderness for future generations to enjoy? As Peter Wild argues in "John Muir: The Mysteries of Mountains," it was to ensure the preservation of the nation's natural beauty that reformers such as John Muir fought for the creation of national parks and forests as places where the pristine beauty of nature would be left undisturbed by the consuming forces of modernization.

Reformers were not the only ones who felt ambivalent about change in twentieth-century America. Ordinary people, too, felt the contradictory attractions of tradition and modernity in their everyday lives. In "Messenger of the New Age," Mary Murphy reveals the magnetic appeal of radio to ordinary citizens during the 1920s. Network entertainment programs, national and international news, and advertising spots opened new worlds to millions of listeners, who embraced the new medium with the same enthusiasm they showed for the motion picture theaters that had begun to appear in their local communities.

While there was much that was attractive in the new age of modernism, there was also much to challenge long-held beliefs. This was especially true of Darwin's theory of evolution, which called into question the biblical account of creation, and the liberal Social Gospel movement, which rejected strict adherence to the Bible and brought a modernized Christianity to the masses. In "Fundamentalism and the Cultural Crisis," George M. Marsden argues that the twin influences of Darwinism and liberal Protestantism marginalized traditional religious beliefs and drove thousands of ordinary people to seek personal certainty through the anti-modern fundamentalist movement.

The Great Depression burned itself into the minds of all who lived through it. In "What the Depression Did to People," Edward R. Ellis captures the human meaning of the Depression and recounts the ways in which ordinary people coped with this unprecedented crisis in their daily lives. While the New Deal attempted to alleviate the worst cases of distress caused by the Depression, as Sarah Deutsch demonstrates in "The Depression, Government Intervention, and the Survival of the Regional Community," even the best-intentioned programs could have unintended negative effects. Looking at the case of Hispanic workers in northern Colorado during the Depression, she argues that rather than helping maintain community life, federal welfare workers and cultural programs undercut family and community efforts to alleviate distress and maintain a long-established way of life.

8

A Bridge of Bent Backs and Laboring Muscles: The Rural South, 1880–1915

JACQUELINE JONES

In the years immediately following the Civil War, southern planters faced an uncertain future. The Union victory ended the slave labor system that planters had relied on since the seventeenth century, and while they were able to forestall a congressional attempt to dispossess former slave owners of their land, that land was useless without the labor necessary for growing and harvesting the cotton, sugar, and tobacco crops that were the source of planter profits. Faced with an immediate and pressing need for low-cost labor, between 1865 and 1880 landowners throughout the South turned to sharecropping and debt peonage as a means to secure a continued supply of agricultural labor. By the end of Reconstruction in 1877, the majority of former slaves, although legally free, were again under the control of white planters.

The working lives of these black sharecroppers were little different from their existence under slavery. This was especially true of freedwomen, who continued to be bound to the double duties of field and household labor long after the end of slavery. Until they abandoned sharecropping and moved northward to take up independent work as laundresses and domestics during World War I, these southern black women lived lives of toil and persistent expectation. Like every member of sharecropping households, women labored long hours to help families survive; but as Jacqueline Jones reveals in this essay, they also lived with the hope that their labor would permit their children to escape the economic and social bondage of postwar southern society.

For black women in the rural South, the years 1880 to 1915 spanned a period between the Civil War era and the "Great Migration" northward beginning with World War I. Although the physical dimensions of their domestic chores and field work had not changed much since slavery, women during this period toiled with the new hope that their sons and daughters would one day escape from their sons and daughters would one day escape from the Cotton South. Maud Lee Bryant, a farm wife in Moncure, North Carolina, spent long days in the fields chopping cotton, wheat, and tobacco, and long nights in the house, washing dishes and clothes, scrubbing floors, and sewing, starching, and ironing. She later recalled, "My main object of working was wanting the children to have a better way of living, that the world might be just a little better because the Lord had me here of something, and I tried to make good out of it, that was my aim." Thus the substance of rural women's work stayed the same compared to earlier generations, while its social context was transformed by the promise, but not necessarily the reality, of freedom.

Black sharecroppers, with the "proverbial unacquisitiveness of the 'rolling stone'," remained outside the mainstream of liberal American society during the years from 1880 to 1915. Their quest for household and group autonomy, like the heavy iron hoes they carried to the cotton fields, represented the tangible legacy of slavery. In an industrializing, urbanizing nation, the former slaves and their children were concentrated in the rural South, and their distinctive way of life became increasingly anomalous within the larger society. Caught in the contradiction of a cash-crop economy based upon a repressive labor system, black households achieved neither consumer status nor total self-sufficiency. Consequently, the lives of black women were fraught with irony; though many had planted, chopped, and picked their share of cotton over the years, they rarely enjoyed the pleasure of a new cotton dress. Though they labored within an agricultural economy, they and their families barely survived on meager, protein-deficient diets. Within individual black households, this tension between commercial and subsistence agriculture helped to shape the sexual division of labor, as wives divided their time among domestic responsibilities, field work, and petty moneymaking activities.

The postbellum plantation economy required a large, subservient work force that reinforced the racial caste system but also undermined the economic status of an increasing number of nonelite whites. By the end of the nineteenth century, nine out of ten Afro-Americans lived in the South, and 80 percent of these resided in rural areas, primarily in the formerly slave Cotton Belt. Blacks represented one-third of the southern population and 40 percent of its farmers and farm laborers, but by no means its only poverty-stricken agricultural group. Up-country yeomen farmers were gradually drawn away from livestock and food production and into the commercial economy after the Civil War. In the process they lost their economic independence to a burgeoning system of financial credit. Yet on a social hierarchy that ranged from planters at the top to small landowners in the middle and various states of tenancy at the bottom—cash renters, share tenants, sharecroppers, and wage laborers—blacks monopolized the very lowliest positions. In 1910 fully nine-tenths of all southern blacks who made their living from the soil worked as tenants, sharecroppers, or contract laborers. Most barely eked out enough in cotton to pay for rent, food, and supplies. They did not own their own equipment, nor could they market their crop independent of the landlord. As the price of cotton declined precipitously near the end of the century, landlords began to insist on a fixed amount of cash—rather than a share of the crop—as payment for rent. Thus individual black households had to bear the brunt of a faltering staple-crop economy.

The black women who emerged from slavery "knew that what they got wasn't what they wanted, it wasn't freedom, really." So they constantly searched for freedom, moving with their families at the end of each year to find better soil or a more reasonable landlord; or, bereft of a husband and grown sons, traveling to a nearby town to locate gainful employment; or raising chickens so they could sell eggs and send their children to school. These women partook of the uniqueness of rural, late nineteenth-century Afro-American culture and at the same time bore the universal burdens and took solace from the universal satisfactions of motherhood. They were the mothers and grandmothers of the early twentieth-century migrants to northern cities, migrants who as young people had been reared in homes with primitive hearths where women of all ages continued to guard the "embers of a smoldering liberty."

THE TRIPLE DUTY OF WIVES, MOTHERS, DAUGHTERS, AND GRANDMOTHERS

For black Americans, the post-Reconstruction era opened inauspiciously. According to Nell Irvin Painter, between 1879 and 1881 as many as twenty thousand rural blacks fled the "young hell" of the Lower South in search of the "promised land" of Kansas. Around this millenarian migration coalesced the major themes of Afro-American history from 1880 to 1915: the forces of terrorism and poverty that enveloped all rural blacks, and the lure of land, education, and "protection for their women" that made them yearn for true freedom. "Rooted in faith and in fear," the Kansas fever exodus consisted primarily of families headed by former slaves desperate to escape neoslavery. Together with their menfolk, then, black women did their best to minimize the control that whites sought to retain over their lives—a "New South" mandate succinctly summarized by the governor of North Carolina in 1883: "Your work is the tilling of the ground, . . . Address yourselves to the work, men and women alike."

In order to understand the roles of black women as workers and household members, it is necessary to examine the methods used by whites to supervise and restrict the options of the family as an economic unit. Although granted relatively more overall freedom than their slave parents,

black men and women in the late nineteenth century had only a limited ability to make crucial decisions related to household and farm management. The nature of the sharecropping system meant that economic matters and family affairs overlapped to a considerable degree. Under optimal conditions, each family would have been able to decide for itself how best to use its members' labor, and when or whether to leave one plantation in search of better land or a more favorable contractual arrangement. These conditions rarely pertained in the Cotton South.

By the early twentieth century, some plantations were so large and efficiently managed they resembled agricultural industrial establishments with hired hands rather than a loose conglomeration of independently operated family farms. The degree to which a household was supervised determined its overall status in southern society, and blacks were systematically deprived of self-determination to a greater degree than their poor white counterparts. For example, in an effort to monitor their tenants' work habits, large cotton planters often employed armed "riders" who were "constantly traveling from farm to farm." As agents of the white landowner, these men kept track of the size of each black family and had the authority to order all "working hands" into the fields at any time. Riders dealt with recalcitrant workers by "wearing them out" (that is, inflicting physical punishment). Indeed, a government researcher noted that southern sharecroppers in general were "subjected to quite as complete supervision by the owner, general lessee or hired manager as that to which the wage laborers are subjected on large farms in the North and West, and indeed in the South." The more tenants a planter had, the larger his profit; hence he would more readily withhold food from a family of unsatisfactory workers, or deny its children an opportunity for schooling, than turn them off his land.

The planter thus sought to intervene in the black farmer's attempt to organize the labor of various family members. Usually the father assumed major responsibility for crop production, and he relied on the assistance of his wife and children during planting and harvesting. But, reported Thomas J. Edwards in his 1911 study of Alabama sharecroppers, if the father failed to oversee the satisfactory completion of a chore, then "the landlord compels every member of his family who is able to carry a hoe or plow to clean out the crops." Some very small households counted on relatives and neighbors to help them during these times; others had to pay the expense of extra laborers hired by the landlord to plow, weed, or chop the cotton on their own farms.

Ultimately a white employer controlled not only a family's labor, but also its "furnishings" and food. By combining the roles of landlord and merchant-financier, he could regulate the flow of both cash and supplies to his tenants. Annual interest rates as high as 25 percent (in the form of a lien on the next year's crop) were not unusual, and tenants had little choice but to borrow when they needed to buy seed, fertilizer, and clothes for the children. Some white men, like the planter who forbade sharecroppers on his land to raise hogs that they would have to buy their salt pork from him, effectively reduced the opportunities for families to provide for their own welfare in the most basic way. To escape this vicious cycle of dependency required a good deal of luck, as well as the cooperation of each household member. The hardworking Pickens family of Arkansas, overwhelmed by debt in 1888, tried desperately to free themselves. Recalled William, the sixth of ten children: ". . . in the ensuing winter Mother cooked and washed and Father felled trees in the icy 'brakes' to make rails and boards [to sell]." Their landlord removed temptation by closing the neighborhood school. Referring to that time, William Pickens remembered many years later that "very small children can be used to hoe and pick cotton, and I have seen my older sisters drive a plow."

Since tenant–landlord accounts were reckoned at the end of each year, sharecroppers had to remain on a farm until they received payment for their cotton (usually in December) or until they had discharged their debt to their employer. The tendency of families to move whenever they had the opportunity—up to one-third left for another, usually nearby, plantation at the end of any one year—caused apprehension among planters who wanted to count on a stable work force for extended periods of time. In the end, the very measures used to subordinate black farmers served as an impetus for them to migrate—to another county, a nearby town, or, after 1916, a northern city. But until alternative forms of employment became available (the lack of free land and transportation halted the exodus to Kansas after a couple of years), most sharecroppers continued to move around to some extent within the plantation economy, but not out of it. Consequently, the annual December trek of sharecropping families from one plantation to another constituted a significant part of Afro-American community life. Some families "were ever on the move from cabin to cabin," prompting the story about the household whose chickens "regularly presented themselves in the dooryard at Christmastime with their legs crossed for tying up before the next morning. . . ." Within such a circumscribed realm of activity, even a neighboring plantation seemed to beckon with opportunity, or at least the possibility of change.

As productive members of the household economy, black women helped to fulfill the economic as well as the emotional needs of their families, factors to consider whenever a move was contemplated. These needs changed over the life course of individual families and clans. So too did the demands upon women fluctuate in the cabin and out in the cotton field, from season to season and from year to year. Thus the responsibilities of wives and mothers reflected considerations related to their families' immediate daily welfare, the fortunes of their kinfolk, and the staple-crop planting and harvesting cycle. Within this constantly shifting matrix of obligations, black women performed housekeeping and childcare tasks, earned modest sums of cash, and worked in the fields.

In their studies of Afro-American life and culture, historians tend to focus on the nuclear family component. However, it is clear that, in rural southern society, the nuclear family (consisting of two parents and their children) frequently cohabited within a larger, rather flexible household. Moreover, neighboring households were often linked by ties of kinship. These linkages helped to determine very specific (but by no means static) patterns of reciprocal duties among household members, indicating that kinship clusters, rather than nuclear families, defined women's and men's daily labor.

For example, a study of the black population in the Cotton Belt (based upon federal manuscript census data for 1880 and 1900) reveals that the "typical" Afro-American household retained certain structural characteristics throughout this twenty-year period. At the core of this household were both a husband and wife (89.6 percent of all households in the 1880 sample, and 87.8 percent in 1900, were headed by a man; 86.4 percent and 82.5 percent, respectively, included both spouses). The typical household remained nuclear, although extended families (that is, those that included blood relations) increased in importance over time (from 13.6 percent in 1880 to 23 percent in 1900). The average household had between four and five members. Significantly, a crude index of local kinship networks suggests that at least one-third of all families lived near some of their relatives.

Contemporary sources indicate that these networks played a large part in determining where sharecroppers' families moved at the end of the year and where small landowners settled permanently. For example, in-laws and distant cousins might try to induce a newlywed couple to join them by coaxing, "Nate, you a young fellow, you ought to be down here workin." Moreover, the spirit of sharing that informed many small communities meant that a woman's chores extended out of her own household and into the larger community; indeed, some neighborhoods were composed entirely of kin, thereby making family and community virtually congruent. A woman might adopt an orphan or a newborn grandchild whose parents had not married. She and her husband helped out on a nearby farm when their neighbors found themselves short-handed. She took over the domestic chores of a sister who had

just had a baby and consulted with other women in her family about the best remedy for a child wracked by fever. If she was particularly skilled in the art of folk medicine, she might serve as an herb doctor and prescribe cures for her neighbors suffering from anything from a toothache to a heartache.

The needs of her kin had a direct bearing upon the number and ages of the people a woman cooked and washed for under her own roof. The household was in reality a "dynamic process" and not a static entity. Although the pattern changed somewhat during the late nineteenth century, in general the younger the husband, the more likely that he and his wife would live alone with their children. Older couples tended to include relatives to a greater degree than did younger couples. These sketchy data suggest that newlyweds quickly, though not necessarily immediately, established independent households and that years later a husband and wife might welcome kinfolk into their home. Perhaps these relatives worked in the fields, taking the place of older children who had left to begin families of their own. Or they might have needed the care and assistance that only a mature household could provide. In any case, it is clear that the boundaries of a household could expand or contract to fill both economic and social-welfare functions within the black community.

Keeping in mind these transformations that occurred over the course of a generation, it is useful to begin a discussion of the farm wife's daily routine with the experience of a young married couple. She and her husband began their life together with very little in the way of material possessions, and they often had to make do with the "sorriest land"—"Land so doggone thin . . . 'it won't sprout unknown peas.'" At least for the first few years, each new baby (there would probably be five or six who would survive infancy) meant an extra mouth to feed and body to clothe while the number of available "hands" in the family stayed the same. Consequently a young wife had to divide her time between domestic tasks and cotton cultivation, the mainstay of family life; she did "a man's share in the field, and a woman's part at home." As Rossa B. Cooley reported of a South Carolina Sea Island family, "Occupation: Mother, farming and housework. Father, farming."

The primitive conditions under which these women performed household chores means that the term housework—when used in the traditional sense—is somewhat misleading. The size and rudeness of a sharecropper's dwelling made it extremely difficult to keep clean and tidy. Constructed by the white landowner usually many years before, the one- or two-room log or sawn-lumber cabin measured only fifteen or twenty square feet. It lacked glass windows, screens to keep out bugs and flies, running water, sanitary facilities, artificial illumination, cupboard and shelf space, and adequate insulation as well as ventilation. Most of the daily business of living—eating, sleeping, bathing—took place in one room where "stale sickly odors" inevitably accumulated. The ashes from a smoky fire used to prepare the evening meal had barely cooled before the children had to "bundle themselves up as well as they might and sleep on the floor in front of the fireplace," while their parents shared a small bed in the same room. Each modest addition to the cabin increased a family's living space and relative comfort—a lean-to, chicken coop–like kitchen; a wooden floor; efficient chimney; sleeping loft for the children; closets and cupboards; or an extra bedroom.

Farm wives had little in the way of time, money, or incentive to make permanent improvements in or around a cabin the family did not own and hoped to leave in the next year or two anyway. One Alabama mother summed up her frustration this way: "I have done dug holes in de ya[r]d by moonlight mo' dan o[n]ce so dat whah I stay at might hab a rose-bush, but I nebber could be sho' whose ya[r]d it would be de nex' yeah." Yet many women remained sensitive to their domestic environment; if they could not always find time to clean up the mud tracked in from outside each day, still they rearranged the house "very nice to meet the great Easter morning," whitewashed it for a Christmas celebration,

dug up flowers in the woods to plant in the yard, or attached brightly colored pictures to the inside walls.

Most families owned few pieces of heavy furniture; modest earnings were often invested in a mule, ox, plow, or wagon rather than domestic furnishings. In any case, a paucity of goods was appreciated when the time came to pick up and move on to another place. Sharecroppers' households also lacked artifacts of middle-class life, such as a wide variety of eating and cooking utensils, books, papers, pencils, bric-a-brac, and clocks. Black rural women relied on a very few pieces of basic equipment in the course of the day; these included a large tub in which to bathe the youngsters and scrub the clothes, a cooking kettle, and a water pail. Their material standard of living was considerably lower than that of mid-century western pioneer families.

The round of daily chores performed by a sharecropper's wife indicates that the arduousness of this way of life bore an inverse relation to its "simplicity." She usually rose with the roosters (about 4 A.M., before other members) to prepare breakfast over an open fire—salt pork (sliced thin and then fried), molasses and fat on cornbread. She either served the meal in the cabin or took it out to family members who were by this time already at work in the field.

During the planting season she joined her husband and children outside at tasks assigned on the basis of sex and age. For example, a typical division of labor included a father who "ran furrows" using a plow drawn by a mule or oxen, a small child who followed him dropping seeds or "potato slips" on the ground, and "at each step the mother covering them with a cumbersome hoe or setting out the plants by piercing holes in the ground with a sharp stick, inserting the roots, and packing the earth with deft movements of the hand." Although she knew as much about the growing cycle as her husband, she probably deferred to his judgment when it came to deciding what she needed to do and when. More than one black person remembered a mother who "done anything my daddy told her to do as far as cultivatin a crop out there. . . ."

Harvest time consumed a substantial portion of each year; two to four cotton pickings lasted from August to December. Like planting techniques, picking had remained the same since the earliest days of slavery, and young and old, male and female, performed essentially the same task. During this period in particular, the Cotton South was remarkable for its resistance to technological innovations compared to the industrial section of the Northeast, or commercial agriculture in the Midwest, a fact that weighed heavily on the shoulders of rural black women. Cotton picking was still such a labor-intensive task, few tenant-farm wives could escape its rigors. The importance of this operation to the well-being of the family—the greater the crop, the more favorable their economic situation at the end of the year—necessitated the labor of every able-bodied person and took priority over all but the most vital household chores.

In the sharecropping family, children were a distinct economic asset. In 1880 nine out of ten southern black wives between the ages of twenty-one and thirty had at least one child aged three or under. Just as the agricultural system helped to influence family size, so the growing season affected an expectant mother's ability to refrain from field work. In 1918 a Children's Bureau report noted that "to some extent, the amount of rest a mother can have before and after confinement is determined by the time of year or by the stage of cotton crop upon which depends the livelihood of the family." The birth of a child represented the promise of better times in terms of augmenting the household's labor supply, but for the time being it increased the workload of other family members and placed additional physical demands on the new mother herself.

Compared to slave women, sharecroppers' wives had more flexibility when it came to taking care of their children during the day. Some women managed to hoe and keep an eye on an infant at the same time. But many, like the mother who laid her baby to sleep on a nearby fence rail, only to return and find "a great snake crawling over the child," found it difficult to divide their attention between the two tasks. Slightly

older children presented problems of a different sort. For instance, the mother of five-year-old John Coleman had to choose between leaving him to his own devices while she worked in the field—he liked to run off and get into mischief in the creek—and coaxing him to help alongside her, "thinning the cotton or corn . . . picking cotton or peas." At the age of six or seven oldest siblings often remained at home to watch over the younger children while their mother labored "in the crop."

In preparation for the main meal of the day (about 11 A.M.), a woman left the field early to collect firewood (which she might carry home on her back) and fetch water from a stream or well. (If she was lucky, she had children to help her with water-toting, one of the worst forms of domestic drudgery; they would follow along behind her, carrying piggins, pails, or cups according to their size.) The noontime meal often consisted of food left over from breakfast, supplemented (if they were fortunate) by turnip or collard greens from the family garden during the months of summer and early fall. The additional time required to fish, hunt for wild game, and pick berries, and the money needed to purchase additional supplies, meant that many sharecropping families subsisted on a substandard, protein-poor diet of "meat, meal, and molasses," especially in the winter and spring. The decline in black fertility rates during the late nineteenth century and the strikingly high child mortality rates during the same period were probably due at least in part to the poor health of rural women and their families.

In the afternoon, work in the fields resumed. Once again, "the house was left out of order [as it was] in the morning, the cooking things scattered about the hearth just as they were used, and the few dishes on the old table . . . unwashed too." Indeed, travelers and social workers often remarked on the dirty dishes and unmade beds that were the hallmark of a sharecropper's cabin. Sympathetic observers realized that women who spent "twelve hours of the day in the field" could hardly hope to complete certain "homemaking" chores. The routine of meal preparation was repeated in the evening. After she collected fire-wood, brought up the water, and milked the cow, a wife began to prepare the final meal of the day. Once the family had finished eating, she might light a pine knot—"No lamps or oil are used unless some one is sick"—but usually family activity ceased around sunset. After a long day of physical labor, "nature overcomes the strongest and sleep is sought by all of the family"—for some, on mattresses stuffed with corn shucks and pine needles and pillows full of chicken feathers.

Few rural women enjoyed respite from the inexorable demands of day-to-day household tasks or the annual cycle of cotton cultivation. Nursing a newborn child and cooking the family's meals; digging, hoeing, and chopping in the fields—these chores dictated the daily and seasonal rhythms of a black wife's life. But they represented only the barest outline of her domestic obligations. On rainy days, or by the light of a nighttime fire, she sewed quilts and mended clothes. "I worked many hours after they was in bed," recalled one mother of nine; "Plenty of times I've been to bed at three and four o'clock and get up at five the first one in the morning." During the day she had to carve out time to grind corn for meal, bathe the children, weed the garden, gather eggs, and do the laundry. Periodically she devoted an entire day to making soap out of ashes and lard or helping with the hog butchering.

At this point, it is important to note that, unlike their slave grandmothers, most sharecropping women did not have the necessary equipment to spin cotton into thread and weave thread into cloth; the expense and bulk of spinning wheels and looms precluded household self-sufficiency in the area of textile production. Ironically, then, although the rural black family lived surrounded by raw cotton, its clothing had to be purchased from a local white merchant. A woman's freedom from the seemingly endless chores of spinning and weaving required a family's increased dependence on credit controlled by whites.

Her involvement with very poor women in the Alabama backcountry at the turn of the century convinced social worker Georgia Washington that "the mother has to hustle all through the winter, in order to get anything" for the family. The "wife and children are worked very hard every year" to pay for the bare necessities, but where "the family is large they are only half fed and clothed. . . ." As a result, most wives attempted to supplement the family income in a variety of ways, few of which earned them more than a few extra cents at a time. Some picked and sold berries or peanuts, while others marketed vegetables, eggs, and butter from the family's garden, chickens, and cow. A "midder" (midwife) found that her services were frequently in demand. Part-time laundresses took in washing and worked at home with the assistance of their older children.

Although modest in terms of financial return, these activities were significant because they yielded small amounts of cash for families that had to rely chiefly on credit. Furthermore, they allowed mothers to earn money and simultaneously care for their small children, and provided them with an opportunity to engage in commercial exchange on a limited basis and in the process gain a measure of self-esteem through the use of shrewd trading skills. This form of work contrasted with their husbands' responsibilities for crop production, which included not only field labor but also monthly and annual dealings with white landowner-merchants. Thus men's income-producing activities took place in the larger economic sphere of a regional cotton market, while women worked exclusively within the household and a localized foodstuff and domestic-service economy.

Husbands preferred that their wives not work directly for whites, and, if they had to, that they labor in their own homes (as laundresses, for example) rather than in a white woman's kitchen. Still, out of economic necessity, a mother's money-making efforts could periodically compel her to leave her house. Although relatively few Cotton Belt women worked regularly as servants for whites (4.1 percent in 1880; 9 percent in 1900), some performed day service during the slack season. In addition, if a black household was relatively large and productive (that is, if it included a sufficient number of "hands" to support itself), a woman might hire herself out to a local planter for at least part of the year. In 1910, 27 percent of all black female agricultural laborers earned wages this way. One Alabama mother managed to combine childcare with wage earning; she took her stepson along when she "went and chopped cotton for white folks." He later recalled, "My stepmother wanted my company; but she also wanted to see me eat two good meals" provided each day by the landowner. As three-quarter hands, women could make about 35 cents per day for "full hours in the field."

Children often helped in and around the house; they supplied additional (though somewhat unpredictable) labor and supposedly stayed within their mother's sight and earshot in the process. Youngsters of five or six also worked in the fields, dropping seeds or toting water. As mentioned earlier, white planters often shaped a family's priorities when it came to the use of children as workers; as a general rule, landowners believed that "the raising of children must not interfere with the raising of cotton," and they advanced food to a household in proportion to its "working hands" and not its actual members. W. E. B. DuBois, in his 1899 study, "The Negro in the Black Belt," found sharecroppers' children to be "poorly dressed, sickly, and cross," an indication that poor nutrition combined with hard work took their toll at an early age. Parents at times hired out children to white employers in order to lessen the crowding at home and bring in extra money.

The sexual division of labor between boys and girls became more explicit as they grew older. For example, some families put all their children to work in the fields with the exception of the oldest daughter. Most girls served domestic apprenticeships under their mothers, but at the same time they learned to hoe and pick in the cotton fields and, in some cases, to chop wood and plow (these latter two were usually masculine tasks). In 1900 over half of all Cotton Belt households reported that at least one daughter

aged sixteen or less was working as a field laborer. Still, girls probably worked in the fields less often, and in proportionately smaller numbers, than boys, and their parents seemed more willing to allow them to acquire an education; school attendance rates among black females remained higher than those among males throughout the period 1880 to 1915, producing an early form of the "farmer's daughter effect." In the fifteen-to-twenty-year age bracket, only seven black males attended school for every ten females. By 1910 literacy rates among young people revealed that girls had surpassed boys in literacy, although the situation was reversed among elderly men and women.

The financial imperatives of sharecropping life produced rates of prolonged dependency for both sexes compared to those of rural wage-earning economies. Black youths who worked on the sugar plantations of Louisiana often grew resentful of having to turn over their wages to their parents, and struck out on their own when they reached the age of fourteen or fifteen. As a result, it was economically feasible for "both boys and girls [to] mate early, take houses, and set up for themselves." On the other hand, sharecroppers' sons could draw upon little in the way of cash resources if they wanted to marry, forcing them "to wait for the home attractions." Men in the Cotton Belt married around age twenty-five, women at age twenty, reflecting, once again, the lessened demands made upon daughters as field workers.

The demographic and economic characteristics of rural black families demonstrate the continuous and pervasive effects of poverty. From 1880 to 1910 the fertility of black women declined by about one-third, due to disease and poor nutrition among females all over the South and their particularly unhealthful living conditions in urban areas. The life expectancy of black men and women at birth was only thirty-three years. If a woman survived until age twenty, she could expect to see one out of three of her children die before its tenth birthday and to die herself (around the age of fifty-four) before the youngest left home. Those women who outlived their husbands faced the exceedingly difficult task of trying to support a farm family on their own. Even women accustomed to plowing with a team of oxen and knowledgeable about the intricacies of cotton cultivation could find the process of bargaining with a white man for seed, supplies, and a sufficient amount of land to be an insurmountable barrier. Many widows relied on the assistance of an older son or other male relative, consolidated their own household with that of neighbors or kin, or moved to the city in search of paid work.

Women headed about 11 percent of all rural black southern households at any one time between 1880 and 1900, but not all of those who managed a farm or supervised the field work of their children were single mothers or widows. Some sharecropping fathers regularly left home to work elsewhere, resulting in a distinction between the "real" (that is, blood) family and the "economic" (cohabitating) household. In the Cotton Belt, men might leave their wives and children to till their land while they hired themselves out to a nearby planter. (In 1910 one-half of all southern black men employed in agriculture earned wages on either a year-round or temporary basis.) This pattern was especially common in areas characterized by noncotton local economies that provided alternative sources of employment for men.

For example, on the South Carolina coast, some black men toiled as day laborers in the rice industry, while others left their farms for Savannah or Charleston in order to earn extra money (usually only a few dollars each week) as stevedores or cotton-gin workers. Phosphate mining in the same area enabled husbands, fathers, and older sons to work together as "dredge han's" and to escape the tedium of rural life. A poor harvest or a natural disaster (like the great hurricane of 1896) affecting the Sea Islands prompted a general exodus of male household members old enough to work for wages; some went north, while most settled for indefinite periods of time in other parts of the South. Sugar

plantations (in Louisiana), sawmills and coal mines (in Tennessee), lumbering and turpentine camps (along the Florida and Alabama coast), brickyards, and railroad construction projects provided income for men who sought to work for cash rather than "credit." While the "real" family never changed, then, the "economic" household responded to seasonal opportunities and to its own specific economic needs.

As older children began to leave a mature family, the economic gains achieved at the height of its productivity gradually slipped away. These established households sometimes took in boarders or relatives to offset the loss of departed offspring. There seemed to be no single pattern of either work or dependency among the rural elderly. For instance, DuBois noted of Black Belt communities in general, "Away down at the edge of the woods will live some grizzle-haired black man, digging wearily in the earth for his last crust; or a swarthy fat auntie, supported in comfort by an absent daughter, or an old couple living half by charity and half by odd jobs."

Widows throughout the South represented extremes of hardship and well-being. An elderly woman living alone sometimes took in a young "mudderless" or "drift" (orphan) for mutual companionship and support. Like Aunt Adelaide, who "received less and less when she needed more and more" once her children left home, some of these women lamented their loss of self-sufficiency: "I ben strong ooman," said Adelaide, "I wuk fo' meself wid me han'. I ben ma[r]sh-cuttin' ooman. I go in de ma[r]sh and cut and carry fo' myself." At the other end of the spectrum was the widow Mrs. Henry; she supported herself by farming and "peddling cakes" until her health failed—or rather, faltered. After that she made a comfortable living selling sweet potatoes, poultry, hogs, and vegetables with the aid of two other women and a child.

Regardless of their physical circumstances, these women formed a bridge of "bent backs and laboring muscles" between "the old African and slavery days, and the sixty difficult years of freedom" for their grandchildren and all younger people in the community. Although men headed individual households, it was not unusual to find an elderly woman presiding over a group of people who in turn cared for her. In Charlotte, North Carolina, the former slave Granny Ann lived alone but "everybody respected" her and "they never would let her cook for herself." She served as spiritual advisor to the neighborhood. To cite another case, according to the 1900 census, Winnie Moore, aged eighty and mother of ten children, lived alone in Perry County, Alabama, with no visible means of support. But at least five nearby households included Moores. Among them was that of John (aged thirty-four) and his wife Sarah (thirty) who had a daughter of twelve named Winnie. Together grandmother and granddaughter Winnie reached from slavery into the twentieth century, and in their lives comingled the anguish of bondage and the ambiguity of freedom.

Although the majority of black rural women were ruled by haggard King Cotton, some followed different seasonal rhythms and work patterns dictated by other forms of commercial enterprise—tobacco and sugar cultivation, truck farming, and oystering. Each of these economies had a distinctive division of labor based on both age and sex. The proximity of processing plants and marketing operations often meant that families employed in such work periodically or in some cases permanently crossed over from agricultural to quasi-industrial labor. For example, in the Piedmont area of Virginia and the Carolinas, and in parts of Kentucky and Tennessee, black people toiled in tobacco fields as hired hands, tenants, or the owners of small family farms. Children performed many of the basic—and most unpleasant—tasks related to the early stages of crop cultivation. Usually boys were hired out for longer periods of time and for a greater variety of operations than were girls. In the tobacco fields closer to home, children's and women's work often overlapped. For example, youngsters of both sexes, together with their mothers, spent long hours stooped over "worming" the plants—that is, examining the underside of each leaf and pinching the head off any worm

found there. Conventional wisdom held that "women make better wormers than men, probably because they are more patient and painstaking."

Unlike cotton planters, white tobacco growers after the war resisted the idea of sharecropping for years, and throughout the late nineteenth century many blacks in the "Old Bright" belt of Virginia and North Carolina worked for wages (60 to 70 cents per day). After 1900, when small tenant farms became more common (a trend linked specifically to the emergence of a single-crop commercial economy), women worked in the fields to a greater extent than they had previously. This change suggested that black men in tobacco-growing regions, like Cotton Belt freedmen, preferred that their womenfolk not perform field work for wages under the direct supervision of whites. However, throughout the late nineteenth and early twentieth century, falling tobacco prices caused increasing numbers of farmers to abandon the land and migrate into nearby towns, where both sexes found menial jobs in tobacco-processing establishments.

The sugar plantation economy of Louisiana, described as a "first cousin to slavery," also relied heavily on wage workers during the postbellum period. A persistent labor shortage in the industry between 1880 and 1900 resulted in "chronic labor disturbances" among workers whose wages were set very low (50 cents a day for women; 65 cents for men) by collusive white employers. In the spring and summer, women hoed in the fields; they plowed and ditched infrequently. The terse remarks made by a sugar plantation owner in his diary one day in 1888 revealed that women who worked under a wage (as opposed to family) system of labor organization remained vulnerable to rape and other forms of sexual abuse at the hands of white men: "Young Turcuit [the assistant overseer] is very objectionable from his 'goings on' with the colored women on the place."

During the grinding season—October through January—hands from all over the state of Louisiana converged on centralized sugar factories. Wages ranged from 25 cents per day for children to 85 cents for women and a dollar for men. Families stayed in company-owned cabins (often converted slave quarters) and made their own decisions about when and how often wives and children should cut cane. Boys began to earn wages around the age of twelve or thirteen, girls not until three or four years later. Women set their own work schedules, much to the disgust of labor-hungry planters. Writing for the Department of Labor in 1902, one investigator found that on the Calumet plantation in St. Mary Parish, "women make only about half-time. During the cultivating season practically none work on Saturdays and very few on Mondays. They do not work in bad weather. During grinding they lay off on Saturdays but generally work on Mondays." In this way families managed to maintain domestic priorities within a wage economy.

In the Tidewater region of Virginia around Hampton Roads and Norfolk, black truck farmers cultivated vegetables to be shipped to distant markets. Along the Atlantic coastline from Virginia to Georgia, oystering families included husbands who worked as gatherers and wives as shuckers. In Chatham County, Georgia, for example, fathers and brothers remained in their home villages during the winter harvest season, while their wives and daughters moved to the factory town of Warsaw to find employment in the seafood processing plants. Family members lived together in the off-season when the men fished and the women took in laundry or picked berries to sell.

Despite the variations in these commercial economies, certain patterns of family organization remained characteristic of blacks in the rural South throughout the period from 1880 to 1915. For most households, a single, sudden misfortune—a flood, a summer drought, high prices for fertilizer, the death of a mule or cow—could upset the delicate balance between subsistence and starvation. Husbands and wives, sons and daughters, friends and kinfolk coordinated their labor and shifted their place of residence in order to stave off disaster—a process that was never-ending. Yet even the poorest families sought to preserve a division of labor between the sexes so that fathers assumed primary responsibility for the financial affairs of the household and mothers oversaw domestic chores first and labored as field hands or wage earners when necessary.

WOMEN'S WORK AND ASPIRATIONS

To outsiders, rural life, set within a larger framework of southern economic backwardness, seemed bleak indeed. DuBois himself asserted that the rural black person's "outlook in the majority of cases is hopeless." Perhaps on the surface the struggle for a living was waged "out of the grim necessity . . . without query or protest," as he suggested. But below that surface ran a deep current of restlessness among even the least fortunate. In St. Meigs, Alabama, Georgia Washington worked with farm wives who "looked pretty rough on the outside." She soon discovered that these mothers were "dissatisfied themselves and anxious to change things at home and do better, but had no idea how or where to begin." They especially wanted the time and resources "to mend or clean up the children before sending them to school in the morning." According to Washington, their "dissatisfaction" was a hopeful sign, proof that they had not succumbed to a paralyzing fatalism.

Two developments in late nineteenth-century southern society—increasing literacy rates and a general urban in-migration among southern blacks—suggest that at least some families managed to wrench themselves from the past and look to the future. Neither books nor a home in the city would guarantee freedom, but they did afford coming generations a way of life that differed in important respects from the neoslavery of the rural South. Because black girls attended school in greater numbers than boys, and because southern towns had disproportionately large black female populations, it is important to examine the relevance of these developments in regard to Afro-American women and their aspirations for their daughters and sons.

It was not uncommon for sharecroppers' children who acquired some schooling later to credit their mothers with providing them with the opportunity to learn. Speaking from experience, William Pickens declared, "Many an educated Negro owes his enlightenment to the toil and sweat of a mother." The saying "chickens for shoes" referred to women's practice of using the money they earned selling eggs and chickens to buy shoes for their children so that they could attend school in the winter. Rossa B. Cooley pointed out that some black mothers were particularly concerned about rescuing their daughters from a fate they themselves had endured. For example, born and raised in slavery, the Sea Island woman Chloe had "one idea" for her daughter Clarissa and that was "an education that meant going to school and away from all the drudgery, the chance to wear pretty clothes any day in the week, and as her utmost goal, the Latin and algebra offered by the early Negro schools in their zeal to prove the capacity of liberated blacks." Female college graduates who responded to a survey conducted by Atlanta University researchers in 1900 frequently mentioned the sacrifices of their mothers, who, like Job, were "patience personified."

Frances Harper, a black writer and lecturer, suggested that black mothers "are the levers which move in education. The men talk about it . . . but the women work most for it." She recounted examples of mothers who toiled day and night in the fields and over the washtub in order to send their children to school. One mother "urged her husband to go in debt 500 dollars" for their seven children's education. This emphasis on women's support for schooling raises the question of whether or not mothers and fathers differed in their perception of education and its desirability for their own offspring.

Although girls engaged in some types of field and domestic labor at an early age, we have seen that parents excused them more often and for longer periods of time (compared to their brothers) to attend the neighborhood school. For instance, the George C. Burleson family listed in the 1900 federal manuscript census for Pike County, Alabama, included four children. Ida May, the oldest (aged sixteen), had attended school for six of the previous twelve months. Her younger brother, Clifford (aged eleven) had worked as a farm laborer all year and had not gone to school at all. In 1910 the Bureau of the Census remarked upon higher female literacy rates among the younger generation by observing, "Negro girls and younger women have received at least such elementary school training as is represented by the ability to write, more generally than have Negro boys and men."

If literate persons prized their own skills highly, they might have felt more strongly about enabling their children to learn to read and write. Apparently, in some rural families the different experiences and immediate concerns of fathers compared to mothers prompted conflicting attitudes toward schooling. Perhaps the experiences of Martin V. Washington were not so unusual. Born in 1878 in South Carolina, Washington grew up in a household composed of his parents and ten siblings. His mother had received a grammar-school education, but his father had never gone to school. "Because of the lack of his education," explained Washington, "my father was not anxious for his children to attend school; he preferred to have them work on the farm." On the other hand, his mother, "who knew the value of an education," tried to ensure that all of her children acquired some schooling.

For blacks in the rural South, even a smattering of education could provoke discontent and thereby disrupt family and community life. Martin Washington's father might have feared that his children would move away; Martin himself eventually emigrated to New York City. Nate Shaw put the matter succinctly: "As a whole, if children got book learnin enough they'd jump off of this country; they don't want to plow, don't want no part of no sort of field work." He believed that the "biggest majority" of literate blacks sooner or later moved to town to find a "public job." If education was a means of personal advancement, then it could splinter families, as young people, eager to flee from the routine of rural life, abandoned the farms of their parents.

The Pickens family of South Carolina moved from the country to the village of Pendleton in the late 1880s. The various factors that shaped their decision revealed how considerations related to both work and schooling attracted people to the towns. (The 1880s represented the peak period of black urban in-migration between 1865 and 1915.) Mrs. Pickens had a great desire "to school the children," but they could hardly attend classes on a regular basis as long as the family's white landlord "would not tolerate a tenant who put his children to school in the farming season." Working together, the Pickenses just barely made ends meet in any case; cotton prices had fallen to the point where a hand earned only 35 or 40 cents a day for picking one hundred pounds.

In Pendleton, the children could attend a better school for longer stretches at a time. Their father relinquished the plow in order to become a "man of all work," and their mother found a job as a cook in a hotel. She preferred this type of employment over field work because it allowed her "somewhat better opportunities" to care for her small children (she probably took them to work with her). William Pickens believed that town life afforded a measure of financial independence for the family, compared to his experiences on a tenant farm where "my father worked while another man reckoned." The young man himself went on to become a scholar and an official of the early National Association for the Advancement of Colored People (NAACP).

By 1910 about 18 percent of the southern black population lived in towns of 2,500 inhabitants or more (an increase of 11 percent over 1860). Since emancipation, small but steadily increasing numbers of former slaves had made their way cityward. As wives, widows, and daughters, black women participated in this gradual migration in disproportionately large numbers. Some women accompanied their husbands to town so that the family as a whole could benefit from the wider variety of jobs available to blacks. Unmarried women—including daughters eager to break away from the "dreary drudgery" of the sharecropper's farm and widows desperate to feed and clothe their children—found an "unlimited field" of jobs, but only in the areas of domestic service and laundering. As a result, all of the major southern cities had an imbalanced sex ratio in favor of women throughout the late nineteenth century. The selection process at work in this population movement, like any other, indicates that black women possessed a spirit of "upward ambition and aspiration" at least equal to that of their menfolk.

Throughout this period, then, some black women demonstrated a restlessness of mind as well as body. In their willingness to move from cabin to cabin and from country to town, they belied the familiar charge that women were more "conservative" then men, less quick to take chances or to abandon the familiar. Perhaps even more dramatic were mothers' attempts to school their children, for in the process they risked losing them. Nate Shaw never went to school because, he thought, "my daddy was scared I'd leave him, so he held me down." Shaw's father had his own priorities, and at least he never had to share the pain felt by a Sea Island mother who read in a note from her self-exiled son, "It pays a man to leave home sometimes, my mother, and he will see more and learn more."

BLACK AND WHITE CULTURE AND MEN AND WOMEN IN THE RURAL SOUTH

Late-nineteenth-century middle-class white women derived their status from that of their husbands. Unproductive in the context of a money-oriented, industrializing economy, and formally unable to take part in the nation's political process, they enjoyed financial security only insofar as their spouses were steady and reliable providers. In contrast, black working women in the South had a more equal relationship with their husbands in the sense that the two partners were not separated by extremes of economic power or political rights; black men and women lacked both. Oppression shaped these unions in another way. The overlapping of economic and domestic functions combined with the pressures imposed by a surrounding, hostile white society meant that black working women were not so dramatically dependent upon their husbands as were middle-class white wives. Within black families and communities, then, public–private, male–female distinctions were less tightly drawn than among middle-class whites. Together, black women and men participated in a rural folk culture based upon group cooperation rather than male competition and the accumulation of goods. The ways in which this culture both resembled and diverged from that of poor whites in the South helps to illuminate the interaction between class and racial factors in shaping the roles of women.

Referring to the world view of Alabama sharecropper Hayes Shaw, Theodore Rosengarten (the biographer-interviewer of Shaw's son Nate) observed that "righteousness consisted in not having so much that it hurt to lose it." Nate himself remembered that his father as a young man had passed up promising opportunities to buy land because "he was blindfolded; he didn't look to the future." Ruled by "them old slavery thoughts," Hayes Shaw knew that

> whenever the colored man prospered too fast in this country under the old rulins, they worked every figure to cut you down, cut your britches off you. So, it . . . weren't no use in climbin too fast; weren't no use in climbin slow, neither, if they was goin to take everything you worked for when you got too high.

Rural black communities that abided by this philosophy sought to achieve self-determination within a limited sphere of action. In this way they insulated themselves from whites and from the disappointment that often accompanied individual self-seeking. They lived like Nate's brother Peter; he "made up his mind that he weren't going to have anything and after that, why nothin could hurt him."

Northern scholars and journalists, as well as southern planters, charged that rural blacks valued freedom of movement, "furious religious revivals," and community holidays—"none of which brings them profit of any sort." A Georgia landowner characterized in this way the philosophy of his tenants, who tended to "dismiss further thought of economy" once they had fulfilled their financial obligations to him: *"dum vivimus vivamus"* ("while we are living let us live"). Some white observers seized upon this theme and warned of its ramifications for the future of American society. Within a growing economy based upon the production of consumer goods, black people's apparent willingness to make do with the little they had represented not so much a moral transgression as a threat to employee discipline on the one hand and incentives to buy on the other. Why should a black husband and father work hard if he was "content with a log cabin and a fireplace, and with corn, bacon, and molasses as articles of food"? How would he profit southern or national economic development if he was satisfied with "merely enough to keep soul and body together"? One contemporary scholar suggested that for the average household head to enjoy a higher standard of living "his wants must be diversified"; otherwise he lacked the impulse to make, save, and spend money. Of course the issue was more complex than the "simple needs" or "wants" of blacks would imply. For example, a northern reporter pointed out that the preachers of the New South gospel of wealth inevitably clashed with the majority of white employers who vowed "to do almost anything to keep the Negro on the land and his wife in the kitchen as long as they are obedient and unambitious workers."

Black settlements in remote areas—especially those that remained relatively self-sufficient through hunting and fishing—experienced the mixed blessings of semiautonomy. These communities existed almost wholly outside the larger regional and national economic system. For example, the people of the Sea Islands who "labor only for the fulfillment of the petition, 'Give us this day our daily bread,' and literally 'take no thought for the morrow,' working only when their necessities compel them," revealed the dilemma of a premodern subculture located within an industrial nation. As independent, self-respecting farmers (a proportionately large number owned their own land), the Sea Islanders remained relatively unmolested by whites and managed to preserve African traditions and folkways to a remarkable degree. Their diet, consisting of fowl, fish, shellfish, and fresh vegetables, was nutritionally superior to that of Cotton Belt sharecroppers. Yet these people lacked proper medical care and the most basic household conveniences. (Water-toting women hailed the installation of a water pump in the early twentieth century as "a most spectacular innovation in domestic economy. . . .") Floods and other natural disasters periodically wrought havoc on their way of life, and pushed young people off the islands and into nearby cities, leaving behind primarily the elderly and the blind.

Even rural communities that lacked the almost total isolation of the Sea Islands possessed a strong commitment to corporatism and a concomitant scorn for the hoarding of private possessions. As government researcher J. Bradford Laws wrote disapprovingly of the sugar workers he studied in 1902, "They have an unfortunate notion of generosity, which enables the more worthless to borrow fuel, food, and what not on all hands from the more thrifty." It is clear that these patterns of behavior were determined as much by economic necessity as by cultural "choice." If black household members pooled their energies to make a good crop, and if communities collectively provided for their own welfare, then poverty and oppression ruled out most of the alternative strategies. Individualism was a luxury that sharecroppers simply could not afford.

Rural folk relied on one another to help celebrate the wedding of a young couple, rejoice in a preacher's fervent exhortation, mark the annual closing of the local school, minister to the ill, and bury the dead. Women participated in all these rites and communal events. In addition, they had their own gender-based activities, as well as societies that contributed to the general good of the community. On the Sea Islands, young women would "often take Saturday afternoon as a time for cleaning the yard or the parlor, for ironing their clothes, or for preparing their hair." (Their

brothers gathered at a favorite meeting place or organized a "cornfield baseball game.") Quilting brought young and old women together for a daylong festival of sewing, chatting, and feasting. Supported by the modest dues of their members, female voluntary beneficial societies met vital social-welfare needs that individual families could not always afford; these groups helped their members to pay for life insurance, medical care, and burial services. Even the poorest women managed to contribute a few pennies a month and to attend weekly meetings. In turn-of-the-century Alabama, "The woman who is not a member of one of these is pitied and considered rather out of date."

The impulse for mutual solace and support among rural Afro-Americans culminated in their religious institutions and worship services. At monthly meetings women and men met to reaffirm their unique spiritual heritage, to seek comfort, and to comfort one another. Black women found a "psychological center" in religious belief, and the church provided strength for those overcome by the day-to-day business of living. For many weary sharecroppers' wives and mothers, worship services allowed for physical and spiritual release and offered a means of transcending earthly cares in the company of one's friends and family. Faith created "a private world inside the self, sustained by religious sentiment and religious symbolism . . . fashioned to contain the world without." "Spiritual mothers" served as the "main pillars" of Methodist and Baptist churches, but they also exercised religious leadership outside formal institutional boundaries; elderly women in particular commanded respect as the standard-bearers of tradition and as the younger generation's link with its ancestors.

Of course, life in "places behind God's back" was shaped as much by racial prejudice as by black solidarity, and the "ethos of mutuality" that pervaded rural communities did not preclude physical violence or overt conflict between individuals. At times a Saturday night "frolic" ended in a bloody confrontation between two men who sought courage from a whiskey bottle and self-esteem through hand-to-hand conflict. Similarly, oppression could bind a family tightly together, but it could also heighten tensions among people who had few outlets for their rage and frustration. Patterns of domestic conflict reflected both historical injustices and daily family pressures. These forces affected black women and men in different ways.

On a superficial level, the roots of domestic violence are not difficult to recognize or understand. Cramped living quarters and unexpected setbacks provoked the most even-tempered of household heads. Like their slave parents, mothers and fathers often used harsh disciplinary techniques on children, not only to prepare them for life in a white-dominated world where all blacks had to act cautiously, but also to exert rigid control over this one vital facet of domestic life. If whites attempted to cut "the britches off" black fathers and husbands, then these men would try to assert their authority over their households with even greater determination. At times that determination was manifested in violence and brutality.

Hayes Shaw epitomized the sharecropping father who lorded over his wives (he married three times) and children. More than once the Shaw children watched helplessly as their father beat their mother, and they too were "whipped . . . up scandalous" for the slightest infraction. Hayes divided his time between his "outside woman"—an unmarried laundress in the neighborhood—and his "regular" family, and he made no effort to conceal the fact. The Shaw womenfolk were hired out or sent to the fields like children, without daring to protest, while Hayes spent his days in a characteristically masculine fashion—alone, away from the house, hunting. According to Nate Shaw, his "daddy'd have his gun on his shoulder and be off on Sitimachas Creek swamps, huntin," after commanding his wife to "Take that plow! Hoe!" The son remembered with bitterness years later that his stepmother (who had borne his father thirteen children) "put part of a day's work in the field" before she died one night.

Hayes Shaw was undoubtedly an extreme example of a domestic tyrant, but he and other husbands like him inspired white and black women community leaders, educators, and social workers to formulate a critique of Afro-American family life in the late nineteenth century. Sensitive to the economic problems confronted by black marriage partners, these observers charged that black men enjoyed certain male prerogatives without the corresponding striving and ambition that those prerogatives were meant to reward. Juxtaposed with this "irresponsible" man was his wife—no doubt a "real drudge," but certainly "the greatest sufferer from the stress and strain attendant upon the economic conditions" faced by all Afro-Americans. The chief problem seemed to stem from the fact that black women played a prominent role in supporting the family in addition to performing their domestic responsibilities. In the eyes of their critics, black men as a group were not particularly concerned about "getting ahead" in the world and thus fell short of their wives' spirit of industry and self-sacrifice.

White teacher–social workers like Rossa Cooley and Georgia Washington and black writers and educators like Anna J. Cooper, Katherine Davis Tillman, Frances Harper, and Fannie Barrier Williams focused on the domestic achievements of poor women and with varying degrees of subtlety condemned their "worthless" husbands. Their critique of black womanhood marked the emergence of the "black matriarchy thesis," for they suggested that the main problem in Afro-American family life was an "irresponsible" father who took advantage of his "faithful, hardworking women-folks." By the mid-twentieth century sociologists had shifted public attention to the "irresponsible" father's *absence;* the relatively large number of single, working mothers in the nation's urban ghettos seemed to lend additional credence to an argument that originally purported to deal with the problems of rural women. Thus the image of the strong, overburdened black mother persisted through the years, and it was usually accompanied by the implicit assumption that women wielded authority over men and children in Afro-American families.

Yet Hayes Shaw's household was never a

"matriarchy." Recent historians who have labeled the postemancipation rural black family "patriarchal" hardly help to clarify the issue. The difficulty in conceptualizing black male–female roles derives from the fact that most observers (whether writing in the nineteenth or twentieth century) have used as their basis for comparison the white middle-class model of family life. Black men headed the vast majority of southern rural families, and they self-consciously ruled their wives and children; hence the use of the term patriarchy to describe family relationships. But these households deviated from the traditional sexual division of labor in the sense that wives worked to supplement the family income, and fathers often lacked the incentive to try to earn money so that they could purchase property or goods and thus advance the family's status. These men worked hard—they had to, in order to survive the ruthlessly exploitative sharecropping system—but most realized that even harder work would not necessarily enable them to escape poverty. Those who confronted this dilemma hardly deserved the epithet "worthless manhood." Still, for the two sexes, relative equality of economic function did not imply equality of domestic authority.

Although a husband and wife each made an essential contribution to the welfare of the household, they were compensated in different ways for their labor. This reward differential reflected their contrasting household responsibilities and produced contrasting attitudes toward work and its personal and social value. As a participant in a staple-crop economy, a black father assumed responsibility for a crop that would be exchanged in the marketplace at the end of the year. He supposedly toiled for future compensation in the form of cash. However, not only did his physical exertion gain him little in the way of immediate reward, in fact he tilled the ground only to repay one debt and to ensure that he would have another in the coming year. Under such conditions, most men took pride in their farming abilities, but worked no more strenuously than was absolutely necessary to satisfy white creditors and keep their own fami-

lies alive in the process.

Their wives, on the other hand, remained relatively insulated from the inevitable frustrations linked to a future-oriented, market economy. For example, women daily performed discreet tasks that yielded tangible results upon completion. Meal preparation, laundering, egg gathering—these chores had finite boundaries in the course of a day. Childcare was a special case, but it had its own special joys. It was an ongoing responsibility that began when a woman had her first baby and ended only years later when her youngest child left home. On a more mundane level, childcare was a constant preoccupation of mothers during their waking hours, and infants' needs often invaded their sleep. Yet a woman's exclusive authority in this area of domestic life earned her emotional gratification. Her husband hardly derived a similar sense of gratification from his responsibility for the cotton crop; he "earned" only what a white man was willing to pay him. Hence the distinction between work patterns simplistically labeled by some contemporary writers as male "laziness" and female "self-sacrifice" actually represented a complex phenomenon shaped by the different demands made upon black men and women and the degree of personal satisfaction resulting from the fulfillment of those demands.

Poor whites in the late nineteenth-century South were also stigmatized by charges of laziness and lethargy; together black and white sharecroppers and tenants endured a form of opprobrium traditionally directed at working people by their employers and social "betters." Like their black counterparts, propertyless whites valued self-sufficiency over cash-crop tenancy, and they too confronted new class relationships established after the war—relationships that turned on mortgages, credit, and crop liens as much as race and kinship. By 1900 over one-third of all whites employed in agriculture were tenants, and even small landowners remained perched precariously on the brink of financial disaster, only a drought or a boll weevil plague away from indebtedness. As many as 90 percent of white farmers in Mississippi, Alabama, and

Georgia owed money to a local financier at the end of the century. A gradual but significant decrease in domestic food production throughout this period meant that few laborers or tenants regardless of race could feed themselves without purchasing supplies from a planter-merchant. Thus all landless farmers, white and black, confronted uncertainties in a period of declining agricultural prices and general economic hardship. It seems likely then that southern poor people as a group deviated from the predominant (that is, white middle-class northern-industrial) culture, a way of life shaped by the powerful ideology of ambition and personal gain.

A comparison of the experiences of poor white and black women in the rural South suggests that to a great extent, class and gender conjoined to determine what all sharecroppers' wives did and how they did it. For example, data on black and white households in the Cotton South for 1880 and 1900 indicate some striking similarities between the family structures characteristic of the two races. For instance, both types of "average" households possessed a male head, and a male head accompanied by his spouse, in the same proportions. Black and white wives shared the same age patterns relative to their husbands. Though slightly larger, white households had a similar configuration compared to black ones and lived near at least some of their kin to the same extent.

Detailed descriptions of the work of poor white rural women are lacking for the nineteenth century. If we assume, however, that these women were no better off than their daughters and granddaughters who continued to live on farms—and there is no reason to believe that they were—then we can extrapolate material about white tenant-farm women in the 1930s to learn about earlier generations. Margaret Hagood's study *Mothers of the South* (published in 1939) suggests that the basic responsibilities of these women had remained the same over the years. Like black women, poor white farm wives bore the domestic burdens that were endemic to the economic system of southern staple-crop agriculture. They married in their late teens and

had an average of six children (although large households of twelve or thirteen were not uncommon). Because the family was constantly in debt to a local merchant, family members felt glad if they broke even at the end of the year. Most women made do with very little cash in piecing together the family's subsistence. They performed all the household chores of washing, sewing, cleaning, cooking, and churning, often with the assistance of their eldest daughter, but a majority also helped out in the cotton or tobacco fields during the busy seasons. Wrote Hagood, "the customary practice is for the father's claim for field work to take precedence over that of the mother for help at the house." These wives often added to the family income with the proceeds they earned from selling eggs, vegetables, or milk. In the Deep South, some couples experienced periodic separations when the wives went off to work temporarily in factories, or when their menfolk found jobs on the levees in the off-season.

In terms of earthly comforts, life offered little more to white tenant-farm wives than it did to blacks; white women too lived in sparsely furnished two- or three-room cabins that lacked running water, and their Cotton Belt families tended to move every three years or so. Mothers were attended by a midwife during childbirth. Predictably, they knew nothing about modern contraceptive techniques, and although they took pride in their child-rearing abilities, they suffered from the consequent drain on their emotional and physical resources. Dreams and fortune-tellers explained the past and predicted the future for many of these illiterate women, but they seemed to lack the religious devotion and denominational loyalties exhibited by black wives and mothers. Undernourished and overworked, they had to remind themselves of the biblical dictate, "Be content with your lot."

In a rural society that honored a code of neighborliness and mutual cooperation, black and white women had few opportunities for interracial contact on any level. Husbands and fathers of both races and all classes observed the ritualized etiquette of southern race relations in the public arena—in town, at the post office, court house, or supply store—but their wives were largely excluded from these encounters. Middle-class white women acted out their own presumptions of racial superiority in their dealings with black servants and laundresses. Tenant-farm wives of course could not afford to employ black women for any length of time or exploit them in a direct way. A few women of the two races did come together in situations that held the promise of enhancing mutual respect and appreciation—for example, when they participated in the Southern Farmers Alliance in the 1880s and 1890s, or when black "grannies" attended white women during childbirth. Yet these opportunities were rare, and for the most part women lacked a formal voice in the politics of interracial protest.

In the end, the fact that the labor of white sharecroppers' wives was so similar to that of their black counterparts is less significant than the social environment in which that work took place. For the outcast group, the preservation of family integrity served as a political statement to the white South. To nurse a child, send a daughter to school, feed a hungry family after a long day at work in the fields, or patch a shirt by the light of a flickering fire—these simple acts of domesticity acquired special significance when performed for a people so beleaguered by human as well as natural forces. If white women also had to make soup out of scraps, at least they and their families remained secure from "bulldosers" (mobs) and Judge Lynch. Finally, and perhaps most important, women of the two races had different things to teach their children about the "southern way of life," its freedoms and its dangers.

Despite the transition in labor organization from slavery to sharecropping, the work of black women in the rural South continued to respond to the same human and seasonal rhythms over the generations. By the early twentieth century, they still structured their labor around household chores and childcare, field and wage work, and community welfare activities. Moreover, emanci-pation hardly lessened the demands made upon females of all ages; young girls worked alongside their mothers, and elderly women had to provide for themselves and their families as long as they were physically able. Although the specific tasks performed by women reflected constantly changing priorities (determined by the cotton-growing cycle and the size and maturity of individual households), the need for a woman to labor rarely abated in the course of a day, a year, or her lifetime.

In its functional response to unique historical circumstances, the rural black household necessarily differed from the late nineteenth-century middle-class ideal, which assumed that men would engage in individual self-aggrandizement. Furthermore, according to this ideal, women were to remain isolated at home, only indirectly sharing in the larger social values of wealth and power accumulation. In contrast, rural black women labored in harmony with the priorities of cooperation and sharing established by their own communities, even as their husbands were prevented from participating in the cash economy in a way that would answer to white-defined notions of masculinity.

Despite the hard, never-ending work performed by rural women—who, ironically, were labeled part of a "lazy" culture by contemporaries and recent historians alike—they could not entirely compensate for the loss of both a husband (through death or another form of permanent separation) and older sons or male relatives who established households on their own. The sharecropping family strove to maintain a delicate balance between its labor resources and its economic needs, and men, as both negotiators in the public sphere and as field workers, were crucial to that balance. Therefore, during the latter part of the nineteenth century, when the natural selection process endemic to commercial crop agriculture weeded out "unfit" households, it forced single mothers, widows, and unmarried daughters to look cityward. Many of them would discover that while the southern countryside continued to mirror the slave past, in the towns that past was refracted into new shapes and images.

9

GENDER AND URBAN POLITICAL REFORM: THE CITY CLUB AND THE WOMAN'S CITY CLUB OF CHICAGO IN THE PROGRESSIVE ERA

MAUREEN A. FLANAGAN

The Progressive movement of the early twentieth century was one of America's most important reform movements. Not only did Progressive measures such as the Children's and Women's Bureaus signal the acceptance of national government intervention in social issues, but nearly every aspect of society was brought under rational, "scientific" scrutiny by Progressive social workers, journalists, and social scientists. Under the umbrella of Progressivism, reformers established settlement houses to shelter the destitute, brought mental hospitals into line with advanced psychiatric practices, cleansed city governments of machine politics and politicians, and further democratized the political system by adding measures for popular referendum and recall.

There was, however, no unified Progressive movement. Rather, Progressivism included many groups with sometimes conflicting and sometimes overlapping agendas for reform. In this essay, Maureen A. Flanagan looks at Progressivism through the lens of gender. Focusing on political reform movements in Chicago, she compares the programs and aims of the upper-middle-class men and women who made up the City Club and the Woman's City Club of Chicago in the second decade of the twentieth century. Although they shared the same class backgrounds, Flanagan finds that these men and women approached urban reform differently. Whether dealing with issues of waste disposal, public education, or police power in the city, men favored a pragmatic, business-oriented approach while women, approaching reform as a public extension of their domestic responsibilities, adopted a broader and more socially informed perspective. As Flanagan demonstrates, reform organizations such as the Woman's City Club gave women an important opportunity to express their political ideas before the advent of female suffrage in 1920.

On one political reform issue after another, the men and women of the Chicago City Clubs disagreed over the means and ends of Progressive Era reform. In the second decade of the twentieth century, the men of the City Club of Chicago, a civic reform organization, were working with businessmen's clubs to implement a vocational education curriculum in the public schools designed to train workers for the benefit of the industry. Simultaneously, the female counterpart of the City Club, the Woman's City Club of Chicago, was cooperating with the Chicago Federation of Labor, the Chicago Federation of Teachers, the Women's Trade Union League, the Woman's party, and the Socialist party of Illinois in sponsoring a talk in Chicago by Congressman David L. Lewis advocating government ownership of the telephones. The men of the City Club strongly opposed any attempt to implement government ownership of utilities as anticapitalist; they also would never have dreamed of cooperating with workers' organizations or the Socialist party on any issue.

It is commonly accepted that male and female reformers in the first two decades of the twentieth century had different agendas for reform; that these differences stemmed primarily from gender concerns is also assumed. Yet historians have rarely compared the political activities of men and women of the same class. Most works on Progressive Era politics and reform concentrate on men, ignoring women's roles, viewing them only as partners with their husbands or assigning them to the periphery of charity and church work. The idea that women were actively concerned with politics is ignored in favor of seeing them as interested in social, not political, causes and reforms. By ignoring women as political reformers, historians assume that women have little or no political history, at least until we can count their votes. As a result, the processes that led women to pursue political activity and political goals in the first place, and the reasons why their political goals differed from men of their own class, have not been examined.

The members of both the Woman's City Club and the City Club were deeply engaged in politi-

cal action of the sort Eric Foner has characterized as concerned with "how power in civil society is ordered and exercised [and] the way in which power was wielded and conceptualized." Feeling assaulted by numerous and vexatious municipal problems, they sought to solve them by changing the structure of government, reorganizing the urban environment, and reallocating power within it. Streets and sidewalks in Chicago were in constant disrepair; the public utilities provided abysmal service; the sewer and garbage collection and disposal systems could not handle the volume of waste produced every day in the city; the public school system was overcrowded, understaffed, and underfunded; the smoke, fumes, and waste from industrial plants polluted the air and ground; a large percentage of the populace lived in crowded, rickety, unsanitary tenement houses that flourished in the face of minimal building regulations; and the city's police force neither controlled crime nor kept the peace. Moreover, in the early twentieth century, municipal governments in the United States often lacked institutional authority for attacking these and other urban problems. Chicago's municipal government was structurally weak, the locus of political power was diffuse and decentralized, and no consensus existed on who should wield power and to what purposes. Such issues as how to collect and dispose of municipal garbage and waste, how to restructure and run the system of public education, and how and to what ends to regulate the use of police power within the city were controversial, and no consensus existed among the citizenry about the appropriate solutions. Because of their different relationships to the urban power structure, to daily life within the city, and to other individuals, when the members of the Woman's City Club confronted these problems, they came to a vision of a good city and specific proposals of how best to provide for the welfare of its residents that were very different from those of their male counterparts in the City Club.

The contrasting approaches of the two City Clubs is particularly significant because in other respects the groups resembled each other. Both were founded as municipal reform organizations, the men's club in 1903 and the women's club in 1910, on the principle that the citizens of a city were responsible for the welfare of the community in which they lived. The two clubs drew their membership largely from the same class of upper-middle-class white men and women within the city. The men were generally businessmen or professionals; often, husbands in the City Club had wives who belonged to the Woman's City Club. Of the 909 married women who joined the Woman's City Club in its inaugural year of 1910–1911, almost 10 percent were married to men who were members of the City Club; five years later, the total percentage had risen to 16. A smaller percentage of women who joined the Woman's City Club were the sisters, mothers, and daughters of men in the City Club. During this same period, 1910–1915, more women joined the Woman's City Club whose husbands had previously been in the City Club and who had either died or dropped membership for other reasons, a circumstance that adds to the picture of a membership drawn from a similar pool of people within the city. Among the leadership of the Woman's City Club, the correlation between husbands and wives belonging to their respective clubs is higher: 55 percent of the married women serving as officers and directors of the Woman's City Club in 1915–1916, for example, were married to men in the City Club; one other officer was the widow of a former City Club member. Of the married women who chaired the club's standing and civic committees, 75 percent had husbands as members of the City Club; and 33 percent of the married women who headed the ward organization committees were married to men in the City Club.

Some of the founding members of the City Club were from the prominent, wealthy Chicago families who had built industrial Chicago: Medill McCormick, John V. Farwell, Jr., Charles R. Crane, Murry Nelson, Jr., and Kellogg Fairbank, for example. But the majority of the membership came from the newer business and professional ranks, which furnished most of the city's middle-class reformers. Among them were real estate

developer Arthur Aldis, manufacturer T. K. Webster, and stationer George Cole; lawyers Walter L. Fisher, Victor Elting, and Hoyt King; university professor Charles Merriam and newspaper editor Slason Thompson. At the Woman's City Club, first-year members included the wives of some of these men—Ruth McCormick, Mabel Fisher, Emma Webster, Mary Nelson, Julia Thompson, and Mary Aldis; the wives of other prominent Chicago business and professional men—Ellen Henrotin, Mary Emily Blatchford, Harriet McCormick, Edith Rockefeller McCormick, Anita McCormick Blaine, Paulette Palmer, and Julia Wolf; and settlement house workers—Jane Addams, Mary McDowell, Anna Nicholes, and Harriet Vittum.

A goodly number of unmarried professional women, including some social workers, belonged to the Woman's City Club. It would be a mistake to assume, however, that the settlement house workers wielded a disproportionate influence over the policies pursued by the club. Of the 1,243 members of the Woman's City Club in 1910–1911, twenty-three listed one of five settlement houses as their residence; two other women were married to male settlement house workers. Five years later, of 2,789 members, forty-three gave their residence as a settlement house with another three married to male settlement house workers. In no year between 1910 and 1916 did settlement house workers occupy more than five of the twenty-eight positions of officers and directors of the Woman's City Club, nor did they hold a higher percentage of chairs of standing, civic, and ward committees. Solidly middle- to upper-class women—either married or widowed—were considerably more numerous than settlement house workers. In 1915, for instance, 388 members listed a residence in the city's affluent twenty-first ward; eighty of these women had husbands or fathers in the City Club. Such prominent Chicago women as Ruth Hanna (Mrs. Medill) McCormick, Ellen (Mrs. Charles) Henrotin, Louise DeKoven (Mrs. Joseph) Bowen, and Elizabeth (Mrs. Charles E.) Merriam, for example, served as vice presidents, directors, and as chairs of standing, civic, and ward committees during the years covered by this study. During the club's first six years, its presidency was held by three prominent Chicago women: Mary (Mrs. H. W.) Wilmarth, Louise DeKoven Bowen, and University of Chicago Professor Sophonisba Breckenridge; and two settlement house workers: Harriet Vittum and Mary McDowell.

It is more difficult to determine how many male settlement house workers may have belonged to the City Club because its membership lists do not give addresses or professions. Raymond Robins and Graham Taylor, two of the city's most prominent settlement house workers, joined the club in early 1904. One or the other of these two men were among the club's thirteen directors its first four years; neither held a higher position, but both men were consistently active in club affairs and programs and in attempting to influence club policies.

Despite the similar constituencies and statements of purpose of the two City Clubs, they took opposing positions on several current municipal issues in a way that reveals profound differences in their conceptions of city government and its responsibility for the general welfare of its residents. For example, the two clubs took very different approaches to the noxious problem of municipal sanitation when the city's contract with the Chicago Reduction Company expired in 1913. Following standard municipal policy at the time, the city had contracted out to this private business most of the task of municipal garbage and waste disposal. The city itself only collected garbage from houses and small buildings, and it hired private contractors to collect from apartment buildings, hotels, hospitals, and other large establishments. It then paid the Chicago Reduction Company $47,500 per year to dispose of the garbage, and the company made profits from selling the by-products produced from the garbage. On the whole, the citizens of Chicago were unhappy with the system. They complained of infrequent garbage collection, of unsanitary and rickety wagons used for collection that leaked garbage and refuse onto the streets

and alleys through which they traveled, of having to separate garbage from other types of waste, and of the reeking fumes emanating from the Reduction Company's plant on the city's near southwest side. When the contract expired, the city had several options to improve service. It could sign a new contract with the Chicago Reduction Company requiring the company to provide better services, it could seek a new company with which to contract, or it could assume direct municipal ownership and operation of all garbage and waste disposal.

The problem of how best to dispose of garbage was part of a larger dilemma faced by the U.S. cities during the early twentieth century over the provision of vital municipal services. It was a dilemma not simply because it involved choosing the best possible means but because there was no agreement among urban residents about what criteria defined the best means. One group wished to replace the system of contracting out (franchising) with municipal ownership and operation of municipal services. Another wanted to retain the present system, albeit more tightly regulated. As everyone involved realized, there was a critical difference between these two positions: with municipal ownership and operation of municipal services, the city government would assume far more power than it currently possessed. It would also deprive private enterprise and the city's businessmen of an arena for profit.

In 1913, both the City Club and the Woman's City Club considered the garbage issue in ways that suggest significant differences between the members of the two clubs. The City Club's approach typified its method of investigating municipal problems. The club constituted a committee and charged it to study the problem, consult with "experts" in the field, and make recommendations to the club as a whole. The club also scheduled meetings to which it invited various people concerned with the problem to present their ideas and recommendations to the general membership. It directed the committee to collect all possible information on garbage dumps, refuse loading stations, ward dump yards, and any and all real property used for the purpose of garbage disposal. The committee was also to visit and inspect the plant used by the Chicago Reduction Company. Most important, the City Club instructed the committee to gain all the information it could about the "financial details of the reduction business."

On the basis of the committee's findings and reports, and a competing bid offered by the Illinois Rendering Company, the City Club firmly supported the option of keeping the system in private hands for financial reasons. The only question in the club members' minds was how to secure the most favorable contract arrangement from one of the two reduction companies. In all its deliberations, the City Club rejected outright the option of municipal ownership, contending that there were no "facts and figures" to show that municipal ownership and operation would be more financially rewarding than private ownership. Under the club's calculations, if the city retained its system of private contractors, it would continue to pay costs of collection and reduction, estimated at nearly $500,000 per year, but would avoid the costs of purchasing and operating a reduction plant. This approach, the City Club argued, would be more fiscally efficient. The City Club also proposed that the one costly item for the city, its collection from private residences, be reduced by making the garbage wagon drivers civil servants.

The City Club carried forward its opposition to municipal ownership when it recommended that its membership oppose an ordinance before the City Council in 1914 to appropriate money for city purchase of the reduction plant, which would then be operated by the city's department of health. Even when the ordinance passed, the club refused to withdraw its opposition. In early 1915, it grudgingly supported a bond issue of $700,000 for the health department, saying that, since the money had already been spent (for the purchase and renovation of the plant), the bonds had to be approved. The City Club, however, never ceased fighting municipal ownership of this and other public utilities.

It was not just its cost–benefit analysis of municipal ownership that motivated the City Club. The debate over garbage disposal also concerned whether to continue with reduction—the disposal method used by both the companies bidding for the city contract—or to shift to the incineration method. When Willis Nance, an alderman and a member of the City Waste Commission, spoke to the City Club, he emphasized that reduction "has proven in certain cities to be of immense value from a commercial standpoint." In Chicago, for example, the profit realized from reduction (a process that rendered an oil product used in the manufacture of soaps) had reached as high as $150,000 per year. "It is a question worth considering if in burning all our waste [that is, incineration] we will not become a bit extravagant in our method." Nance admitted that incineration plants were virtually odorless, that because the extreme heat destroyed almost everything this method was certainly sanitary, and that the heat generated by burning refuse could be used to create electricity for the city. Yet Nance, and the City Club, rejected these considerations in favor of reduction. In its refusal to consider creating a municipally owned and operated garbage system, and its support of reduction over incineration, the City Club remained solidly on the side of private profit and limited municipal power over city services. The club did not even investigate possible long-term savings to the city of buying and operating the disposal equipment. Implicit in its stance was the notion that the good of the city lay in maximizing private profits from the provision of municipal services and minimizing governmental involvement.

The Woman's City Club, on the other hand, favored both municipal control over and incineration of garbage on the grounds that they would maximize the healthiness of the urban environment. The Woman's City Club did not concentrate on fiscal details but directed Mary McDowell to explore the variety of sanitation methods used in the United States and in Europe. McDowell, a settlement house worker and chair of the club's Committee on City Waste, undertook an extensive tour of waste disposal operations on both continents in 1913. On her return, she addressed the men's club about her findings. Her tour had convinced her that incineration was a more efficient and sanitary way to dispose of garbage. All the incineration plants she had visited, she told her audience, were free of noxious fumes, the heat from incineration went to generate electricity, and the hardened ash left as a by-product was being used in Europe for street paving. She could see little to recommend in reduction and told the men of the City Club that it was wrong to think of garbage removal as a business rather than a question of health and sanitation. By thinking of it as a business, they failed to consider, for instance, that, because a reduction plant could only handle pure garbage, citizens had to perform the unhealthy task of sorting pure garbage from unreducible refuse before it could be collected. Reduction, she bluntly told them, "fascinates the business man in America because you can extract money out of the garbage."

Incineration was only one facet of the overall program for garbage collection and disposal reform favored by the members of the Woman's City Club. These women wanted to centralize power through the municipal ownership and operation of waste facilities, the same system specifically rejected by their male counterparts. After the city purchased the reduction plant in 1914, the men continued to decry the lack of facts and figures available to show whether municipal ownership could be profitable. The women responded by showing that it was indeed profitable. In contrast to the men of the City Club, who advocated maximizing private profits—as high as $150,000—while minimizing municipal expenditures, the women showed that the city had made a profit of almost $6,000 in the year after it purchased the reduction plant. According to their calculations, once the initial outlay had been made to purchase equipment, the possibilities of a small yearly profit for the city existed. Moreover, while they never advocat-

ed waste or careless expenditure of municipal finances, they did not see profit as the primary issue. As debate continued during 1915, the Woman's City Club's Committee on City Waste stressed the primacy of health over economics. Where garbage disposal was concerned, announced the club, "the true measure of its efficiency in such work is not the financial returns to be received, but the character of the service given."

In 1916, the Woman's City Club made municipal ownership and operation of all garbage and waste collection and disposal a provision of its Woman's Municipal Platform for Reform. Later that year, the club proposed additionally that the city institutionalize garbage collection and disposal in a new municipal bureau, opposing a new bond issue of $2 million that neither provided for purchase and development of collection equipment nor established this municipal bureau. Unlike the men of the City Club, these women believed that service and the good health and sanitation of the city should be the priority for settling this issue. They rejected claims that municipal garbage disposal would not work, wondering aloud "why a municipality should not use the same sense in running their business that a packing plant does."

On the issue of public education, the differences between the City Club and the Woman's City Club were, if anything, even more pronounced. For a number of years, the City Club had been seeking to increase the business efficiency of the school system by implementing a type of education "more in accordance with the demands of modern society and business conditions." In 1908, in response to the statement of Superintendent of Schools Cooley that "instruction in the elementary grades of the city schools was hopelessly academic and unable to fit the mass of the children for the vocation upon which they were to enter," the City Club constituted a subcommittee to investigate the possibilities of instituting a curriculum stressing vocational education. The club followed its general operating premise that every issue should be scientifically investigated—a task made easier by its wealth—and hired an outside investigator, E. A. Wreidt of the University of Chicago, to pursue this issue for them.

The City Club was seeking a system of vocational education that would better train students for industrial jobs. This system, the club decided after some consideration, could best be established by businessmen and the board of education working together to design a program "directing school children toward proper occupations, and securing additional training for these children in the occupations themselves," while they were still in school. To secure the requisite funding and administration, the City Club supported various measures in the state legislature. It especially liked a bill introduced by the Illinois Bankers' Association to give state support to schools providing vocational education within the general school curriculum.

As was true of the City Club's attitude toward garbage and waste disposal, its proposals for vocational education, intended to create a dependable industrial work force, reflected members' preoccupation with financial reward for business. The subcommittee on vocational education declared industrial education "urgent if not imperative if we are to attain a place in the world's commerce commensurate with our possibilities and opportunities." Whether children or parents wanted this innovation did not concern the City Club. If anyone objected, he or she was accused of selfishness. The club's resolution in support of vocational education declared that "the nurture of intelligent skill in our hand workers is but increasing our effectiveness in industrial production. Certainly any measure looking to this end should have the hearty support of all classes of our citizens. What is good for the whole people can not possibly work harm to any section of our country."

The Woman's City Club also supported vocational education but of a different type and for different means and ends. These women used no rhetoric about the productivity and advancement of industrial society. They were concerned instead with the fate of the individual child within the school and industrial work systems. The Woman's City Club did not establish a new subcommittee to study the problem, and they could not afford outside experts. Working jointly with more than two hundred women from thirty women's clubs across the city, the Woman's City Club approached the issue of vocational education with two goals in mind. The first was to find ways to keep children in school beyond age fourteen (the mandatory age limit for schooling) in order to educate and prepare them for better-paying jobs. These women believed it a social and personal tragedy that thousands of children left school every year to enter "low-grade industries, untrained, unguided, and unguarded." They wanted children to understand "that the earning capacity of those who have had a technical or commercial training is much greater than those who have completed only the eighth grade." Their second goal was to provide advice and guidance to schoolchildren once they were ready to leave school and seek work. Children, the Woman's City Club believed, needed "help in choosing a job so as to prevent the wastage that comes to them and the employers from their own haphazard choice."

To help carry out both these goals, in 1911 the Woman's City Club, along with the Chicago Woman's Club and the Association of Collegiate Alumnae, formed the Bureau for Vocational Supervision. The bureau took a personal interest in schoolchildren, working directly to place them in appropriate jobs when they left school and then to follow their subsequent progress. It also established a scholarship committee to raise funds to keep needy children between the ages of fourteen and sixteen in school "until they have acquired enough education, training and physical strength to guarantee them some chance of success in the industrial world." Scholarship money could be used for books, carfare, or as a stipend to replace the income a needy family could have earned from having a child leave school at fourteen; a book-loan fund was also established. The women's organizations, unlike their male counterparts, were always low on funds. The bureau raised the scholarship and book-loan monies through pledges of $1 a month from their memberships.

The positions of the City Club and the Woman's City Club on two additional aspects of education reform also invite comparison. One is the question of whether to establish a system of vocational education separate from general education. Both groups opposed this proposition—which had been introduced into the state legislature with the avid support of the Commercial Club of Chicago—but for different reasons. The City Club thought a dual system would make it difficult to attract students into vocational education. Fearing that vocational education was viewed negatively by much of the U.S. society, the club preferred that it be offered within the common schools as a separate curriculum. The Woman's City Club, on the other hand, emphatically rejected a separate system of vocational education as discriminatory. Speaking before the club, Agnes Nestor, a glove worker who at the age of eighteen had led her fellow women workers in a successful strike, and who was both a labor organizer with the Women's Trade Union League and member of the Woman's City Club, urged her audience to reject a separate system of education. She reminded club members that while children might be trained for work in school, they deserved the privilege of cultural training as well as the practical. The women agreed. They passed a resolution stating, "All the children of the community, whether rich or poor are entitled . . . to the benefits of general education for citizenship . . . [and] the children who are to become efficient workmen must comprehend their work in relation to science, art, and to society in general."

The second aspect of education reform over which the two clubs differed was that of maximum classroom size. After visiting public schools and talking to teachers, the Woman's City Club insisted that there be no more than thirty children to a classroom and urged the City Club to support this goal, or at the very least, some definite limit to classroom size. The women further declared that they would "insist that Chicago can

afford and must have adequate facilities and a sufficient teaching force to insure a maximum of thirty in high school courses." In other words, the principle of reduced class size demanded the municipality find and allocate the money to implement the changes. The City Club, for its part, refused to support any specific limits on class size, either the thirty initially proposed or the limits of forty-two and twenty-eight in elementary and secondary classrooms that the Woman's City Club later suggested as alternatives. In a letter to the women, the City Club sympathized with the idea of reducing the size of classrooms. It preferred, however, "to go into the question of the proper number of children under each teacher . . . with some care" and to make a future recommendation "based on the best evidence which can be obtained through the country after a rather careful search as to the maximum number of children that can be efficiently taught by a single teacher."

The two organizations also clashed over the issue of police power in the city, especially police activities during labor strikes. Although the men of the City Club, unlike the members of the more ardent antilabor business clubs such as the Commercial Club, did not advocate or condone police violence against strikers, they were loath to condemn it when it happened. After a controversial strike in February 1914 by waitresses from the restaurant workers' union against the Henrici restaurant, the club confined itself to "investigating" both sides of the issue. During the strike, more than one hundred of the striking waitresses had been arrested on the picket line, and the restaurant owners had secured a court injunction against picketing. On both issues—the injunction and the arrests—the chairman of the club's Committee on Labor Conditions, Frederick S. Deibler, presented a noncommittal report to the general membership. It acknowledged that the courts recognized the right to peaceful picketing and conceded that, in general, this was good for labor relations, but it also pointed out that courts could rule against picketing on the grounds that such activity "had threatened irreparable injury to property." How to determine whether to issue an injunction was best left to the courts. If in this particular case a judge had found just cause in enjoining the Henrici strike, Deibler implied, that decision ought to be accepted by the club and all citizens. He neither challenged the court's ruling nor questioned the prevailing idea that workers' rights to picket should be restricted to peaceful actions that caused no harm to property. The latter limitation was particularly important. Implicit in that notion was the protection of companies from the loss of any business or trade as a result of picketing.

Deibler did show more doubt about the propriety of the arrests of the striking waitresses and their treatment by the police. "When all the circumstances surrounding the dispute are concerned," he told the club members, "it is difficult to account for the necessity of 119 or more arrests." It looked, he reported, as if the police had been determined to halt the picketing, whatever the legal rights of the waitresses. He expressed doubts about the validity of the restaurant's claim that it had to employ private detectives, who were used against the strikers, in order to protect its property. However, he refused to condemn either the police or the owners for their actions. Deibler's report merely suggested that police violence during strikes and the restaurant's use of private police during this particular strike did not help labor–business relations. The Henrici strike provoked no sentiment within the City Club to modify the exercise of police powers, at least as far as these affected labor activities.

By contrast, members of the Woman's City Club were actively involved in the strike itself: trying to resolve it and promoting reform of police powers. Several of these women, including Ruth Hanna McCormick (the wife of Medill McCormick, congressman, former publisher of the *Chicago Tribune,* and founding member of the City Club), had walked the picket lines with the striking waitresses. Based on its experiences, the Woman's City Club accused the police and businessmen of brutality, demanded that police-

women be assigned to protect the picketers, and asked that all private guards be withdrawn.

That police violence seemed endemic to labor situations in Chicago appalled the members of the Woman's City Club. At the mass meeting of the club called to consider the Woman's Municipal Platform in March 1916, they roundly condemned the 1,800 arrests made by police and private guards during the garment worker's strike of 1915. "It is time we challenged such things," Agnes Nestor told the assembly. "[The strikers] have come to this country because it holds out a promise to them. They come seeking freedom . . . and instead of that, they find they are exploited; and when they go on strike to protest against conditions, they are arrested . . . They are arrested at the suggestion of the employer." The women attending the meeting agreed with Nestor; they adopted a plank opposing the extraordinary use of police power against workers. "We condemn the practice of giving police power to private guards whose employment during industrial disputes we believe increases disorder," read the plank. "We protest against the illegal arrest of persons engaged in patrolling the district where a strike is in progress." This last referred to the police practice of arresting private citizens who were walking the picket lines in order to protect the striking workers from police brutality.

Nestor was a working-class woman. The vast majority of women attending the meeting were not, and many were married to men who were employers. This did not keep them from sharing Nestor's sentiments, nor had it in the past. Six years earlier during a strike by the garment workers, Louise DeKoven Bowen, the wealthy Chicago reformer who chaired the meeting in 1916, had declared her sympathies to be on the side of the workers and their right to organize and protest.

As part of their municipal platform, the Woman's City Club also demanded that the city create a municipal strike bureau. This bureau would require the office of chief of police to act as mediator in strikes, instead of acting on the behalf of employers, and would ban the use of private guards. The club declared that, while injustices or wrong-headedness might exist on the part of both employer and employee in labor disagreements, the workers' actions were quite often valid and justified. It advocated mediation, negotiation, and police protection of strikers rather than police power to arrest and abuse them. The men of the City Club, by contrast, were oriented to the needs and desires of businessmen on this issue as on most others. At a discussion meeting held to consider the proposed strike bureau, they listened to the attorney for the Illinois Manufacturers' Association speak against the measure as an infringement on the rights of business. There is no evidence that the City Club held a different opinion or that it ever seriously considered supporting a municipal strike bureau.

It has been a prevailing idea of Progressive Era historiography that middle-class business and professional men, such as the members of the City Club, became municipal reformers because they had developed a citywide vision. This vision resulted from their realization that, as business affairs were conducted increasingly on a citywide basis, they needed to reform the entire urban structure in order to protect these affairs. In Chicago, the men of the City Club viewed the city primarily as an arena in which to do business, and they advocated municipal reforms intended to protect and further the aims of business. If business and businessmen prospered, they argued, the city and the rest of its inhabitants would ultimately prosper. Thus, while they designed solutions for municipal problems that would, in practice, most directly profit one class, they argued that the benefits would spread through the remainder of the city. On one issue after another, they made fiscal efficiency and financial profitability the criteria for evaluating proposals for change.

I have argued elsewhere that, by the turn of the century, a broad range of urban residents, not just elite white males, had developed often-conflicting visions of the city as a whole. The vision pursued by the members of the Woman's City Club has not been studied, in large part because of the tendency in Progressive Era political history to study men. That the women of the Woman's City Club had a citywide vision is apparent in their arguments and proposals for garbage disposal, public education, and the uses of police power. For them, municipal problems required solutions that guaranteed the well-being of everyone within the city, regardless of their immediate implications for business. The Woman's Municipal Platform of 1916 laid out the club's position on franchises, schools, housing, public health and sanitation, police and crime, among others. Underlying it was the belief that all municipal problems had to be solved before the city would be a good place in which to live.

One must, however, ask why the members of the Woman's City Club took strikingly different positions on municipal issues from the men of the City Club. As mentioned earlier, the different vision of the women of the Woman's City Club cannot be explained simply as one that the settlement house workers imposed on the rest of the membership. No one, we assume, forced Ruth McCormick to march the picket lines with the striking waitresses in 1914 in the company of Hull House resident Ellen Gates Starr. As president of the club, Louise DeKoven Bowen willingly took the lead in designing and promoting the Woman's Municipal Platform. Where the settlement house workers may well have made an impact on the Woman's City Club was in their skill in political organizing. Kathryn Kish Sklar's recent work on the activities of the women at Hull House suggests that the settlement house milieu gave women "a means of bypassing the control of male associations and institutions," one in which "women reformers were able to develop their capacity for political leadership free from many if not all of the constraints that otherwise might have been imposed on their power by the male-dominated parties or groups." The activities of the Woman's City Club were the next step in the progression of building political leadership.

Twenty-five years after the founding of Hull House, these Chicago women had gained more in the political arena than just the right to vote.

In explaining why middle-class men and women had such different views of the city, and of political reform, it is also not sufficient to attribute the Woman's City Club positions to a received female culture both traditional and limited. Paula Baker has argued for the influence of a female culture, the basics tenets of which were shaped in the early nineteenth century. This female culture, emanating from a belief in the "special moral nature of women," compelled women to work to "ensure the moral and social order" of their surroundings, first through voluntary organizations and then government agencies. Women's efforts in the Progressive Era were thus, according to Baker, an extension of the pursuit of a morality-based social reform in which women passed "on to the state the work of social policy that they found increasingly unmanageable." But the Woman's City Club did not speak about the higher morality of women. Mary McDowell described the club's work as "a constructive fight for better things, for higher standards, for a sense of collective responsibility for public safety and public morals . . . Civic patriotism with a living daily sacrifice is the need of the hour." Louise DeKoven Bowen, during her term as president of the Woman's City Club, proclaimed that the club, "should act not only as a spotlight turned on our community . . . but it should also serve as an agency to correct the evils depicted and to guide women in their efforts to make of their citizenship a constructive force in the city's life."

Further, even if Woman's City Club members may have learned from their mothers to concern themselves with the welfare of the poor, these received ideas do not explain the political strategies and the specific municipal proposals they developed in response to the problems of early twentieth-century Chicago. There is a crucial distinction between ideas received from previous generations and those that individuals create out of their own experiences. Received ideas had nothing to say about labor unions, for example, or

municipal efficiency and municipal ownership. We know that businessmen, working out of their personal experiences of life and business in the city, changed their conception of politics and municipal government over the course of a generation. Women went through the same process. But, as women's daily experiences were different from men's, they came to different conclusions about the direction political reform should take in Chicago.

The majority of men in the City Club were businessmen who drew on their professional experiences to design urban reform agendas. They were accustomed to thinking in terms of profitability and fiscal efficiency, of assessing a problem through the slow but steady accumulation of facts, and of seeking solutions that were best for themselves and their businesses. Their proposals for solving the problems of garbage disposal, public education, and police power make clear that they came easily to see as best for the city what was best for business and businessmen.

The primary daily experience for most middle-class women, on the other hand, was the home. Women were used to organizing a home environment that ensured the well-being of everyone in the family. When they entered the political arena, they sought to achieve the same objective. "The struggle within the city is a fight for the welfare of all the children of all the people," declared Mary McDowell. The *Bulletin* decreed that women "must form a citywide organization. We must unite forces for the common good and act together." "Suppose we had a system of municipal relief," asked DeKoven Bowen, "which is built upon the principle that the community is one great family and that each member of it is bound to help the other, the burden of support falling on all alike?" Thus women applied their experience of how the home worked to what a city government should try to achieve.

The different gender experiences of the members of the City Club and Woman's City Club also shaped the recruitment and activities of the club. To begin with, members of the City Club established more rigorous membership requirements than did the Woman's City Club. Before joining the City Club, any proposed member had to have his name submitted along with "facts and references indicating his fitness for membership and facilitating corroborative inquiry among the members." One negative vote was enough to blackball a prospective member. The admission requirements were strict, not because the purpose of the club was to make business contacts (as was the case with the Commercial Club) but to ensure that men whose opinions might differ dramatically from the majority did not have access to the club. "The chief function of the club," read an early circular, "is to promote the acquaintance, the friendly intercourse, the accurate information and personal co-operation of those who are sincerely interested in practical methods of improving the public life and affairs of the community in which we live." This sentiment was echoed by founding member Walter Fisher, who wrote that membership was "confined to those who are sincerely interested in practical methods of improving public conditions." Careful admission requirements gave the City Club the leeway to define sincere interest and practical methods as it wished to keep out those with whom its members might disagree. Entry into the Woman's City Club was easier. The club seems to have assumed that most women could contribute to its work, for all that was needed was nomination by one club member who believed that the nominee sympathized with the objectives of the organization. Without records of who was proposed for membership, or who was turned down, no definitive statement can be made about the City Club's membership practices. It is clear, however, that the City Club grew more slowly than did the Woman's City Club. From an initial membership of 335 in 1903–1904, the City Club reached approximately 2,400 members in 1916; the members of the Woman's City Club numbered around 1,250 in its inaugural year of 1910–1911 and stood at approximately 2,800 for 1915–1916.

Similarly reflective of their different experiences are the methods by which the two clubs investigated municipal problems. As business-

men, the members of the City Club were accustomed to experiencing firsthand only parts of the problem they were investigating. Employees often gathered facts and figures for the employer. Although social workers were members of the City Club, it is doubtful that the majority of the club members ever saw the places social workers lived and worked because the City Club carried on much of its work within its own quarters. In contrast, the women focused on grass-roots activities out in the city itself. The Woman's City Club leaders directed members to organize according to their city ward (in its membership lists, the club provides the ward each woman lived in). They also instructed them to go out into the wards to investigate street, alley, and sidewalk conditions; housing, schools, and churches; infant mortality rates, numbers of children, and juvenile delinquency; parks, playgrounds, dance halls, saloons, hotels, jails, and courts. A personal investigation of the garbage problem convinced the female reformers that only municipal ownership and operation of the means of garbage disposal would work well enough. Whether municipal ownership was the most financially profitable way to dispose of garbage was not their first concern; they asked whether it was the best way to promote the health and sanitation of the individuals whose neighborhoods they visited. When the answer seemed to be yes, they demanded municipal ownership.

Gender experiences, finally, help explain why the Woman's City Club, and women involved in municipal reform movements throughout the country, used the term "municipal housekeeping" to describe their activities—a more complicated metaphor than has previously been acknowledged. The women of the Woman's City Club were not just attempting to keep the city clean, as they did their homes. They had tried that approach years earlier, for example, in 1894–1895 when Jane Addams had organized women to go out and clean the streets themselves when the city was doing little about the problem. Rather, from their recognition of what it took to keep a home running, and running for the benefit of all its members, they developed ideas about how a good city should be run for the benefit of all its members. To characterize its work, the club talked in terms of "the Links that Bind the Home to City Hall," with city hall in the middle, linked by chains to fourteen pairs of squares describing municipal activities and bureaus that affected life in the city.

The home and all life within the city, they argued, were inextricably "chained" to city hall. As one might expect, their illustration of these links includes the "traditional" female concerns about food inspection, factory safety, and clean air. But the two squares that depict the power of the city to license marriage and register birth showed that these women had became conscious of the power of the state to regulate and control their lives. "Whether she [the club member] likes it or not, the city government invades the privacy of her family life in the interests of the whole city," pointedly noted an essayist in the club's bulletin. Marriage and birth may be viewed as primarily female concerns, but, without a political agenda to organize, investigate, and promote political municipal reforms in these and other areas, women had no say in that city government or over how it affected the home.

Using a term such as "municipal housekeeping" enabled women to become involved in every facet of urban affairs without arousing opposition from those who believed woman's only place was in the home. Moreover, by depicting the city as the larger home, the women were asserting their right to involve themselves in every decision made by the Chicago city government, even to restructure that government. They supported the creation of a municipal strike bureau, for instance, in order to institutionalize within government protection for workers from businessmen. When the club sought to institutionalize

municipal ownership and operation of garbage disposal, it was advocating a radical change in Chicago's city government, for municipal ownership would dramatically change the political purposes and structures of city governments. In attempting to redefine what was economic in the political system, it came into direct conflict with established, male-dominated institutions. In its positions on these issues, the Woman's City Club had thus moved beyond reliance on moral suasion to sophisticated participation in the political system.

I do not mean to suggest that gender was the only point of reference for these women or that they were political radicals. They wished to have the city control certain public services, but they did not vote for socialists; they belonged to the Women's Trade Union League but not the Industrial Workers of the World. They also tended to believe that theirs was the only appropriate municipal vision for women and that part of their task was to educate women of other classes to their point of view. Undoubtedly, there were people in the neighborhoods and institutions they visited who did not always welcome their presence. But, because of their gender experiences, the Woman's City Club members were more open to the possibilities of cross-class alliances than were most of their male counterparts. These experiences also brought them to a different vision of good city government. Woman's City Club members seldom equated the good of the business community with the good of the citizenry as a whole. Instead, members of the Woman's City Club viewed the city as they had viewed their homes, a place where the health and welfare of all members should be sought.

10

JOHN MUIR: THE MYSTERIES OF MOUNTAINS

PETER WILD

The final phase of America's westward expansion involved the exploration and settlement of the far western frontier. From the end of the Civil War through the early twentieth century, hundreds of thousands of native-born and immigrant Americans flooded into the region between the Rocky Mountains and the Pacific Coast to begin new lives as farmers and small-town businesspeople. But unlike America's earlier frontiers, the Far West brought more than farmers and shopkeepers. The region's dense forests and rich mineral deposits also attracted eastern lumber and mining companies intent on exploiting these lucrative natural resources. By the turn of the century, years of unrestricted logging, hydraulic mining, and careless dam-building threatened to destroy the natural beauty of America's last frontier.

This heedless exploitation of the wilderness of the Far West did not go unchallenged, however. Beginning in the 1880s, scientists, and government officials joined together in a national conservation movement that sought to preserve the country's wilderness areas for the enjoyment and education of future generations of Americans. If any one man symbolized the conservationist impulse, it was the Scottish immigrant, John Muir. Explorer, nature writer, and general spokesman for wilderness America, Muir played a pivotal role in popularizing the cause of conservation in America. In this biographical essay, Peter Wild traces Muir's love of nature to the restrictions of his early life and follows his efforts to preserve America's wilderness as a counterweight to modern industrial society.

I must explain why it is that at night, in my
  own house,

Even when no one's asleep, I feel I must
  whisper.

Thoreau and Wordsworth would call it an
  act of devotion. . . .

—*Reed Whitemore*

At sunset in the Sierras some hikers chant John Muir's words: "I am always glad to touch the living rock again and dip my head in high mountain air." To them John Muir is a hero, the high priest of those who escape to the wilderness.

And well he might be. By tradition Americans long for the freedom of wilderness, a wilderness fast disappearing. Muir said that all he needed to flee was to "throw some tea and bread in an old sack and jump over the back fence." How can the schedule-bound and traffic-weary commuter not envy the man who, as Yosemite's cliffs collapsed around him, rushed into the night shouting, "A noble earthquake, a noble earthquake!" At times he seems one of the daring Americans who, we like to imagine, led us West through our short history. We prefer our heroes dressed in a simple guise, but with a vigor and joie de vivre just beyond our ken.

The danger is that Muir tends to become lost in his mythology, some of it his own making. A closer look shows him a complex man, like others capable of gloom and hesitation. After years of private struggle and doubt, he beat his conflicting practical and mystical bents into an unusually consistent and powerful personality. Yet the most dramatic events of his life are indeed telling, though often not fully appreciated.

One of the most famous of these, a catastrophe that ended in a spiritual change, occurred in 1867. While he adjusted a new belt in an Indianapolis carriage factory, a file flew from his hand, blinding his right eye. Soon after, the other eye went dark as though in sympathetic reaction. For weeks he lay in agony: "My days were terrible beyond what I can tell, and my nights were if possible more terrible. Frightful dreams exhausted and terrified me." Muir was twenty-nine, an age of trial and decision for many prophets.

Up to this time, chances for a lucrative but unsatisfying career as an inventor contended with his love of extended wanderings through the woods. In his blindness he saw an answer: if his eyes healed he would give up tinkering with man's inventions and devote his life to "the study of the inventions of God." As he tossed in his room, slowly his sight returned. Significantly, he described his deliverance in religious terms: "Now had I arisen from the grave. The cup is removed, and I am alive!" From then on he would consistently equate God with light.

Likeable and talented, Muir was asked by his employers Osgood & Smith to stay on. However, a promotion to foreman, a raise, shorter hours, and a future partnership couldn't sway him. Lifting his pack containing a change of underwear and a few favorite books, he was off. His goal was to walk the thousand miles across the South—no mean feat in the bandit-ridden forests after the Civil War—to the tip of Florida, and from there to hitch a ride by boat to the Amazon. In the words of his biographer, Linnie Wolfe, he was resolved to become "one of God's fools." Yet as dramatic as the file incident might appear, the resulting conversion was neither simple nor complete. The five-month trip provided him with the time and space to mull over conflicts that had troubled him since childhood.

John Muir was born in Dunbar, Scotland, in 1838. Over the years his father's zealousness crossed the blurred line into a religious fanaticism the merchant brought with him when he settled his family in America. Daniel Muir sat in his homestead reading the Bible while his sons labored in the Wisconsin fields. When they returned weary at the end of the day, he beat them for sins they might have committed. To him books, paintings—even an adequate diet—smacked of the Devil. Precocious John, however, discovered that he could do with only a few hours sleep; in the darkness of early morning he'd secretly crawl down into the cellar to read and to whittle a variety of curious clocks.

Though Daniel scowled when he found out about the inventions, neighbors urged his son to exhibit them at the State Agricultural Fair. At the age of twenty-two, suffering his father's parting anger, John shouldered his pack stuffed with strange devices and headed for the state capital. There in the Temple of Art, Madison's citizens marveled at the youth from the backwoods, whose early-rising machine whirred and creaked to propel the reluctant sleeper out of bed.

But Muir found more than local fame in Madison. Like many an aspiring American youth, he strolled with opening eyes among the buildings of the nearby university, envious of the students who had stepped into a larger world of intellectual opportunity. Sometime later he enrolled with money earned from odd jobs, to spend two and a half pleasant years at the University of Wisconsin. There, after glimpsing the cosmos through his courses, he amused the other students with the devices that clicked and wheezed through their bizarre paces in his room at North Hall.

Restlessness overtook him in the spring of 1863, and he wandered through Canada, then back again into the Midwest. He was by now in his mid-twenties, a late bloomer tinged with guilt that he hadn't done more with his life. Far from being simply an enjoyable interim, however, the time spent in Madison would change and serve him more profoundly than he realized. In the frontier's atmosphere of intellectual democracy, Muir had made friends. His professors ignored the long hair and careless dress of the country boy and offered him confidence in his eccentric development. Dr. Ezra Carr and his wife Jeanne had graciously opened their Madison home and their private library to Muir. On the scientific side, Professor Carr instilled his students with Louis Agassiz's theory that a great Ice Age had carved out much of the northern hemisphere's topography. This grounding in science would result in Muir's first public controversy and his fame in California's Sierras. As for philosophy, both Carr and his wife were self-appointed missionaries of Ralph Waldo Emerson's transcendental ideas. They believed that through the oneness of nature a person could arrive intuitively at spiritual truth, if not ecstasy. It was just what young Muir needed to assuage his guilt and to justify wandering as a spiritual adventure.

And so with his boyhood and Madison as backgrounds, the dropout sat writing in his notebook among the palmettos and sand dunes of Florida's west coast, recording his thoughts and working his philosophical and personal conflicts into a unified view, the basis for future publications. He saw nature as a whole, a unity in flux. Man should stand in nature's temple, witnessing the eternal "morning of creation" occurring all about him. Emerson would have applauded the imagery, yet Muir went beyond the Concord philosopher. Unlike the flights of the cerebral Emerson, Muir's arose from perceptions grounded in science and elemental experiences in nature. Whether collecting specimens or hanging perilously by his fingertips from some yet unclimbed peak, he recognized that "a heart like our own must be beating in every crystal and cell" of the surrounding wilderness. Muir's ability to survive, botanize, and philosophize in the wilds was a rare power.

As his thinking developed, he realized—as Emerson did not—that if nature is a holy place, then civilization, with its sheep, axes, and dynamite, is the infidel, the wrecker in the temple. As Thomas Lyon has pointed out, the view represents a reversal of Muir's boyhood Calvinism. God, not the Devil, is to be found in the wilderness. Nature, not man, is the center of a timeless universe. With this in mind, Muir set his spiritual sights south on the Amazon basin; there he could glory in a nature steaming and writhing in the speeded-up processes of the jungle. But the semitropical winds already had blown him ill. Wracked by malaria, he turned back at Havana, Cuba, in hopes that the Sierra cold would purge his blood. The retreat made all the difference to a beginning conservation movement that as yet had no heroes.

In the early spring of 1868, the former inventor stepped off the boat in San Francisco. All around him that bustling city of commerce—a commerce based largely on resources hauled out of the interior—displayed "the gobble gobble school of economics." In a typical Muir scene, he told of stopping a carpenter to ask the fastest way out of town. Puzzled, the workman inquired where he wanted to go. Muir replied, "Anywhere that is wild." About the time that John Wesley Powell was bounding through the unknown Grand Canyon in his little boat, Muir was beginning a decade of Sierra exploration.

At first he supported himself by coming down out of the mountains to work on sheep ranches. The job disgusted him, and he branded the bleating, overgrazing creatures, degenerate cousins of the noble bighorns living high in his range of light, "hooved locusts." Eventually he chose Yosemite as a home base. Though accessible only by foot or horse, the striking canyon scenery attracted the more rugged variety of tourist. Muir took a job operating the sawmill for one of the two expanding hotels—with the stipulation that he would work only on wind-downed logs. On the sunny side of the valley, the sawyer built a little cabin for himself, complete with a wild fern growing inside and a brook running through it. Except for intermittent concessions to working for a few supplies, he was at peace, free to wander and enjoy the unexplored peaks.

Despite his pleasure in solitude, it should not be supposed that Muir was a cranky malcontent. Though he could chide people with his Scottish humor, he enjoyed company; if he had any social fault beyond his slipshod dress, it was his garrulousness. When in the mood around a camp fire, Muir could hold forth on the glories of the surroundings long after foot-weary companions wished they were in their sleeping bags. Even before he was stirring up the public in print, with the help of friends he had become something of a celebrity, something of the "John of the Mountains" figure that persists to this day. Professor and Mrs. Carr of Madison days had moved to the University of California. They sent a stream of vacationing writers and scientists—many of them eminent personages from the East—knocking on the Hutchings Hotel door, asking to be shown Yosemite's wonders by the only authority on them, ragtag John Muir. He more than satisfied tourist expectations of a romantic character of the Wild West.

As he befriended these Eastern visitors, the amateur naturalist made connections that would serve him in future conservation battles. He guided scientific expeditions and showed off the valley to his aging Concord guru. Emerson added the young transcendentalist to his list of "My Men," but he seemed a little taken aback by all the wilderness, so much more wild than his modest Massachusetts woods. Whether intentionally or not, Muir charmed Viscountess Thérèse Yelverton, victim of a scandalous English divorce tangle, who viewed him as a transcendental noble savage. She wanted him to run away with her to Hong Kong, but to his credit he gently turned her aside. However, she continued the romance on a unilateral basis, writing the novel *Zanita*, which featured John Muir as its Pre-Raphaelite hero.

More importantly, in later years he camped out with President Theodore Roosevelt, who happened to be scanning the nation for places to preserve. In his boyish enthusiasm, TR declared that he had a "bully" time with Muir—a man who if pressed would admit that in attempting to scale Mount Whitney he had danced the Highland fling all night to keep from freezing in the –22° cold. Yet California, the bellwether of America, was fast filling with settlers and developers. John Muir's rugged peace could not last long. In one of several striking shifts in his life, he exchanged it for a public career as a writer and for a reputation that holds to this day as the nation's foremost protector of wilderness.

As a late bloomer, John Muir wrote his first article at the age of thirty-four, his first book at fifty-six. Drawing heavily from the journals kept throughout his adult life, he tended to poeticize the facts. Then, too, his mysticism slowed him down; he found his adventures so spiritually satisfying that writing about them gave only a secondary thrill. "Ink cannot tell the glow that lights me at this moment in turning to the mountains," he explained. On the other hand, his beliefs eventually compelled him to write in defense of nature; and, when the writing fire burned in him, he was far more than the reluctant author. A scientific wrangle provided the first spark.

California's State Geologist, Josiah D. Whitney, applied the popular cataclysmic theory of geology to Yosemite. Basically, Whitney maintained that in a dramatic shift of the earth's crust the floor had suddenly fallen out of the valley, creating the present gorge. Schooled in Agassiz's contrary glacial theory and believing in the slow processes of nature espoused by Emerson, Muir viewed Whitney's pronouncement as an affront. By the early 1870's proprietary feelings about the Sierras ran deep in Muir. He, after all, knew his "range of light" far better than any geologist, regardless of his lack of degrees and professional standing. Glaciers grinding over eons had carved out Yosemite, not a super earthquake. As it turned out, Muir happened to be right, though there was at least as much emotion as science on both sides of the debate.

Urged by visiting scientists supporting his minority opinion, he sent off "Yosemite Glaciers." When the New York *Tribune* not only published the article but paid him for the effort, it set the practical side of his Scottish mind to whirling. At the time, journalism offered far more lucrative returns than it does today; writing might be an alternative to his periodic bondage at the sawmill—as well as a vehicle for rebuffing exploiters. Boosted by influential contacts, his articles, both celebrating his country and warning the public of its imminent demise, won the praise and concern of readers of the *Overland Monthly,* *Harper's,* and the *National Geographic.* Unlike many of the nature writers of the time, Muir grounded his rhapsody in the details of personal experience. He took readers with him from one detailed Sierra adventure to the next. Here he is edging along a cliff face to get a grand view of plunging Yosemite Creek:

> . . . the slope beside it looked dangerously smooth and steep, and the swift roaring flood beneath, overhead, and beside me was very nerve-trying. I therefore concluded not to venture farther, but did nevertheless. Tufts of artemisia were growing in clefts of the rock near by, and I filled my mouth with the bitter leaves, hoping they might help to prevent giddiness. Then, with a caution not known in ordinary circumstances, I crept down safely to the little edge, got my heels well planted on it, then shuffled in a horizontal direction twenty or thirty feet until close to the out-plunging current, which, by the time it had descended thus far, was already white. Here I obtained a perfectly free view down into the heart of the snowy, chanting throng of comet-like streamers, into which the body of the fall soon separates.

It is perhaps a bit difficult for an age sated with television spectacles to appreciate the impact of his revelations, based on the union of the physical and spiritual. Upon considering a new Muir manuscript, one editor declared that he almost felt as if he had found religion. On the mystical side, the poetry of Muir's words had the ecstatic ring of a man who was "on the side of the angels and Thoreau," as Herbert Smith describes him. Muir was having the best of two worlds: new economic freedom allowed him to garner material for magazines while he enjoyed trips to Utah, Nevada, and Alaska.

Yet there was a hitch; at the age of forty, "John of the Mountains" longed for a home life. Again his friends came into play, this time in match-making. Jeanne Carr introduced Muir to Louie Wanda Strentzel, eligible daughter of a wealthy medical doctor exiled from Poland. The match was not as unlikely as it first sounds. Despite his wanderings, Muir could carry himself like a gentleman; by this time he was a writer of some note; he knew the value of money and had $1,000 in the bank. It took patience and subtle urgings on the part of Mrs. Carr, but in the middle of April, 1880, John Muir married Louie Strentzel. The groom's literary abilities lapsed into cliché, however, when he expressed his genuine domestic joy: "I am now the happiest man in the world!"

For a wedding present, Dr. Strentzel gave his new son-in-law an orchard and a house in Martinez, across the bay from San Francisco. Perhaps middle-aged Muir needed a rest from freezing on mountaintops and eating monk's fare from a bread bag. Whatever the case, his old farming instinct asserted itself. With the exception of significant trips to Alaska, in the next few years he stayed fairly close to home, laboring in the vineyards that provided the modest fortune that would support his final and most important years of activism. To his credit, though Muir showed astute business sense, he also was generous with his money, supporting relatives, giving heavily to charity. "We all loved him," said a friend, "for his thoughtfulness for others." And Muir loved the banter and refuge of a comfortable household, one much different from that of his severe childhood.

John Muir's grapevines prospered, but his health and writing, cut off from the strength of the Sierras, suffered. In a way that might not be fashionable today, his wife rearranged her life to deal with the problem. Louie insisted that he spend July through October, the slack season for orchardmen in Contra Costa County, trying to regain his vital contact with the mountains. Though she loved music, when he was laboring in his study, she kept her piano closed. Editors hadn't forgotten Muir; joined by his wife, they connived to get him out into the wilderness and his pen working again.

In time they succeeded in rebaptizing Muir with his old power—redoubled when Robert Underwood Johnson of *Century Magazine* took him on a camping trip to see what unrestrained sheep and lumbermen had done to his beloved Yosemite. The plots of his friends worked just in time; the 1880's and 1890's marked the first cohesion and substantial victories of the early conservation movement. Pen in hand and backed by Johnson, the aging mountain man stood at its forefront. In 1890 the Eastern press reprinted his articles "Treasures of the Yosemite" and "Features of the Proposed Yosemite National Park." Telegrams and letters flooded Congressmen's offices. Saving Muir's old stamping grounds became a cause célèbre of national proportions. Congress reacted to the outcry for government preservation—a novel idea. Forced by

popular pressure to ignore commercial interests opposing the plan, it created Yosemite National Park and provided a cavalry detachment to patrol the area. Muir and Johnson took advantage of the public's ire at its loss of scenic places and of its hope for saving what remained of them. Through writing and lobbying, in the same year they compelled a publicity-conscious Congress to add Sequoia and General Grant to the growing list of National Parks.

Things were going well for conservation. Supported by a core group of activists, including the young forester Gifford Pinchot in the East, the Enabling Act of 1891 allowed timberlands to be set aside by executive order. Before he left office, President Harrison created the forerunners of the National Forests by designating 13,000,000 acres of public land as Forest Reserves. Through these years, editor Johnson continued to be the man behind the somewhat shy John Muir. Individual concerns, however deep, could be effective in the political maelstrom only through united effort, Johnson urged. In 1892 Muir gathered a number of prominent Californians into a San Francisco law office to incorporate the Sierra Club, an organization Muir led until his death. One of the earliest citizen groups of its kind, the Club continues in the tradition of its founder to "explore, enjoy, and preserve" the country's resources. To support the movement, Muir was writing, writing—*The Mountains of California* (1894), *Our National Parks* (1901), *My First Summer in the Sierra* (1911)—for a public that looked to the written word as a guide for its judgments.

Yet in the seesaw of politics, for a time it looked as if the new Forest Reserve system—if not the new National Parks—might be lost. Those whose livelihoods depended on exploiting the natural heritage were quick to call in political debts and mount an effective counterattack. By then, however, other magazines followed the example of *Century* with strong stands for conservation. And from John Muir's pen came prose with a stentorian thunder that echoed the fire and brimstone of his childhood. Readers opening the August, 1897, issue of the *Atlantic Monthly* found both their religion and patriotism at the stake:

> The forests of America, however slighted by man, must have been a great delight to God; for they were the best he ever planted. The whole continent was a garden, and from the beginning it seemed to be favored above all the other wild parks and gardens of the globe. . . . Everywhere, everywhere over all the blessed continent, there were beauty, and melody, and kindly, wholesome, foodful abundance.

Muir knew his rhetoric. After presenting an historical survey of America's forests, comparing their abuse with the stewardship of Germany, France, and Switzerland, he concluded with a poetic appeal for firm government action:

> Any fool can destroy trees. They cannot run away; and if they could, they would still be destroyed,—chased and hunted down as long as fun or a dollar could be got out of their bark hides. . . . Through all the wonderful, eventful centuries since Christ's time—and long before that—God has cared for these trees, saved them from drought, disease, avalanches, and a thousand straining, leveling tempests and floods; but he cannot save them from fools,—only Uncle Sam can do that.

Only ignorance and greed could challenge Muir's plea. There were successes—passage of the Lacey Antiquities Act of 1906, for example. Its provisions allowed creation of National Monuments by Presidential decree. Because of Muir's urging, Roosevelt set aside Petrified Forest and parts of the Grand Canyon. And Muir, at the age of seventy-four, would fulfill his youthful urge to explore the Amazon. But in the last years John Muir fought his most significant and agonizing battle—and lost.

In 1913, after years of bitter feuding, Congress voted to dam the Hetch Hetchy Valley, fifteen miles northwest of Yosemite, in order to provide water and power for San Francisco. Like so many plans touted by politicians as cure-alls, Hetch Hetchy proved a miserable, unnecessary boondoggle, a windfall for a few, with the public paying the bills. It hurt Muir that his friend and ally of the past, Forest Service Chief Gifford Pinchot—his eye always on use rather than preservation—joined its loudest promoters. Worse still, the Hetch Hetchy project violated the purpose of a National Park. Muir knew that it was a commercial wedge into an ideal, a wedge that has since been sunk into other parks. In Wolfe's words, Muir "was a prophet of the shape of things to come."

Yet to a reform-minded nation, the lost Hetch Hetchy Valley, whose beauty had once rivaled Yosemite's, became a symbol, part of John Muir's legacy. Stung by its mistake, Congress three years later passed a comprehensive National Parks bill. In 1914 "John of the Mountains" died, but he had shown the way to Aldo Leopold, Enos Mills, and Stephen Mather—and to thousands of others.

11

FUNDAMENTALISM AND THE CULTURAL CRISIS

GEORGE M. MARSDEN

The late twentieth century has witnessed the global resurgence of religious fundamentalism. Affecting developed and developing nations alike, these religious movements have aimed at the restructuring of governments and societies according to strict interpretations of the basic texts of Islam, Judaism, Hinduism, and Christianity. While social scientists disagree on the root cause of this fundamental revival, almost all agree that these movements are in large part a reaction to the workings of modern society. Anxious about the disruptions brought by social and economic change and uncertain about their immediate and long-term future, these analysts argue, many people find in fundamentalism a set of rules to guide them in the conduct of their everyday lives.

If this search for certainty during periods of social disruption helps to explain the rise of fundamentalism at the close of the twentieth century, it applies equally well to the rise of American fundamentalism during World War I and the immediate postwar years. As the United States became a modern society in the early twentieth century, growing numbers of Americans began to take stock of the immense social changes that industrialization and urbanization had wrought in their country. For many people, the unprecedented scale of change and the seemingly endless social problems it generated called into question the benefits of modernization. Among these people were men and women who used as their social yardstick not only traditional, small-town values and the tenets of American republicanism but the social teachings of biblical Christianity.

Religious values had long been an integral part of American reform movements. As George M. Marsden argues in this essay, early-twentieth-century fundamentalism was both a reaction to the modernization of American society and an attempt to restore American government and society to what its proponents saw as true Christian principles. Reacting to their increasingly marginal role in American life, Protestant evangelicals created fundamentalism as a reform movement that would make biblical Christianity the center of national life.

From Fundamentalism and American Culture: The Shaping of 20th Century Evangelicalism, 1870–1925 *by George M. Marsden (New York: Oxford University Press, 1980). Copyright © 1980 by Oxford University Press, Inc. Reprinted by permission.*

Between 1917 and the early 1920s American conservative evangelicals underwent a dramatic transformation. In 1917 they were still part of the evangelical coalition that had been dominant in America for a century. Some theological conservatives, premillennialists, and revivalists were often warning against the modern tendencies of their liberal, postmillennial, or Social Gospel opponents; but all of these groups operated within the same denominations and interdenominational agencies, and at times still cooperated. Occasionally the anti-liberals became rather strident, but the relative moderation of *The Fundamentals* was more characteristic of the conservative tone of the time. After 1920 conservative evangelical councils were dominated by "fundamentalists" engaged in holy warfare to drive the scourge of modernism out of church and culture.

Two factors help to explain this remarkable shift from moderation to militancy. One is that more aggressive and radical forms of theological liberalism had developed. Fundamentalists themselves occasionally explained the phenomenon thus, and their claim had some basis. Clearly, however, fundamentalism was more than a reaction to theological change. After 1920 fundamentalism became conspicuously associated with a major component of social and political alarm—most evident in the effort to save American civilization from the dangers of evolutionism. This perception of cultural crisis, in turn, appears to have created a greater sense of theological urgency. Thus, fundamentalist theological militancy appears intimately related to a second factor, the American social experience connected with World War I.

The most important clue to understanding the impact of the war on fundamentalism is the lack of a distinctive social or political stance in the emerging anti-modernist movement before World War I. Although a variety of traditions was represented, most of the movement's leaders in fact expressed relatively little interest in political or social issues. Most retained to some degree the idea that the strength of the American Republic was rooted in Christian principles, and

they encouraged legislation for select causes. Yet for a variety of reasons they had scruples against deep political involvement. So while on the whole their tendencies were politically conservative, no particular position or interest characterized the movement.

The initial reactions of the proto-fundamentalists to World War I confirm this point. Almost as wide a variety of responses appeared among these adamantly conservative Protestants as in any group in America. Some were patriots or super-patriots; others were opposed to all wars. Still others displayed only moderate patriotism, expressly qualified by first allegiance to God.

One had only to look at the two most popular individuals connected with fundamentalism to see something of the pre-war variety of opinion. William Jennings Bryan, although not a typical fundamentalist in either his political activism or his brand of politics, distinguished himself in 1915 by resigning as Wilson's Secretary of State rather than take steps that might lead to war. A peace advocate rather than a pacifist, he reluctantly but dutifully supported the war after it was declared in April, 1917. Yet throughout the war he avoided the rabid anti-German hysteria that had possessed most Americans by 1918.

Billy Sunday, on the other hand, competed with George M. Cohan and Teddy Roosevelt for the position of most extravagant patriot. Although Sunday had little interest in the war until the United States joined it, he soon concluded that zeal for the Gospel and patriotic enthusiasm should go hand in hand. It apparently did not strain his principles (which included premillennialism and opposition to the "social gospel") to conclude in 1917 that "Christianity and Patriotism are synonymous terms and hell and traitors are synonymous." As the war effort accelerated he used the rhetoric of Christian nativism to fan the fires of anti-German furor and was famous for sermons that ended with his jumping on the pulpit waving the flag. "If you turn hell upside down," he said, "you will find 'Made in Germany' stamped on the bottom." Praying before the House of Representatives in 1918 he advised God that the Germans were a "great pack of wolfish Huns whose fangs drip with blood and gore."

Between Bryan and Sunday were many conservative Protestants whose degree of patriotism does not seem to have been much different from that of the American public generally. For example, the conservative Baptist journal *The Watchman-Examiner* avoided commenting on the war for a long time before March 1917. The Baptist tendency to avoid politics may account for this. When the editor, Curtis Lee Laws, broke the silence in March 1917, he defended "pacifists" (meaning peace advocates) but said "pacifists are not 'peace-at-any-price' men." With Woodrow Wilson he agreed "we must prepare for war, however much we hate it." During the war, although the magazine's support was unquestionable, it was not extravagant in the context of the excesses of the day.

The conservative Presbyterian weekly *The Presbyterian,* by way of contrast, possibly because of its postmillennial leanings, emphasized the importance of religion and morality for civilization and had few scruples about war. Government was ordained to wield the sword, which was the only way to keep the peace. War would cease only at the coming of Christ, meaning apparently "when the world is evangelized." In the meantime, "The conflict is one between Jehovah and Prince of Darkness. Right and wrong cannot compromise."

During the war conservative Baptists and conservative Presbyterians, together with virtually all Americans, became far more politically oriented, and by late 1918 their journals were filled with vigorous commentaries on the war. Aside from this important politicization, however, there was nothing especially remarkable in the development of their wartime views. At the end of the war their position, although more ostentatiously patriotic, was nevertheless consistent with their prewar attitudes.

The premillennialists, however, were not only politicized by the war, but for some the war experience involved a remarkable change in their view of the nation. This development is so dramatic, and the premillennialists played such a central role in organizing fundamentalism immediately after the war, that a close look at their wartime views is most helpful for understanding the relationship between fundamentalism and its cultural context.

Premillennialism taught that no trust should be put in kings or governments and that no government would be specially blessed by God until the coming of the King who would personally lead in defeating the forces of Satan. Although opinions varied, many premillennialists of the radically anti-worldly type followed the logic of this teaching to a pacifist conclusion. The dispensationalist journal *Our Hope,* for instance, was out-and-out pacifist at the beginning of the war. Its reasoning, however, was not that of Bryan or the humanitarians who opposed war because they favored peace. Rather, this thoroughly antipolitical attitude consistently emphasized the hopelessness of all efforts to solve the world's problems through political efforts, whether pacifist or military. Bryan, they thought, was chasing illusions. Referring in 1913 to his proposal for a world court of arbitration, editor Arno C. Gaebelein said that such was typical of "man's plans during 'man's day.'" "'Peace and safety' is what the world and apostate Christendom wants to hear." "Sudden judgment," Gaebelein prophesied, "will someday bring the terrible awakening."

When this prediction was in a sense fulfilled by the catastrophic European events of the next year, *Our Hope* took little interest, except to say that the war was a sure sign the end times were close. The conflict was important, however, in that it provided some more pieces to be fit into the prophetic puzzle. Gaebelein was intrigued by the question of whether German ambitions for empire might represent the beginning of the predicted re-forming of the Roman Empire. A thoroughgoing literalist, Gaebelein thought not, since Prussia and the greater part of present-day Germany had never been within the boundaries of the original Roman Empire. The most revealing of the speculations concerning the combatants was *Our Hope*'s prediction in 1916 concerning Russia, then part of the allied powers toward which the United States was leaning. It "is known to every close student of prophetic portions of the Bible," Gaebelein affirmed, "that this power of the North will play a prominent and to herself fatal part during the predicted end of this age." The apparent confirmation of this prediction in the Bolshevik Revolution of the next year, combined with preexisting prejudice against socialism, resulted eventually for Gaebelein, as we shall see, in a fierce anti-communist partisanship.

When the United States entered the war in the spring of 1917, Gaebelein was still intent on his neutralist, "signs of the times" and "I told you so" course. "It has doubtless awakened rudely from their dreams many who had not conceived that such a war was possible," he wrote in July. The Dictator and the Anti-Christ, he added, should be expected shortly. As to premillennialist service in the war, *Our Hope* published as late as September 1917 a thorough exposition of the question "Should a Christian Go to War?" in which the answer was clearly "No." Quoting the passages that advocated peace in the New Testament (and dismissing more easily than did most American Protestants any relevance of examples of divinely ordained warfare from the Old Testament dispensation), the author said, "The very question well-nigh answers itself." Christians should separate themselves from the world, should not enter politics nor vote, and should not "set to 'improve the world.'" On the other hand, they must obey the powers that be when governmental commands do not go against God's word, and they must pray for their government (which in any case is more effective than fighting). So the answer was that Christians must serve, but without fighting. "There are lines of duties as clerical, ambulance service on the field of battle, ministering to the wounded and dying in the hospitals—ministering *Christ*, as we minister to the body."

While *Our Hope* continued into 1917 to confine itself to reading the signs of the times, *The King's Business*, then the leading premillennial

journal, was more typical of the tension in the movement between other-worldly prophecy and genuine concern for the political direction of this world. *The King's Business* was in a sense a continuation of the work of *The Fundamentals*, having been recommended as such in the concluding number of that series. The journal was published by the Bible Institute of Los Angeles, which at that time prospered with the Stewart brothers' oil money under the leadership of Reuben Torrey.

During the two years preceding America's entry into the war its editors firmly and repeatedly announced their total opposition to the war. "At the present time," they said in a typical statement, "all other interests seem sacrificed to the monstrous war god." Warfare was inevitable (prophecy made it clear that this war would not be the last), yet it was still terribly wrong. Indeed, the lead editorials of August 1915 could have been taken from the pages of the most sentimental liberal-pacifist journal. There is 'neither Greek nor Jew,' . . . English, German, or American," said the editors; hence "we must never forget we are brethren, and we must show our love for one another in every way possible." This sentiment is especially poignant in the face of the editor's note that they have lost a fine Christian friend on the Lusitania; still they steadfastly maintain that "'Vengeance' belongs to God, not to us. . . . Our part is to feed our hungry enemy (Rom. XII: 20) and to 'overcome evil with good.'" These high sentiments could, moreover, be translated into political action. The editors advised in the spring of 1916 that Teddy Roosevelt should be opposed because a vote for TR would be a vote for war. In remarkable contrast to later fundamentalist opposition to unholy alliances, *The King's Business* in 1916 was willing to quote Bertrand Russell at length on the anti-war issue and to reprint an entire peace sermon by liberal Protestant spokesman Henry Sloan Coffin.

The European war, by widespread testimony, sharpened interest in prophetic teachings even outside the usual perimeters of the premillennial camp. A remarkable example of this is found in the socially active, theologically conservative *Christian Herald*. When the European war broke out in 1914, peace became the overwhelming preoccupation of *The Christian Herald;* in contrast to *The King's Business,* however, this interest was framed in post-millennial terms which identified the progress of humanity with the advance of the kingdom. "World-wide philanthropy, international friendship, arbitration, popular education and advance in scientific hygiene, even the regulation of trusts," the editors had said on the eve of the war, "must all be included among the ideals toward which we have been reaching of late years." But there is another, they added, "—remote, illusive, but finer than all else—the vision of world-peace." During the period prior to America's entry into the war in April of 1917, *The Christian Herald* continued to advocate peace. In the meantime, however, the editor, George Sandison, apparently altered his eschatology drastically. By January 1917 he stated that "we are living in a time of prophetic fulfillment, though just now how far that fulfillment may reach no man knows. . . ." "No one," he went on, "on this side of the Atlantic . . . occupies so high a position" in this field of prophetic interpretation as James M. Gray of Moody Bible Institute. Recent articles by Gray had "been widely read and universally appreciated" and now a new series, "The Mountain Peaks of Prophecy," was "certain of a still larger audience." For the next three years until the end of Sandison's editorship, *The Christian Herald* was (as it had been at its inception) a predominantly premillennial journal.

The dramatic wartime increase in interest in premillennialism created alarm among liberals and precipitated what may be the strangest episode in the development of fundamentalism. Beginning in 1917, for several years the theologians at the University of Chicago Divinity School led a fierce assault on premillennial teaching. These attacks, directed largely against their cross-town rival, Moody Bible Institute, were the first stage of the intense fundamental-

ist–modernist conflicts. In retrospect it seems utterly bizarre that one of the liberals' main accusations during the war was that premillennialism bred a lack of patriotism and hence was a threat to the national security.

Whether the Chicago polemics were motivated primarily by theological or nationalist zeal is difficult to say. The question is probably unanswerable because to the modernists at Chicago the progress of Christianity and the progress of culture were so intimately bound together that the two were always considered together. "Modernism," in fact, meant first of all the adaptation of religious ideas to modern culture. So when the modernists affirmed the immanence of God, they characteristically meant that God is revealed in cultural development. The corollary was that human society is moving toward realization of the kingdom of God. These principles, and especially this last, represented (as we have seen) new versions of postmillennialism; the spiritual progress of the kingdom could be seen in the progress of culture, especially democratic cultures in Europe and America.

World War I was a tremendous challenge to this faith in the progress of both culture and kingdom. European culture, for all its faults, had generally been viewed—together with its American offspring—as the best hope for the world. Now it seemed bent on destroying itself. When America was drawn into the war, liberal Protestants—like their conservative brethren— were divided. A fair number had at least some reservations about America's entry into the war and some of these continued simply to see the issue as war versus universal peace. Many others, however, viewed the war as a struggle for democratic civilization (and hence, in the long run, peace) against autocracy. Those who took this view were subject to the extreme and extravagant enthusiasm that swept the American people generally. For these modernists a war to ensure the safety of democracy and to end war, exactly fit the logic of their hopes for the kingdom.

At the Divinity School of the University of Chicago patriotism seemed unrestrained, especially in its treatment of premillennialism. Shailer Mathews, Dean of the Divinity School, launched the attack in 1917 in a widely distributed pamphlet, "Will Jesus Come Again?" castigating premillennialism on theological, Biblical, and historical grounds. Shirley Jackson Case, Professor of Early Church History, soon followed suit with a more extensive study, *The Millennial Hope: A Phase of War Time Thinking*, published in January of 1918. As the title implied, Case explained millennialism—in fact tried to dismiss it—on historicist grounds, showing how such thinking often became popular in times of crisis. He also noted, by way of introduction, that the current upsurge of premillennialism was especially dangerous, as it "strikes at the very heart of all democratic ideals" by denying human responsibility for the reform and betterment of society.

Case told the press that his motive for publishing was his growing concern about the spread of premillennial ideas, about which the Divinity School received "many communications" every week. Case was convinced that the immediate cause of the millennialists' rise was a sinister conspiracy. "Two-thousand dollars a week is being spent to spread the doctrine," he told reporters. "Where the money comes from is unknown, but there is a strong suspicion *that it emanates from German sources. In my belief the fund would be a profitable field for governmental investigation.*"

These sensational charges were not offhand or unrepresentative remarks, but were just what they now seem to be—outright expressions of wartime paranoia. This becomes clear from a survey of Shailer Mathew's journal, *The Biblical World*. In 1918 this scholarly publication might just as well have been called *The Biblical War*, filled as it was with the idealism of the crusade. On the home front the premillennialists were the chief enemy. During 1918 and 1919 most issues of the journal contained at least one major feature attacking premillennialism. The editor even seemed willing to use unfounded charges and innuendo in order to cast the premillennialists in the worst light. An essay in May 1918 was prefaced by a reproduction of a letter from a Liberty Loan speaker who complained that premillennial evangelists were undermining enthusiasm for the war. The writer suggested that perhaps this movement, like the I.W.W., was financed by German money. The letter, said the editor, speaks for itself.

Shirley Jackson Case repeated these accusations and added some of his own in the most hysterical attack of the series, "The Premillennial Menace," published in June. "The principles of premillennialism," he said, "lend themselves to the purpose of I.W.W. propaganda. . . .When one regards the present world as irremediably bad, it is only a short step to the typical I.W.W. tirade against existing institutions." But the burden of his message was that premillennialism threatened both the American war cause and the fundamental premise of modernist theology. "The American nation," said Case, "is engaged in a gigantic effort to make the world safe for democracy." Hence, "it would be almost traitorous negligence to ignore the detrimental character of premillennial propaganda." This posed an inestimable danger to both religion and culture because "In the name of religion we are told that the world cannot appreciably be improved by human efforts." Mathews prefaced this contribution with similarly extreme remarks about the dangers of premillennialism to both religion and patriotism, adding (in an apparent effort to associate evangelical premillennialists with Russellites) a newspaper report "that several of the leaders of one of these movements have been found guilty of disloyal utterances and sentenced to imprisonment."

Such acrimony indicated the extent to which the war fanned the smoldering coals of theological debate. For premillennialists and other doctrinal militants, of course, it did not take much provocation to unleash fierce controversy. The liberals had been traditionally the party of peace, tolerance and comprehensiveness. During and immediately after the war, however, liberals seemed openly ready to seek a showdown. *The Christian Century*, for instance, was as active as *The Biblical World* in attacking the premillennialists, running a twenty-one article series on the subject during the war.

The premillennialists uniformly responded by denying any disloyalty and by reiterating their case for the Biblical source of their views; yet the liberal attacks had also opened the way for an important line of counterattack. The liberals had insinuated that premillennialism might be tainted by German gold. *The King's Business* responded: "While the charge that the money for premillennial propaganda 'emanates from German sources' is ridiculous, the charge that the destructive criticism that rules in Chicago University "emanates from German sources' is undeniable." This quickly became one of the most effective and widely-repeated accusations among opponents of liberal theology. Probably the most forceful statement of this idea came from W. H. Griffith Thomas, British premillennial scholar and Professor of Old Testament at Wycliffe College in Toronto since 1910. A loyal citizen of the British Empire, Thomas had been decrying the evil connection between German theology and German militarism since early in the European war. In a particularly vitriolic essay written just as the war was ending, he dealt with the subject of "German Moral Abnormality." After ten pages of atrocity anecdotes (which by then were commonplace in American propaganda) he spent another half-dozen pages quoting patriotic sentiments taken from German sermons. He pointed out the self-evident incredibility of these sentiments in the light of the atrocities. How could one explain "these (let us put it mildly) aberrations"? Corrupt German Biblical scholarship was at the root of the astounding moral collapse of German civilization.

The radical dispensationalist journal *Our Hope* likewise attributed German militarism directly to German theology. "Every word of this is true," remarked Arno C. Gaebelein in reference to a suggestion that if the churches in other countries had "'entered the conflict against German rationalism fifty years ago, as loyalty to Christ demanded, this most destructive and hideous of wars could never have occurred.'" This observation had important implications for the home front as well. "'The new theology has led Germany into barbarism, and it will lead any nation into the same demoralization.'" The conservatives at Princeton Seminary, who had long been lonely voices in warning against the dangers of German "rationalism," saw a similar meaning in the demise-of-civilization motif. William B. Greene, at the seminary opening in the fall of 1918, described "the Present Crisis in Ethics," particularly as evince in Germany's conduct of the war, as related to (among other things) rationalism, evolutionary naturalism, and the philosophy of Nietzsche. Premillennialist Howard W. Kellogg stressed these same themes in a less restrained address given at the Bible Institute of Los Angeles during the same summer. "Loud are the cries against German Kultur . . . ," he declaimed. "Let this now be identified with Evolution, and the truth begins to be told." The truth, he suggested, was that this philosophy was responsible for "a monster plotting world domination, the wreck of civilization and the destruction of Christianity itself."

These ideas, and the cultural crisis that bred them, revolutionized fundamentalism. More precisely, they created it (although certainly not *ex nihilo*) in its classic form. Until World War I various components of the movement were present, yet collectively they were not sufficient to constitute a full-fledged "fundamentalist" movement. The cultural issue suddenly gave the movement a new dimension, as well as a greater sense of urgency. During the 1920s the point was constantly reiterated that the argument between fundamentalists and modernists was not merely a theological debate (theological debate would not have created much fervor among Americans). The contention was that the whole moral course of civilization was involved. Evolution became a symbol. Without the new cultural dimension it is unlikely that the debate over Darwinism could have been revived in the spectacular way it was or that fundamentalism itself would have gained wide support. Americans had just fought a war that could be justified only as a war between civilization and barbarism. German barbarism could be explained as the result of an evolutionary "might is right" superman philosophy. The argument was clear—the same thing could happen in America.

This insight transformed the premillennialist movement in a dramatic way. Before World War I many premillennialists had stayed aloof from cultural concerns and all were skeptical of any plans concerned merely with the future of civilization. By the end of the war their strongest line of attack on modernism committed them to a position which put forward the survival of civilization as a principal concern. This position accentuated the long-standing paradox in the thinking of American premillennialists. As premillennialists they had to say that there was no hope for culture, but at the same time they were traditional American evangelicals who urged a return to Christian principles as the only cultural hope.

The latter emphasis, which had been largely (though never entirely) suppressed among premillennialists, re-emerged in full strength during the summer of 1918. This transformation of a group that had included many pacifists can be understood only in view of the extreme pressure of propaganda and public opinion toward patriotic excess. Liberals and conservatives alike found the force of popular sentiment irresistible. Even that staunch journal of peace, *The Christian Herald,* had by 1918 (though at the same time temporarily embracing premillennialism) succumbed to the characteristic American patriotism of that year, going so far as to praise Lutheran schools for giving up the teaching of German.

Some of the most adamant premillennial advocates of political noninvolvement likewise succumbed. *Our Hope* provides the most striking example. It should be recalled that this ardently premillennialist journal had shown little interest in the war prior to American involvement and in September of 1917 had answered "no" to the question "should a Christian go to war?" By April 1918 the war was becoming a godly cause. Citing the American government's claim that this was a defensive war provoked by a scheming, dishonest Germany, *Our Hope* concluded: "These are

unanswerable arguments. There is an element of righteousness which any right thinking man cannot fail to see and which is, we believe, in harmony with the righteous government of God." By July the wartime rhetoric and call to arms was fully developed. Wrote Arnold Gaebelein:

> If we had not done so the German warships would probably be bombarding our coast by this time and the hellish program of murder, pillage, and rapine would soon be carried out on our soil. . . . And now it is the solemn duty of everyone to do all and to give all in this cause and stand by the government, so the hosts of evil may be speedily defeated.

James M. Gray and his *Christian Workers Magazine* of Moody Bible Institute did not have to travel as far to arrive at the same patriotic destination. In 1917 Gray attempted to maintain a balanced position and had published articles on both sides of the question whether Christians might participate in war. He himself favored dutiful support of the war on the grounds that magistrates were ordained by God. He insisted, however, that Christians' attitude toward the Germans should be "malice toward none." But with the revelations in the spring of 1918 concerning German war aims and alleged atrocities Gray also came to see America's war effort as a totally righteous cause:

> Hitherto we have felt it to be the Christian's duty to serve his government in this conflict even to the taking up of arms, but now this secondary obligation, strong as it is, fades out of sight in the thought of our responsibility to God as the executioners of His avenging justice.

The King's Business, which of all the standard premillennial journals had campaigned most vigorously against military preparedness, had a more difficult struggle with the war issue; but in 1918 it too came to the same conclusion. In 1917 the California-based journal had warned against the disastrous and demoralizing effects of war, and urged Christians to "love our enemies," even if they were Germans. By early 1918, however, the editors were beginning to believe that the Kaiser's capacity for evil rivaled that of the most notorious precursors of the anti-Christ, and that he might even be in some sort of league with both the Pope and Mohammedans. By May 1918 they got to the point of relating the Kaiser directly to the devil. Ignoring the traditional premillennial condemnation of the Constantinian ideal of church and state united in Christian culture against the infidels, *The King's Business* quoted with unqualified approval:

> The Kaiser boldly threw down the gage of battle—infidel Germany against the believing world—Kultur against Christianity—the Gospel of Hate against the Gospel of Love. Thus is Satan personified—"Myself and God." . . . Never did Crusader lift battle-ax in holier war against the Saracen than is waged by our soldiers of the cross against the German.

The editors of *The King's Business* used a traditional Puritan and evangelical theme to justify this apparent reversal of their views. During 1917 the editors had made the point (useful for evangelism) that no nation was righteous and none could receive God's blessing without repentance. In 1918 this principle provided an opportunity to abandon, more or less gracefully, earlier misgivings about the war. Woodrow Wilson called for a day of prayer and fasting on Decoration Day, May 30, 1918. The editors saw this as America's only hope. Americans responded to this call, the editors believed, in a most laudable fashion. Now the editors were convinced that they had simply been wrong about the demoralizing effects of war. The war had brought out courage and dedication that they had never thought possible. But the key had been repentance. In a Thanksgiving editorial written before the war ended, *The King's Business* attributed the success of the American war effort primarily to the Decoration Day of prayer and fasting:

> This day was very widely observed, far more widely and earnestly we admit than we thought it would be, and God heard the prayers that went

up on that day, heard them in a way that has made the whole world wonder.

In fact the day of fasting had coincided remarkably with the beginning of the effective American contribution to the war (Château-Thierry was June 4) and the dramatic reversal of the German offensive. So now these premillennialists sounded as convinced as mid-nineteenth-century evangelicals that God was on the side of America. "God had done wonderful things for this nation."

Only at the official prophetic gatherings was the tradition of staying clear of politics still in evidence. Thus, at the two major prophetic conferences held in 1918, patriotic themes were kept in the background. Instead, the most engrossing political topic was the capture of Jerusalem by the British General Allenby. To a student of prophecy this was immensely more important than anything else that the allies did, since it cleared the path for the fulfillment of the predicted return of the Jews to Palestine.

Significantly, however, the one speaker at either of these conferences to consider at any length the more general social and political questions was William B. Riley. Riley, as we have seen, exemplified the primary tension in premillennial cultural attitudes. Since early in his career he had been wrestling with the political implications of social issues. During his long Minneapolis pastorate, begun in 1897, he championed some progressive reforms and defended the right of ministers to deal with "secular" subjects. He also had been a vocal opponent of the Spanish American War. But when World War I broke out, he defended it on the basis of the Christian's "dual citizenship." Americans should be loyal both to the "heavenlies" and to the United States, the latter loyalty entailing an obligation to defend civilization against barbarism.

Nevertheless, at the Philadelphia Prophecy Conference of 1918, even though Riley had two sons in the war he still was able to qualify the implications of patriotism. He spoke eloquently for charity toward the poor, but he warned that the self-sacrifice and heroism of the war should not create any illusions concerning human nature or any hopes for salvation of society without Christ. Similarly, while clearly supporting the American cause, he warned against allowing patriotism to revive unqualified confidence in American idealism. "'Make the world safe for democracy,'" he said, "is a sentiment with which "we have no controversy." "But," he immediately added, "who will rise, and when will he come to *make democracy safe for the world?*" Only "the blood of the Son of God" could change human nature sufficiently for that. Preachers should not allow "the modern voices to lead them to substitute democracy for a divinely appointed plan of divine REDEMPTION. . . ."

Although pointing to modern tendencies that might be dangerously strengthened by the war, Riley, along with other premillennialists, saw in the war a central lesson about the welfare of society. For the past fifty years the trend had been toward the exaltation of man. Darwinism, not simply as a biological theory, but as a progressive evolutionary philosophy, was the best evidence of this trend. German "Kultur," where the doctrine of evolution had bred the twin evils of modernism and militarism, showed the inevitable result of such doctrines. Riley, it seems, had long been searching for a way in which to show how Christianity involved concern for society as well as for individuals. Now the war focused and clarified the issues and showed where the battle to save American civilization must be met.

World War I saw the rise of William B. Riley to leadership in the fundamentalist movement—a fact doubtless related to his ability to articulate the urgency of the cultural crisis. In 1919 he was the chief organizer of the World's Christian Fundamentals Association, the principle organization of the premillennial wing of the fundamentalist movement. Unlike any of the premillennialist organizations immediately preceding it, this new fundamentalist body expressed strong concern for the condition of American society. As in conservative-evangelical anti-German wartime rhetoric, evolution and modernism were tied together and seen as a cultural as well as a specifically religious threat. Out of these con-

cerns, to which anti-communism was soon added, fundamentalist super-patriotism began to grow. Thus a movement that had characteristically claimed that loyalty was not owed to kings and nations, and had been sufficiently apolitical in 1917 to be suspected of disloyalty, became sufficiently patriotic to make the defense of Christian civilization in America one of its major goals.

The war brought closer together individuals who held a variety of opinions on the proper relationship of Christianity and culture. Both radical and moderate premillennialists now gave greater importance to the preservation of civilization. American evangelicals, typified by Bryan, had always given Christian civilization top priority, and now they believed it to be gravely threatened. Postmillennialist confessional conservatives, represented by Princeton or by *The Presbyterian,* tempered their hope for civilization with Calvinist views of innate human depravity. Important points of disagreement remained and would continue to surface. Now, however, all had a shared interest in the cultural question and all regarded the state of American civilization with a mixture of hopeful loyalty and increasing alarm.

An overwhelming atmosphere of crisis gripped America during the immediately postwar period. The year 1919 especially was characterized by a series of real as well as imagined terrors. The disruption caused by massive demobilization and postwar economic adjustments was compounded by a number of acrimonious labor disputes and strikes and by a series of terrorist bombings. There was alarm over rapidly deteriorating moral standards and a deep suspicion of foreign influence. The immediate reaction was to focus on the sinister implications of the strikes and terrorism and to rechannel the enormous emotional force of wartime patriotism against a different foreign enemy—Bolshevism. In this "Red Scare," a real but limited threat excited near hysteria. Clearly it was part of the general psychological disorientation of the nation. Americans had been whipped into a frenzy of wartime enthusiasm. Abruptly the war ended, leaving behind a directionless belligerence which sought a new outlet. It seemed as though the people needed an enemy, one that could account for the disruptions on the home front.

The continued ambivalence of most premillennialists in this highly charged atmosphere of national crisis is well suggested by the two accompanying cartoons, which first appeared in *The King's Business* during the summer of 1919. The first, on the cover of the July issue, while intimating an ideal of Christian civilization, points only toward a future hope. The other, from the preceding issue is aimed at more immediate solutions to social problems.

These reactions to the widely proclaimed Bolshevik threat were not unusual in the atmosphere of acute paranoia which prevailed throughout the country in the summer of 1919, and do not necessarily indicate that premillennialism had become politicized by this time. But the tension between the deep disturbance awakened by cultural trends and the attempt to continue to respond only in the realm of prophecy and evangelism was more acute than ever. This is evident in the *Christian Worker's Magazine* of July 1919, in which editor James M. Gray identified the pressure to join the League of Nations as "the third greatest crisis" in the nation's history. Gray averred that to join the League would be to commit "national suicide," and urged his readers to send for the literature of Henry Watterson's "League for the Preservation of American Independence," which portrayed the League as incompatible with the "fundamentals of American independence." Yet, having yielded thus far to the desire to save the nation, Gray clearly was embarrassed and attempted to disclaim that he was suggesting anything more than prayer. "We have no position to maintain and are not taking sides," said Gray, "for this is a political more than a religious question, but we are urging our readers to reflect, . . . and above all to pray that the God of nations . . . may rule . . . that no harm may come to our nation and that His will may be done in the world." By the time of the national election the next year, Gray dropped even this pretense of neutrality. He made it clear that both for reasons of national welfare (it would

lead to war) and because of prophetic warnings (the league probably was condemned as the latter-day revival of the Roman Empire) Christians should do all they would to oppose the League.

Ironically, the premillennial publication that reacted most strongly to the threat of Bolshevism was the radical anti-cultural journal *Our Hope,* in which the war seemed to have created a heightened political consciousness. Although the editor, Arno C. Gaebelein, stuck to the sign-of-the-times format, his alarm about the political situation was clearly immediate and very real. For Gaebelein the pieces of the prophetic puzzle had suddenly fallen into place with the dramatic fulfillment of a prophecy. In 1916, before the Revolution, he had predicted that Russia (the "great power of the North") would "play a prominent and to herself fatal part during the predicted end of this age. . . ." Now the Bolshevik Revolution made it clear what that role would be. In the "danger of Bolshevism," the bombings and attempted bombings of 1919, he now could see clearly that "The Beast Lifts the Head in Our Land." The government had been naïve and lax with respect to radicalism, and Americans should now expect not less but more lawlessness as "the full power of the god of this age—Satan—" is revealed. On the same subject a year later, he pictured Americans as confronted with a life or death choice between civilization and communism. *"We are going through a reconstruction period,"* he said, ". . . and either we are coming out of it as a family of nations in which rich and poor alike will have been chastened, and in which each citizen will accord to his fellowman the same rights and privileges that he wants for himself, or the reconstruction period will expire by *giving birth to a World Communist Internationale,* in which our civilization and religion *will be totally destroyed!!!*"

A sense of doom was created by apparent confirmations of premillennial pessimism in the daily news, and heightened by growing dismay about the moral condition of the nation. Premillennialists shared with many conservative Americans the conviction that the moral foundations of the nation were rapidly crumbling.

Statistics documented the rise in crime rates. Many Americans now flaunted the vicious habits often condemned by evangelical preachers. Young men and even women were openly smoking—*The King's Business* spoke of "The Yellow Peril of America." It was particularly galling that churches accepted such changes. Methodist church choirs, for instance, allowed young women to display "brazen bared knees." "Who is responsible for this change in custom from the bended knee . . . ?" queried *The King's Business*. Dancing, once an abomination to the Methodists, was now allowed even in their churches.

All of these various postwar phenomena could easily be seen as related to one another. In November 1919 the Reverend Oliver W. Van Osdel, a prominent premillennialist pastor in Michigan, did just that in a sermon on the signs of the times. Van Osdel decried everything from such classic sins as selfishness, covetousness, and greed, to the League of Nations, the celebration of the anniversary of the Armistice by public dancing in the streets, and gymnasiums and moving pictures in the churches. In an impressionistic way he summed up a fairly typical reaction to the complexity of the events and their relationships:

> Sometimes people ask what are the objections to dancing and theaters and card playing and such things; they say these are not to be severely condemned; but you will notice that the people who indulge in these worldly things are always loose in doctrine . . . the two go together, and when you find people indulging in worldliness they become loose in doctrine, then apostasy easily creeps in, the union of Christendom becomes possible and probably will be united through corrupt doctrine under one head, the Pope of Rome.

One indication that many premillennialists were shifting their emphasis—away from just evangelizing, praying, and waiting for the end time, toward more intense concern with retarding degenerative trends—was the role they played in the formation of the first explicitly fundamentalist organization. In the summer of 1918, under the guidance of William B. Riley, a num-

ber of the leaders in the Bible school and prophetic conference movement conceived the idea of the World's Christian Fundamentals Association. The first conference of the new agency was held in May 1919. It differed from earlier prophecy conferences primarily in the wider range of topics discussed. There was a program of well-worn Bible school lectures in defense of the faith and featuring some premillennialism. More important, a tone of urgency prevailed at the 1919 meetings. "The Great Apostasy was spreading like a plague throughout Christendom," declared the conference organizers. "Thousands of false teachers, many of them occupying high ecclesiastical positions, are bringing in damnable heresies, even denying the Lord that bought them, and bring upon themselves swift destruction." The Bible "was wounded in the house of its friends;" cardinal doctrines "were rejected as archaic and effete; false science had created many false apostles of Christ; indeed they were seeing that 'Satan himself is transformed into an angel of light.'" Yet, said the promoters, there was a "widespread revival—not a revival in the sense of great ingatherings resulting from evangelistic effort, but a revival of interest in and hunger for the Word of God." Indeed, the premillennial leaders had some reason for this hope, which was part of the crusading mood of the moment. The WCFA meeting in Philadelphia was reportedly attended by six thousand people and was only one of a series of conferences held in various cities in 1919. Whereas a few years earlier the vast publication campaign of *The Fundamentals* had produced little perceptible effect, now the Fundamentals conference was the spark that helped to generate a nationwide movement.

While for most premillennialists it was a departure to direct intense energy toward the organization of a counterattack on the degenerative trends in churches and culture, among the Presbyterian conservatives the cultural crisis of 1917–1920 served only to intensify existing concerns and efforts. Of the groups with a major role in the formation of classic fundamentalism, the Presbyterians had the most highly developed view of the connection between religion and culture. They had long linked the progress of truth to the progress of morality and civilization, and the connection between theological decline and the demise of civilization was one with which they were quite familiar. The urgency of this concern had already been expressed in the alarmist preamble to the "five points" of 1910. With respect to organizing against modernism, Presbyterian conservatives were already in the field in 1919—indeed their representatives had been battling one or another sort of infidelity in America for close to two hundred years.

The unsettling years 1919 and 1920, however, served to accentuate the cultural dimension of the crisis for the doctrinaire Presbyterians and to bring out expressions of the same concerns felt in other circles. Writing early in 1920, David S. Kennedy, editor of the popular voice of Presbyterian militancy, *The Presbyterian,* reiterated and summarized his own recent analysis of "The American Crisis." His statement, stressing the moral implications of this crisis, epitomizes the view of the nation that was coming to prevail throughout the conservative evangelical community:

> It must be remembered that America was born of moral progenitors and founded on an eternally moral foundation. Her ancestors were Christian of a high order, purified by fire, and washed in blood. Her foundation is the Bible, the infallible Word of God. The decalogue written by the finger of God is her perfect guide in her religious and social life. There had been some weakening of this moral standard in the thought and life of America. This is the result of an age of luxury within and freedom from conflict from without. There is but one remedy: the nation must return to her standard of the Word of God. She must believe, love and live her Bible. This will require the counteraction of that German destructive criticism which has found its way into the religious and moral thought of our people as the conception and propaganda of the *Reds* have found their way with poisoning and overthrowing influence into their civil and industrial life. The Bible and the God of the Bible is our only hope. America is narrowed to a choice. She must restore the Bible

to its historic place in the family, the day school, the college and university, the church and Sabbath-school, and thus through daily life and thought revive and build up her moral life and faith, or else she might collapse and fail the world in this crucial age. . . .

One result of the rapid spread of this type of thinking among conservative Protestants was the formal organization of an anti-modernist protest in the Northern Baptist Convention. This was the actual occasion of the invention of the term "fundamentalist." Curtis Lee Laws, editor of a prominent Baptist paper, *The Watchman Examiner,* coined the word, and defined "fundamentalists" as those ready "to do battle royal for the Fundamentals." He and 154 other signatories called for a "General Conference on Fundamentals" to precede the yearly meeting of the Northern Baptists. They expressed "increasing alarm" over "the havoc which rationalism is working" in the churches, which were also affected by "a widespread and growing worldliness."

As the term "fundamentalist" suggests, Laws's primary concern, as well as of the organizers of parallel fundamentalist movements at the time, was doctrinal. This point is worth emphasizing, because it might be supposed that fundamentalism was *primarily* a response to social and political conditions. It was not. First of all it was what its proponents most often said it was—a response to the spread of what was perceived as false doctrine. After the war these suspect teachings were presented more widely, openly, and aggressively, reflecting a new openness and enthusiasm generated by a changed social setting. It is true that the crusading spirit of the war, together with the urgency of cultural alarm that followed, contributed to the intensity of the fundamentalist reaction. It also served to provide, as had been pointed out, a new cultural dimension to the movement. Nevertheless, these observations, although important, should not obscure the fact that for the fundamentalists the fundamental issues were theological.

Theology, however, did impinge upon other areas of the national culture—perhaps most observably in the schools and colleges. Most American colleges had been established by evangelical Protestants, and even the public schools had been dominated by Protestant ideas. In the half century since the Civil War, the schools had generally experienced a revolutionary secularization. Accordingly, those who were now organizing strategy for dealing with the religious dimensions of the cultural crisis saw the schools as an important arena for battle. William B. Riley in 1918 founded a paper entitled *Christian Fundamentals in School and Church*, which gave priority to the school issue. Here was a religious issue for which it was easy to rally support. Qualms about political involvement and establishments of religion could easily be forgotten when speaking about the schools. *The King's Business,* for example, which often printed remarks like "there is no such thing as Christian Civilization in any nation on earth today," could with respect to the education issue observe that in the public schools the Devil was dispensing "a Satanic poison that threatens the very foundations of the Republic," and made a plea for an all-out campaign to "MAKE THE COUNTRY SAFE FOR CHILDREN."

At the pre-convention conference of conservative Northern Baptists in 1920, the school issue was the primary focus in planning for action at the Convention itself. J.C. Massee, president of the new fundamentalist group (who had spoken also at the 1919 premillennialist WCFA Conference), warned against false teachers in Baptist colleges and seminaries. Massee declared that, even if an institution be nine-tenths sound, if it permitted *any* false teachings, "it remains unsafe until it has purged itself of that source of pernicious percolating poison." The schools, he said, were strongly affected by the general "drift away from the ancient landmarks" (a key phrase referring to strict Baptist principles), by "modernism in theology," "rationalism in philosophy," and "materialism in life." These could no longer be regarded as merely disturbing and were now dangerous and destructive. Massee's call for action was vivid, even if his imagery is laid on with a heavy hand:

If we would save them, we must cease now to let Philistine teachers plow with our educational heifer, lest our denominational Samson, stripped of the goodly garments of his faith and virtue, fall under the witchery of a scholastic Delilah, and be permanently shorn of his strength, blinded as to his spiritual eyes, and bound to the unspeakable service of godless and mocking masters.

Most of the speakers at the Baptist conference concentrated on questions of fundamental doctrines and/or strictly ecclesiastical issues. Another premillennialist, A. C. Dixon, must take credit for explicitly extending their concerns to the whole of American civilization. The logical necessity for this extension had already been established by wartime rhetoric. Dixon, former editor of *The Fundamentals,* and recently returned from serving in Spurgeon's former church in London, now clearly articulated the connections among the school issue, the future of civilization, and theological decline, with particular emphasis on the role of evolution. Evolution was not only a clear question of naturalism versus supernaturalism, theory versus fact, it was a part of "the conflict of the ages, darkness versus light, Cain vs. Abel, autocracy vs. civilized democracy." Greek philosophers, descended from Cain, had first developed evolutionary theory between 700 and 300 B.C. Darwin had added to this the idea of survival of the fittest, which Dixon described as giving "the strong and fit the scientific right to destroy the weak and the unfit." In Germany Nietzsche expanded this doctrine, and together with the German attacks on the Bible as the proper basis for civilization, this led inevitably to the barbaric German atrocities of World War I. By contrast, American civilization was founded on the Bible, Plymouth Rock, separation of church and state (a Baptist shibboleth), democracy and freedom, and the principles of Abraham Lincoln. Americans always stood with the weak and the oppressed against the oppressors. They had freed the slaves, "delivered little Cuba from her strong oppressor," and come to the rescue of Britain and her allies in the World War, "defending the weak against the aggression of the strong." America had won the victory of prohibition "over the oppressive powers of the drink traffic." Here Dixon, although a premillennialist, harked back to postmillennial visions of a democratic America leading the world to the triumph of righteousness. The agenda for the next evangelical crusade was an attack on the anti-democratic, "might is right," Bible-denying philosophy of evolution.

The sense of social crisis also brought to the fore a new type of fundamental leader, the moral reformer. William B. Riley's rise to the leadership of the movement is, as has been already mentioned, evidence of this trend. The subsequent emergence of William Jennings Bryan as a prominent spokesman for fundamentalism fits the same pattern. It was in keeping with the direction the movement was taking that a politician should come to represent it. In fact, the optimistic Bryan could really add little—beside the prestige of his support—to the combination of patriotism, evangelism, and Biblicism already articulated by a premillennialist such as A. C. Dixon. The fusion of these traditions suggests, however, that fundamentalism represented a new combination of revivalist, conservative, and premillennial traditions, united in an effort to bind together once again the many frayed strands of evangelical America.

Although the career of Frank Norris of Texas could be used to illustrate this same point, John Roach Straton of New York City perhaps comes closest to the "ideal type" of the fundamentalist moral reformer. Straton came to Calvary Baptist Church in New York in the spring of 1918. He was a Southerner, rather well educated, who had held several other major city pastorates. In his early career he was an ardent champion of both moral and social reform, attacking not only notorious vices such as prostitution and the use of alcohol, but also advocating some more progressive causes, such as women's and children's labor reform, wage reform, fair housing, and prison reform. During this period, although he preached a traditional Gospel of salvation, he was not a premillennialist in any significant sense and

often sounded more like a postmillennialist believer in progress.

Soon after his arrival in New York, the two major characteristics of his later career appeared: his social message became focused almost entirely on notorious vices, and he emerged as a prominent card-carrying premillennial fundamentalist. His social program is evident in his nationally published sermon of the summer of 1918, "Will New York Be Destroyed if it Does not Repent?" in which he attacked the vice, gluttony, gaming, and indecency of New York's hotels and cabarets, comparing the city with Nineveh, Babylon, Sodom, Gomorrah, and (drawing upon more recent history) San Francisco before the earthquake. Although Straton pictured New York as facing an impending doom, there was still no trace of premillennial prophecy in his message. Rather, he suggested that "the destiny of the human race for hundreds of years to come is in the balance." Despite the lack of explicit premillennialism in his prophetic preaching of 1918, by 1919 Straton had identified himself with premillennial fundamentalism and was in fact a speaker at the first WCFA conference.

Premillennialism seems not to have dampened Straton's zeal to expose and eradicate the immorality of his time. The most sensational period in his career, in fact, commenced in the spring of 1920 with a highly publicized raid and exposé of vice in the Times Square area. During the succeeding years Straton supplied the New York newspapers with a steady stream of sensational attacks on vice, including everything from Sabbath desecration to ballroom dancing and prize fighting. Such attacks helped to tie fundamentalism to the popular idea of the Puritan tradition as morally repressive. One observer described Straton as "like Oliver Cromwell in a nightclub, or Bishop Asbury at the Saratoga races." Straton's own view of the situation is caught in the title of his two most sensational books: "The Menace of Immorality in Church and State" (1920) and "Fighting the Devil in Modern Babylon" (1929).

Despite this latter title, Straton never quite made up his mind whether the United States was

Babylon or the New Israel. Perhaps he thought of New York City as Babylon in the midst of Israel. At any rate, despite his non-stop prophecies of doom, he always remained a full-fledged patriot. Indicating that "the deadliest danger now confronting America is the union of irreligion and political radicalism," he declared:

> Can anyone doubt that God had lodged with us in this free land the ark of the convenant of humanity's hopes? So surely as God led forth ancient Israel for a unique and glorious mission, so does he seem to have raised up Christian America for such an hour as this.

Straton's impetus for his fierce attacks on the dance, theaters, and other worldly amusements seems to have been a sense that Christian America was losing touch with its foundation in Biblical teaching. The Bible, he said, in the context of a typical attack on dancing, "is the foundation of all that is decent and right in our civilization." Thus it was consistent for Straton to identify himself with the central fundamentalist cause—the defense of the fundamental doctrines of the faith. For Straton, whether attacking vice or debating modernists, the key issue was the same—the all-importance of Scripture. Frequently he made the accusation that attacks on the Bible would lead to lawlessness and ultimately to the total demise of civilization. At this point the theological aspect of fundamentalism merged with its concern for the social and moral welfare of the nation. The battle for the Bible was a battle for civilization.

By the end of 1920 most Americans had recovered from the most extreme manifestations of crisis mentality and were set on course for a return to "normalcy." Fundamentalists too were committed to a return to the *status quo ante bellum,* but they wished to revive an evangelical theological consensus that had in fact been gone for at least a generation. Such a quest for normalcy could hardly be satisfied by a vote for Harding. Moreover, while the postwar sense of crisis was apparently only a temporary disruption for most Americans, for fundamentalists it was the beginning of a crusade. They began to organize precisely at the time of the crisis in 1919 and 1920, and as a result they institutionalized and preserved important parts of the outlook of that era of intense feeling and opinion.

12

MESSENGER OF THE NEW AGE: STATION KGIR IN BUTTE

MARY MURPHY

Before 1920, newspapers and magazines defined the limits of mass media in the United States. Until the end of World War I, Americans had learned about national and international events, sports contests, and the offerings of the new consumer culture by reading the columns of their local newspapers, by perusing the pages of such magazines as *Saturday Evening Post* and *Harper's Weekly*, or by browsing through nationally circulated catalogs such as those distributed by Sears, Roebuck and Montgomery Ward. This all changed during the 1920s, however, as radio stations proliferated throughout the nation. First thought of as a public medium of education and moral uplift, by the end of the decade radio took on a new aspect as local stations and national networks began accepting commercial advertisements as a regular part of their programming. For the first time, Americans—even those living in the remotest parts of the country—could listen to "live" news coverage and participate in a national culture of consumption focused on the sale of an ever-increasing variety of goods.

In this essay, Mary Murphy uses the letters written by listeners to Station KGIR in Butte, Montana, to explore the impact that radio had on the lives of ordinary people. These letters, the equivalent to "letters to the editor" written to local newspapers, provide a rare opportunity to get inside the thoughts of people for whom sources are usually all but unobtainable.

As these letters reveal, KGIR listeners, like Americans everywhere, enthusiastically welcomed the new medium into their homes. On remote ranches and in small towns, families gathered around the radio to listen to news, sports, and especially the comedy and drama programs broadcast by the national networks. Even the Great Depression failed to curtail the appeal of commercial radio in Butte, as radio helped to lift the spirits of local listeners and made people realize that they weren't alone in dealing with economic distress. During the 1930s, Murphy argues, radio became a companion for millions of Americans and created a national mass culture that altered the nation in fundamental ways.

"Messenger of the New Age: Station KGIR in Butte." Montana: The Magazine of Western History, *39 (Autumn, 1989), pp. 52–63. Reprinted by permission of the publisher.*

Was dead from the waist both ways till I tuned in
on KGIR but now hot dog I could climb a cactus
bush sixty eight feet high with a panther under
both arms trim my toe nails with a forty-five when
I reached the summit slide back to earth without
a scratch hot dawg whoopee cmon have one with
us fellas wine for the ladies n everything.

With that classic western accolade greeting its
inaugural program, radio station KGIR arrived in
Butte, Montana, on February 1, 1929, just ahead
of the Great Depression. It performed a dual,
sometimes contradictory function during that
economic crisis. In a time of almost universal
belt-tightening, the allure of the radio impelled
people to buy receivers on credit, and commercial programming bombarded listeners with
advertisements designed to increase their desire
for consumer goods. But the radio also provided
a source of comfort, news, and entertainment for
the unemployed and underemployed who could
no longer afford movies, vacations, restaurant
meals, and other pleasures of the consumer society. A radio was a substitute for many of the
leisure activities that people gave up during those
hard years, but it also prepared them to indulge
freely in consumerism once good times returned.
Through network programming, KGIR introduced Butte listeners to a developing national
culture, while also giving considerable air time to
local performers and shows. In this way, Butte's
first commercial radio station created an amal-
gam of news and entertainment that celebrated
local talent and served community groups, while
exposing its audience to programs of national
popularity and significance.

KGIR was Edmund B. Craney's brainchild.
Until it began broadcasting, the only radio signals
emanating from Butte were those of amateur
operators. Arriving in Butte in 1927, Craney saw
a potential market and applied for a commercial
broadcast license. With wide-ranging and far-
sighted interests, Craney was the first station
owner in Montana to affiliate with a national network, the National Broadcasting Company, in
1931. KGIR also became the flagship of a
statewide network of radio stations known as the

Z-Bar. In accordance with his own personal philosophy, Craney attempted through radio to
instill in citizens of the Big Sky a sense of themselves as Montanans, rather than as isolated residents of an archipelago of small towns and cities.

Radio was the medium of communication of
the 1920s and 1930s. The nation's first radio station, KDKA, Pittsburgh, broadcast the results of
the Harding–Cox presidential election in 1920
and began regularly scheduled programs in 1921.
Early radio fans were attracted not so much by
regular transmissions or even the content of programs, but by the romance of distance. Radio
telescoped the vast expanses of the West, bringing to rural dwellers the sounds of the city, facilitating communication between towns and outlying ranches, easing the loneliness of isolated
lives. Edward P. Morgan, an Idahoan who
became a broadcast commentator in Washington,
D.C., dated the start of his love affair with radio
to his father's purchase of a DeForest set in the
mid-1920s. "My night sounds had been the sharp
haunting bark of coyotes," Morgan remembered,
"but now the boundaries of my world suddenly
dilated far beyond the sagebrush hills of Idaho,
and through the hissing swish of static, like a bell
pealing in a snowstorm, came the sweet, waver-
ing voices of KHJ, Los Angeles, KDKA,
Pittsburgh, and, one enchanted evening, Havana,
Cuba."

While entrancing, the signals from distant stations were irregular and spurred some
Montanans to build local stations. Without the
resources common in metropolitan areas, commercial radio in the state developed slowly and
sporadically. Between 1922, when KDYS,
Montana's first commercial station, debuted in
Great Falls, and 1929, when KGIR went on the
air in Butte, small stations opened in Havre,
Missoula, Vida, Kalispell, and Billings. Programs
depended on local talent and leaned heavily
toward stock and grain market reports, coverage
of school sports, updates on the weather, and
direct messages to farm and ranch families.

Throughout the 1920s, commercial radio was
distinctly non-commercial. Advertising agencies,

sponsors, radio manufacturers, and broadcasters viewed the new medium as an educational tool, an avenue of cultural uplift. Sponsors limited their advertising to modest announcements of who was paying for the program at its beginning and end, or they attached brand names to orchestras and performers, such as the A & P Gypsies, the Lucky Strike Orchestra, and the Best Food Boys. Owen D. Young, chairman of General Electric and RCA, announced in 1926 that he considered the companies' new subsidiary, NBC, to be "semi-philanthropic."

By 1929, advertisers' insistence on sponsorship had faded. The advertising industry had mushroomed during the 1920s; its successful cultivation of a consumer society fed its continued growth. Agencies realized that the intimacy of radio offered an unprecedented opportunity to personalize advertising, and they discovered that listeners did not mind commercials. Listeners often heard the ads as part of the entertainment, and pollsters had found that what radio fans wanted was entertainment. Advertisers began to design commercials as part of the show and to listen to radio station managers who advised: "Ditch Dvorak. They want 'Turkey in the Straw.'"

Radio in Butte bypassed the semi-philanthropic days of the 1920s. When the Symons Company of Spokane announced its intention to start up KGIR, the *Montana Free Press* reported that the station would be "frankly a commercial proposition." Ed Craney, KGIR's manager, had been involved in the radio business for seven years when he came to Butte. Already an amateur operator when he graduated from high school in Spokane in 1922, Craney got a job running a radio parts store owned by lawyer Thomas W. Symons, Jr. As in many small metropolitan areas, the absence of good radio signals in Spokane made it difficult to sell receiving sets, so Craney and Symons started their own radio station to boost equipment sales. KFDC, Spokane went on the air in October 1922, one of the more than fourteen hundred stations that received licenses from the Department of Commerce in 1922–1923. Business picked up, and the two men expanded their sales to western Montana. It was

during the course of his sales trips that Craney pinpointed Butte, "a real rip-roaring town," as a plum site for a new station.

Craney received a license for KGIR in 1928 and began construction on the station late that year. He built studios in the third floor of Shiner's furniture store in uptown Butte and, to make sure the transmitter's antenna was fully supported, rigged it from Shiner's roof across the street to the roof of the opposite building. Radio fans avidly followed Craney's progress and geared up for the initial broadcast, scheduled for January 31. Shiner's offered a special price on "Freshman" radios, and the *Butte Daily Post* promised a free crystal set to any boy or girl who enrolled three new subscribers to the paper. Craney later claimed that radio dealers told him they sold three thousand crystal sets during the first week of broadcasting.

On the night of January 31, Butte listeners tuned in to a recording of the "Star Spangled Banner" and the dedication of the station by the Catholic bishop, a Methodist minister, and a rabbi. Then followed twelve hours of musical selections and orations performed by men, women, and children from the Butte area, directed by three prominent Butte music teachers. Hundreds of letters and telegrams sent to the station the next day testified to listeners' delight.

About a month after KGIR's debut, Craney arranged to broadcast Herbert Hoover's inauguration. It was KGIR's first hookup with NBC and more than any other event illustrated the radio fever that gripped Butte. Days before the broadcast, a festive spirit infused the city, as radio owners planned "inauguration breakfasts" so that friends and relatives could gather to eat and drink and listen to Hoover's swearing-in. On inauguration day, crowds massed outside the stores of radio dealers who had hung loudspeakers on their buildings. The Butte Radio Club and the Montana Stock and Bond Company hosted open houses for listeners. Restaurants and department stores aired the broadcast for diners and shoppers. Public and Catholic high school students listened in their auditoriums. Two thousand seventh and eighth graders heard the program over a loudspeaker installed in the Broadway Theater and cheered as the bands passed the reviewing stand in Washington D.C. The following day, the *Montana Standard,* which had absorbed most of the cost of the program, reported: "The inauguration was made actual, vital—something a great deal more than a remote happening . . . it was as if the listener here were standing among the throngs on the capital lawn. . . ."

The inauguration broadcast stimulated radio sales in Butte. Orton Brothers music store, which had lamented that "the only difficulty in recent months has been to obtain a sufficient number of sets to supply the demands of our customers," announced the imminent arrival of a major shipment of new radios. One trainload of four thousand Majestic receivers, the "biggest single shipment of radio receivers ever routed to the northwest," arrived at the Butte depot on March 23. Butte business directories had listed no radio dealers during the 1920s; by 1930 there were five, and by 1934 seven were serving the city's fans. People added radios to the list of durable goods, such as automobiles and furniture, that they purchased on installment plans. They accepted indebtedness for the delights provided by the radio and the ability of KGIR to link Butte to a larger world in ways more intimate and immediate than newspapers, traveling theater, or even the movies.

Between 1929 and 1931, before KGIR affiliated with NBC and began receiving nationally syndicated programs, the station explored the potential of broadcasting from Butte. Management created fanciful promotions to multiply advertising revenues, engaged local talent who performed in the station's studios, supplementing the phonograph records and occasional transcriptions that formed the bulk of programming, increased coverage of local events, and groped toward a determination of listeners' pleasures. Craney's unfamiliarity with Butte led to some gaffs that other staff members caught. A few months after its debut, for example, the station began a request hour. One night when Craney

was running the program, his salesman Leo McMullen came in and asked what he was doing. Craney replied, "We're having request hour." "Request hour, hell," replied McMullen, "you're advertising every whore in Butte." "Gladys at 2 Upper Terrace" and "Dorothy at 8 Lower Terrace" had quickly discovered the commercial benefits of local broadcasting.

Most broadcasts, however, were aboveboard. Local celebrities like Howard Melaney, the "singing fireman" of the Northern Pacific Railway, joined a roster of performances by the Camp Fire Girls, the Rocky Mountain Garden Club, and other civic groups. In May 1929, KGIR observed National Music Week with a special choral broadcast of eighty-five Butte mothers and daughters. Craney solicited local groups to put on their own shows. The Marian White Arts and Crafts Club proudly noted that "our radio station" wanted programs from the club's various departments and promptly responded with short talks three times a week. In the fall of 1929, KGIR broadcast the Rotana Club's Montana Products Dinner from the Masonic Temple, a gala evening celebrating Montana-grown products, speeches, and music.

Beginning in 1929 Craney had appealed to NBC for "programs of national importance" and sought affiliate status with the network. He described the isolation of many Montana listeners who "can receive no other station than KGIR and many of them depend on our station for the newspaper can reach them only from 24 to 72 hours late." NBC was concentrated in the East. At the time of Craney's request it had extended its service to only a few cities west of the Mississippi and feared the unprofitability of a hook-up in a small market like Montana. Craney persuaded Senator Burton K. Wheeler to intercede; and NBC, hoping to please an increasingly powerful politician, partially accommodated Craney. On November 28, 1931, KGIR affiliated with NBC, although the network supplied only an incomplete roster of programs to the station.

Despite the new shows available through NBC, Craney continued to solicit local talent sponsored by local advertisers and to balance commercial broadcasting with community service. One of the most successful programs of the 1930s was the amateur hour sponsored by Symons Department Store. Ray Schilling, advertising manager for the store, decided to test the powers of radio, and Symons scheduled a sale and advertised only on KGIR; nothing appeared in the newspapers. The response was overwhelming, and Schilling was converted. He and his brother then developed Butte's own amateur hour—a fad that was sweeping the radio world during the mid 1930s. Art Chappelle played his accordion on the amateur hour; and shortly thereafter Craney approached Art's father, the owner of Chappelle's Cleaning Works, to sponsor a fifteen-minute program of Art's accordion music. Art, who during high school had a band called the Whirlwinds and still moonlighted as a musician in addition to driving his father's delivery truck, was happy to oblige. Three times a week he stopped his truck at the KGIR studio, brought in his accordion, and played a selection of polkas and waltzes. Often he performed melodies popular with Butte's ethnic communities—an entire selection of Italian music, or Irish, Polish, or Finnish songs. Art played requests, signed an occasional autograph, and was delighted when he dropped off someone's dry cleaning and they said, "I just heard you on the radio!"

While hundreds of Butte residents performed on KGIR, thousands participated in station-sponsored contests or wrote unsolicited letters. In 1930, Craney began conducting listeners' surveys to determine the average number of hours each radio receiver was turned on each day (in 1930, ten hours; in 1937, nine and a half); how many hours it was tuned to KGIR (in 1930, seven hours; in 1937, eight and a half); what the favorite programs were and why; and what suggestions for new programs and new sponsors listeners might have. The responses that have been preserved reveal a wealth of detail about the likes and dislikes of Butte's radio audience and the role that radio played in the lives of KGIR listeners during the darkest days of the Great

Depression. For instance, Craney determined that jazz and old-time string-band melodies were Butte's favorite kind of music and that comedy programs eased the worries of economic hard times.

Through the polls and the success of a few new programs, broadcasters and advertisers across the country discovered that during the Depression audiences wanted lighter fare than classical music and Department of Agriculture reports. The tremendous popularity of "Amos 'n' Andy" demonstrated the potential audience for comedy programs. Advertising agencies, who were producing most shows by the 1930s, experimented with transposing to radio many of the genres already present in popular literature— western, detective stories, serialized melodramas—as well as developing new formats like amateur hours and quiz shows.

Soap operas, churned out in assembly-line style, dominated air time between ten o'clock in the morning and five o'clock at night. Criticized by some for encouraging neuroses in housewives, "washboard weepers" also had their defenders in those who interpreted them as morality plays, easily digested lessons in good and evil. A national study discovered that despite the far-fetched story lines, women found the serials useful sources of information regarding interpersonal relationships. Listeners drew from the dramas some "dos and don'ts" of child-rearing, dating, and marriage. They saw in the characters reflections of people in their own families, or they put themselves in analogous situations and hoped to pattern their behavior to attain similarly successful outcomes. One young woman who followed a soap opera argument between a jealous boy and his girlfriend, observed: "that is just like my boyfriend . . . listening to the stories like that makes me know how other girls act and listening to the way the girl argued I know how to tell my boyfriend where he can get off at." A Butte woman wrote KGIR that her favorite program was the serial "One Man's Family," because "I have a younger brother like Jack and I have grown to understand his ways listening to Jack and Claudia talk." Another testified about the same program: "it is a thirty-minute picture of American life that might as well have been taken in Butte."

Historians of radio have noted how directly and personally Americans responded to the new medium. Listeners welcomed broadcasters into their family circle; and through their letters to stations, fans created a democratic dialogue of praise, criticism, and suggestion in which they conveyed a sense of themselves as direct participants in the broadcast experience. Stations and the networks encouraged fans to correspond with them. During the early 1930s, more than two-thirds of all NBC programs explicitly requested audiences to write in, and the volume of mail was phenomenal. In 1926, NBC received 383,000 communications; in 1929, one million; and in 1931, seven million. CBS claimed that it received over twelve million pieces of mail in 1931.

Much of the mail to stations during the 1930s was in response to free offers of prizes in exchange for a cereal box top or come other evidence of the purchase of a sponsor's product. Pictures of Little Orphan Annie, magnet rings, slide whistles, and Tom Mix decoder rings kept the mail bags of America full during the Depression. During the 1937 Christmas season, KGIR offered a free prize for every letter to Santa Claus it received. For a seasonal program, selected letters were read on the air, interspersed with chatter between Santa and his helpers. After two such shows, the station had received three thousand letters and exhausted its grab bag. Hoping to slow the flow of mail, it asked that future letters include a sales receipt from a station advertiser. Three thousand more letters poured in. Broadcasters' invitations to the radio audience encouraged a letter-writing habit that ranged from participating in contests to conveying intimate thoughts and opinions to the President of the United States. Ed Craney confirmed that at times the largest volume of mail received by KGIR was in response to a program sponsored by the Farmers' Union, which discussed New Deal legislation and urged people to write to President Roosevelt.

During the mid-1930s, KGIR kept a tally of the mail it received: 5,770 in 1934 and 23,065 in 1938. Butte women outnumbered men two to one as correspondents, paralleling national trends in which women outdistanced men who wrote radio fan mail. National studies also determined that lower income people and those with little education wrote the most letters to radio stations, radio stars, and advertisers. The small number of letters to KGIR that were saved, 165 of them from 1933 and 1935, tends to support that claim. Nevertheless, Butte was a working-class community, and it is natural that the majority of letters to KGIR would have come from working-class households. Of the 15,322 men employed in Butte in 1930, 62 per cent of them were engaged either in mining or manufacturing, in contrast to the 10 per cent employed as professionals or in clerical positions. Of those whose occupations could be determined, miners compromised 31 per cent of the adult males who wrote letters preserved by the in KGIR's files. Of the remaining adult male writers, only one was a management position. A few women married to professionals, managers, and business owners also sent their opinions to the station. Eighty per cent of the adult women writers, however, were wedded to working-class men or were themselves wage-earners.

National studies estimated that the majority of letter-writers wrote to stations in response to contests. But KGIR correspondents sent as many unsolicited letters and replies to surveys that did not promise any material reward as they did to prize offers. During nine months in 1934, the station received 2,121 survey responses, compared to 2,071 responses to offers. In 1935, the number of letters seeing prizes was only 76 more than the 6,253 other letters received. Clearly, KGIR listeners believed that it was not only appropriate, but perhaps also necessary, to share their opinions with station management.

Gratuitous advice, pungent criticism, and heartfelt best wishes accompanied both thoughtful and absurd suggestions. Some wrote to say that KGIR was the "only half-way decent program on the air," others to warn that it was playing too much jazz and should "crowd the trash off the air." George Hardesty, a carpenter, conveyed most eloquently the fondness that many listeners felt for their radios and for KGIR. Writing in 1933, Hardesty described his radio as a powerful spur to the imagination and spoke of the relief it delivered during the psychologically bleak days of the 1930s:

> There was a time when I saw a Movie twice a week, but not in these slim times. And with my radio, I really can't say that I mind so much. Any evening there are shows come to me over KGIR, but Wednesday evening when Sherlock Holmes unravels his mysteries, I am positive I don't miss my shows. I can see the two old gentlemen, as if they were in my room, poreing over their G. Washington Coffee [the show's sponsor]. Certainly I am entirely unaware of a depression when one of these life and death mysteries is on, and honestly, anything that can make me do that is worth a lot. Thats one of the reasons I like it, perhaps the main one.

All over the country radio fans attested to the cheering effects of comedy and drama programs during the Depression, and the Butte audience was no exception. The character that elicited far and away the most responses from KGIR listeners was Ed Wynn's "Fire Chief," sponsored by Texaco. Fans wrote: "He will cure the worst case of the Blues and even make you forget the Depression"; "Ed sure keeps the radio audience in an uproar from start to finish, which is just what is needed by all of us during these trying times . . ."; "It is humorous and produces a '*good laugh*' which I consider necessary to offset the serious problems of this strenuous life of ours." Wynn's show provoked some poignant compositions on the part of fans. Young Harry Lonner sent in this dispatch:

> A dance orchestra is on the air. Dad is reading the newspaper. Ma is busy with some sewing or other household task. Sis and I are doing schoolwork. Suddenly, comes the shrill scream of a siren! The clang of bells! Ed Wynn is on the air! Dad lets the newspaper drop in his lap, Ma comes into the parlor and sits close to the radio; and Sis and I stop our schoolwork. . . . Dad, Sis and I grin and chuckle after every joke, but Ma laughs till her sides ache. This is the one big reason why I like the Texaco Program. For fifteen minutes Dad forgets about his job, Ma quits worrying about how she is going to pay the bills, and I am happy to see them happy. Old Man Depression is forgotten and Happiness is King.

Time and again writers expressed gratitude that they had been able to buy their radios during good times, because now they were their only source of pleasure and news. Using empathy and imagination, radio listeners transported themselves, however briefly, from their surroundings. Listening to the travails of Little Orphan Annie made "our troubles so small compared to our more unfortunate fellow beings." The radio compensated those not able to travel during the vacation season—even though unemployment guaranteed "most of us are having quite a long vacation"—by taking them to the Mountains of the Moon of the jungles of Malaya and Africa. And the radio was democratic. As Ted Wilson, a clerk at Southside Hardware, remarked: "it is a A one entertainment equally alluring for the rich or poor."

By the 1930s, radio had become part of many people's daily lives, a companion that did more than lift the blues of the Depression. Mrs. George McCoy wrote KGIR that the comedy of an early morning show, "The Gazooks," along with three cups of coffee "make it possible to face the horrors of the new day with a smile." Mrs. Nellie Sacry chronicled a day "beginning with the Gazooks—who help us get up better natured for you can't be grumpy when someone makes you laugh." Her eight-year-old son waited at the door with his coat on to dash out to school as soon as "Cecil and Sally" was over, and the family's day continued through the "Music Box" at dinner time. Mrs. George Hardesty praised the sweet music that calmed her frayed nerves after a day of housework and made her "a better me, to meet my husband and family."

Radio fans took programs far more seriously and invested them with more importance than advertising men or writers ever imagined. They accepted radio almost uncritically, as a wise seer who provided advice, pleasure, and testimonials for reliable products. Listeners wrote amazingly innocent and intimate letters to fictional characters and national corporations. Mrs. J. W. Larson, a miner's wife, lauded a children's program sponsored by General Mills:

> Personally, Skippy's program has helped me a great deal. My little girl is four years old, she can't tell time yet, but she never lets me forget Skippy. Skippy has taught her to brush her own hair and not to forget to clean her theeth [sic] and fingernails. Before Skippy was on the air I couldn't get her to eat any cereal, but now I have no trouble. She don't get Wheaties very often now, as her father isn't working. But she eats her oatmeal every morning. She had Wheaties every morning when her Dad was working.

Craney's calls during the 1930s for new programs and sponsors elicited a wide variety of suggestions and documented the energy and thought that many listeners put into "their station." More than one person thought a show relating tales of Butte and Montana history would be entertaining. Mrs. T. H. Wilkinson suggested having pioneers relate their experiences of settling the area or perhaps retelling some tales of hunting and fishing. "After all," she concluded, "Butte is a good old town and just full of good stories to tell." H. C. Howard proposed a different way of exploring Montana, a series of "short enthusiastic talks" recounting the "delights of motoring in Montana and describing each week some historical or scenic spot that is little known in the state and describing how it is reached, the condition of the roads to this spot and various points of interest along the route." The show would be accompanied by popular music and paid for by service stations, hotels, auto camps, or businesses patronized by tourists.

Housewives recommended programs that would interest them during the day: a morning exercise routine, advice to young housekeepers on arranging furniture, reports on new clothing styles, a menu contest of meals "that the average housewife could afford to serve." From Mrs. Adah Daugherty, wife of a salesman, came a letter that could have gotten her a job in any advertising agency:

> There are things dear to the heart of every woman, and dearest of these things is her personal appearance. If she could go to the radio and tune in on a beauty talk that would deal with any phase of a woman's face, hair, figure, hands, and feet, I dare say that only the door bell could draw her away. These things she might be able to get in the advertisements in the current magazines, or an occasional article, but the busy woman has very little time for reading. There is a psychological difference between reading the printed word, and hearing the same spoken. The latter catches the instant attention and is retained longer. With this given by some firm or firms in Butte, and the talk read by a woman, it would prove most effective.

Mrs. Daugherty continued with a discussion of possible sponsors and a reflection on the future of advertising: "Radio is the new means of advertising, and is here to stay. More and more firms are going to adopt clever methods of advertising, and owing to the depression, more vigorous methods." She acknowledged that the intrinsic worth of the product was immaterial and that by appealing to women's vanity a manufacture could successfully peddle anything. "Woman is eternally looking for the foundation of youth . . . she will be a susceptible listener to a program on beauty talks, and the firm to which she is listening will be the one to gain." And in words reminiscent of the personal testimony advertisements that were popular in magazines of the time, she concluded: "I am a woman. I know."

Mrs. Daugherty was unusual in analyzing the advertising industry's relationship to radio with such perspicacity. The overwhelming majority of listeners who wrote the station and mentioned sponsors conveyed a simple gratitude that corporations were providing them with so many hours of delight. Some avowed they enjoyed the advertising as much as the programming. Mrs. Henry Webking claimed that "the K.G.I.R. announcer tells us so much about the firm and its products during the course of the program, and in so few well chosen words, that we really enjoy the advertising and absorb it as much as we do the request numbers." Fans appeared to feel that the least they could do to demonstrate their appreciation was to buy the sponsor's product. Margaret Carolus, who enjoyed the Jack Benny program paid for by Jello, found the advertising so compelling "that it has encouraged me to eat and like Jello—though I had never cared for it before." Clarence Roper testified that smoking Edgeworth tobacco gave him as much of a thrill as the music on the Edgeworth program. Ruth O'Brien begged KGIR to "keep Orphan Annie on the radio for a little ten-year-old like me" and promised, "I'll drink lots and lots of Ovaltine."

Such promises and testimonials are weighty evidence of the power that advertisers exerted on the radio audience. Craney's device for generating new ideas may have provided the kernels for only a few marketable programs, but it reaped a harvest of radio fans participating actively in their own seduction by consumer culture. The lure of winning a prize coaxed them into experimenting with the language of sales, extolling the virtues of any and all products. The impetus of a contest may have led listeners to embellish their appreciation of certain products, but the internal structure of their letters, the way in which they linked product use to their daily lives, and the effort by which men, women, and children sat down to write lengthy missives—often much longer than that required or desired by contest rules—testify to the earnestness with which most correspondents wrote.

When Helen and Robert Lynd observed the popularity of radio in Middletown in the early 1920s, they also hypothesized that radio, along with national advertising and syndicated newspapers, would act to standardize much of Middletown's culture. Writer Dorothy Johnson certainly found that to be the case in Montana:

Everybody, all over, could listen to the same demagogues, howl at the same comedians, make a fad of the new slang. Everybody with a radio . . . suddenly was sophisticated, part of the great outside world. . . . Listeners became addicts, so accustomed to having sounds of any old kind coming into the house that they were nervous when it was quiet. . . . For better or worse, the quiet, the isolation, the parochialism was gone.

KGIR brought those forces of homogenization to Butte. Yet, throughout the 1930s, the station continued to air programs that spotlighted local talent, that extolled the unique virtues of the Montana landscape, that caused listeners to feel an allegiance to their local station—not only gratitude to national sponsors. As much as fans appreciated syndicated shows, they loved listening to themselves and their neighbors more. Jim Harmon declared that "the very stuff of radio was imagination," and KGIR permitted citizens to let their imaginations run riot. Symons's amateur hour nourished the dreams of local performers. Neighbors guessed at the hidden messages conveyed by songs on the request hour. Families gathered around the radio to listen to their sons and daughters sing, play in jazz bands, and recite poetry. Members of Butte's different ethnic communities waited for special holiday programs that featured their musical heritage. Private delights, broadcast over the air, assumed a cloak of public importance.

The effect that radio had on listeners is evident in the long and pleasurable memories that people associate with KGIR. Mona Daly "vividly" recalled in 1988 the afternoon in the 1930s on which her voice teacher at the Webster school chose her and a classmate to go to the KGIR studio and sing a duet of "Juanita"—"a definite thrill." Fifty years after he first heard the melodies, Jacob Jovick could name eighty-one songs that KGIR played on the request hour and thirty-one different programs that he listened to and apologize because "there were others I don't recall."

Ed Craney, his small staff, and the KGIR audience composed a score that harmonized strains of local, regional, and national culture. Craney had hoped that radio would make Montanans "realize that there was more in Montana than the little town that they lived in." To gain that end, he invited Montanans' participation in his enterprise. Miss May Gates of Opportunity was one of twenty-four would-be news editors who volunteered their services to pass on the tidings of their communities to the KGIR audience. KGIR's listeners thus had access not only to national news, New York opera, and southern string-band music, but also to "all the news and gossip that is told each evening at the Opportunity store"—and in stores in Butte, Melrose, Rocker, Deer Lodge, Twin Bridges, and a handful of other communities in KGIR's broadcast radius. KGIR introduced its audience to nationally standardized programs that some analysts feared would erase the cultural diversity of America. The station's commitment to airing the voices of its own region, however, guaranteed a medley of cultural expression. Listeners greeted radio's first decade in Butte with uncritical pleasure. KGIR became a source of delight, education, and emotional relief to thousands weathering the Great Depression, and May Gates spoke for many when she exclaimed, "What a wonderful invention the radio has been."

13

WHAT THE DEPRESSION DID TO PEOPLE

EDWARD R. ELLIS

The American economy has a long history of cyclical recessions and depressions dating back to the eighteenth century. But none of the depressions could compare in severity or longevity to that which struck Americans between 1929 and 1941. Following a decade of unprecedented prosperity, which saw the rapid expansion of consumer goods production and the introduction of consumer credit to pay for these goods, the Great Depression took Americans by surprise. What had gone wrong?

Modern historians and economists now view the Depression as the consequence of underconsumption—that is, the overproduction of goods for sale and the lack of buyers with sufficient wages to purchase them. But to the unemployed workers, the dispossessed farmers, and their families, the Depression—whatever its cause—was the most disastrous event of their lives. By 1931, over 11 million workers, nearly a third of the labor force, were unemployed, and the average farm income had declined to 60 percent of 1929 levels. In this essay, Edward R. Ellis provides a wide panorama of life during the Depression, surveying its effects on the rich as well as the poor. He finds that the Great Depression scarred the lives of all people, regardless of social class, and shaped the outlook of everyone who lived through it.

From A Nation in Torment: The Great American Depression, 1929–1939 by Edward Robb Ellis (New York: Putnam, 1970). Copyright © 1970 by Edward Robb Ellis. Reprinted by permission of The Putnam Publishing Group.

The Depression smashed into the nation with such fury that men groped for superlatives to express its impact and meaning.

Edmund Wilson compared it to an earthquake. It was "like the explosion of a bomb dropped in the midst of society," according to the Social Science Research Council Committee on Studies in Social Aspects of the Depression.

Alfred E. Smith said the Depression was equivalent to war, while Supreme Court Justice Louis D. Brandeis and Bernard Baruch declared that it was worse than war. Philip La Follette, the governor of Wisconsin, said: "We are in the midst of the greatest domestic crisis since the Civil War." Governor Roosevelt agreed in these words: "Not since the dark days of the Sixties have the people of this state and nation faced problems as grave, situations as difficult, suffering as severe." A jobless textile worker told Louis Adamic: "I wish there would be war again." In a war against a foreign enemy all Americans might at least have felt united by a common purpose, and production would have boomed.

Poor and rich alike felt anxious and helpless.

Steel magnate Charles M. Schwab, despite his millions and the security of his Manhattan palace, freely confessed: "I'm afraid. Every man is afraid." J. David Stern, a wealthy newspaper publisher, became so terrified that he later wrote in his autobiography: "I sat in my back office, trying to figure out what to do. To be explicit, I sat in my private bathroom. My bowels were loose from fear." Calvin Coolidge dolorously told a friend: "I can see nothing to give ground for hope."

Herbert C. Pell, a rich man with a country estate near Governor Roosevelt's, said the country was doomed unless it could free itself from the rich, who have "shown no realization that what you call free enterprise means anything but greed." Marriner Eccles, a banker and economist who had *not* lost his fortune, wrote that "I awoke to find myself at the bottom of a pit without any known means of scaling its sheer sides." According to Dwight W. Morrow, a Morgan associate, diplomat and Senator: "Most of my friends think the world is coming to an end—that is, the

world as we know it." Reinhold Niebuhr, the learned and liberal clergyman, said that rich "men and women speculated in drawing-rooms on the best kind of poison as a means to oblivion from the horrors of revolution."

In Youngstown, Ohio, a friend of Mayor Joseph L. Heffernan stood beside the mayor's desk and said: "My wife is frantic. After working at the steel mill for twenty-five years I've lost my job and I'm too old to get other work. If you can't do something for me, I'm going to kill myself." Governor Gifford Pinchot of Pennsylvania got a letter from a jobless man who said: "I cannot stand it any longer." Gan Kolski, an unemployed Polish artist from Greenwich Village, leaped to his death from the George Washington Bridge, leaving this note: "To All: If you cannot hear the cry of starving millions, listen to the dead, brothers. Your economic system is dead."

An architect, Hugh Ferriss, stood on the parapet of a tall building in Manhattan and thought to himself that the nearby skyscrapers seemed like monuments to the rugged individualism of the past. Thomas Wolfe wrote: "I believe that we are lost here in America, but I believe we shall be found." Democratic Senator Thomas Gore of Oklahoma called the Depression an economic disease. Henry Ford, on the other hand, said the Depression was "a wholesome thing in general."

Obviously, the essence of a depression is widespread unemployment. In one of the most fatuous remarks on record, Calvin Coolidge said: "The final solution of unemployment is work." He might have added that water is wet. Senator Robert Wagner of New York called unemployment inexcusable.

A decade before the Crash the British statesman David Lloyd George had said: "Unemployment, with its injustice for the man who seeks and thirsts for employment, who begs for labour and cannot get it, and who is punished for failure he is not responsible for by the starvation of his children—that torture is something that private enterprise ought to remedy for its own sake." Winston Churchill now used the same key word, "torture," in a similar comment: "This problem of unemployment is the most torturing that can be presented to a civilized society."

Before Roosevelt became President and named Frances Perkins his secretary of labor, she was so pessimistic that she said publicly it might take a quarter century to solve the unemployment problem. A Pennsylvania commission studied 31,159 workless men and then reported that the typical unemployed man was thirty-six years old, native-born, physically fit and with a good previous work record. This finding contradicted Henry Ford's belief that the unemployed did not want to work.

However, the Pennsylvania study was *not* typical of the unemployed across the entire nation. Negroes and aliens were the last hired and the first fired. Young men and women were graduated from high schools and colleges into a world without jobs. Mississippi's demagogic governor and sometime Senator, Theodore G. Bilbo, vowed the unemployment problem could be solved by shipping 12,000,000 American blacks to Africa. The United Spanish War Veterans, for their part, urged the deportation of 10,000,000 aliens—or nearly 6,000,000 more than the actual number of aliens in the United States. Some noncitizens, unable to find work here, voluntarily returned to their homelands. With the deepening of the Depression, immigration dropped until something strange happened in the year 1932: More than three times as many persons left this country as entered it. No longer was America the Promised Land.

The Depression changed people's values and thus changed society.

The Chamber of Commerce syndrome of the Twenties became a mockery in the Thirties. Business leaders lost their prestige, for now it had become apparent to all Americans that these big shots did not know what they were talking about when they said again and again and again that everything would be all right if it were just left to them. Worship of big business was succeeded by greater concern for human values. The optimism of the speculative decade was replaced by the pessimism of the hungry decade,

by anguished interest in the problem of having enough food on the table.

People eager to make a big killing in the stock market had paid scant attention to politics, but now they wondered about their elected representatives and the kind of political system that could permit such a catastrophe to happen. Indifference gave way to political and social consciousness. Dorothy Parker, the sophisticate and wit, cried: "There is no longer I. There is WE. The day of the individual is dead." Quentin N. Burdick, who became a Senator from North Dakota, said long after the Depression: "I guess I acquired a social conscience during those bad days, and ever since I've had the desire to work toward bettering the living conditions of the people." Sylvia Porter, who developed into a financial columnist, said that while at Hunter College she switched from English to economics because of "an overwhelming curiosity to know why everything was crashing around me and why people were losing their jobs."

People lost their houses and apartments.

Franklin D. Roosevelt said: "One of the major disasters of the continued depression was the loss of hundreds of thousands of homes each year from foreclosure. The annual average loss of urban homes by foreclosure in the United States in normal times was 78,000. By 1932 this had increased to 273,000. By the middle of 1933, foreclosures had advanced to more than 1,000 a day."

In New York City, which had more apartments than private houses, there were almost 200,000 evictions in the year 1931. During the first three weeks of the following year there were more than 60,000 other evictions. One judge handled, or tried to handle, 425 eviction cases in a single day! On February 2, 1932, the *New York Times* described the eviction of three families in the Bronx:

Probably because of the cold, the crowd numbered only about 1,000, although in unruliness it equalled the throng of 4,000 that stormed the police in the first disorder of a similar nature on January 22. On Thursday a dozen more families are to be evicted unless they pay back rents.

Inspector Joseph Leonary deployed a force of fifty detectives and mounted and foot patrolmen through the street as Marshall Louis Novick led ten furniture movers in to the building. Their appearance was the signal for a great clamor. Women shrieked from the windows, the different sections of the crowd hissed and booed and shouted invectives. Fighting began simultaneously in the house and in the street. The marshal's men were rushed on the stairs and only got to work after the policemen had driven the tenants back into their apartments.

In that part of New York City known as Sunnyside, Queens, many homeowners were unable to meet mortgage payments and were soon ordered to vacate. Eviction notices were met with collective action, the residents barricading their doors with sandbags and barbed wire, flinging pepper and flour at sheriffs who tried to force their way inside. However, it was a losing battle; more than 60 percent of Sunnyside's householders lost their homes through foreclosure.

Harlem Negroes invented a new way to get enough money to pay their rent. This, as it came to be called, was the house-rent party. A family would announce that on Saturday night or Thursday night they would welcome anyone and everyone to their home for an evening of fun. Sometimes they would print and distribute cards such as this: "There'll be plenty of pig feet / And lots of gin; / Jus' ring the bell / An' come on in." Saturday night, of course, is the usual time for partying, while Thursday was chosen because this was the only free night for sleep-in black domestics who worked for white people. Admission to a house-rent party cost 15 cents, but more money could be spent inside. A festive mood was established by placing a red bulb in a light socket, by serving food consisting of chitterlings and pigs' feet and by setting out a jug of corn liquor. These parties often went on until daybreak, and the next day the landlord got his rent. The innovation spread to black ghettos in other big cities across the land, and some white people began imitating the Negroes.

In Chicago a crowd of Negroes gathered in front of the door of a tenement house to prevent the landlord's agent from evicting a neighborhood family, and they continued to stand there hour after hour, singing hymns. A Chicago municipal employee named James D. O'Reilly saw his home auctioned off because he had failed to pay $34 in city taxes at the very time the city owed him $850 in unpaid salary.

A social worker described one pathetic event: "Mrs. Green left her five small children alone one morning while she went to have her grocery order filled. While she was away the constable arrived and padlocked her house with the children inside. When she came back she heard the six-weeks-old-baby crying. She did not dare to touch the padlock for fear of being arrested, but she found a window open and climbed in and nursed the baby and then climbed out and appealed to the police to let her children out."

In widespread areas of Philadelphia no rent was paid at all. In this City of Brotherly Love evictions were exceedingly common—as many as 1,300 a month. Children, who saw their parents' distress, made a game of evictions. In a day-care center they piled all the doll furniture in first one corner and then another. One tot explained to a teacher: "We ain't got no money for the rent, so we's moved into a new house. Then we got the constable on us, so we's moving again."

In millions of apartments, tension mounted and tempers flared toward the end of each month, when the rent was due. Robert Bendiner, in his book *Just Around the Corner*, wrote about conditions in New York City:

> Evictions and frequent moves to take advantage of the apartment market were as common in middle-income Washington Heights as in the poor areas of town, and apartment hopping became rather a way of life. My own family moved six times in seven years. . . . Crises occurred monthly, and several times we were saved from eviction by pawning leftover valuables or by my mother's rich talent for cajoling landlords. On one more than routinely desperate occasion she resorted to the extreme device of having one of us enlarge a hole in the bathroom ceiling and then irately demand-

ing repairs before another dollar of rent should be forthcoming.

In moving from one place to another, some families left their furniture behind because it had been brought on the installment plan and they were unable to meet further payments. Time-payment furniture firms owned warehouses that became crammed with tables and chairs and other items reclaimed from families without money. Whenever a marshal, sheriff or constable evicted a family from a house or apartment, the landlord would simply dump the furniture on the sidewalk. If the installment company failed to pick it up, each article would soon be carried away by needy neighbors.

What happened to people after they were dispossessed? Many doubled up with relatives—or even tripled up, until ten or twelve people were crammed into three or four rooms. Human beings are like porcupines: they like to huddle close enough to feel one another's warmth, but they dislike getting so close that the quills begin pricking. Now, in teeming proximity to one another, the quills pricked and relatives quarreled bitterly.

The Depression strained the family structure and sometimes shattered it. Well-integrated families closed ranks in the face of this common danger and became ever more monolithic. Loosely knit families, on the other hand, fell apart when the pressures on them became too great.

After a man lost his job, he would trudge from factory to factory, office to office, seeking other employment, but after weeks of repeated rejections he would lose heart, mutely denounce himself as a poor provider, shed his self-respect and stay at home. Here he found himself unwelcome and underfoot, the target of puzzled glances from his children and hostile looks from his wife. In the early part of the Depression some women simply could not understand that jobs were unavailable; instead, they felt there was something wrong with their men. In Philadelphia one unemployed man begged a social worker: "Have

you anybody you can send around to tell my wife you have no job to give me? She thinks I don't want to work."

The idle man found himself a displaced person in the household, which is woman's domain, and in nameless guilt he crept about uneasily, always finding himself in the way. He got on his wife's nerves and she on his, until tension broke in endless wrangles. If the man tried to help by washing dishes and making beds, he lost status in the eyes of the rest of the family.

The Depression castrated some men by dethroning them from their position as the breadwinner and the head of the family. Ashamed, confused and resentful, they became sexually impotent. In Western culture a man tends to think of himself in terms of the work he does, this self-identity being what Jung calls his persona. Man does. Woman is. To rob a man of his work was to rob him of his idea of himself, leaving him empty and without much reason for living. The displacement of the man as the head of the family and the way some women moved in to fill this vacuum were described sensitively by John Steinbeck in his novel *The Grapes of Wrath*. This great book tells the story of the flight of the Joad family from the dust bowl of Oklahoma to the green valleys of California:

> "We got nothin', now," Pa said. "Comin' a long time—no work, no crops. What we gonna do then? How we gonna git stuff to eat? . . . Git so I hate to think. Go diggin' back to a ol' time to keep from thinkin'. Seems like our life's over an' done."
>
> "No, it ain't," Ma smiled. "It ain't, Pa. An' that's one more thing a woman knows. I noticed that. Man, he lives in jerks—baby born an' a man dies, an' that's a jerk—gets a farm an' loses his farm, an' that's a jerk. Woman, it's all one flow, like a stream, little eddies, little waterfalls, but the river, it goes right on. Woman looks at it like that. We ain't gonna die out. People is goin' on—changin' a little maybe, but goin' right on."

Some adolescent girls felt their fathers' agony and tried to comfort them with lavish expressions of love, much to the embarrassment of the man and the uneasiness of his wife. This did emotional damage to father, mother and the young girl, whose fixation on her father retarded her normal interest in boys her own age.

Strife between parents, together with the realization that it cost money to marry and have babies, resulted in a decision by many young people to postpone their weddings. One young man joined the Communist Party and swore he never would marry or have children under "the present system." Unable to repress their human needs, however, young men and women made love secretly and guiltily, regarding pregnancy as a disaster. Despite an increase in the sale of contraceptives, the abortion rate rose, and so did venereal disease. The birthrate dropped.

It has been estimated that the Depression postponed 800,000 marriages that would have occurred sooner if it had not been for hard times. Margaret Mead, the noted anthropologist, argued that there was nothing wrong about letting girls support their lovers so they could marry sooner. Surprisingly, there even was a decline in marriages among members of the *Social Register*. Liberals and feminists pointed out that half of all births were in families on relief or with incomes of less than $1,000 a year; they strongly advocated birth control. Who could afford babies when a sixty-one-piece layette cost all of $7.70? Gasps of horror arose when it was reported in Illinois that a sixteenth child had been born to a family on relief.

Housewives suffered as acutely as their husbands. Many had to send their kids to live with relatives or friends. Others took part-time jobs, while a few wives actually became temporary whores to earn enough money to keep the family going. Lacking money for streetcars and buses, without the means to buy clothes to keep them looking attractive, they remained cooped up in their homes until their nerves screamed and they had nervous breakdowns.

All too often their men simply deserted them. A California woman said: "My husband went north about three months ago to try his luck. The first month he wrote pretty regularly. . . . For five weeks we have had no word from him. . . . Don't know where he is or what he is up to."

A young man who lived in the French Quarter of New Orleans was solicited by five prostitutes during a ten-block stroll, each woman asking only 50 cents. In Houston a relief worker, curious about how the people were getting along, was approached by one girl after another. For the benefit of an insistent streetwalker, the man turned his pockets inside out to prove that he had no money. Looking at him ruefully, she said: "It doesn't cost much—only a dime!"

The close relationship between poverty and morals shocked Franklin D. Roosevelt, who told reporters about an investigator who went to southeastern Kentucky: "She got into one of those mining towns," Roosevelt said, "and started to walk up the alley. There was a group of miners sitting in front of the shacks, and they pulled down their caps over their faces. As soon as she caught sight of that she walked up and said, 'What are you pulling your caps down for?' They said, 'Oh, it is all right.' 'Why pull your caps down?' They said, 'It is sort of a custom because so many of the women have not got enough clothes to cover them.'"

The Depression made changes in the country's physical appearance.

Fewer pedestrians were to be seen on the streets since many men did not go to work and women shopped less frequently; for lack of warm clothing and fuel, many people stayed in bed most of the day during winter. The air became cleaner over industrial cities, for there was less smoke from factory chimneys. The downtown business districts of most cities had long rows of empty shops and offices. Trains were shorter, and only rarely did one see a Pullman car. However, gas stations multiplied because millions of Americans drove their battered family cars here and there in endless quest of work. In conflicting attempts to solve their problems, farmers moved into town while city folks moved into the country to build their own houses and grow their own food. More and more blacks were seen in northern cities as desperate Negroes fled from the hopeless South. Telephones were taken out of homes, and mail deliveries were lighter. Houses and stores, parks and fences sagged and lapsed into unpainted, flaked ugliness for want of money to make repairs.

In his novel called *You Can't Go Home Again,* Thomas Wolfe described a comfort station in front of New York City Hall:

> . . . One descended to this place down a steep flight of stairs from the street, and on bitter nights he would find the place crowded with homeless men who had sought refuge there. Some were those shambling hulks that one sees everywhere, in Paris as well as in New York. . . . But most of them were just flotsam of the general ruin of the time—honest, descent, middle-aged men with faces seamed by toil and want, and young men, many of them mere boys in their teens, with thick, unkempt hair. These were the wanderers from town to town, the riders of freight trains, the thumbers of rides on highways, the uprooted, unwanted male population of America. They drifted across the land and gathered in the big cities when winter came, hungry, defeated, empty, hopeless, restless, driven by they knew not what, always on the move, looking everywhere for work, for the bare crumbs to support their miserable lives, and finding neither work nor crumbs. Here in New York, to this obscene meeting place, these derelicts came, drawn into a common stew of rest and warmth and a little surcease from their desperation.

Heywood Broun devoted a column to a description of a slum in San Antonio, Texas:

> . . . The Church of Guadalupe stands upon the fringe of what had been described to me as the most fearsome slum in all America. It covers four square miles. At first I thought that the extreme description might have been dictated by local pride. It was my notion to protest and say, "Why, we in New York City know worse than that." But after we had gone up the third back alley I had to confess defeat gracefully.
>
> You can see shacks as bad as these in several States, but I do not know of any place where they have been so ingeniously huddled together. This is flat, sprawling country, and there is much of it, and so it seems devilish that one crazy combination of old lumber and stray tin should be set as a flap upon the side of another equally discreditable. I did not quite comprehend the character of the alley until I discovered that what I took to be a toolhouse was a residence for a family of eleven people.
>
> And these are not squatter dwellings. People pay rent for them, just as if a few rickety boards and a leaky roof constituted a house. They even have evictions and go through the solemn and obscene farce of removing a bed and a frying pan as indication that the landlord's two-dollars-and-a-half rent has not been forthcoming. . . .
>
> Back at the Church of Guadalupe, the priest said, "I have other letters from those who fight federal housing because they like their rents." He tossed over an anonymous message, which read, "I could start a story that there is a priest who writes love letters to young girls and gives jewels to women of his congregation."
>
> "Doesn't this worry you?" one of us asked.
>
> "No," said the priest. "Last month we buried thirty-nine persons, mostly children, from this little church alone.
>
> "I am worried," he said, "about people starving to death."

Louis Adamic and his wife were living with her mother in New York City in January, 1932. Born in Yugoslavia, now a naturalized American, he was a writer, a tall young man with a look of eager curiosity in his eyes. One cold morning at seven forty-five the doorbell rang, and Adamic, thinking it was the postman, opened the front door. In his book called *My America,* he told what happened next.

There stood a girl of ten and a boy of eight. They had schoolbooks in their arms, and their clothing was patched and clean, but hardly warm enough for winter weather. In a voice strangely old for her age, the girl said: "Excuse me, mister, but we have no eats in our house and my mother she said I should take my brother before we go to school and ring a doorbell in some house"—she swallowed heavily and took a deep breath—"and ask you to give us . . . something . . . to eat."

"Come in," Adamic said. A strange sensation swept over him. He had heard that kids were ringing doorbells and asking for food in the Bronx, in Harlem and in Brooklyn, but he had not really believed it.

His wife and her mother gave the children some food. The girl ate slowly. Her brother bolted his portion, quickly and greedily.

"He ate a banana yesterday afternoon," said his sister, "but it wasn't ripe enough or something, and it made him sick and he didn't eat anything since. He's always like this when he's hungry and we gotta ring doorbells."

"Do you often ring doorbells?"

"When we have no eats at home."

"What made you ring our bell?"

"I don't know," the girl answered. "I just did."

Her name was Mary, and her brother's name was Jimmie. They lived in a poor neighborhood five blocks away.

Mary said: "We used to live on the fourth floor upstairs and we had three rooms and a kitchen and bath, but now we have only one room downstairs. In back."

"Why did you move downstairs?"

The boy winced.

"My father," said the girl. "He lost his job when the panic came. That was two years ago. I was eight and Jimmie was six. My father he tried to get work, but he couldn't, the depression was so bad. But he called it the panic."

Adamic and the two women were astonished at her vocabulary: "panic" . . . "depression."

"What kind of work did your father do?"

"Painter and paperhanger. Before things got so bad, he always had jobs when his work was in season, and he was good to us—my mother says so, too. Then, after he couldn't get any more jobs, he got mean and he yelled at my mother. He couldn't sleep nights and he walked up and down and talked, and sometimes he hollered and we couldn't sleep, either."

"Was he a union man?"

"No, he didn't belong to no union."

"What did your father holler about?"

"He called my mother bad names."

At this point in the conversation, Adamic

wrote, the little girl hesitated, and her brother winced again. Then she continued: "Uh . . . he was angry because my mother, before she married him, she was in love with another man and almost married him. But my mother says it wasn't my father's fault he acted mean like he did. He was mean because he had no job and we had no money."

"Where's your father now?"

"We don't know. He went away four months ago, right after Labor Day, and he never came back, so we had to move downstairs. The landlord didn't want to throw us out, so he told my mother to move in downstairs."

Between sips of milk the girl said her mother did household work whenever she could find a job, but earned very little money this way. A charity organization had been giving her $2.85 a week, but lately it had stopped. Mary did not know why. Her mother had applied for home relief, but had not yet received anything from that source.

The boy stopped eating, turned to his sister and muttered: "You talk too much! I told you not to talk!"

The girl fell silent.

Adamic said: "It's really our fault, Jimmie. We're asking too many questions."

The little boy glared and said: "Yeah!"

In Detroit someone gave another little girl a nickel, which seemed like such a fortune to her that she agonized three full days about how best to spend it.

In Erie, Pennsylvania, a seven-year-old boy named Tom received a tiny yellow chick as an Easter present. Using some old chicken wire, he built a coop for his pet beneath the back step to the house and fed and tended it carefully. His father was an unemployed molder, and the family often ate nothing but beans. Time passed. Now the little chick had grown into a full-sized chicken. One day Tom's father announced that the boy's pet would have to be killed and served for Sunday dinner, since everyone was hungry. Tom screamed in horrified protest but was unable to prevent his father from taking his chicken into the backyard and chopping off its head. Later that day the family sat around the table feasting on fowl, while the boy hunched in his chair, sobbing.

There was another boy who never forgot a scene from his childhood days during the Depression. He lived in a small town in Iowa. Every so often a train would stop there for a few minutes, and a man would get out carrying bags of buttons. He would distribute these buttons to waiting farmers and their wives, collect the cards to which they had sewn other buttons, pay them a meager sum for their labor, get back into the train and depart. This trivial piecework provided them with the only income they could get.

President Hoover was foolish enough to let himself be photographed on the White House lawn feeding his dog. This picture did not sit well with Americans who were hungry, suffering from malnutrition or even starving to death. Several times Hoover denied that there was widespread undernourishment in the nation, but he depended on unreliable statistics. Comedian Groucho Marx, who was closer to the people, said he knew things were bad when "the pigeons started feeding the people in Central Park." However, it was no laughing matter.

In Oklahoma City a newspaper reporter was assigned to cover state relief headquarters. Walking into the building one morning, he ran into a young man he had met through his landlady. This fellow offered the reporter some candy. The reporter did not want the candy but accepted it lest he hurt the other's feelings. As they stood and chewed, a social worker approached them.

"We don't allow any eating in here," she said.

The reporter, who thought she was jesting, made a wisecrack.

"We don't allow any eating in here," she repeated sternly. "Some of these applicants haven't had any breakfast. We make it a rule among ourselves never to eat or drink Cokes in front of them."

Ashamed of himself, the reporter mumbled an apology and slunk behind a beaver-board wall.

He wanted to throw away the morsel of candy remaining in his hand but felt that this would be even more sinful with hungry people so near.

Arthur Brisbane, the rich columnist and editor, walked into a Manhattan restaurant and ordered two lamb chops. When he had finished the first one, he looked longingly at the second but was too full to eat it, too. After much thought he summoned a waiter.

"What happens if I don't eat this chop?" Brisbane asked. "Will you take it back?"

"No, sir. We can't do that, sir."

"But what will you do with it? Will it be thrown away?"

"Not at all, sir. We give the leftovers to poor people."

Brisbane sighed in relief, nodded approvingly, paid his check and left.

In 1933 the Children's Bureau reported that one out of every five children in the nation was not getting enough of the right things to eat. A teacher in a coal-mining town asked a little girl in her classroom whether she was ill. The child said: "No. I'm all right. I'm just hungry." The teacher urged her to go home and eat something. The girl said: "I can't. This is my sister's day to eat." In the House of Representatives, during a debate about appropriations for Indians living on reservations, a Congressman said that eleven cents a day was enough to feed an Indian child. A Senate subcommittee learned that the president of a textile firm had told his workers they should be able to live on six cents a day.

AFL President William Green said: "I warn the people who are exploiting the workers that they can only drive them so far before they will turn on them and destroy them. The are taking no account of the history of nations in which governments have been overturned. Revolutions grow out of the depths of hunger."

Sidney Hillman, president of the Amalgamated Clothing Workers of America, appeared at a Senate hearing in 1932 and was told that it was not yet time to give federal relief. Angrily, he cried: "I would ask by what standards are we to gauge that time! Must we have hundreds of thousands of people actually dead and dying from starvation? Must we have bread riots? What is necessary to convince them that there is a need for federal and speedy relief?"

The Communists took up the slogan: "Starve or fight!"

At the University of Pennsylvania a prim audience was shocked to hear Daniel Willard, president of the B & O Railroad, say: "While I do not like to say so, I would be less than candid if I did not say that in such circumstances I would steal before I would starve."

Obviously, less fortunate Americans agreed. Petty thievery soared. Children hung around grocery stores begging for food. Customers emerging from groceries had bundles snatched from their arms by hungry kids, who ran home with the food or ducked into alleys to gobble it as fast as they could. Small retail stores had their windows smashed and their display goods stolen. Grown men, in groups of two or three, walked into chain store markets, ordered all the food they could carry and then quietly walked out without paying for it. Chain store managers did not always report these incidents to the police for fear that publicity would encourage this sort of intimidation. For the same reason the newspapers engaged in a tacit conspiracy of silence.

However, newspapers did not mind reporting that in Manhattan a debutante supper for 600 guests at the Ritz-Carlton cost $4,750. On nearby Park Avenue, beggars were so numerous that a well-dressed man might be asked for money four or five times in a ten-block stroll. President Hoover not only denied that anyone was starving, but said: "The hoboes, for example, are better fed than they ever have been. One hobo in New York got ten meals in one day."

People of means thought up ways to protect themselves from panhandlers and from begging letters. Boston's mayor, James M. Curley, had a male secretary named Stan Wilcox, who was adept at brushing off approaches. Whenever a beggar asked if he had a quarter, Wilcox would reply: "Heavens, no! I wouldn't dream of taking a drink at this hour!" Alfred E. Smith received the

following letter from Milwaukee: "This is unusual, but I am in need. Would you send me $2,500, as this is the amount I am in need of. I will give you as collateral my word of honor that I will repay you if possible. If not, let the good Lord repay you and he will also pay better interest."

Governor Gifford Pinchot of Pennsylvania flatly declared that starvation was widespread. Among the many pathetic letters he received was this one: "There are nine of us in the family. My father is out of work for a couple of months and we haven't got a thing eat [sic] in the house. Mother is getting $12 a month of the county. If mother don't get more help we will have to starve to death. I am a little girl 10 years old. I go to school every day. My other sister hain't got any shoes or clothes to wear to go to school. My mother goes in her bare feet and she crys every night that we don't have the help. I guess that is all, hoping to hear from you."

Bernard Baruch, who felt burdened by the thought of his wealth, got a desperate letter from his cousin, Fay Allen Des Portes, who lived in his home state of South Carolina. "The horrible part of the whole situation," she wrote to him, "is these poor starving people here in our midst. The banks can't let anyone have money, the merchants are all broke; the farmers can't let the poor Negroes on the farm have anything to eat. I don't know what is going to happen. I have about four hundred Negroes that are as absolutely dependent upon me as my two little boys, but I can't help them any more and God knows what is going to happen to them."

John L. Lewis, president of the United Mine Workers, once said to a group of mine operators: "Gentlemen, I speak to you for my people. I speak to you for the miners' families in the broad Ohio valley, the Pennsylvania mountains and the black West Virginia hills. There, the shanties lean over as if intoxicated by the smoke fumes of the mine dumps. But the more pretentious ones boast a porch, with the banisters broken here and there, presenting the aspect of a snaggle-toothed child. Some of the windows are wide open to flies, which can feast nearby on garbage and answer the family dinner call in double-quick time. But there is no dinner call. The little children are gathered around a bare table without anything to eat. Their mothers are saying, 'We want bread.'"

A writer named Jonathan Norton Leonard described the plight of Pennsylvania miners who had been put out of company villages after losing a strike: "Reporters from the more liberal metropolitan papers found thousands of them huddled on the mountainsides, crowded three or four families together in oneroom shacks, living on dandelion and wild weedroots. Half of them were sick, but no local doctor would care for the evicted strikers. All of them were hungry and many were dying of those providential diseases which enable welfare workers to claim that no one has starved."

In 1931 four New York City hospitals reported 95 deaths from starvation. Two years later the New York City Welfare Council said that 29 persons had died from starvation, more then 50 others had been treated for starvation, while an additional 110 individuals—most of them children—had perished of malnutrition. In one routine report the council gave this picture of the plight of one family in the Brownsville section of Brooklyn: "Family reported starving by neighbors. Investigator found five small children at home while mother was out looking for vegetables under pushcarts. Family had moved into one room. Father sleeping at Municipal Lodging House because he could get more to eat there than at home and frequently brought food home from there in pockets for children and wife. Only other food they had for weeks came from pushcarts."

A family of fourteen was on relief in Kewanee, Illinois, the hog-raising center of the Midwest. The family was given $3 worth of groceries a week, and of course this food soon ran out. After giving the last crumbs to the children, the adults would exist on nothing but hot water until they received their next grocery allotment.

In Chicago a committee investigated city garbage dumps and then reported: "Around the truck which was unloading garbage and other refuse were about 35 men, women and children. As soon as the truck pulled away from the pile all of them started digging with sticks, some with their hands, grabbing bits of food and vegetables."

Edmund Wilson described another Chicago scene: "A private incinerator at Thirty-fifth and La Salle Streets which disposes of garbage from restaurants and hotels, has been regularly visited by people, in groups of as many as twenty at a time, who pounce upon anything that looks edible before it is thrown into the furnace. The women complained to investigators that the men took unfair advantage by jumping on the truck before it was unloaded; but a code was eventually established which provided that different sets of people should come at different times every day, so that everybody would be given a chance."

A ballad called "Starvation Blues" was sung by some of the poor people of America during the Depression.

Prentice Murphy, director of the Children's Bureau of Philadelphia, told a Senate committee: "If the modern state is to rest upon a firm foundation, its citizens must not be allowed to starve. Some of them do. They do not die quickly. You can starve for a long time without dying."

Scientists agree that a person can starve a long time without dying, but this is what it is like to starve to death: After a few days without food the stomach cramps and bloats up. Later it shrinks in size. At first a starving child will cry and eat anything to ease hunger pains—stuffing his mouth with rags, clay, chalk, straw, twigs, berries and even poisonous weeds. Then, as the child weakens, his cries change to whimpers. He feels nauseated. All the fat is being burned from his body. This burning produces acidosis. The fruity odor of acetone can be smelled on the breath, and it also appears in the urine. When starvation reaches this point, nature becomes kinder. The child grows listless and sleepy. The bulging eyes are sad and dull. Now body proteins have been depleted, while the water and electrolyte balance has been destroyed. Degeneration of the vital organs, such as the liver and kidneys, proceeds in earnest. By this time the child lacks all resistance to diseases and may be killed by some infection.

John Steinbeck has told how he survived the early part of the Depression before he became a famous author. "I had two assets," he wrote. "My father owned a tiny three-room cottage in Pacific Grove in California, and he let me live in it without rent. That was the first safety. Pacific Grove is on the ocean. That was the second. People in inland cities or in the closed and shuttered industrial cemeteries had greater problems than I. Given the sea, a man must be very stupid to starve. That great reservoir is always available. I took a large part of my protein food from the ocean.

"Firewood to keep warm floated on the beach daily, needing only handsaw and ax. A small garden of black soil came with the cottage. In northern California you can raise vegetables of some kind all year long. I never peeled a potato without planting the skins. Kale, lettuce, chard, turnips, carrots and onions rotated in the little garden. In the tide pools of the bay, mussels were available and crabs and abalones and that shiny kelp called sea lettuce. With a line and pole, blue cod, rock cod, perch, sea trout, sculpin could be caught."

The sale of flower seeds shot up as Americans, tired of the ugliness of their lives, turned to the beauty of homegrown flowers. As might have been expected, there was widespread cultivation of vegetable gardens. Many did this on their own, while others received official encouragement. Big railroads rented garden plots for their workers. The United States Steel Corporation used social workers and faculty members of Indiana University to develop an extensive garden project for its workers in Gary, Indiana. In New York State, in the summer of 1933, jobless men and women were tending 65,000 gardens. The city of Detroit provided tools and seed for "thrift gardens" on empty lots, an idea which Mayor Frank Murphy said he had borrowed from Hazen S. Pingree. During the Panic of 1893 Pingree had

been the mayor of Detroit, and confronted with a city of jobless men, he provided them with gardens to cultivate—"Pingree's Potato Patches," receiving national attention.

Now, in the present emergency, Henry Ford ordered all his workmen to dig in vegetable gardens or be fired. Out of his imperious command there developed what the Scripps-Howard Washington *News* called 50,000 "shotgun gardens." Rough-grained Harry Bennett, chief of Ford's private police, supervised this vast project and kept a filing system on all Ford employees. If a man had no garden in his own backyard or on some neighborhood lot, he was assigned a patch of earth somewhere on Ford's 4,000 acres of farmland around Dearborn, Michigan. Each workman had to pay fifty cents to have his strip plowed.

More than one-third of the men employed in Ford's Dearborn plant lived 10 to 20 miles away, and some protested that since they did not own a car they would have to spend an extra two hours daily just traveling to and from their allotted patches. A Bennett henchman would snarl: "Why don't-cha buy a car? You're makin' 'em, ain't-cha?" Bone-weary workmen who simply couldn't muster the energy to toil on their garden plots soon were brought into line by Bennett's personal deputy, Norman Selby, the former boxer "Kid McCoy."

In the spring of 1932 the Community Council of Philadelphia ran out of private funds for the relief of needy families. Eleven days elapsed before this relief work could be resumed with public funds, and many families received no help during this interim. A study was made to find out what had happened when food orders stopped.

One woman borrowed 50 cents from a friend and bought stale bread at 3 1/2 cents per loaf. Except for one or two meals, this was all she could serve her family throughout those eleven days.

A pregnant mother and her three children could afford only two meals a day. At eleven o'clock in the morning she would serve breakfast, which consisted of cocoa, bread and butter. This left everyone so hungry that the mother began advancing the time of their evening meal, which was just one can of soup.

Another woman scoured the docks, picking up vegetables that fell from produce wagons. Fish vendors sometimes gave her a fish at the end of the day. On two separate occasions her family went without food for a day and a half.

On the day the food orders stopped, one family ate nothing all day. At nine o'clock that night the mother went to a friend's house and begged for a loaf of bread. Later she got two days' work at 75 cents a day. With this pittance she bought a little meat. Then, adding vegetables picked up off the street, she made a stew which she cooked over and over again each day to prevent spoilage.

One family ate nothing but potatoes, rice, bread and coffee, and for one and a half days they were totally without food.

Hunting jackrabbits to feed the family became a way of life among farmers and ranchers. This gave birth to a Depression joke reported by John Steinbeck in *The Grapes of Wrath*. One man said to another: "Depression is over. I seen a jackrabbit, an' they wasn't nobody after him." The second man said: "That ain't the reason. Can't afford to kill jackrabbits no more. Catch'em and milk'em and turn'em loose. One you seen prob'ly gone dry."

Audie Murphy was born on a Texas farm five years before the Crash, the son of very poor parents. Almost as soon as he could walk, he began hunting game for the family. Since shells were expensive, every shot had to count. Aware of this, Audie Murphy developed into an expert marksman—so expert that when he was a GI during World War II, he killed 240 Nazis and emerged as the most decorated American soldier of the war.

Wheat growers, bankrupted by drought, talked about heading for Alaska to kill moose to fill their growling bellies. In the timberlands of the great Northwest some desperate men set forest fires so that they would be hired to extinguish them, while in big cities other men prayed for heavy snowfalls to provide them with shoveling jobs. When some Pittsburgh steel mills reopened briefly, the steelworkers called back to their jobs were too weak from hunger to be able to work.

At the age of eleven Cesar Chavez, who later won renown as a Mexican-American labor leader, fished and cut mustard greens to help keep his family from starving.

Charles H. Percy, who wound up a multimillionaire and a United States Senator, never forgot what it was like to be a poor boy in Chicago during the Depression: "I remember a great feeling of shame when the welfare truck pulled up to our house. And you talk about cheating! Once they delivered us 100 pounds of sugar by mistake. My father wanted to return it, but my mother said, 'God willed us to have it,' and she wouldn't give it up." She swapped some of the sugar for flour and helped tide the family over by baking cookies that little Chuck Percy peddled door to door.

Americans under the stress of the Depression behaved with dignity that varied in terms of their religious backgrounds, their mental images of themselves and their rigidity or flexibility. Brittle people snapped, while the pliant bent and survived.

In Georgia a blind Negro refused all relief, harnessed himself to a plow like a mule and tilled the fields, day after day. In Pittsburgh a father with starving children stole a loaf of bread from a neighbor, was caught, hanged himself in shame. In Youngstown, Ohio, a father, mother and their four sons preferred to starve rather than accept charity. Before they died, their condition was discovered by a neighbor who happened to be a newspaper reporter. They were existing on fried flour and water.

Charles Wayne also lived in Youngstown. He had been a hot mill worker for the Republic Iron and Steel Company until he was laid off. For the next two years he was unable to get any kind of work. Now a fifty-seven-year-old man, workless, hopeless, unable to feed his wife and ten children, he climbed onto a bridge one morning. He took off his coat, folded it neatly, then jumped into the swirling Mahoning River below. Instinct caused him to swim a few strokes, but then he gave up and let himself drown. Later his wife sobbed to reporters: "We were about to lose our home and the gas and electric companies had threatened to shut off the service."

An elderly man receiving $15-a-week relief money for his large family went out each day, without being asked, to sweep the streets of his village. "I wan't to do something," he said, "in return for what I get." A graduate of the Harvard Law School, now old and almost deaf, gladly took a $15-a-week job as assistant caretaker at a small park.

Rather than accept charity, a New York dentist and his wife killed themselves with gas. He left this note: "The entire blame for this tragedy rests with the City of New York or whoever it is that allows free dental work in the hospital. We want to get out of the way before we are forced to accept relief money. The City of New York is not to touch our bodies. We have a horror of charity burial. We have put the last of our money in the hands of a friend who will turn it over to my brother."

John Steinbeck wrote: "Only illness frightened us. You have to have money to be sick—or did then. And dentistry also was out of the question, with the result that my teeth went badly to pieces. Without dough you couldn't have a tooth filled."

Shoes were a problem. Upon reaching home, poor people took off their shoes to save wear and tear. Middle-class people bought do-it-yourself shoe-repair kits. Those unable to afford the kits would resole their shoes with strips of rubber cut from old tires. Some wore ordinary rubbers over shoes with holes in their bottoms. A miner's son, Jack Conroy, told what a hole in a shoe could mean to a man walking the streets looking for work: "Maybe it starts with a little hole in the sole; and then the slush of the pavements oozes in, gumming sox and balling between your toes. Concrete whets Woolworth sox like a file, and if you turn the heel on top and tear a pasteboard inner sole, it won't help much. There are the

tacks, too. You get to avoiding high places and curbstones because that jabs the point right into the heel. Soon the tack has calloused a furrowed hole, and you don't notice it unless you strike something unusually high or solid, or forget and walk flat-footed. You pass a thousand shoe-shops where a tack might be bent down, but you can't pull off a shoe and ask to have *that* done—for nothing."

Keeping clean was also a problem, since soap cost money. Steinbeck washed his linen with soap made from pork fat, wood ashes and salt, but it took a lot of sunning to get the smell out of sheets. As the sale of soap declined across the nation, its production was reduced. Procter & Gamble did not lay off its workers, as it might have done under the circumstances, but put them to work cutting grass, painting fences and repairing factories until soap production began to rise again.

Steinbeck wrote a short story called "Daughter" about a sharecropper who shot and killed his own daughter because he had no food to give her. This could not be shrugged off as mere fiction, for in Carlisle, Pennsylvania, a starving man named Elmo Noakes actually suffocated his three small daughters rather than see them starve.

The Depression scarred many young men and women who later became celebrities or who already were well known. Jack Dempsey, former heavy-weight boxing champion of the world, became so strapped for money that at the age of thirty-six he got himself sufficiently back into shape to fight fifty-six exhibition bouts. Babe Ruth, always a big spender, tried to supplement his income by opening a haberdashery on Broadway but lost his own shirt after five months.

Clifford Odets wrote his first play while living on ten cents a day. Lillian Hellman, who later became a renowned playwright, earned $50 a week as a script reader for Metro-Goldwyn-Mayer. William Inge, who also won fame as a playwright, acted in tent shows during the

Depression, long afterward recalling: "We actors considered ourselves fortunate if we earned five dollars a week. Sometimes the farmers of Kansas would bring in flour and meat as barter for admission to Saturday matinees."

Songwriter Frank Loesser learned from his parents that they had lost all their money. He took any job he could get, including screwing the tops on bottles of an insecticide. He also worked as a spotter for a chain of restaurants, getting seventy-five cents a day plus the cost of each meal for reporting on the food and service. Later he reminisced: "I used to eat twelve times a day. When you're poor, you're always hungry from walking around so much."

Danny Thomas performed in saloons, but finally even this kind of work came to an end. The chance of getting another job seemed so slim that he considered giving up show business. In desperation, he prayed to St. Jude, the patron saint of the hopeless, and the next day he landed a job in Chicago that proved to be the turning point of his career.

Ralph Bellamy almost starved to death in the basement of a Greenwich Village apartment. Cary Grant was working in Hollywood as an extra. Dana Andrews worked four years as a gas station attendant in Van Nuys, California. Robert Young was employed as a soda jerk, grease monkey and truck driver. Ray Milland, living on credit in Hollywood, was about to go to work in a garage when he landed a part in a movie called *Bolero*. In Chireno, Texas, a twelve-year-old girl named Lucille Ann Collier began dancing professionally to help the family finances; later she grew into a long-legged beauty and won fame under the name of Ann Miller. In the Bronx a four-year-old girl named Anna Maria Italiano sang for WPA men working on a nearby project; today she is known as Anne Bancroft.

Victor Mature set out for Hollywood in 1935 at the age of seventeen, with $40 in cash and a car loaded with candy and chewing gum. He drove for five days and slept in his automobile each night, and by the time he reached the film capital he was almost broke. To his father in Louisville he wired: ARRIVED HERE WITH 11 CENTS. His father, an Austrian scissors grinder who had taken up refrigerator selling, wired back: FORTY-THREE YEARS AGO I ARRIVED IN NEW YORK WITH FIVE CENTS. I COULD NOT EVEN SPEAK ENGLISH. YOU ARE SIX CENTS UP ON ME.

The effect of the Depression on Hollywood extras was told by Grover Jones to an amused courtroom in a trial concerning Metro-Goldwyn-Mayer. Jones, once an extra and then a scriptwriter, gave this entertaining testimony: "They wanted eighty Indians, and I got the job only because I knew how to put on what they called bolamania—burnt umber and raw umber mixed. But they made me a chief. That meant I didn't have to go naked. I could wear a suit, you see. And at that time I was convinced I was fairly smart. So there were now eighty-one Indians. I had never seen a camera during all those months, because I was always in the background, waiting over in back of the hill for the call to come over the hill on the horses to rescue the child. And I had never been on horses. So we sat on these horses, each confiding in the other, and none of them had ever been on horses, except we were all hungry. Finally the man said, 'Now look, when you hear shooting I want you all to come over the hills, and I want some of you to fall off the horses.' Well, in those days they paid three dollars extra for a man who would fall off a horse, because it is quite a stunt. So we waited until finally we got the call to come over the hill, and somebody shot a gun off—and eighty-one Indians fell off their horses."

There was nothing surprising about the fact that men would risk injury or death by falling off a horse to earn an extra $3 a day. People felt that if they could just live through the Depression, they could endure anything else life had to offer. To *endure* was the main thing. Many took pay cuts without a murmur. A young man just out of college with a Bachelor of Journalism degree accepted a job on a newspaper at exactly *nothing* per week; a month later he was grateful to be put on the payroll at $15. Graduate engineers worked as office boys. College graduates of various kinds ran elevators in department stores. Unemployed architects turned out jigsaw puzzles. One jobless draftsman, Alfred Butts, used his spare time to invent the game of Scrabble.

Young men who might have grown into greatness chose, instead, to seek the security of civil service jobs, becoming policemen, firemen, garbage collectors. Fewer sailors deserted from the Navy. Enlistments rose in all branches of the nation's military establishment. When Congress voted a 10 percent pay cut for all federal employees, President Hoover secretly asked the Senate to make an exception for soldiers and sailors, because he did not wish to rely on disgruntled troops in case of internal trouble.

Women and children toiled for almost nothing in the sweatshops of New York City, welfare workers reporting these grim examples:

- A woman crocheted hats for 40 cents a dozen and was able to make only two dozen per week.
- An apron girl, paid 2 1/2 cents per apron, earned 20 cents a day.
- A slipper liner was paid 21 cents for every seventy-two pairs of slippers she lined, and if she turned out one slipper every forty-five seconds she could earn $1.05 in a nine-hour day.
- A girl got half a cent for each pair of pants she threaded and sponged, making $2.78 a week.

Connecticut's state commissioner of labor said that some sweatshops in that state paid girls between 60 cents and $1.10 for a fifty-five-hour week. In Pennsylvania men working in sawmills were paid 5 cents an hour, men in tile and brick manufacturing got 6 cents per hour, while construction workers earned 7 1/2 cents an hour. In Detroit the Briggs Manufacturing Company paid men 10 cents and women 4 cents an hour, causing auto workers to chant: "If poison doesn't work, try Briggs!" Also in Detroit, the Hudson Motor Car Company called back a small-parts assembler and then kept her waiting three days

for a half hour of work, forcing her to spend 60 cents in carfare to earn 28 cents.

Two Marine fishermen put out to sea at four o'clock one morning and did not return to port until five o'clock that afternoon. During this long day of toil they caught 200 pounds of hake and 80 pounds of haddock. They burned up eight gallons of gas at 19 cents a gallon and used 100 pounds of bait costing two cents a pound. For their catch they were paid one cent a pound for the hake and four cents a pound for the haddock. Thus they earned less than two cents an hour for their day's work.

Meantime, Henry Ford was declaring: "Many families were not so badly off as they thought; they needed guidance in the management of their resources and opportunities." Ford needed no guidance. He managed to transfer 41 1/2 percent of stock in the Ford Motor Company to his son, Edsel, without paying a cent in inheritance or estate taxes.

Ford, who liked to boast that he always had to work, declared in 1930 that "the very poor are recruited almost solely from the people who refuse to think and therefore refuse to work diligently." Roger W. Babson, the statistician, pontificated two years later: "Better business will come when the unemployed change their attitude toward life." Most rich men were quick to moralize.

The concept of hard work was central to capitalism and the Protestant ethic. Americans had been raised on a diet of aphorisms praising work and self-reliance. Benjamin Franklin said: "God helps them that help themselves." The Bible insisted: "In the sweat of thy face shalt thou eat bread." Thomas Carlyle said: "All work, even cotton-spinning, is noble; work alone is noble." Elizabeth Barrett Browning wrote: "Whoever fears God, fears to sit at ease." It was either Bishop Richard Cumberland or George Whitefield (no one is sure) who first said: "Better to wear out than to rust out." Most Americans agreed, but now in these Depression times men did sit at home and rust, through no fault of their own, losing the fine edge of their skills.

Idle, dispirited, hungry, defeated, withdrawn, brooding—people began to feel that somehow they were to blame for everything, that somehow, somewhere, they had failed. Maybe the Depression was punishment for their sins. After all, Protestant Episcopal Bishop John P. Tyler attributed it to the lack of religion. Perhaps Christians, if they wished to be good Christians, should bow to fate by accepting Christ's words that "to everyone that hath shall be given; and from him that hath not, even that which he hath shall be taken from him." But some found it difficult to find comfort in a sermon preached by the Reverend William S. Blackshear, an Episcopalian clergyman, in the bleak year of 1932. Blackshear said in part: "Christ was happy to be at the banquets of the rich. It was at such a place that the woman broke the vial of costly ointment and anointed His feet. There were those who cried out for the improvident and rebuked the woman, saying that this should have been converted into cash and given to the poor. It was then that Christ spoke on the economic plan, 'The poor ye have always with you.'"

This kind of sermon, representing conservative Protestantism, offended liberal clergymen. Forced by the Depression to rethink their values, they began searching for a new theology. Some began with the premise that if the church were to serve any purpose or perform realistically, it had to divorce itself from economic and political values. This developing viewpoint was expressed with crystal clarity by H. Richard Niebuhr, a pastor and a brother of Reinhold Niebuhr. He wrote:

> The church is in bondage to capitalism. Capitalism in its contemporary form is more than a system of ownership and distribution of economic goods. It is a faith and a way of life. It is faith in wealth as a source of all life's blessings and as the savior of man from his deepest misery. It is the doctrine that man's most important activity is the production of economic goods and that all other things are dependent upon this. On the basis of this initial idolatry it develops a morality in which economic worth becomes the standard by which to measure all other values and the eco-nomic virtues take precedence over courage, temperance, wisdom and justice, over charity, humility and fidelity. Hence nature, love, life, truth, beauty and justice are exploited or made the servants of the high economic good. Everything, including the lives of workers, is made a utility, is desecrated and ultimately destroyed. . . .

Other dissenters noted the supremacy of capitalism over every other value in the fact that church property was exempt from taxation. State constitutions and special statutes declared that no real estate taxes could be levied on church-owned properties, such as the church building itself, parochial schools, parsonages, the parish house and cemeteries. Why? A Missouri Supreme Court decision said that "no argument is necessary to show that church purposes are public purposes."

But was this really true? The United States of America was a Christian nation nominally, but not legally. No single religion, sect or church was recognized as the established church. Although the phrase "separation of church and state" does not appear in the Constitution of the United States or in that of any state but Utah, the idea for which it stands is found in the constitutional provisions against religious tests and in the words of the First Amendment: "Congress shall make no law respecting an establishment of religion. . . ."

During the Depression some liberal Christians, agnostics, atheists and others fretted about the special status given churches and church property. A few scholars recalled that President Ulysses S. Grant had said: "I would suggest the taxation of all property equally, whether church or corporation, exempting only the last resting place of the dead, and possibly, with proper restrictions, church edifices." Dissenters objected on principle to the exemption of church property, regarded this as an indirect subsidy by the state to religion and pointed out that personal taxes might be less if churches bore their share of the tax burden.

They got nowhere. At the core of capitalism was the belief that God looked with favor on the rich. This idea had been expressed as long ago as

1732 by one of J. P. Morgan's ancestors, the Reverend Joseph Morgan, who sermonized: "Each man coveting to make himself rich, carries on the Publick Good: Thus God in His Wisdom and Mercy turns our wickedness to Publick Benefit. . . . A rich Man is a great friend of the Publick, while he aims at nothing but serving himself. God will have us live by helping one another; and since Love will not do it, Covetousness shall."

J. P. Morgan himself flatly told a Senate committee: "If you destroy the leisure class you destroy civilization." When reporters pressed for a definition of the leisure class, Morgan said it included all who could afford a maid. In 1931, according to *Fortune* magazine, there still were 1,000,000 families with servants. One wealthy family announced that it had solved its Depression problem by discharging fifteen of its twenty servants—although the family members showed no curiosity or concern about the fate of the unemployed fifteen.

John Jacob Astor came of age in 1933 and thereupon inherited about $4 million. Nonetheless, he dabbled at a job in a downtown Manhattan brokerage house. Before long he quit with the explanation: "I didn't finish until five o'clock and by the time I got uptown it was six. And then I had to get up early the next morning." At a later date Astor was employed briefly by a shipping firm, and when he quit this second job, he commented: "I have discovered that work interferes with leisure." He was a representative of that leisure class which Morgan felt must be maintained to save civilization.

When Dwight Morrow was running for governor of New Jersey, he said: "There is something about too much prosperity that ruins the fiber of the people. The men and women that built this country, that founded it, were people that were reared in adversity." Morrow made this statement and died before Adolf Hitler declared: "It was poverty that made me strong." Joseph P. Kennedy, a busy member of the leisure class, felt that the rich had to make some sacrifices. Writing about the Depression, Kennedy said: "I am not ashamed to record that in those days I

felt and said I would be willing to part with half of what I had if I could be sure of keeping, under law and order, the other half."

One member of the enormously wealthy Du Pont family seems to have been out of touch with reality. An advertising agency wanted his company to sponsor a Sunday afternoon radio program, but this Du Pont rejected the idea, saying: "At three o'clock on Sunday afternoons everybody is playing polo."

Everybody except the millions of Americans gobbling the last morsel of food from their plates in the fear that it might be their last meal—a habit that persisted in some people down through the next three decades. As Sinclair Lewis commented in his novel *It Can't Happen Here,* people were so confused, insecure and frustrated that they hardly could do anything more permanent then shaving or eating breakfast. They were tortured with feelings of inadequacy and guilt.

A young Alabama school teacher with eight years of tenure was fired after the Wall Street Crash. Eager to work, willing to take any job however low in the social scale, she became a maid in a private home. However, upon learning that she would be expected to work seven days a week, getting room and board but no wages, she quit. Then she took a job in a convalescent home which paid her room and board and $3 a week, but soon the home closed for lack of funds. The gentle schoolteacher completely lost faith in herself, confessing to a caseworker: "If, with all the advantages I've had, I can't make a living, then I'm just no good, I guess!"

Forty experienced secretaries found work after being unemployed a year, but the first few days on the job they were unable to take dictation from their bosses without weeping from sheer nervousness. After seeking employment for a long time, a man finally landed a job and became so overwrought with joy that he died of excitement. A corporation executive was given the nasty chore of firing several hundred men. A kind and compassionate person, he insisted on talking to each of them personally and asking what plans each had for the future. In a few months the executive's hair had turned gray.

The Depression began to erode freedom.

Some Americans, a little more secure than others, asked harsh questions. How about finger-printing everyone on relief? Was it proper for a man on relief to own a car—even if he needed it to try to find work? Wasn't it wrong to sell liquor to the head of a family on relief? Did anyone owning a life insurance policy deserve relief? Should reliefers be allowed to vote? Did they deserve citizenship?

In New Orleans a federal judge denied citizenship to four qualified persons because they were on relief and therefore, in the judge's words, "unable financially to contribute to the support of the government." In California another judge withheld citizenship from Jacob Hullen; in response to the judge's questions Hullen had said he believed in municipal or federal ownership of public utilities.

In New York City, one cold and rainy day, the police arrested 38 men who had taken shelter in the Pennsylvania Railroad's ferry terminal on Cortlandt Street. All were marched to the nearest police station. Fifteen of them, able to prove that they had a few nickels and dimes in their pockets, were released. The other 23 men, who did not have a cent on them, were led before a magistrate, who sentenced them to jail for vagrancy. Newspaper stories about this obvious injustice raised such a hullabaloo, however, that the 23 prisoners soon were freed.

Robert Morss Lovett, a professor of English literature at the University of Chicago, wrote in his autobiography:

An example of the injustice meted out to foreign-born workers involved a Yugoslav named Perkovitch. When conditions were at their worst in 1932–33 the unemployed on the West Side [of Chicago] were in the habit of crossing the city to the South Side where food was sometimes available from bakeries, disposing of yesterday's bake, and where, at least, the garbage was more lavish.

One morning these itinerants were picked up by the police and held at the station house on the absurd pretext that a revolution was planned. Perkovitch told me that he and about one hun-

dred others were kept in the basement all day without food. Once a lieutenant with a bodyguard of patrolmen raged through the room, striking and kicking the men in an ecstasy of sadism. At six the prisoners were released with no charges.

Paul D. Peacher, the town marshal of Jonesboro, Arkansas, arrested a group of Negro men without cause and forced them to work on his farm. A federal grand jury indicted him under Title 18 of the Anti-Slavery Act of 1866 for "causing Negroes to be held as slaves" on a cotton plantation. This was the first case ever tried under the slavery statute. A county grand jury absolved Peacher, but the federal Department of Justice would not drop the case. Now the marshal was forced to stand trial—this time before a *federal* jury. Taking the witness chair in his own behalf, he denied that he had done anything wrong. However, the jury disagreed with him and found him guilty. Peacher was sentenced to two years in prison and fined $3,500. He appealed, lost his appeal, paid the fine and accepted a two-year probationary sentence.

Someone asked Eugene Talmadge, the governor of Georgia, what he would do about the millions of unemployed Americans. Talmadge snarled: "Let'em starve!" It made him happy when the city fathers of Atlanta put unwanted nonresidents in chain gangs. When some textile workers went on strike in Georgia the governor had barbed-wire concentration camps built and threw pickets into them. Frank Hague, the mayor and ruthless boss of Jersey City, called for the erection in Alaska of a concentration camp for native "Reds."

Wise and temperate men worried about the growing loss of liberty in America, the land of the free and the home of the brave. George Boas, a professor of philosophy, sadly said: "It is taken for granted that democracy is bad and that it is dying." Will Durant, busy writing his many-volumed *Story of Civilization*, asked rhetorically: "Why is it that Democracy has fallen so rapidly from the high prestige which it had at the Armistice?"

14

THE DEPRESSION, GOVERNMENT INTERVENTION, AND THE SURVIVAL OF THE REGIONAL COMMUNITY

SARAH DEUTSCH

Franklin D. Roosevelt's New Deal was a watershed in American history. Beginning shortly after he took office in 1933, Roosevelt and his advisors fashioned a distinctively American welfare state to combat the worst abuses of the Depression. The New Deal record was an impressive one: it established price supports in agriculture, fashioned a National Recovery Administration to direct new industrial growth, provided jobs for the unemployed through the Civilian Conservation Corps and the Works Progress Administration, insured bank deposits, and established social welfare programs through the Social Security Administration. The New Deal eased the pain of the Great Depression for millions of ordinary Americans and paved the way for further liberal reforms in the following two decades.

Yet despite good intentions, New Deal programs did not always achieve their goals; at times, they even made matters worse. Such was the case with the Hispanic farm workers of northern Colorado. Every spring and summer since the 1880s, men from the Hispanic farm villages of northern New Mexico had supplemented the income of their wives' landholdings by working as miners, farm laborers, and railroad workers in Colorado. Far from disrupting the local community, these annual migrations became part of a complex and highly cohesive regional community that expanded and contracted according to the demands of the labor cycle. This pattern changed during the 1920s, however, when traditional railroad and mining jobs dried up and whole families were forced to leave New Mexico to take the only work available: harvesting sugar beets in northern Colorado. Carrying their community traditions with them, these migratory families quickly rebuilt a Hispanic community along the Colorado Front Range that was as strong and vital as the one they had left behind.

In this essay, Sarah Deutsch follows the shifting fortunes of this regional community during the Great Depression. As she shows, culturally insensitive New Deal officials and the cultural biases of the federal Hispanic Arts Program served to erode, rather than enhance, the community supports and cultural cohesion that had brought the Hispanic community through the rigors of migration and the worst hardships of the depression.

A Great Western Sugar Company spokesman labelled 1929 the "worst year in beet history." Things would not get better for a long time. That year an early freeze cost some growers nearly all their crops and some laborers all their wages. Drought and the national Depression took over where the freeze left off. In 1930, Colorado harvested 242,000 acres of beets. Five years later, it harvested only 140,000. Four-fifths of the beet-growers in the Arkansas Valley had gone bankrupt, and beet farms on the South Platte were sold for taxes or were repossessed. The demand for beet labor in Colorado fell more than 45 percent. Anglo growers tended their own beets, if they still had any, or hired newly eager Anglo laborers. The largest single source of employment in the villagers' regional system threatened to disappear.

But even for those who had it, employment was no guarantee of survival. New contracts demanded that beetworkers bear more of the risk; employers defaulted on old contracts, and wages plummeted. Wages in northern Colorado beets fell from $27 an acre in 1930 to $12.37 in 1933. In 1934, the median family earnings came to only $250 a year. The reduced cost of living absorbed only a small fraction of the decline. It still took about $1000 for a family of five to survive. Workers had to seek government or private relief even while they worked beets.

Chicanos kept pace with the upward spiral of those unemployed and on relief in Colorado as it rose from 9093 families on federal emergency unemployment relief in October 1932 to 56,461 the following February. Even the Hispanic strategy of a multi-source income could not save them from the depredations of the Depression. Other agricultural wages fell, railroads let their maintenance slip, and the coal mines of both northern and southern Colorado hired fewer men for fewer days each year. Those who had broken out of these traditional occupations found no refuge. Chicano construction workers, factory hands, truck drivers, waitresses, musicians, and even representatives of the few Chicano clerical workers in northern Colorado also suffered from unemployment.

As the Depression attacked the nation and eliminated Hispanic jobs, it threw Hispanics back on the resources of the Hispanic village heartland or on the communities they had managed to erect on the northern edge of the Anglo-Hispanic frontier. It tested the vulnerability of Hispanic communities both in the villages and on the periphery, and it called into question the efficacy of the strategies Hispanics had evolved. The regional community could not survive such an onslaught unchanged.

As Anglos and Hispanics struggled to control developments and relations on the Anglo-Hispanic frontier, they generated new forces, new strategies, and new adaptations. By analyzing first the breakdown of the regional community strategy and of the village as refuge, and then turning to new strategies emerging in Hispanic communities, and finally examining the impact of government policies on job and sexual structures, the way in which the intersection of these often competing strategies and cultures shaped the future of the cross-cultural region becomes clear.

"People on the farm were better off than downtown," remembered a Hispanic woman who lived in northern Colorado during the Depression; "we had our gardens." In contrast, she remembered "an aunt in Fort Collins, they were living on the soup line; we could hardly visit them because they barely had enough for themselves. . . . [W]e would go after meals. They felt bad." The few farmers who still hired Chicanos rarely let them winter on the farm. As a result, more than half of northern Colorado's Chicano beetworkers joined the unemployed Chicanos wintering in towns and cities. Almost none had cash or gardens, and all had to pay rent.

Relief seemed the only hope of obtaining the income essential to the survival of the local Chicano communities and the larger regional community linked to them. It was far from perfect. Private agencies often collapsed under the relief load. And even after the federal government stepped in, its Works Progress Administration never absorbed all the unemployed. Moreover, its relief appropriations tended to provide only a portion, often less than half, of what people needed for subsistence.

As opportunities for subsistence evaporated, the north became an ineffective part of the regional community. Fear of losing their resident status and so losing any relief benefits immobilized some Chicano families, but individuals and families with fewer children or with land to the south sought refuge from unemployment and new competition by retreating to the Hispanic villages of southern Colorado and northern New Mexico. Most of them would not venture north again for nearly a decade.

The Depression disrupted migration patterns and strategies Hispanics had followed for ten, fifteen, and even twenty-five years. Only the skeleton of the regional migratory pattern survived. Villagers continued to visit relatives established at the perimeters of the regional community. A few men still managed to find work herding sheep or working beets in Colorado or Wyoming, and their wives, like one woman near Embudo, New Mexico, were considered "fairly well off." But it was not enough. In the 1920s the 14,000 Hispanic families in northern New Mexico's Upper Rio Grande Valley sent seven to ten thousand individuals north for work each year. In the early 1930s, they sent only two thousand. Those sent earned only about one-third as much as they had before. Persistence led to disaster for Hispanics who exhausted their credit on job-seeking in the north and found no jobs. With such reduced participation, the framework of the regional community could survive, but the original function of the regional community, Hispanic village survival and autonomy, was less secure.

Two actions in particular reinforced the retreat to the villages and underscored the loss of Chicano control over the dynamics of the regional community: the repatriations in the early 1930s and the 1936 Colorado border closing. In 1929, the federal government attempted to increase its control over Mexican immigration. It enhanced penalties for illegal immigration, enlarged the Immigration and Naturalization Service Border Patrol, and adopted "administrative restriction":

the more rigorous enforcement of existing laws. But pressure for legislated restriction continued unabated, like the Depression; three Mexican-quota bills appeared before the House Committee on Immigration in the spring of 1930. As economic conditions further deteriorated, destitute and stranded Chicanos became increasingly visible on relief rolls. Impatient local social-service agencies took matters into their own hands. From 1930 to 1935, with and without the aid of local Mexican consulates and Mexican funds, relief agencies in Colorado engineered the departure of approximately 20,000 Mexicans and their often United States–born children. Across the Mid- and Southwest similar actions sent approximately 400,000 Chicanos to Mexico, "repatriating" them.

Whether the majority left "absolutely voluntarily," the victims only of "homesickness" and unemployment, or whether they felt the force of "polite coercion" via threats of removal from welfare or even deportation—both views documented and held by contemporary observers and historians—whole communities disappeared from Colorado and elsewhere. The movement south stood in stark contrast, at its peak in May 1932, to the years of a healthy regional community, when each May had witnessed the greatest number of Chicano arrivals.

Much to the chagrin of the relief agencies and county commissioners, Chicanos continued to appear and reappear on county relief rolls in northern Colorado. "It was agreed and understood that these people were to remain in Mexico," complained the Weld County Board of Commissioners to the Commissioner-General of Immigration. But, contrary to the promises of the labor importers in the 1910s and 1920s, the Chicanos refused to disappear when unwanted.

The solutions offered by taxpayers and politicians became more extreme as sugar, sheep, and railroad companies continued to recruit Hispanic labor in New Mexico, despite the growing number of Chicanos on relief. By March 1935, Governor Johnson of Colorado was proposing to round up all aliens in the state and deport them himself if federal immigration officials would not. Two months later, he ordered alien beetworkers out of the state and had local sheriffs in southern Colorado turn them back at the New Mexico border. Despite a protest from the Mexican Ambassador and the blatant illegality of his actions, Johnson merely increased the effectiveness of his policy. The following April he called out the National Guard and declared martial law along Colorado's southern border.

United States citizenship afforded Chicanos no protection from Johnson's blockade against "aliens." Spanish Americans as well as Mexicans found themselves under arrest, as a group at Colorado Springs did—even one hundred miles inside the state—and they numbered among the over five hundred would-be laborers turned back by troops in the next ten days. Twelve Spanish Americans from northern New Mexico's Abiquiu and Peñasco were taken from a train, loaded in trucks and dumped out on the prairie at the New Mexico line. Hispanic reactions at the border, according to an Albuquerque newspaper report, "ranged from tears to indignation." The regional community had been cut in half.

Other states had closed their borders to block Anglo dustbowl migrants, but both those who favored and those who opposed Colorado's action labored under no illusion as to the targets. "We are right behind you," wrote a Mr. and Mrs. Williams to the Governor, "in your move to keep the Mexican race out of our state." Anglo employers beseeched the governor to end the blockade, as it kept out the "Mexicans from New Mexico" on whom they relied for herding, lambing, harvesting, and section maintenance.

Before the blockade, Spanish Americans had asked the governor for protection against the importation of alien labor. They favored deportation and voiced resentment over the presence of Mexican aliens on relief rolls. The actual blockade, however, was another story. While Governor Johnson's administration insisted that the blockade protected "the Colorado Spanish-American working class as well as all of Colorado labor" by reducing the labor supply, Spanish American loy-

alties were not bound by state lines. As the blockade continued, and stories of Spanish Americans suffering harassment surfaced, more conservative Hispanic groups and individuals in New Mexico and Colorado joined the radical Spanish Speaking Workers League in protest. They had wanted to shut out aliens, but they resented having "citizens of this government turned back and refused entry to the state of Colorado merely because they were of Spanish decent." They resented both this denial of Spanish American membership in the United States polity, and the arbitrary fragmentation of the region. Even the Beet Workers Union, local no. 20,190 of Greeley, whose Anglo vice president had spoken at first in favor of the blockade, joined the opposition.

Spanish American outrage in Colorado and New Mexico helped end the blockade, but Hispanics were powerless to repair the migrant webs. The blockade had been an effective if illegal symbol of a more permanent problem. Few Spanish Americans tried again to cross the border even after the departure of the National Guard. In terms of demography and economy, the regional community had become more its parts than their sum.

The Hispanic beetworkers who participated in what contemporary observers called "a wholesale retreat . . . to the villages and their land," knew that their four or five acres of irrigated land held the promise of only an inadequate livelihood, but they also believed that these acres held "a house and a garden spot that would help cushion the shock from the collapse of practically all demand for their labor." In the event, the cushion proved none too soft. The winter of 1931/32 brought to northern New Mexico unprecedented snows that left livestock marooned, frozen, or starved to death. The melted snow provided welcome moisture, and optimistic farmers planted accordingly, but hailstorms and grasshoppers destroyed much of the crop. Then began a prolonged drought, the worst the area had ever suffered, according to one agricultural extension agent. Renewed vigilance on behalf of the Pueblo Indians led, in addition, to the transfer of some range land from villages to Pueblos and to increased stringency regarding pasturage quotas for other Indian land previously used as free range. Clearly a retreat to purely pastoral activities would not suffice.

In those areas of northern New Mexico less affected by the drought and less dependent on livestock, returning migrants increased their cash crops and began selling their produce directly. During a peak month in 1930, joint trucking ventures and roadside booths brought a total of three thousand dollars to Rio Arriba County farmers. All too soon, however, the market for their chief commercial crops, chili and apples, collapsed from increased competition. As state relief agents reported families in the county "verging on starvation," Rev. Julian Duran concluded, "None of the products our people have to sell are worth very much." As one resource after another failed the villagers, Duran trenchantly observed, "[T]here is a heaven and a hell to economics, as most of us have found out since 1929."

The failure of cash-earning alternatives within the villages intensified the impact of the regional community's collapse. Before the Depression, village migrants had earned two million dollars a year. In 1935 they earned only about $350,000. By mid-decade, 60 percent of the Spanish Americans in northern New Mexico villages were receiving government aid. In some villages every family appeared on the relief roll. Tax delinquency rose from 32.4 percent of the levy in 1928 to 65 percent in 1932. As more Anglos from Texas and Oklahoma drifted into the villages in the early 1930s, they brought with them the specter of Hispanic dispossession.

The villages had proven unequal to their role as refuge. Returning migrants found themselves in much the same straits as those who had settled permanently in the north. Only the larger economy of the regional community had sustained the villages as a viable retreat for Hispanics. With no demand for their labor, the villagers could not retain control over their interactions with the larger, Anglo-dominated economy. Family networks had not disappeared. They still aided their members through adoption of children and exchange of produce, and passed on information about jobs and relief. But the demands of a cash economy exposed the limits of networks dependent entirely on what were now non-cash-earning families. Relief proved as poor a substitute in the villages as it did in northern Colorado. Agencies, both public and private, ran out of funds. The Red Cross stepped in only in cases of crop failure, not of monetary shortage, and where many land-owning villagers at a single site claimed need, relief agents tended to view them with great suspicion. Villagers adamantly asserted their rights. They held mass meetings to protest ethnic discrimination and planned to march on the bank when threatened with foreclosure. They protected their core as best they could, and neither mortgaged nor sold vital, irrigated lands and gardens. But the Depression severely curtailed their power to assert, protect, and control. Like the Hispanics in the north, they would have to find new strategies of autonomy and survival to replace the regional community.

Chicanos in New Mexico and Colorado, stranded when the high tide of 1920s' prosperity ebbed, headed for cities and towns. They joined the seasonal laborers evicted by farmers for the winter, but they stayed in the city year round. In Denver, for example, the number of Chicanos trebled during the 1930s while other groups remained static. These urban Chicanos retained village mores, much to the exasperation of welfare workers. They shared what relief they received among kin and other community networks, and Hispanic stores that grew up within these communities came to rely, as had those in the villages, on the relief orders of their clientele. Church membership and participation rose, accompanied by a proliferation of sects that reached into the villages.

The new, relatively sedentary population in Denver and on the edges of rural towns reinforced the stable core emerging in northern Colorado's Chicano settlements in the 1920s and as lines to the villages frayed spurred an increasing sense of local community. These communities, like the ones in the southern Colorado coal camps and the 1920s beet colonies, were different from the villages. They were even more vulnerable to tides of the larger economy because they lacked a separate economic base, however insufficient. But they served other functions, provided other kinds of support and collectivity, as the shared relief and church membership implied.

Stability, though not necessarily entirely the product of choice, had benefits. Despite reports throughout the region that Chicanos lacked sufficient clothing, shoes, paper, and pencils, and despite the need for children's labor to provide additional income or child care for working mothers, increased stability led to increased Chicano enrollments in schools not only in northern Colorado, but in southern Colorado and northern New Mexico. As in other parts of the nation among similar groups, lack of wage-earning alternatives for the children, free school lunches, and the warmth of school buildings may all have played a role in greater enrollment. More children throughout the country went past the fifth and even the eighth grades for the first time. The proportion of enrolled Chicanos who were in Denver's senior high school, for example, rose from less than 2 percent in 1930 to over 5 percent seven years later. In Rio Arriba County, New Mexico, the Spanish American high-school enrollment almost doubled between 1933 and 1935 alone. For Chicanos, however, the greater school enrollments and persistence did more than reflect greater stability. They meshed with a determination to gain broader opportunities within the Anglo society and economy as the retreat to the Hispanic world of the villages became less and less beneficial or even possible.

This determination together with the increased size and stability of urban settlements also intensified the 1920s' trend toward a more formally organized, assertive Chicano community in northern Colorado. Mutualistas [mutual benefit societies], lobbying groups, and unions grew. Whereas in the 1920s a lone individual had initiated a civil rights suit, during the 1930s an organization was formed to file lawsuits against public discrimination. And the Spanish American Citizens Association now had branches throughout southern and northern Colorado. It endorsed and bargained with political candidates, cooperated with organized labor, held mass meetings, and defended the rights of Chicano workers. In 1933 its Denver membership totaled 1100, and in 1934, its annual convention hosted one hundred delegates. Adapting to the fragmentation of the regional community, Chicanos reorganized along lines suited to their new economic, social, and political dilemma.

Even non-labor organizations usually had some connection with labor or saw their interests as allied, but as in Texas and California, Chicano labor organizations particularly grew, both in membership and in activity. Communists—who adopted a resolution late in 1930 to form local Agricultural Workers Unions across racial lines—and the A.F.L. worked to organize and stimulate the grass-roots upheaval among beetworkers that had resulted, in part, from the disruption of the regional community and from Anglo attempts to manipulate movements within that community. Together, they built on the beetworker unions formed in the late 1920s and made the agricultural labor movement in Colorado second only to that in southern California as the most active of the decade.

Chicanas joined Chicanos in the unions and protests of the 1930s. Though they did not achieve the prominence of Chicanas in cities such as Los Angeles and San Antonio, with a large female semi-industrial sector, they joined the attempt to redefine the terms of their northern existence. Hispanic women in New Mexico and Colorado addressed union rallies of miners and beetworkers, joined picket lines, and went to jail. Some politically active Hispanic women lobbied for better wages; Mrs. Mauricio Trujillo of Gardner and Mrs. Aurelia Sanchez of Frederick agitated in W.P.A. unions, and Helen Lucero organized against police brutality in Denver. For these women, mutuality of interests between the sexes and in occupational patterns overcame a tradition which placed interethnic contact in the male sphere, and their actions returned these women, even in northern Colorado, from the margin to the center of community life.

Myriad difficulties beset any attempt to organize Chicano beetworkers. Though at least one Hispanic beet local moved with its constituents from Walsenburg, Colorado, in the winter to Vale, South Dakota, in the summer, few were so successful in maintaining contact with workers. Even when they wintered in the north, beetworkers usually changed residence during the beet season. In addition, in most areas in the 1930s, Anglos as well as Hispanics performed beet labor, and ethnic tensions arose within mixed and between rival ethnically-based locals. Moreover, members often lacked the money for dues; hostile city and county officials canceled scheduled meeting places and jailed union leaders, whom they designated as outside agitators, on charges of vagrancy; and neither the sugar companies nor the growers admitted responsibility for bargaining with labor.

Despite all these difficulties and several particularly low points, at least some locals, many of which remained independent throughout the decade, agitated each year. Conferences attempting to build ever larger and more effective coalitions at the state and national level convened in Colorado with great persistence. In 1930 a beet-union conference hosted 200 delegates with a Colorado constituency placed at 7500 workers. Six years later, a conference of 120 delegates appointed committees to meet with the growers, the company, and W.P.A. officials. In 1937, the movement culminated in a broadly based national convention in Denver from which emerged the United Cannery, Agricultural and Packing and Allied Workers of America (UCAPAWA) under a C.I.O. (Congress of Industrial Organizations) charter. At least ten of the one hundred delegates represented the purported 8000 Colorado beetworker members.

The persistence of these organizational efforts, like the political organizations and mutu-

alistas, measured the declining effectiveness of the regional community as a viable strategy. As avenues of retreat and aid were cut off and Chicano beetworkers formed increasingly permanent communities in the north, they sought newer, more confrontational organized means, such as these unions, to gain some control over their conditions and interaction with the Anglo economy and society.

Beet unions demanded wage increases, an end to growers withholding pay, and that the sugar company guarantee payment of wages by the growers. Beyond these monetary items, the unions sought adequate housing, drinking water, and garden plots large enough for a family food supply. They also demanded the right to conduct all negotiations where the majority of the laborers belonged to a union, and non-discriminatory work relief and hiring policies. Together these demands would have increased the economic base for Chicanos in the north until it more nearly approximated that of the Hispanic villages in the south, and increased their control over their environment.

They seldom won any of these demands from the growers. Yet although they threatened almost every year, only in 1932 did they actually strike. It was perhaps the legacy of this strike that prevented them from repeating it.

In response to massive wage reductions in early 1932, a new beetworkers' committee called a strike for May 16. The United Front Committee represented a coalition under radical leadership of the surviving politically and ethnically varied grass-roots beet locals in Colorado, and it attempted an unprecedented scale of organizing to culminate in the first state-wide beetworkers' strike. Mass meetings were held the Sunday before the strike, and the following Monday carloads of Chicano organizers toured the beetfields. They persuaded quite a few of the workers to declare themselves on strike and to walk off the field. Some accusations of intimidation were made but none were confirmed. As in the 1920s, the areas near the coal mines in Weld County, the Chicano clusters on the edges of rural towns, and the beet colonies contained the most enthusiasts. Coal-mining areas had the most exposure to union organizing in the mines. Clusters and colonies—more permanent Chicano settlements—shared the most homogeneity in ethnicity and class, and there a sense of neighborhood, of common interest, had grown deepest.

Many Anglos claimed the strike leaders were outsiders. Weld County and Greeley officials and the press labeled them "oily tongued" communists and agitators from Denver. But four of those jailed on May 17 for investigation of such charges turned out to live in Greeley's own Hispanic colony. The twenty-four Chicanos arrested three days later not only were local, but represented, with six women and ages ranging from 22 to 73, a wide sector of the Chicano community.

As the strike continued, tensions rose. Deputies began to patrol beetfields in the coal-mine section of the county. When they arrested seventeen more Chicanos and one Anglo on the twenty-first, strike leaders protested at open-air meetings. The Greeley Hispanic colony, a union stronghold, hosted a Communist party meeting. These colonists felt themselves pushed farther and farther outside the Anglo community. Farmers armed themselves, and "squads of deputy sheriffs and volunteers" arrested unarmed "rioters." Repatriations also continued, and strike leaders were jailed for twenty to thirty days. A Communist journal claimed that 18,000 beetworkers had gone on strike in Colorado. But by May 30, the fields were quiet, the beet tenders were back at work, and none of their aims had been achieved.

The strike was plagued from the beginning with more than arrests or red-baiting. Even before the strike began, the *Greeley Daily Tribune* reported that "local men were free with the prediction that for every man that joins the strike there would be two to take his place," and at least one farmer replaced his troublesome "Mexican" beet labor with "Anglo-Saxons." And beyond that, the area the strikers attempted to cover was too wide, too difficult to police, and their resources too small, the Hispanic settlements too vulnerable. The union had promised food during the strike, but failed to provide it, and in the northern enclaves there was no alternate source of wages or subsistence.

Of course the failure of the strike did not mean that Chicanos found labor organizing a useless strategy, a useless alternative or addition to the retreat to the villages. At least eight Hispanic beet-labor locals survived in Colorado into the 1940s. And the leftist Liga Obrera de Habla Española, or Spanish Speaking Workers Union, established with the aid of the I.W.W. in the Colorado beetfields in 1928, also survived. It retained branches in Denver and other parts of northern Colorado. And it even reached the remote Hispanic villages of the Upper Rio Grande, traveling with its members along the now fragile routes of the regional community to become the largest lay organization there.

Although its members undertook no regional action, the Liga exemplified the way in which the region's Chicanos used their labor organizations most effectively in the 1930s: as pressure groups. It had branches also in Gallup, Las Vegas, and Santa Fe, New Mexico, and became increasingly demonstrative and political. In 1935 the Liga's eight thousand New Mexico members succeeded in defeating a New Mexico criminal syndicalism bill. And two years later members occupied the Chicago governor's office. In the villages, Hispanics saw the Liga as powerful enough to force its demands on political authorities, to gain for the villagers more relief and work projects, and so they flocked to its standard.

In Colorado the beet-labor unions lobbied with some success for their constituents. In 1933, beet-labor leader Leo Rodriguez of Fort Lupton hitch-hiked to Washington to testify on low wages and child labor. After the 1934 Jones-Costigan Act extended the Agricultural Administration Act to cover sugar beets, Rodriguez and other union leaders petitioned for on-site hearings and represented beet labor at those hearings. They also kept pressure on the federal government and relief officials between the invalidation of that act and the passage of the Sugar Act in 1937. They policed the enforcement of wage determinations and policies, and kept beet-labor conditions before the public eye.

Despite their inability to force a settlement on the beetgrowers or the sugar company, Chicanos had achieved at least a limited measure of success in creating a strategy for confronting the Anglo economy that did not depend on the survival of the regional community. As the efficacy of the ethnically based regional community declined, Chicanos in both Colorado and New Mexico turned to a more class-based solidarity.

The unions, the growth in school enrollment, and the burgeoning organization of Chicano settlements in northern Colorado all pointed to a Chicano effort to replace the fragmented regional community with other means to achieve some control over their fate. But federal intervention as well as interference on the local level limited this new effort. In a context of general economic disaster, overstretched budgets and unrest, when faced with the enhanced militance of the non-disappearing "Mexicans" and the potential threat to order from the increasingly radical nature and persuasiveness of their unions, local, state, and federal governments, too, adopted new strategies. Repatriations, state border closings, and Immigration and Naturalization Service investigations of Liga members were only the most obvious.

A contributing factor in the formation of government policies was the ongoing tension between Anglos and Hispanics, a tension exacerbated by the economic crisis as the two groups became rivals for scarce resources. While increased enmity and growing urban concentrations did lead to some new efforts to reduce these tensions—for example the Denver Interracial Commission's adoption of the issue in 1935—many Anglos throughout Colorado and New Mexico, in company with many Spanish Americans, blamed the nation's ills on the Mexicans. Unlike the Spanish Americans, however, the Anglos continued to confound Chicano citizens with Mexican aliens. After all, had not

"Mexican" officially been designated a race in the 1930 census? It was not a matter of citizenship. Mexican and Spanish American alike were now "Mexican." The "White Trade Only" signs which still graced shop windows in Greeley, Fort Collins, and other cities excluded all Chicanos—both Spanish American and Mexicans. Public recreation facilities were occasionally segregated, clubs almost always so, and some towns did not allow Chicanos to build or live within their borders. The Ku Klux Klan again demonstrated in sugar-beet towns; handbills that warned "ALL MEXICANS AND ALL OTHER ALIENS TO LEAVE THE STATE OF COLORADO AT ONCE BY ORDERS OF COLORADO STATE VIGILANTES" floated over not just Mexican neighborhoods but the Spanish American colony in Greeley in 1936. The persuasiveness of Anglo hostility toward Mexicans and, by association, Spanish Americans, emerged fully when a 1940 questionnaire distributed to 915 junior and senior high school students in a "representative" Colorado county elicited the information that 31 percent of the students would not grant Mexicans United States citizenship, 35 percent would not allow them in the same school room, and 42 percent not in the same church. Forty-eight percent would not accept a Mexican as a friend, 69 percent would not accompany one to a social function, and 94 percent would not marry one. These tensions were not, however, geographically limited. Even in the heavily Hispanic areas of New Mexico and the San Luis Valley, Chicanos faced similar problems. Hardship had clearly not made the Chicano and Anglo communities as one.

The universality of the hostility portended a more or less uniform attitude across the region regarding Chicano employment and relief. Employment agencies, public and private, encountered difficulty placing their Chicano clients because, as they reported, "an employer will often refuse to take a Spanish-speaking person unless a special effort is made by the placement officer," The jobs Chicanos found tended to be on public relief projects or in poorly paid domestic work.

Hispanic dependence on public works projects, in turn, led Anglos to label W.P.A. projects in the Arkansas Valley "Mexican Projects," and the state sales tax, the "Mexican bonus." It seemed to some that Chicanos actually received preference over Anglos for work relief. This possibility appalled Anglos who saw Chicanos as un-American. "Keep our Americanism," pleaded one irate Fort Collins citizen who reported that the "Mexicans" would not or could not "speak American." Colorado's Spanish American heritage had made no impression on these Anglos. An outraged Rocky Ford resident posited that the relief load in the Arkansas Valley town was half Chicano; "[T]he skunks," he warned, "are claiming now that they were born in the United States." If Chicanos, wherever they were born, however persistent, were not to be part of the United States polity in the prosperity of the 1920s, they certainly would not be admitted during the Depression.

Many Anglos, including relief officials, took the less overtly resentful line that relief was actually damaging to Chicano recipients. Freddy Falogrady, secretary of the National Reemployment Service in Las Animas County, a county one-third to one-half Spanish American, revealed that "the greater number of those receiving relief are Spanish Americans, and the Chairman of our relief committee feels, and we believe justly so, if these people are not held down to the minimum of help from Federal Relief, they will settle down to live on the country for the rest of their lives and it will be impossible to persuade them to work even when conditions are better." Continuing to label local Spanish Americans in the same way they had for at least thirty years, as "childish" in their attitude toward money, passive, complacent, resistant to progress, and incapable of any but common or manual labor, Anglos in Colorado and New Mexico saw government relief as reinforcing these tendencies which, many believed, lay at the root of Hispanic need even more fundamentally than did the Depression. "Before the advent of the WPA," claimed a naïve Anglo graduate student at the University of Mew Mexico, "the people of Rio Arriba County were on the whole self supporting. . . . Since the inauguration of the WPA there has been a noticeable decrease of small farms and an increased dependency on the relief agencies." Other Anglos were dismayed to find that once Hispanics discovered the possibilities of relief, they demanded food, medical care, and clothes for the children. "I believe they could easily become quite inclined to beg," concluded one teacher.

Along with this sense of the peculiar moral vulnerability of Chicanos went a greater fear on the part of some Anglos that the existence of relief work endangered the survival of that facet of the regional community which served Anglo employers. It threatened the reliance of Hispanics on beet, railroad, and sheepherding labor and to destroy the region's system of low-wage labor. "All Mexicans who refuse to work in the beet fields," demanded a Denver Anglo, "should be cut off from *all* relief. We have coddled them entirely too long and they think they have us bluffed."

Indeed, beetworkers did try to exploit this new opportunity to better their condition. Year-round government work relief allowed increased stability, a highly desirable condition since the decline of the regional community. Beginning in 1934, however, federal policy was to remove potential beetworkers from relief rolls in the early spring, several weeks before beetwork began. Harry Hopkins, in charge of the Federal Emergency Relief Administration, explained that after "very careful consideration" the administration had concluded the policy was "necessary in order to overcome the reluctance on the part of these people to move off relief rolls when employment does become available." Yet Chicanos knew that the end of the beet season would find them again in need and with no certainty of regaining work relief or any other employment. Forcing these workers to migrate for seasonal labor threatened their local relief status as residents; it also meant either a return to abbreviated school years for their children or leaving their families behind for work at wages lower than those the work relief paid, wages too low for year-round survival. Nor could these workers rely, as they had earlier, on village kin to make up the difference. Contrary to popular Anglo opinion, observers found among villagers and ex-villagers "general dissatisfaction with remaining dependent upon the generosity of the Governmental agencies," but in a situation where it required the work of four family members for an entire season—from May to early November—to equal the annual wage of a single worker on a relief work wages, Chicanos, particularly those with small families, resisted being forced to accept jobs in the private sector at less than subsistence wages. The increasingly organized Chicano workers attempted to use their work relief jobs to allow them to survive while pressuring growers and other employers for higher wages. They resisted being forced to participate in an Anglo version of the regional community's migratory labor which held few benefits for Hispanics.

In the interests of stability and of maintaining the status quo ante, however, government relief agencies could not allow themselves to be governed by sympathy for the beetworkers' new strategies. Hopkins added to his explanation a warning: "The Relief Administration cannot take part in any efforts to influence the wages in such fields which are outside its own Work Division activities." In the years following, as federal work relief directors continued to drop beetworkers long before beetwork became available, they reiterated that they were "not interested in the terms of the beet labor contract offered by farmers." Administrators publicly ignored the effect their timely removal of workers had on the bargaining power of those workers, and argued that springtime reductions in W.P.A. rolls affected all states and all ethnic and racial groupings. But in Colorado, at least, the greatest impact of those reductions fell on the Chicano workers, and covert discrimination in this area was recognized by all parties, however often they publicly denied it. Terry Owens, District W.P.A. Director for Pueblo, Colorado, confided to his regional administrator, "I cannot help but feel that our procedures in this matter have been eminently

fair and intelligent," but, he admitted, "the fact that other nationalities are not acceptable to the sugar beet farmers may be interpreted as racial discrimination." Paul Shriver, on the other hand, as state W.P.A. director, was "not particularly proud of the way in which it was handled." "Men were laid off on the assumption that they were beet laborers," he explained, "because of their names—Spanish and Mexican."

The federal government adopted as the official view the myth that only Chicano labor would or could perform beet and other underpaid work. What had been a convenient rationale in the private sector for the continued importation at low wages of Chicano workers in the 1920s now became a government rationale for reducing the work relief load. Equally important, the government's adoption of this rationale perpetuated and legitimized discrimination on ethnic lines already prevalent in northern Colorado's labor market. By April 1937, when the beetworkers were at the height of their organizing, the W.P.A. of both New Mexico and Colorado had already agreed, in conference with the sugar companies who threatened to return to active recruitment of out-of-state labor, to "make available" qualified beet labor. With federal manipulation of relief jobs governing the ebb and flow of migration and the wages received, the government was perpetuating the migratory and economic aspects of the regional community at the same time that Hispanics were rejecting them.

Chicano individuals and organizations protested these relief policies. Spanish Americans demanded, "Why should only the Spanish Americans be sent when they like the rest have been born and raised right here in the United States?" And one World War I veteran bitterly complained that "only in times of war and during elections are we noticed . . . after that we have no country or no flag." A sympathetic but powerless Paul Shriver explained, "We have to work this thing out realistically. We are working under a capitalist system in this country." The W.P.A.'s Director of Labor Relations in Washington added, "The law is on the side of the sugar companies and there is nothing we can do about it."

The Jones-Costigan Act of 1934 could be seen as a compromise between the government's rigid relief policies and the laborers' demands. It stipulated that in order to receive full benefits, a grower had to pay beet labor in full; the Secretary of Agriculture could set minimum wages in the event of a dispute; and the growers had to accept the Secretary of Agriculture's decisions as adjudicator. In 1935 an amendment was passed that restricted the use of child labor. After an initial year of confusion and indecision, rates for 1935 were set at $19.50 per twelve-ton acre, a great increase over the $14 of the previous year, though less than beetworkers' demands. But the Sugar Act passed in 1937 to replace that which the Supreme Court invalidated the previous year lacked the provision empowering the Secretary of Agriculture to enforce a minimum wage or to adjudicate disputes between growers and labor.

In the absence of wage-enforcement power, the act had less to offer the beetworkers. Even the child-labor provisions proved a mixed blessing. In 1939 child labor in northern Colorado declined to 12 percent of beetworkers' children aged six to fourteen, as compared to 73 percent in 1920, and, as a result, children stayed in school for more of the school year. But a social worker at the Greeley Hispanic colony explained the drawbacks: "By the time the fathers employ men to do the labor which the children used to do, the money is out of the family and the children do not have the food, clothing, and warmth that they used to have." Wages rose slightly after 1937, but each spring, 78 percent of beet families found themselves living on store credit, 11 percent of relief, and 4 percent on advances from the grower. Thirty-eight percent still ended the season with no cash on hand after settling bills. Federal action taken via the Sugar Acts may have restored conditions to the status they had before the Depression, but it had not improved on them. Through both its relief policies and the Sugar Acts the federal government had sustained the economic structure of the regional community and had hindered any attempts, whether Chicano or Anglo, to alter the relations it imposed.

In the same vein, New Deal jobs programs reflected less the aspirations of Hispanics than the old order Hispanics were trying to escape. While alterations in power dynamics and resources on the Anglo-Hispanic frontier encouraged Hispanics to depend less on their enclaves and more on winning a better and more permanent place in the larger society through such avenues as unions and education, New Deal jobs programs had their own definition of Hispanic improvement. The New Deal's focus on improvement within the confines of the old order, in the name of stability and neutrality, like their relief policies regarding beetworkers, frustrated new Hispanic strategies and aspirations. The conundrum appeared with particular clarity with regard to gender.

As it did elsewhere and for other women, the New Deal's jobs programs tended to reinforce older labor patterns rather than to create new patterns for Hispanic women. Trends that had begun in the 1920s as a result of greater school attendance and political opportunities continued. By 1937 Hispanic women teachers in Rio Arriba County outnumbered the Hispanic men at last. And the ranks of Hispanic clerical and health workers increased. Hispanic women in Hispanic culture areas also continued to be politically active. (At least five Hispanic women were in the New Mexico state legislature in the 1930s.) A substantial village could still support a few teachers, a seamstress, a laundress, a postmistress, and a midwife, and women still maintained their own bartering economy; they worked in each other's fields, plastered, and traded fruit and vegetables. Packing, sorting, and stringing chili brought a cash income to many women, and a few others ran family stores.

In the 1930s, as they had before, however, particularly landless and urban Hispanic women faced limited cash-earning opportunities. Plagued by discriminatory hiring practices of stores and offices, lack of education and English, poverty, and increased Anglo competition, they could make little headway in improving their labor-market choices. In the cities a few worked in canneries or as waitresses. But for the rest, earning cash still meant taking in laundry or doing domestic service, and many women did both.

Across the nation, women beset by declining alternatives and disappearing incomes sought housework, and the proportion of employed women in domestic service went up during the 1930s for the first time in this century. Chicanas were part of the trend and suffered from it. Sixty-five percent of unmarried Chicanas between the ages of fifteen and nineteen worked outside the home both in suburban Albuquerque and in Denver, almost two-thirds of them in low-paying housework or cleaning. Even in the villages it became increasingly common for a daughter or a mother to do housework for wages. Prospective employers continued to greet them with both distrust and the expectation that they would work for a lower wage than other domestic servants. And the relative difficulty with which employment services placed Chicanas bore out that Chicanas in Denver, at least, seeking wage-work in increasing numbers, continued to find the market for their labor even more constricted than for Hispanic men or for Anglo women.

Into this fairly static picture came the New Deal's work programs. As in other states, the work programs became embroiled in state and local politics, triggering a constant barrage of angry and contradictory letters from Hispanics and Anglos, males and females alike. But although Hispanic politicians did exploit these new opportunities for patronage, Hispanic men and women, even in areas of Hispanic majorities, remained underrepresented in these programs at all levels. A work project in Rio Arriba County, for example, a county 90 percent Hispanic, had no Hispanic supervisors. Although Hispanics numbered an unusually high 35 percent of the project's 45 skilled workers, they comprised 87 percent of the 139 unskilled laborers.

Hispanic women, too, found that New Deal jobs programs offered them less than it offered their neighbors. A few Hispanic women participated in sexually mixed work projects, and at least two rural school projects employed women plasterers, but the director of women's work in New Mexico, Helen Dail Thomas, felt obliged to apologize "that we have so few purely women's work projects to report." The paucity was not, in her view, her fault, or that of the program. "During the summer, practically all of the women are busy working in the gardens," she explained, and, in any case, "our native women are not good sewers."

The most fundamental reason New Mexico lacked work projects for Hispanic women, however, lay beyond either gardens, often suffering from drought in any case, or ignorance of needle-craft. It lay in the same perspective which differentiated relief needs of Anglo and Hispanic beet-workers. Margaret Reeves, New Mexico State Relief Administrator in 1933 and 1934, baldly replied to a query sent by Ellen Woodward, Director of Women's Work in Washington, "I do not believe that there should be many more women working in New Mexico, nor many more projects for women than we have at present. You may know that seventy per cent of the population of this state is Spanish-Speaking. . . . I feel that women projects are better adapted to Anglo-American communities and to industrial areas." While Reeves claimed to have made a "special effort to help the man of the family to employment," she insisted that Spanish American mothers, because of the large families (somewhat exaggerated by Reeves), were "badly needed in the home." Apparently Anglo mothers, in her view, were not. Sympathetic observers, while recognizing the declining resources of the villagers, also believed that Hispanics were habituated to a less expensive diet and standard of living than most Anglos and so, in their view, "needed" fewer of the scarce dollars relief directors had to spend.

Although Reeves and Thomas both soon disappeared from the scene, Woodward continued to find New Mexico's Hispanic women's projects inadequate. In late 1936, for example, spurred by complaints received from women on sewing projects, she questioned "most emphatically whether we should sanction part-time employment, even in New Mexico where the situation in connection with the Mexican women is quite unique."

Woodward was not blind to the racial issue. "It seems to me," she explained to the regional director at Salt Lake City, "that when we did not lower the standard in the southern states where the problem of the negro women is so acute it was a great pity to discriminate against the Mexican women in New Mexico." But Woodward bowed, in this instance, to the greater authority of the woman on the spot, Mrs. Andrews, who contended that the W.P.A. program's wage, which could reach fifty-five dollars per month in urban centers, lured women from their private employment at three to five dollars per week or fifteen cents per hour. It led to "far more women certified than it would be possible for us to work if we worked them full time." Part-time employment, with its reduced wages, she argued, would not only lessen the incentive to leave other low-paying jobs, but would increase the number of women the project could reach. Andrews insisted that though a few had complained, the majority of women preferred the new arrangement as it gave them more time at home. As with the relief policies of Colorado in regard to beetworkers, the aim was not to change the economic structure, but to sustain it. And by giving more cash-earning jobs to men, the New Deal sustained a pattern where village men, preferring work to relief and desperate for cash, left the gardens and irrigated lands in the hands of women. For landless, unmarried, and urban women, however, the Anglo and male bias brought few rewards.

This is not to deny that New Deal jobs programs offered desperately needed employment and some lasting benefits to Hispanics. New Deal agencies provided modern technical and professional training for some Hispanic men and women, and hired a few Hispanic men and women to administer extension programs among Spanish Americans. In general, however, New Deal programs, when they placed Hispanic women at all, tended to channel them, as they did minority women elsewhere, into traditional or marginal occupations. In rural areas, crafts projects that employed both men and women were often seen particularly as a way to produce

added income for the difficult-to-place women. In urban centers, besides the ubiquitous sewing projects and despite the fact that some young Hispanic women earned as little as fifty cents a week doing housework, W.P.A. officials argued for and won household-training projects. Mary Isham, State Director of Women's Activities for Colorado in 1935, contended, "[W]e have many girls from Spanish speaking and negro families whom we greatly desire to do something worthwhile for in the way of permanent training." The most suitable permanent training for Chicanas seemed to Isham, as to others in previous decades, training for domestic service, though Chicanas disliked the work so much that the programs went begging for candidates. Even the National Youth Administration, which sometimes offered training in office skills, had most of its Hispanic female participants in Colorado and New Mexico making quilts and mattresses, cleaning, and in domestic training. George Bickel, Assistant State Director of the W.P.A. for Colorado, justified this use of N.Y.A. funds as appropriate to the future he foresaw for San Luis Valley's Hispanics. "Many of the valley's youth," he claimed, "have little to anticipate in life save an existence of peonage. The average Spanish-American girl on the NYA program looks forward to little save a life devoted to motherhood often under the most miserable circumstances." Heading neither for higher education nor industry, such a Hispanic girl, Bickel argued, "must have opportunity to learn and work in a program of sewing, budget management, commodity usage, and personal hygiene." For the boys, too, Bickel envisioned the future as static in terms of occupational mobility: "these boys will be sheepmen, tenant farmers, laborers and craftsmen. Our challenge is to help them from relief to self sufficiency in these fields." What Bickel and his New Deal cohorts seemed to want for Chicanos and Chicanas, as one Nambé Community School teacher expressed it, was "to improve but not to change" conditions. But the stipulation of stasis frustrated evolving Hispanic strategies and limited the improvement that such New Deal programs could achieve.

The 1930s had brought new Anglo and Hispanic strategies. Like the arts program, most faded with the decade. By 1939, for example, only six UCAPAWA locals still organized beetworkers in northern Colorado. In 1941, UCAPAWA abandoned the field. Yet grievances remained. The Farm Security Administration revealed that most beet-labor houses in northern Colorado still lacked "adequate waste disposal facilities, refrigeration, or indoor toilets, while two thirds had leaky roofs and were without proper drainage," and in Denver 89 percent of Spanish Americans resided in substandard housing. Fewer than 11 percent of Denver Hispanics owned their homes, as compared to 34 percent of black and 41 percent of Anglo residents, and half the Chicanos still depended on WPA work, a proportion five times that of any other racial or ethnic group. In rural areas, investigators reported in 1943 that "practically none have acquired self-subsisting farms." Infant mortality among Denver's Chicanos remained at almost three times that among Anglos. And a 1945 Department of Labor report concluded that conditions in the beetfields showed no improvement notwithstanding federal government regulations. Despite federal programs and new Anglo services, the Depression had witnessed little progress in the northern Colorado Chicano community.

Continuing isolation in northern Colorado, poverty, substandard housing, and lack of non-seasonal employment opportunities there help to explain why sociologist Kalervo Oberg found Hispanics in 1940 still looking to their New Mexican villages rather than outside them for their life's center. "As poor and insecure economically as the Spanish-American undoubtedly is, he still holds tenaciously to a community life that offers him more than he can find elsewhere." Yet these northern New Mexico communities had weathered the Depression little better. In 1941 an El Cerrito resident told investigators, "[T]he people here are worse off than they have ever been in their lives." Despite federal rehabilitation, crafts, and other programs, their farms were still too small or too dry to provide a living;

they continued to lack adequate grazing land; and steady wage work remained elusive. After seven years of federal subsidies through work projects and relief, the investigators reported, basic conditions remained unchanged.

Both in the villages and in northern Colorado, some Chicanos had benefited from the increased schooling that greater stability coupled with child-labor laws had made possible. In addition, literacy programs, workers' education, and other federal outreach programs that hired Hispanics to serve Hispanics, although established only late in the 1930s, did help foster leaders and organized community groups in some localities. These government-sponsored community organizations could supplement the dwindling, more radical grass-roots unions that, in contrast, the government (local, state, and federal) as well as employers had discouraged. But the new organizations were limited in scope and aims, and most of the Hispanics would have to await the greater prosperity and opportunities of the 1940s to garner any reward for their increased education.

The federal government had intervened at almost every level of the regional community during the Depression, from work-relief policies in northern Colorado to crafts programs in the villages, from rural rehabilitation to midwifery, in the name of welfare, stability, and order. Health and nutrition officials, home economic and agricultural agents, literacy and cooperative teachers had entered Hispanic communities, each "missionary" bringing with him or her a cultural message. Yet the pattern that remained after 1940 was not that of stabilized and self-sufficient Anglo-style communities. And even the alternate patterns Chicanos themselves had been building, based on unions and other community organizations, lay diminished or in disarray. The Chicano organizations that had not suffered at the hands of federal and local investigators by having leaders arrested or deported called off their struggles for Chicano rights for the duration of the Second World War. The "rehabilitated" villagers returned to seasonal labor, while the youths, "interested," as New Mexico's director of vocational education found, "in learning more lucrative trades than traditional craftsmanship," turned eagerly to the war industries. What remained, after all, was the migratory and interdependent pattern of the regional community. As late as 1979 anthropologist Paul Kutsche observed the regional community still operating in the New Mexican villages: "a network promoting the survival of its members in a variety of subsistence situations. . . . Those more established on the periphery provide bases for migrating kinsmen seeking work or education." Had the regional community survived the Depression despite federal intervention or because of it?

World War I had given a brief glimpse of what the federal government could accomplish in the way of Americanization given enough money, attention, and time. But in the 1930s the aims were different. Just as Chicanos were forming new strategies less dependent on the regional community with its migratory patterns and ethnic isolation, the federal government began working instead to maintain it. Undermining stability in the north by manipulation of migration patterns through relief timing, the federal government also fostered ethnic distinction through crafts and village rehabilitation programs. A homogenized America no longer seemed the government's ultimate goal. This new federal policy was a major reason not only for the survival of the villages and Hispanics as a group apart but for the limited success of the new Chicano strategies.

By the end of the 1930s, the villagers, men and women alike, had lost, at least temporarily, much of their remaining autonomy, their ability to choose for themselves among income opportunities and cultural adaptations. This loss of autonomy had not come, as might have been expected, through assimilation. It had come through government "preservation" of Hispanic village culture. When the kinship and regional strategies proved inadequate to the task, the federal government helped sustain both the villages and the migratory patterns. It adopted private methods of labor discrimination and cultural patronage to do so, though it also returned wages closer to the admittedly inadequate level of the mid-1920s. Tempered by Hispanic resistance, bureaucratic inefficiency, and limited funds, the government thus suspended the dynamic of Hispanic culture, including the growth of alternatives to the regional community strategy. In effect in the 1930s the government succeeded in taking over the regional community erected on the Anglo-Hispanic frontier and used it to restore order, despite economic dislocation. What had begun as a Hispanic strategy to retain autonomy and cultural control became, in other hands, an instrument against both. But, ironically, the government also thus suspended the destruction of the villages as a separate culture. And it was largely due to this federal intervention that the regional community survived the 1930s at all.

PART THREE

A RESILIENT PEOPLE

The post–World War II generation lived through a unique era in the nation's history. Driven by the world's strongest economy, protected by the world's preeminent military establishment, and enjoying unprecedented personal prosperity at home, ordinary people and national leaders alike looked forward to living in what one observer dubbed the "American Century." In the end, however, that century would last a mere 20 years. By 1967, the costs of the Vietnam War pushed the nation's economy into an inflationary spiral; during the 1970s, foreign products made serious inroads into American markets; and in 1974, the Vietnam War ended in American withdrawal and defeat. Pressed economically, national pride diminished by failure in Vietnam, the United States witnessed a resurgence of conservatism that threatened the existence of the liberal welfare state.

Conservatism was nothing new in American life, however. During World War II itself, many ordinary people supported the government's decision to violate the property rights and civil liberties of Japanese Americans. In "The Decision for Mass Evacuation," Roger Daniels reconstructs the process by which the government deprived tens of thousands of Japanese Americans of their property and forcibly transported them to inland internment camps for the duration of the war. As he shows, the relocation policy was a political ploy with heavy anti-Asian overtones and had little to do with the threat posed by overwhelmingly loyal Americans of Japanese ancestry.

Sacrifice on the battlefield was taken for granted by all Americans during World War II, but sacrifice on the home front was a different matter. As Mark H. Leff shows in "The Politics of Sacrifice on the American Home Front," ordinary men and women readily accepted the need for personal sacrifice, but at the political and business level, interest groups battled continuously to minimize the extent of their own losses. Like internment, sacrifice on the home front was a thoroughly political process.

By the late 1940s, the American people found themselves fighting a "Cold War" against international communism, with an enormous impact on the nation's social and political life. In "Rebels Without a Cause," Nils Kristian Bogen analyzes the impact of the Cold War on the youth culture of the postwar era. He argues that the anti-Communist crusade of Senator Joseph McCarthy served to dampen the reformist impulses of postwar youth and, in the process, created an alienated but materialistic youth culture in the 1950s.

The unprecedented prosperity of the immediate postwar decades created a virtual revolution in consumer goods and in the consumption patterns of ordinary Americans. One result was the creation of what Kenneth T. Jackson calls a "Drive-In Culture," based on a precipitous rise in automobile ownership during the postwar years. By the 1960s, motels and drive-in restaurants, movies, banks, and even churches were a regular part of everyday life in the United States.

One of the truly momentous developments of the postwar era occurred in the realm of race relations. As record numbers of African Americans moved from the South during World War II and gained better-paying jobs in defense industries and greater power and acceptance in northern and western cities, they began to demand an end to discrimination and segregation throughout the nation. In "The Paul Robeson–Jackie Robinson Saga," Ronald A. Smith looks at the problems of racial acceptance before the civil rights movement of the 1960s. Comparing the divergent public careers of Paul Robeson and Jackie Robinson, he concludes that conformity to mainstream ideals lay at the heart of social acceptance.

The collapse of postwar prosperity in the late 1960s and early 1970s cast a lengthening shadow over the lives of ordinary Americans. As wages failed to keep pace with inflation, growing numbers of married women with preschool-aged children were forced into the labor market simply to maintain the postwar standard of living. The political fallout of economic decline was immediate and long-lived. In "The Overthrow of LBJ," Allen J. Matusow argues that the combination of a faltering economy and the failure of the United States to achieve a decisive victory in Vietnam brought down one of the most powerful political leaders of the postwar era. Between 1968 and 1992, increasing numbers of Americans turned to the right, electing conservative Democrats and Republicans who promised in one way or another to restore the postwar prosperity and international dominance of the United States. In "Ronald Reagan—The Movie," Michael Rogin examines the ways in which the most successful of these conservative politicians employed popular culture to gain his political and economic ends. In Ronald Reagan and his successor, George Bush, voters found a comfortable reassertion of the receding "American Century." But by the 1992 election, it was clear that ordinary people judged "photo opportunities" and Cold War rhetoric poor substitutes for workable economic and social policies that would restore the health of American society.

15

THE DECISION FOR MASS EVACUATION OF THE JAPANESE AMERICANS

ROGER DANIELS

From 1939, when World War II broke out in Europe, to December 1941, mainstream opinion in America was avowedly isolationist. The war was widely thought to be a European concern, the price that European states had to pay for their "corrupt" system of power politics. But when Japanese naval aircraft attacked and destroyed much of the American fleet at Pearl Harbor on December 7, 1941, popular isolationism quickly changed to demands for prompt retaliation.

In Washington, Franklin D. Roosevelt responded quickly to the Japanese attack, asking Congress on December 9 for a declaration of war. But America was militarily unprepared to proceed against the Japanese, for much of its Pacific forces had been destroyed at Pearl Harbor. Moreover, America's European allies were in desperate straits by 1942; excepting Switzerland, Luxembourg, and Sweden, all of continental Europe was under Axis control and Germany was poised for a major assault upon a staggering Britain.

Faced with this situation, Roosevelt saw America's first duty as the rescue of Britain and the defeat of the fascist forces in Europe. Only then, reasoned Roosevelt, would the United States have sufficient time to arm itself for a concentrated campaign against Japan. But while he developed this European strategy, Roosevelt also had to respond to the growing public clamor for an immediate military response to the Japanese attack.

Caught between these conflicting demands, Roosevelt looked to symbolic attacks against the Japanese to satisfy domestic demands and to gain support for his war strategy. Thus, in early 1942, Roosevelt authorized air raids on Tokyo, and in February of the same year he signed an executive order giving the Army authority to remove all people of Japanese descent, many of whom were American citizens, from the western United States. In this essay, Roger Daniels traces the ways in which government officials conspired to deprive thousands of Japanese Americans of their constitutional rights.

From Concentration Camps: North America *by Roger Daniels (Melbourne, FL: Krieger, 1981), pp. 42–73. Reprinted by permission of Krieger Publishing Company.*

December 1941 was a month of calamities which saw West Coast opinion harden against the Japanese; during January, as the war news got worse and worse and it became apparent that the Japanese audacity at Pearl Harbor would not be quickly avenged, the national climate of opinion, and Congressional opinion in particular, began to veer toward the West Coast view. That this climate had to be created is shown by an examination of the *Congressional Record*. Not only was there no concerted strong feeling exhibited against the Japanese Americans, but in the first weeks after Pearl Harbor members of the California delegation defended them publicly. (The only trace of hostility shown by a California solon in early December was a telephone call that the junior senator, Democrat Sheridan Downey, made to the Army on the night of December 7 suggesting that De Witt prompt Governor Olson to declare some sort of curfew on "Japs.") On December 10, for example, Bertrand W. Gearhart, a four-term Republican congressman from Fresno and an officer of the American Legion, read a telegram professing loyalty to the United States from an Issei leader in his district whom Gearhart described as an "American patriot." Five days later, when John Rankin (D-Miss.), the leading nativist in the lower house, called for "deporting every Jap who claims, or has claimed, Japanese citizenship, or sympathizes with Japan in this war," he was answered by another Californian, Leland M. Ford, a Santa Monica Republican:

> These people are American-born. They cannot be deported . . . whether we like it or whether we do not. This is their country. . . . [When] they join the armed forces . . . they must take this oath of allegiance . . . and I see no particular reason at this particular time why they should not. I believe that every one of these people should make a clear, clean acknowledgment.

Despite the lack of Congressional concern, by the end of December momentum was gathering for more drastic action against the Japanese and against enemy aliens generally. On December 30 the Justice Department made the first of many concessions to the military, concessions that had little to do either with due process or the realities of the situation. On that date Attorney General Biddle informed the Provost Marshal General's office that he had authorized the issuance of search warrants for any house in which an enemy alien lived, merely on the representation that there was reasonable cause to believe that there was contraband on the premises. Contraband had already been defined to include anything that might be used as a weapon, any explosive (many Issei farmers used dynamite to clear stumps), radio transmitters, any radio that had a shortwave band, and all but the simplest cameras. For the next few months thousands of houses where Japanese lived were subjected to random search. Although much "contraband" was found (most of it in two Issei-owned sporting goods stores), the FBI itself later stipulated that none of it was sinister in nature and reported that there was no evidence at all that any of it was intended for subversive use. But the mere fact of these searches, widely reported in the press, added to the suspicion with which the Japanese were viewed. These searches, like so much of the anti-Japanese movement, were part of a self-fulfilling prophecy: one is suspicious of the Japanese, so one searches their houses; the mere fact of the search, when noticed ("the FBI went through those Jap houses on the other side of town"), creates more suspicion.

For individual Japanese families, these searches intensified the insecurity and terror they already felt. One fifteen-year-old girl in San Jose, California reported what must have been an all-too-routine occurrence:

> One day I came home from school to find the two F.B.I. men at our front door. They asked permission to search the house. One man looked through the front rooms, while the other searched the back rooms. Trembling with fright, I followed and watched each of the men look around. The investigators examined the mattresses and the dresser and looked under the beds. The gas range, piano and sofa were thoroughly inspected. Since I was the only one at home, the F.B.I. questioned me, but did not procure sufficient evi-

dence of Fifth Columnists in our family. This made me very happy, even if they did mess up the house.

Concurrent with its more stringent search order, the Department of Justice and the Provost Marshal General's office decided to send representatives to De Witt's headquarters in San Francisco; the two men sent—James Rowe, Jr., Assistant Attorney General and a former Presidential assistant, and Major (later Colonel) Karl R. Bendetsen, chief of the Aliens Division, Provost Marshal General's office—were key and mutually antagonistic figures in the bureaucratic struggle over the fate of the West Coast Japanese. Rowe, during his short visit in California, exercised a moderating influence on the cautious General De Witt, who often seemed to be the creature of the last strong personality with whom he had contact. Bendetsen represented a chief (Gullion) who wanted not only exclusion of the Japanese from the West Coast but also the transfer of supervisory authority over all enemy aliens in the United States from the civilian control of the Department of Justice to the military control of his office. Bendetsen soon became the voice of General De Witt in matters concerning aliens, and was well rewarded for his efforts. A graduate of Stanford Law School, he had gone on to active duty as a captain in 1940, and in the process of evacuating the Japanese he would gain his colonel's eagles before he turned thirty-five. After Bendetsen's arrival, Gullion arranged with De Witt that the West Coast commander go out of normal channels and deal directly with the Provost Marshal on matters concerning aliens. The result of this seemingly routine bureaucratic shuffle was highly significant; as Stetson Conn has pointed out, the consequence of this arrangement was that "the responsible Army command headquarters in Washington [that is, Chief of Staff George C. Marshall and his immediate staff] had little to do during January and February 1942 with the plans and decisions for Japanese evacuation."

Telephone conversations and correspondence between De Witt's headquarters and the Provost Marshal General's office in late December and early January reveal the tremendous pressures that the soldiers were putting on the civilians. According to General Gullion, the Justice Department's representatives, James Rowe, Jr., and Edward J. Ennis, were apologetic about the slowness of the Justice Department, an apparent criticism of their chief, the Attorney General. At about the same time Gullion was complaining that "the Attorney General is not functioning" and threatened to have Secretary Stimson complain to the President. De Witt was, as usual, vacillating. Within the same week he told the Provost Marshal General's office that "it would be better if . . . this thing worked through the civil channels," but a few days later insisted that "I don't want to go after this thing piecemeal. I want to do it on a mass basis, all at the same time."

The arrival of Bendetsen at De Witt's San Francisco headquarters seemed to strengthen the West Coast commander's resolve. Before Bendetsen left Washington he had drafted an Executive Order transferring authority over aliens to the War Department, but the Provost Marshal General's office felt that since the Justice Department's representatives were so apologetic, it "wasn't quite fair" to take over without giving them a chance to come up to the Army's standards. Shortly after his arrival in San Francisco, Bendetsen drafted a memo that quickly became the guideline for De Witt's policy. It called for an immediate and complete registration of all alien enemies, who were to be photographed and fingerprinted. These records were to be kept in duplicate, one set to be kept in the community in which the alien resided, the other in a central office. The purpose was to set up what Bendetsen called a "Pass and Permit System." Doubtful that the Attorney General would agree to all this, Bendetsen's memo concluded with what had become the refrain of the Provost Marshal General's men: if Justice won't do it, the War Department must.

The next day, January 4, in a conference at his Presidio headquarters attended by Rowe, Bendetsen, and representatives of other federal departments and officials in local government, De Witt made some of his position clear, stressing, as he always did to civilians, what he called the military necessity.

> We are at war and this area—eight states—has been designated as a theater of operations. I have approximately 240,000 men at my disposal. . . . [There are] approximately 288,000 enemy aliens . . . which we have to watch. . . . I have little confidence that the enemy aliens are law-abiding or loyal in any sense of the word. Some of them yes; many, no. Particularly the Japanese. I have no confidence in their loyalty whatsoever. I am speaking now of the native born Japanese— 117,000—and 42,000 in California alone.

One result of this conference was that the Department of Justice agreed to go further than it had previously: enemy aliens were to be re-registered under its auspices, the FBI would conduct large-scale "spot" raids, something De Witt was particularly eager for, and, most significantly, a large number of restricted, or Category A, zones would be established around crucial military and defense installations on the Pacific Coast. Entry to these zones would be on a pass basis. Assistant Secretary of War John J. McCloy later described this program as "the best way to solve" the West Coast alien problem.

> . . . establish limited restricted areas around the airplane plants, the forts and other important military installations . . . We might call these military reservations in substance and exclude everyone— whites, yellows, blacks, greens—from that area and then license back into the area those whom we felt there was no danger to be expected from . . . Then we can cover the legal situation . . . in spite of the constitution. . . . You may, by that process, eliminate all the Japs [alien and citizen] but you might conceivably permit some to come back whom you are quite certain are free from any suspicion.

In addition to the Category A zones, there were to be Category B zones, consisting of the rest of the coastal area, in which enemy aliens and citizen Japanese would be allowed to live and work under rigidly prescribed conditions.

Although De Witt and the other Army people were constantly complaining about the slowness of the Justice Department, they quickly found that setting up these zones was easier said than done. De Witt did not forward his first recommendations for Category A areas to the War Department until January 21, more than two weeks after the San Francisco conference.

On January 16 Representative Leland Ford, the Santa Monica Republican who had opposed stern treatment for the Japanese on the floor of the House in mid-December, had changed his mind. Ford had received a number of telegrams and letters from California suggesting removal of Japanese from vital coastal areas—the earliest seems to have been a January 6 telegram from Mexican American movie star Leo Carillo—and by mid-January had come around to their point of view. He urged Secretary of War Henry L. Stimson to have "all Japanese, whether citizens or not, . . . placed in inland concentration camps." Arguing that native-born Japanese either were or were not loyal to the United States, Ford developed a simple test for loyalty: any Japanese willing to go to a concentration camp was a patriot; therefore it followed that unwillingness to go was a proof of disloyalty to the United States. Stimson and his staff mulled over this letter for ten days, and then replied (in a letter drafted by Bendetsen, now back from the Pacific Coast) giving the congressman a certain amount of encouragement. "The internment of over a hundred thousand people," Stimson wrote, "involves many complex considerations." The basic responsibility, Stimson pointed out, putting the finger on his Cabinet colleague Francis Biddle, has been delegated to the Attorney General. Nevertheless, the Secretary continued, "the Army is prepared to provide internment facilities in the interior to the extent necessary." Assuring Ford that the Army was aware of the dangers on the Pacific Coast, Stimson informed him that the military were submitting suggestions to the Justice Department, and advised him to present his views to the Attorney General.

The same day that Ford wrote Stimson, January 16, another federal department became involved in the fate of the West Coast Japanese. Agriculture Secretary Claude Wickard, chiefly concerned with increasing farm production— "Food Can Win the War" was his line—called a meeting in his office at which the War, Labor, Navy, Justice, and Treasury Departments were represented. He had become alarmed over investigative reports from his agents on the West Coast, who were concerned both about the fate of the Japanese and the threat to food production. Wickard had been informed that although violence against the Japanese farmers was an isolated phenomenon, greatly exaggerated by the press, nevertheless it was quite clear that the Japanese rural population was "terrified."

> They do not leave their homes at night, and will not, even in the daytime, enter certain areas populated by Filipinos. The police authorities are probably not sympathetic to the Japanese and are giving them only the minimum protection. Investigation of actual attacks on Japanese have been merely perfunctory and no prosecutions have been initiated.

The federal officials then concluded that the whole "propaganda campaign" against the Japanese was essentially a conspiracy designed to place Japanese-owned and leased farm lands into white hands; the real aim was to "eliminate Japanese competition." Wickard's West Coast representatives urged him to take positive steps both to maintain agricultural production and to preserve and protect the property and persons of the Japanese farmers.

Wickard's action was not exactly along the lines recommended by the men in the field. He did urge immediate federal action "so that the supply of vegetables for the military forces and the civilian population will not be needlessly curtailed." But Wickard also felt that the fears and suspicions of the general public—particularly the West Coast public—should be taken into account. He seemed to envision a sort of large agricultural reservation in the central valleys of California on which the Japanese could "carry on their normal farming operations" after being removed from "all strategic areas." In this way,

Wickard felt, the country could protect itself from "possible subversive Japanese activities," provide "limited protection to all Japanese whose conduct is above suspicion," and at the same time "avoid incidents that might provide an excuse for cruel treatment for our people in Japanese occupied territory." As for the agricultural lands in the coastal area which the Japanese had tilled, Wickard suggested that Mexicans might be brought in to replace them.

Also, by mid-January, the urban Japanese, if not terrorized as were their rural cousins, were feeling more and more hopeless and demoralized. An occasional militant like James Y. Sakamoto, a Japanese American Citizen League (JACL) official in Seattle, could indignantly protest against Representative Ford's evacuation proposal which went out on the Associated Press wire on January 21.

"This is our country," Sakamoto pointed out, "we were born and raised here . . . have made our homes here . . . [and] we are ready to give our lives, if necessary, to defend the United States." Ford's drastic measures, he insisted, were not in the best interests of the nation. But even a Nisei leader like Sakamoto felt compelled to admit that there was some kind of subversive danger from the older generation of Japanese. The Seattle Nisei, he stated, were "actively cooperating" with the authorities "to uncover all subversive activity in our midst" and, if necessary, he concluded, the Nisei were "ready to stand as protective custodians over our parent generation to guard against danger to the United States arising from their midst." One of the standard complaints quite properly raised by Americans in denouncing totalitarian regimes is that their police states turn children against their parents; it is rarely remarked that, in this instance at least, such too was the function of American democracy.

But for those really in charge, the agonizing distinctions between father and son, between alien and citizen, were essentially irrelevant. By mid-January, perhaps as a way of answering the points made by Representative Ford, Chief of Staff George C. Marshall ordered the Provost

Marshal General's office to prepare a memorandum on the West Coast Japanese situation. Bendetsen, the natural drafter for such a report, called General De Witt to ask what his attitude would be if "the Department of Justice still fails to do what we think they ought to do?" De Witt, who felt that things would work out, was nevertheless apprehensive about the continuing potentialities for sabotage and other subversive activities. "We know," he told Bendetsen, "that they are communicating at sea. . . ." De Witt actually knew no such thing, as no evidence existed of such communication, but he undoubtedly believed it. Then, in a classic leap in what Richard Hofstadter has styled the paranoid style, the West Coast commander insisted that "the fact that we have had [not even] sporadic attempts at sabotage clearly means that control is being exercised somewhere." Here then was the "heads I win, tails you lose" situation in which this one Army officer was able to place more than 100,000 innocent people. There had been no acts of sabotage, no real evidence of subversion, despite the voices that De Witt kept hearing at sea. Yet, according to this military logician, there was a conspiracy afoot not to commit sabotage until America dropped its guard. Ergo, evacuate them quickly before the conspiracy is put into operation.

The next day, January 25, the long-awaited report on the attack on Pearl Harbor made by the official committee of inquiry headed by Supreme Court Justice Owen J. Roberts was released to the press just in time for the Sunday morning papers, though it is dated two days earlier. In addition to its indictment of the general conditions of unreadiness in the Hawaiian command, the board reported, falsely, as it turned out, that the attack was greatly abetted by Japanese spies, some of whom were described as "persons having no open relations with the Japanese foreign service." It went on to criticize the laxity of counterespionage activity in the Islands, and implied that a too close adherence to the Constitution had seriously inhibited the work of the Federal Bureau of Investigation. The publication of the report was naturally a sensation; it

greatly stimulated already prevalent rumors that linked the disaster to wholly imaginary fifth column activities by resident Japanese. Perhaps the most popular was the yarn that University of California class rings had been found on the fingers of Japanese pilots shot down in the raid. Even more ridiculous was the story that the attacking pilots had been aided by arrows, pointing at Pearl Harbor, which had been hacked into the cane fields the night before by Japanese workers. The absurdity of this device—a large natural harbor containing dozens of war vessels, large and small, is highly visible from the air—seems to have occurred to few. The Roberts Report provided a field day for those who had long urged more repressive measures and a more effective secret police unfettered by constitutional restrictions. Congressmen like Martin Dies of Texas, then head of the House Committee on Un-American Activities, insisted, in and out of Congress, that if only people had listened to them, the disaster at Pearl Harbor could have been averted. More significantly, it gave an additional argument to those who were pressing for preventive detention and must have given pause to some who had been urging restraint.

On January 25 Secretary Stimson forwarded to Attorney General Biddle recommendations that General De Witt had made four days earlier, calling for total exclusion of enemy aliens from eighty-six Category A zones and close control of enemy aliens in eight Category B zones on a pass and permit system. As this proposal involved only aliens, the Justice Department quickly agreed and made the first public, official announcement of a mass evacuation on January 29, to be effective almost a month later, on February 24. This relatively modest proposal would have moved only about 7000 aliens in all, and fewer than 3000 of these would have been Japanese. At about the same time it announced the appointment of Tom C. Clark (who later became Attorney General under Truman and then an Associate Justice of the Supreme Court) as Coordinator of the Alien Enemy Control Program within the Western Defense Command. Clark flew to the West Coast the next day.

A few days before Stimson's recommendation to Biddle, the top echelons of military command, for the first time, began to become aware of the kinds of proposals that were emanating from De Witt's headquarters. General Mark W. Clark (then a brigadier on the General Staff and later a major commander in the European Theater) was instructed to prepare a memorandum for the President on the subject of "enemy aliens" in the Western Theater of Operations. The day after Stimson's letter to Biddle requesting the announcement of Category A and B areas, General Clark recommended that no memorandum be sent unless the Attorney General's action should "not be all that is desired." Clark's memorandum was read by Chief of Staff George C. Marshall, who noted on it "hold for me until Feb. 1." The top brass was satisfied with a very modest program, involving the forced removal, without detention, of a very few aliens. Clark's memorandum made no mention of citizens at all.

But if the top brass were satisfied, De Witt, Bendetsen, and Gullion were not. And neither were the leading public officials in California. On January 27 De Witt had a conference with Governor Culbert Olson and related to Washington, probably accurately:

> There's a tremendous volume of public opinion now developing against the Japanese of all classes, that is aliens and non-aliens, to get them off the land, and in Southern California around Los Angeles—in that area too—they want and they are bringing pressure on the government to move all the Japanese out. As a matter of fact, it's not being instigated or developed by people who are not thinking but by the best people of California. Since the publication of the Roberts Report they feel that they are living in the midst of a lot of enemies. They don't trust the Japanese, none of them.

Two days later, De Witt talked with Olson's Republican Attorney General Earl Warren. (De Witt thought his name was Warner.) The California Attorney General, who was then preparing to run for governor against Olson in November, was in thorough agreement with his

rival that the Japanese ought to be removed. This was not surprising. Warren was heir to a long anti-Japanese tradition in California politics and the protégé of U. S. Webb, a long-time Attorney General of California (1902–1939) and the author of the 1913 California Alien Land Act. Warren had been intimately associated with the most influential nativist group in the state, the Joint Immigration Committee, but shortly after he became Attorney General in 1939 he prudently arranged to have his name taken off the Committee's letterhead, although he continued to meet with them and receive copies of all documents and notices. Because of his later prominence, some have tried to make too much of Warren's very minor role in pressing for an evacuation. He did add his voice, but it was not yet a very strong one and it is almost inconceivable that, had any other politician held his post, essentially the same result would not have ensued.

On the very day of Biddle's formal announcement of the A and B zones, De Witt and Bendetsen worked out a more sweeping scheme, which Bendetsen would present to an informal but influential meeting of congressmen the next day. After a rambling conversation—De Witt was rarely either concise or precise—Bendetsen, always the lawyer in uniform, summed it up neatly:

Bendetsen: . . . As I understand it, from your viewpoint summarizing our conversation, you are of the opinion that there will have to be an evacuation on the west coast, not only of Japanese aliens but also of Japanese citizens, that is, you would include citizens along with alien enemies, and that if you had the power of requisition over all other Federal agencies, if you were requested you would be willing on the coast to accept responsibility for the alien enemy program.

De Witt: Yes, I would. And I think it's got to come sooner or later.

Bendetsen: Yes, sir, I do too, and I think the subject may be discussed tomorrow at the congressional delegation meeting.

De Witt: Well, you've got my viewpoint. You have it exactly.

The next day, January 30, the Japanese question was discussed in two important meetings, one in the White House and one on Capitol Hill. In the Cabinet meeting fears were expressed about the potentially dangerous situation in Hawaii. General Marshall penned a short memo to General Dwight D. Eisenhower, then a member of his staff, telling him that Stimson was concerned about "dangerous Japanese in Hawaii." Justice Roberts had told the War Secretary that "this point was regarded by his board as most serious." Several Cabinet members, but particularly Navy Secretary Frank Knox, were greatly disturbed at what they considered the laxity with which the Hawaiian Japanese were treated. As early as December 19, a previous Cabinet meeting had decided that all Japanese aliens in the Hawaiian Islands should be interned, and put on some island other than Oahu, where the major military installations were located.

At the other end of Pennsylvania Avenue, the focus was on the West Coast Japanese. Bendetsen, along with Rowe and Ennis from the Justice Department, attended a meeting of the Pacific Coast House delegation. (A joint meeting between the congressmen and the six senators was already scheduled for the following Monday.) The subject was what to do about the Japanese. Although Bendetsen officially reported to his superiors that he "was present as an observer," it is clear from his telephone conversations with General De Witt, both before and after the meeting, that he went as an advocate for the policies that he and his boss, General Gullion, had been proposing. Bendetsen called De Witt right after the meeting and told him what they both considered good news.

> They asked me to state what the position of the War Department was. I stated that I could not speak for the War Department. . . . They asked me for my own views and I stated that the position of the War Department was this: that we did not seek control of the program, that we preferred it be handled by the civil agencies. However, the War Department would be entirely willing, I believed, [to assume] the responsibility provided they accorded the War Department, and

the Secretary of War, and the military commander under him, full authority to require the services of any federal agency, and required that that federal agency was required to respond.

De Witt liked this. "That's good," he responded. "I'm glad to see that action is being taken . . . that someone in authority begins to see the problem." What he particularly liked was the delegation to himself of full power over civilian agencies. He had had problems with civilians already, particularly civilians in the Federal Bureau of Investigation whose West Coast agents, as we have seen, refused to respond positively to De Witt's imaginary alarms and excursions. As De Witt envisioned it, "Mr. [J. Edgar] Hoover himself as head of the F.B.I. would have to function under the War Department exactly as he is functioning under the Department of Justice."

Bendetsen, naturally, encouraged De Witt to grab for power. "Opinion is beginning to become irresistible, and I think that anything you recommend will be strongly backed up . . . by the public." De Witt and Bendetsen agreed that protestations of loyalty from the Nisei were utterly worthless. As De Witt put it:

> "There are going to be a lot of Japs who are going to say, 'Oh, yes, we want to go, we're good Americans and we want to do everything you say,' but those are the fellows I suspect the most."
>
> "Definitely," Bendetsen agreed. "The ones who are giving you only lip service are the ones always to be suspected."

The Congressional recommendations were immediately sent to Secretary Stimson by the senior California representative, Clarence Lea, a Santa Rosa Democrat first elected in 1916. Although they did not specifically call for removal of American citizens of Japanese ancestry, the delegation did ask that mass evacuation proceed "for all enemy aliens and their families," which would have included most of the Nisei. Later the same day, Provost Marshal General Gullion called De Witt to get some details straight. He was chiefly interested in how far De Witt proposed to move the evacuees. De Witt did not know, but he did point out to Gullion that within California "one group wanted to move them entirely out of the state," whereas another wanted "them to be left in California." After receiving these assurances from De Witt, Gullion began to wonder where the Army was going to put 100,000 people, and, perhaps for the first time, fleetingly realized that "a resettlement proposition is quite a proposition." The following day, Bendetsen, acting for his chief, had the Adjutant General dispatch telegrams to Corps Area commanders throughout the nation asking them about possible locations for large numbers of evacuees. Bendetsen suggested some possible sites: "agricultural experimental farms, prison farms, migratory labor camps, pauper farms, state parks, abandoned CCC camps, fairgrounds."

By the end of the month De Witt was able to make his position a little clearer. When Bendetsen asked whether or not he contemplated moving citizens, De Witt was emphatic.

> I include all Germans, all Italians who are alien enemies and all Japanese who are native-born or foreign born . . . evacuate enemy aliens in large groups at the earliest possible date . . . sentiment is being given too much importance. . . . I think we might as well eliminate talk of resettlement and handle these people as they should be handled . . . put them to work in internment camps. . . . I place the following priority. . . . First the Japanese, all prices [sic]. . . as the most dangerous . . . the next group, the Germans . . . the third group, the Italians. . . . We've waited too long as it is. Get them all out.

On Sunday, February 1, exactly eight weeks after Pearl Harbor, Assistant Secretary of War John J. McCloy, Gullion, and Bendetsen went to a meeting in Attorney General Francis Biddle's office. Biddle, who was seconded by James Rowe, Jr., Edward J. Ennis, and J. Edgar Hoover, had been concerned about the increasing pressure for mass evacuation, both from the military and from Congress, and about a crescendo of press criticism directed at his "pussyfooting," some of which was undoubtedly inspired by

the military. Biddle presented the Army men with a draft of what he hoped would be a joint press release. Its crucial sentences, which the military refused to agree too, were

> The Department of War and the Department of Justice are in agreement that the present military situation does not *at this time* [my emphasis] require the removal of American citizens of the Japanese race. The Secretary of War, General De Witt, the Attorney General, and the Director of the Federal Bureau of Investigation believe that appropriate steps have been and are being taken.

Biddle informed McCloy and the others that he was opposed to mass evacuation and that the Justice Department would have nothing to do with it. Rowe, remembering his early January visit to De Witt's headquarters, said that the West Coast commander had been opposed to mass evacuation then and wondered what had changed his mind. According to Gullion, Rowe, after some uncomplimentary remarks about Bendetsen, complained about the hysterical tone of the protests from the West Coast, argued that the western congressmen were "just nuts" on the subject, and maintained that there was "no evidence whatsoever of any reason for disturbing citizens." Then Biddle insisted that the Justice Department would have nothing at all to do with any interference with civilians. Gullion, admittedly "a little sore," said: "Well, listen, Mr. Biddle, do you mean to tell me if the Army, the men on the ground, determine it is a military necessity to move citizens, Jap citizens, that you won't help us?"

After Biddle restated his position, McCloy, again according to Gullion, said to the Attorney General: "You are putting a Wall Street lawyer in a helluva box, but if it is a question of the safety of the country [and] the Constitution. . . . Why the Constitution is just a scrap of paper to me."

As the meeting broke up, it was agreed that the Army people would check with the "man on the ground," General De Witt. As soon as they got back to their office, Gullion and Bendetsen made a joint phone call to the West Coast commander. They read him the proposed press release and, when the crucial sentences were reached, De Witt responded immediately: "I wouldn't agree to that." When asked specifically whom he did want to evacuate, the answer was "those people who are aliens and who are Japs of American citizenship." Then Gullion cautioned De Witt:

> Now I might suggest, General, Mr. McCloy was in the conference and he will probably be in any subsequent conference . . . he has not had all the benefit of conversations we have had with you—if you could give us something, not only in conversation but a written thing . . . stating your position.

De Witt agreed to do this. Then Bendetsen summarized the Justice Department's point of view:

> . . . they say . . . if we recommend and it is determined that there should be an evacuation of citizens, they said hands off, that is the Army's job . . . they agree with us that it is possible from . . . a legal standpoint. . . . They agree with us that [the licensing theory] could be . . . the legal basis for exclusion. . . . However we insist that we could also say that while all whites could remain, Japs can't, if we think there is military necessity for that. They apparently want us to join with them so that if anything happens they would be able to say "this was the military recommendation."

De Witt stated, "they are trying to cover themselves and lull the populace into a false sense of security."

When questioned about the details of the evacuation, De Witt blustered: "I haven't gone into the details of it, but Hell, it would be no job as far as the evacuation was concerned to move 100,000 people."

Actually, of course, it was a tremendous job, and even in such a relatively simple matter as the designation of Category A (prohibited to aliens) and Category B (restricted to aliens) zones, De Witt's staff had botched the job. Bendetsen had to call Western Defense Command headquarters and point out that although they had permitted limited use by enemy aliens of the San

Francisco–Oakland Bay Bridge (the bridge itself was Category B), all the approaches to the bridge were classified Category A, and thus prohibited.

Two days after the conference in Biddle's office both Assistant Secretary of War McCloy and General George C. Marshall made separate calls to De Witt. McCloy, and presumably Stimson and Marshall, had become concerned that De Witt and the Provost Marshal's office were committing the Army to a policy that the policy makers had not yet agreed to. McCloy was blunt:

> . . . the Army, that means you in the area, should not take the position, even in your conversations with political figures out there [favoring] a wholesale withdrawal of Japanese citizens and aliens from the Coast. . . . We have about reached the point where we feel that perhaps the best solution of it is to limit the withdrawal to certain prohibited areas.

Then, incredibly to anyone who has read the transcripts of his conversations with Gullion and Bendetsen (which were apparently not then available to McCloy), General De Witt denied that he had done any such thing: "Mr. Secretary . . . I haven't taken any position."

This, of course, was a palpable lie. What the cautious commander knew, however, was that he had never put any recommendations on paper, and that General Gullion was not likely to produce the telephone transcripts because they showed him and his subordinates pressing for a policy that had not yet been officially sanctioned.

General Marshall's call was terse and businesslike; the extract of it which he furnished to the Secretary of War is worth quoting in full, both because of what it does and what it does not say.

Marshall:	Is there anything you want to say now about anything else? Of course we're on an open phone.
De Witt:	We're on an open phone, but George, I can talk a little about this alien situation out here.
Marshall:	Yes.
De Witt:	I had a conference yesterday [February 2]

with the Governor [Olson] and several representatives of the Department of Justice [Tom C. Clark] and the Department of Agriculture with a view to removal of the Japanese from where they are now living to other portions of the state.

Marshall: Yes.

De Witt: And the Governor thinks it can be satisfactorily handled without having a resettlement somewhere in the central part of the United States and removing them entirely from the state of California. As you know the people out here are very much disturbed over these aliens, and want to get them out of the several communities.

Marshall: Yes.

De Witt: And I've agreed that if they can get them out of the areas limited as the combat zone, that it would be satisfactory. That would take them about 100 to 150 miles from the coast, and they're going to do that I think. They're working on it.

Marshall: Thank you.

De Witt: The Department [of Justice] has a representative out here and the Department of Agriculture, and they think the plan is an excellent one. I'm only concerned with getting them away from around these aircraft factories and other places.

Marshall: Yes. Anything else?

De Witt: No, that's all.

Marshall: Well, good luck.

That same day, February 3, there was an hour-and-a-half meeting between Stimson, McCloy, Gullion, and Bendetsen. (It is not clear whether the phone conversations between McCloy and De Witt and Marshall and De Witt preceded, followed, or straddled this meeting.) The next day Provost Marshal Gullion reported, somewhat dejectedly: " . . . the two Secretaries [Stimson and McCloy] are against any mass movement. They are pretty much against it. And they are also pretty much against interfering with citizens unless it can be done legally."

What had apparently happened was that De Witt, understanding from the McCloy and Marshall phone calls that the War Department

was, as he put it, "afraid that I was going to get into a political mess," and under great pressure from Governor Olson and Tom C. Clark to allow a limited, voluntary, compromise evacuation within California, trimmed his position accordingly. Clark, a strong and vigorous personality, seemed to have great influence over the general, who described him as "a fine fellow . . . the most cooperative and forceful man I have ever had to deal with. He attacks a problem better than any civilian I have ever had contact with."

Clark was clearly playing an independent role, and his position was somewhere between that of the Provost Marshal's office and that held by his own chief, the Attorney General. The plan that he sponsored or supported in the February 2 conference in Sacramento with Governor Olson and De Witt called for a conference between Governor Olson and leading Japanese Americans which would result in a voluntary resettlement in the central valleys of California where the Japanese could augment agricultural production. As De Witt explained the Clark-Olson plan to an unhappy Gullion:

> Well, I tell you, they are solving the problem here very satisfactorily. . . . I have agreed to accept any plan they propose to put those people, Japanese Americans and Japanese who are in Category A area in the Category B area on farms. . . . We haven't got anything to do with it except they are consulting me to see what areas I will let them go into. . . . Mr. Clark is very much in favor of it . . . the people are going to handle it locally through the Governor and they are going to move those people to arable and tillable land. They are going to keep them in the state. They don't want to bring in a lot of negroes and mexicans and let them take their place. . . . They just want to put them on the land out of the cities where they can raise vegetables like they are doing now.

The Provost Marshal General's men were disgusted with this turn of events. Not only were their plans being thwarted by the civilians who ran the Army—Stimson and McCloy, who were thinking in terms of creating "Jap-less" islands of security around a few key installations like the

Consolidated-Vultee aircraft plant in San Diego, the Lockheed and North American plants in Los Angeles, and the Boeing plant in Seattle—but even their former ally, General De Witt, the all-important man on the ground who alone could make authoritative statements about "military necessity," had now deserted their cause. As Colonel Archer Lerch, Gullion's deputy, put it:

> I think I detect a decided weakening on the part of Gen. De Witt, which I think is most unfortunate. . . . The idea suggested to Gen. De Witt in his conference with Gov. Olson, that a satisfactory solution must be reached through a conference between the Governor and leading Jap-Americans, savors too much of the spirit of Rotary and overlooks the necessary cold-bloodedness of war.

If pressure for evacuation within the Army seemed to be weakening, stronger and stronger outside forces were being brought into play. On February 2 and 3, in separate meetings, representatives and senators from all three Pacific Coast states agreed to coordinate their efforts. Serving as coordinator of these anti-Japanese efforts was Senator Hiram W. Johnson of California, who, in the mid-1920s, had masterminded a similar joint Congressional effort which brought about elimination of a Japanese quota in the Immigration Act of 1924. Johnson was actually more concerned about the defense of the West Coast—he feared a Japanese invasion—and complained bitterly to one of his political intimates that "the keenness of interest in the Japanese question far overshadowed the general proposition of our preparedness."

Back in California, Governor Culbert Olson went on the air on February 4; his speech could only have further inflamed public opinion. Disseminating false information that probably came from his conference two days previously with General De Witt and Tom Clark, he warned the already frightened people of California that

> it is known that there are Japanese residents of California who have sought to aid the Japanese enemy by way of communicating information, or

have shown indications of preparation for fifth column activities.

Loyal Japanese, he insisted, could best prove their loyalty by cooperating with whatever the authorities asked them to do. Then, in a vain attempt to reassure the public, he went on to say that everything would be all right. He told of his conference with De Witt and announced, without of course giving any specifics, that

> general plans [have been] agreed upon for the movement and placement of the entire adult Japanese population in California at productive and useful employment within the borders of our state, and under such surveillance and protection . . . as shall be deemed necessary.

The next day the mayor of Los Angeles, Fletcher Bowron, outdid the governor in attempting to arouse passions. After pointing out that the largest concentration of Japanese was in Los Angeles, he turned on the venom:

> Right here in our own city are those who may spring to action at an appointed time in accordance with a prearranged plan wherein each of our little Japanese friends will know his part in the event of any possible attempted invasion or air raid.

He then argued that not only Japanese aliens but citizens of Japanese descent, some of whom were "unquestionably . . . loyal," represented a threat to Los Angeles. Disloyal Nisei, he argued, would loudly proclaim their patriotism. "Of course they would try to fool us. They did in Honolulu and in Manila, and we may expect it in California." Bowron's answer, or course, was mass internment for all Japanese, citizens and aliens alike. From favorable references to Tom Clark, he seems to have been willing to go along with the De Witt–Olson–Clark plan of labor camps within California. Bowron also tried to take care of constitutional and ethical scruples:

> If we can send our own young men to war, it is nothing less than sickly sentimentality to say that

we will do injustice to American-born Japanese to merely put them in a place of safety so that they can do no harm. . . . We [in Los Angeles] are the ones who will be the human sacrifices if the perfidy that characterized the attack on Pearl Harbor is ever duplicated on the American continent.

In a follow-up statement the next day, Bowron put forth the interesting proposition that one of the major reasons that Japanese could not be trusted was that Californians had discriminated against them:

The Japanese, because they are unassimilable, because the aliens have been denied the right to own real property in California, because of [immigration discrimination against them], because of the marked differences in appearance between Japanese and Caucasians, because of the generations of training and philosophy that makes them Japanese and nothing else—all of these contributing factors set the Japanese apart as a race, regardless of how many generations have been born in America. Undoubtedly many of them intend to be loyal, but only each individual can know his own intentions, and when the final test comes, who can say but that "blood will tell"? We cannot run the risk of another Pearl Harbor episode in Southern California.

And, that same week, in Sacramento, Attorney General Earl Warren presided over a meeting of some one hundred and fifty law enforcement officers, mostly sheriffs and district attorneys. According to a federal official who attended the meeting:

In his opening remarks, Mr. Warren cautioned against hysteria but then proceeded to outline his remarks in such a fashion as to encourage hysterical thinking. . . . Mr. [Isidore] Dockweiler, Los Angeles District Attorney . . . , asserted that the United States Supreme Court had been packed with leftist and other extreme advocates of civil liberty and that it was time for the people of California to disregard the law, if necessary, to secure their protection. Mr. Dockweiler finally worked himself into such a state of hysteria that he was called to order by Mr. Warren. . . . The meeting loudly applauded the statement that the

people of California had no trust in the ability and willingness of the Federal Government to proceed against enemy aliens. One high official was heard to state that he favored shooting on sight all Japanese residents of the state.

Despite relative claim in the press until the end of January, a government intelligence agency (the civilian Office of Government Reports) informed Washington that "word of mouth discussions [continue] with a surprisingly large number of people expressing themselves as in favor of sending all Japanese to concentration camps." By the end of January, the press "flared up again" with demands growing "that positive action be taken by the Federal Government. This awakening of the press has increased the verbal discussions that never ceased." By early February the Los Angeles *Times,* never friendly to the Japanese Americans, as we have seen, could no longer find human terms to describe them. All Japanese Americans, the *Times* insisted editorially, were at least potentially enemies: "A viper is nonetheless a viper wherever the egg is hatched—so a Japanese-American, born of Japanese parents—grows up to be a Japanese, not an American."

Henry McLemore, the nationally syndicated columnist, put into words the extreme reaction against Attorney General Francis Biddle, whom Californians (probably with some prompting from the military and militant congressmen) had made the chief target of their ire. Biddle, McLemore reported, couldn't even win election as "third assistant dog catcher" in California. "Californians have the feeling," he explained, "that he is the one in charge of the Japanese menace, and that he is handling it with all the severity of Lord Fauntleroy."

With this kind of encouragement in the background, Provost Marshal Gullion and his associates continued to press for mass action against the West Coast Japanese despite the fact that the officers of General Headquarters, directly under Marshall, were now trying to moderate anti-Japanese sentiment among members of Congress. On February 4, an impressive array of military personnel attended the meeting of West Coast congressmen: Admiral Harold R. Stark, Chief of Naval Operations; Brigadier General Mark W. Clark of General Headquarters (who had become Marshall's "expert" on the West Coast Japanese, even though just hours before he was to appear at the meeting he had to ask Bendetsen, "Now what is this Nisei?"); Colonel Hoyt S. Vandenberg of the Army Air Corps; and Colonel Wilton B. Persons, Chief of the (Congressional) Liaison Branch. According to Colonel Persons' report, Senator Rufus Holman of Oregon was the chief spokesman, and in pressing for an evacuation, he stressed the point that the people on the West Coast were "alarmed and terrified as to their person, their employment, and their homes." Clark then gave the congressmen the first truly military appraisal of the situation that they had received. Summarizing General Headquarters' findings, he told them that they were "unduly alarmed" and speculated that, at worst, there might be a sporadic air raid or a commando attack or two, and that while an attack on Alaska "was not a fantastic idea," there was no likelihood of a real onslaught on the West Coast states.

The day after General Clark's moderate presentation, the Provost Marshal began to try to bring Assistant Secretary of War McCloy around to his point of view. On February 5 he wrote McCloy that although De Witt had changed his mind, he (Gullion) was still of the view that mass evacuation was necessary. The De Witt–Olson–Tom Clark idea of voluntary cooperation with Japanese American leaders, the Provost Marshal General denounced as "dangerous to rely upon. . . ." In a more detailed memo the following day (February 6) he warned McCloy of the possible grave consequences of inaction:

> If our production for war is seriously delayed by sabotage in the West Coastal states, we very possibly shall lose the war. . . . From reliable reports from military and other sources, the danger of Japanese inspired sabotage is great. . . . No halfway measures based upon considerations of economic disturbance, humanitarianism, or fear of

retaliation will suffice. Such measures will be "too little or too late."

This shrewd appeal—"too little and too late" was a journalistic slogan that all too accurately described the general tenor of anti-Axis military efforts to that date—was followed by a concrete program that had been drawn up by Gullion and Bendetsen, and that the Provost Marshal General formally recommended. Somewhat short of total evacuation, it still would have involved moving the vast majority of West Coast Japanese. The plan consisted of four steps, as follows:

> *Step 1.* Declare restricted areas from which all alien enemies are barred. [This had already been done by Biddle, although it would not go into effect until February 24.]
> *Step 2.* Internment east of the Sierra Nevadas of *all* Japanese aliens, accompanied by such citizen members of their families as may volunteer for internment. [Since a majority of the Nisei were minors this would have included most of the citizen generation.]
> *Step 3.* The pass and permit system for "military reservations." [This would result, according to Gullion, in excluding citizens of Japanese extraction, "without raising too many legal questions."]
> *Step 4.* Resettlement. [Neither Gullion nor anyone else, as we shall see, had worked this out in any detail. According to the Provost Marshal General, it was "merely an idea and not an essential part of the plan."]

By February 10, however, Gullion and Bendetsen, the latter now back on the West Coast to strengthen General De Witt's resolve, seemed to have convinced McCloy, somehow, that a mass evacuation was necessary, although Secretary Stimson still clung to the idea of creating islands around strategic locations, an idea that the Provost Marshal General's men were sure he had gotten from General Stilwell. Bendetsen insisted that safety "islands" would not prevent sabotage: "if they wanted to sabotage that area, they could set the outside area on fire. They could still cut water lines and power lines." According to Bendetsen he had been over that ground twice with McCloy, who seemed to agree, and who had told Bendetsen that he would call him back after he had had another talk with the Secretary.

The next day, February 11, 1942, was the real day of decision as far as the Japanese Americans were concerned. Sometime in the early afternoon, Secretary Stimson telephoned Franklin Roosevelt at the White House. Shortly after that call, McCloy phoned Bendetsen at the Presidio to tell him the good news. According to McCloy:

> . . . we talked to the President and the President, in substance, says go ahead and do anything you think necessary . . . if it involves citizens, we will take care of them too. He says there will probably be some repercussions, but it has got to be dictated by military necessity, but as he puts it, "Be as reasonable as you can."

McCloy went on to say that he thought the President would sign an executive order giving the Army the authority to evacuate. He also indicated there was at least some residual reluctance on the part of Secretary Stimson, who wanted to make a start in Los Angeles, concentrating on areas around the big bomber plants. McCloy indicated that he thought he could convince the Secretary that the limited plan was not practicable. In his conversation with McCloy, Bendetsen had talked about evacuating some 61,000 people, but in talking to Gullion about an hour later, he spoke of evacuating approximately 101,000 people.

By February 11 the Provost Marshal's men had the situation all their own way. Assistant Secretary McCloy, who had been "pretty much against" their view just a week before, had been converted, and through him, Secretary Stimson and the President, although the latter probably did not take too much persuading. Bendetsen was again in San Francisco, and helping General De Witt draft what the Western Defense commander called "the plan that Mr. McCloy wanted me to submit." Although, in retrospect, it seems clear that the struggle for mass evacuation was over by then, not all the participants knew it yet.

Among those in the dark were the staff at General Headquarters, particularly General Mark Clark who had been assigned to make the official military report on the advisability of mass evacuation. Early on February 12 he called De Witt, and when told that an evacuation, to include citizens of Japanese descent, was in the works, he expressed disbelief. His own official memorandum, completed at about that time, had reached opposite conclusions, and deserves quoting at length, because it alone represents official military thinking on the subject.

General Clark's report concluded:

> I cannot agree with the wisdom of such a mass exodus for the following reasons:
>
> (a) We will never have a perfect defense against sabotage except at the expense of other equally important efforts. The situation with regards to protecting establishments from sabotage is analogous to protecting them from air attack by antiaircraft and barrage balloons. We will never have enough of these means to fully protect these establishments. Why, then, should we make great sacrifices in other efforts in order to make them secure from sabotage?
>
> (b) We must weigh the advantages and disadvantages of such a wholesale solution to this problem. We must not permit our entire offensive efforts to be sabotaged in an effort to protect all establishments from ground sabotage.
>
> I recommend the following approach to this problem:
>
> (a) Ascertain and designate the critical installations to be protected in each area and list them according to their importance.
>
> (b) Make up our minds as to what means are available for such protection and apply that protection as far as it will go to the most critical objectives, leaving the ones of lesser importance for future consideration, or lesser protection.
>
> (c) Select the most critical ones to be protected and delimit the essential areas around them for their protection.
>
> (d) Eject all enemy aliens from those areas and permit entrance of others by pass only.
>
> (e) Only such installations as can be physically protected in that manner should be included in this category. For example, it is practicable to do

this in the case of the Boeing Plant, Bremerton Navy Yard and many other similar vital installations. In other words we are biting off a little at a time in the solution of the problem.

(*f*) Civilian police should be used to the maximum in effecting this protection.

(*g*) Federal Bureau of Investigation should be greatly augmented in counter-subversive activity.

(*h*) Raids should be used freely and frequently.

(*i*) Ring leaders and suspects should be interned liberally.

(*j*) This alien group should be made to understand through publicity that the first overt act on their part will bring a wave of countermeasures which will make the historical efforts of the vigilantes look puny in comparison.

It is estimated that to evacuate large numbers of this group will require one soldier to 4 or 5 aliens. This would require between 10,000 and 15,000 soldiers to guard the group during their internment, to say nothing of the continuing burden of protecting the installations. I feel that this problem must be attacked in a sensible manner. We must admit that we are taking some chances just as we take other chances in war. We must determine what are our really critical installations, give them thorough protection and leave the others to incidental means in the hope that we will not lose too many of them—and above all keep our eye on the ball—that is, the creating and training of an offensive army.

Here was truly "stern military necessity." The General Staff officer, who probably reflected Marshall's real view, would have moved very few Japanese, not because he was a defender of civil liberty, or even understood what the probabilities for sabotage really were, but because, it did not seem to him, on balance, that the "protection" which total evacuation would provide was worth its cost in military manpower and energy. But military views, as we have seen, were not the determinants of policy; political views were. The real architects of policy were the lawyers in uniform, Gullion and Bendetsen. Their most highly placed supporters, McCloy and Stimson, were two Republican, Wall Street lawyers.

Very late in the game, and often after the fact, a very few New Dealers tried to influence the President to take a more consistently democratic approach to the Japanese. On February 3 Archibald MacLeish, then Director of the Office of Facts and Figures, a predecessor of the Office of War Information, wrote one of Roosevelt's confidential secretaries suggesting that the President might want to try to hold down passions on the West Coast. His office, he said, was "trying to keep down the pressure out there." He enclosed, for the President, a statement of Woodrow Wilson's that he thought might be useful. During the other world war, Wilson had said, in a statement highly appropriate to the West Coast situation:

> . . . I can never accept any man as a champion of liberty either for ourselves or for the world who does not reverence and obey the laws of our beloved land, whose laws we ourselves have made. He adopted the standards of the enemies of his country, whom he affects to despise.

Getting no response from the White House, MacLeish tried the Army six days later. "Dear Jack," the libertarian poet wrote McCloy, "In my opinion great care should be taken not to reach a grave decision in the present situation on the representations of officials and pressure groups alone. The decision may have far-reaching effects."

MacLeish's efforts were, of course, fruitless. Much more influential was the authoritarian voice of America's chief pundit, Walter Lippmann. Writing from San Francisco in a column published on February 12, the usually detached observer who has so often been on the unpopular side of issues, was, in this instance, merely an extension of the mass West Coast mind. In an essay entitled "The Fifth Column on the Coast," Lippmann wrote:

> . . . the Pacific Coast is in imminent danger of a combined attack from within and without . . . . It is a fact that the Japanese navy has been reconnoitering the coast more or less continuously. . . . There is an assumption [in Washington] that a citizen may not be interfered with unless he has committed an overt act. . . . The Pacific Coast is

officially a combat zone: Some part of it may at any moment be a battlefield. And nobody ought to be on a battlefield who has no good reason for being there. There is plenty of room elsewhere for him to exercise his rights.

The pundit's thinkpiece drew a lot of notice. Westbrook Pegler, delighted at finding a respectable man urging what he had long urged, chortled:

Do you get what he says? This is a high-grade fellow with a heavy sense of responsibility. . . . The Japanese in California should be under armed guard to the last man and woman right now [even Pegler didn't like to talk about children]—and to hell with habeas corpus until the danger is over. . . . If it isn't true, we can take it out on Lippmann, but on his reputation I will bet it is all true.

In the War Department, Marshall sent a copy of Lippmann's column to Stimson, and Stimson sent it to McCoy, and it was undoubtedly read in the White House. It was read in the Justice Department too. Long-suffering Attorney General Francis Biddle, former law clerk to Justice Holmes, civil libertarian, and New Dealer, was finally stirred to respond by Lippmann's column. In his memoirs, published in 1962, deeply regretting the whole affair, Biddle wrote:

. . . if, instead of dealing almost exclusively with McCloy and Bendetsen, I had urged [Stimson] to resist the pressure of his subordinates, the result might have been different. But I was new to the Cabinet, and disinclined to insist on my view to an elder statesman whose wisdom and integrity I greatly respected.

What Biddle did not reveal, however, was that he himself had given Stimson a kind of green light. In a letter written on February 12, the Attorney General voiced his distaste for the proposed evacuation, particularly of citizens, but assured Stimson that

I have no doubt that the Army can legally, at any time, evacuate all persons in a specified territory

if such action is deemed essential from a military point of view. . . . No legal problem arises when Japanese citizens are evacuated, but American citizens of Japanese origin could not, in my opinion, be singled out of an area and evacuated with the other Japanese.

Then Biddle, Philadelphia lawyer that he was, told Stimson how he thought it could be done.

However, the result might be accomplished by evacuating all persons in the area and then licensing back those whom the military authorities thought were not objectionable from a military point of view.

Five days later, on February 17, Biddle addressed a memorandum to the President, a memorandum that was, in effect, a last-gasp effort to stop the mass evacuation that was being planned. Biddle apparently was unaware that Roosevelt had given Stimson and McCloy the go-ahead signal almost a week before. The Attorney General opened with a statement about the various West Coast pressure groups and Congressmen who were urging the evacuation. He then singled out Lippmann and Pegler, and argued that their concern about imminent invasion and sabotage was not borne out by the facts. Biddle then maintained, rather curiously, that "there [was] no dispute between the War, Navy and Justice Departments," and warned that the evacuation of 93,000 Japanese in California would disrupt agriculture, require thousands of troops, tie up transportation, and raise very difficult questions of resettlement. Then, in an apparent approval of evacuation, Biddle wrote, "If complete confusion and lowering of morale is to be avoided, so large a job must be done after careful planning."

Then, in a parting blast, directed specifically at Lippmann, Biddle attacked columnists acting as "Armchair Strategists and Junior G-Men," suggested that they were essentially "shouting FIRE! in a crowded theater," and warned that if . . . riots occurred, Lippmann and the others would bear a heavy responsibility.

But Biddle could have directed his attack much closer to home. Not only his Cabinet colleagues but some of his subordinates were doing more than shouting. Three days before the Attorney General's letter, Tom C. Clark, of his staff, assured a Los Angeles press conference that the federal government would soon evacuate over 200,000 enemy aliens and their children, including all American-born Japanese, from areas in California vital to national defense.

On February 13, the Pacific Coast Congressional delegation forwarded to the President a recommendation for evacuation that was fully in line with what Stimson and McCloy were proposing. They recommended, unanimously:

> the immediate evacuation of all persons of Japanese lineage and all others, aliens and citizens alike, whose presence shall be deemed dangerous or inimical to the defense of the United States from all strategic areas . . . such areas [should] be enlarged as expeditiously as possible until they shall encompass the entire strategic areas of the states of California, Oregon and Washington, and the Territory of Alaska.

Finally, on Thursday, February 19, 1942, a day that should live in infamy, Franklin D. Roosevelt signed an Executive Order that gave the Army, through the Secretary of War, the authority that Gullion and Bendetsen had sought so long. Using as justification a military necessity for "the successful prosecution of the war," the President empowered the military to designate "military areas" from which "any or all persons may be excluded" and to provide for such persons "transportation, food, shelter, and other accommodations as may be necessary . . . until other arrangements are made." The words Japanese or Japanese Americans never even appear in the order; but it was they, and they alone, who felt its sting.

The myth of military necessity was used as a fig leaf for a particular variant of American racism. On the very day that the President signed the order, a conference at General Headquarters heard and approved an opposite opinion. Army Intelligence reported, officially, that it believed "mass evacuation unnecessary." In this instance,

at least, the military mind was superior to the political: the soldiers who opposed the evacuation were right and the politicians who proposed it were wrong. But, why did it happen?

Two major theories have been propounded by scholars which ought to be examined. Almost as the evacuation was taking place, administrators and faculty at the University of California at Berkeley took steps to set up a scholarly study of the relocation in all its aspects. With generous foundation support and with the cooperation of some of the federal officials most responsible for the decision (for example, John J. McCloy), the "Japanese American Evacuation and Resettlement Study" was set up under the directorship of Dorothy Swaine Thomas, then a University of California Professor of Rural Sociology and a skilled demographer. Her staff included a broad spectrum of social scientists, but curiously did not include either professional historians or archivists. Professor Thomas' own volumes did not seek to determine responsibility for the evacuation, but two volumes that flowed out of the project did: Morton Grodzins, *Americans Betrayed* (Chicago, 1949) and Jacobus tenBroek, Edward N. Barnhart, and Floyd Matson, *Prejudice, War, and the Constitution* (Berkeley and Los Angeles, 1954). Grodzins felt that the major cause of the evacuation was the pressure exerted by special interest groups within California and on the Pacific Coast generally. The "western group," he wrote, "was successful in having a program molded to its own immediate advantage made national policy." Professors tenBroek, Barnhart, and Matson vigorously disputed the Grodzins thesis: for them, the responsibility was General De Witt's, and, they argued, his decision was based essentially on his "military estimate of the situation."

Five years later a professional historian, Stetson Conn, then a civilian historian for the Department of the Army and later the Army's Chief of Military History, published an authoritative account of what really happened, as far as the military was concerned. He found in the contemporary evidence "little support for the argument that military necessity required a mass evacuation" and pointed, accurately, to the machinations of Gullion and Bendetsen and their success in bending the civilian heads of the War Department to their will.

The question that remains to be answered is why the recommendation of Stimson and McCloy was accepted by the nation. Grodzins' pressure groups were, of course, important, but even more important than the peculiar racism of a region was the general racist character of American society. The decision to evacuate the Japanese was popular, not only in California and the West, but in the entire nation, although only on the West Coast was it a major issue in early 1942.

The leader of the nation, was, in the final analysis, responsible. It was Franklin Roosevelt who in one short telephone call passed the decision-making power to two men who had never been elected to any office, saying only, with the politician's charm and equivocation: "Be as reasonable as you can." Why did he agree? Probably for two reasons: in the first place, it was expedient; in the second place, Roosevelt himself harbored deeply felt anti-Japanese prejudices.

As to expediency, it is important to remember what the war news was like in early 1942. It was a very bad time for the military fortunes of the United States and its allies. The Japanese had landed on the island of Singapore on February 8, on New Britain on the 9th, and were advancing rapidly in Burma. Roosevelt was concerned, first of all with winning the war, and secondly with unity at home, so that he, unlike his former chief, Woodrow Wilson, could win the peace with the advice and consent of the Senate. He could read the Congressional signs well and knew that cracking down on the Japanese Americans would be popular both on the Hill and in the country generally. And the last thing he wanted was a rift with establishment Republicans like Stimson and McCloy; New Dealers like Biddle and MacLeish could be counted on not to rock the boat.

But, in addition, Franklin Roosevelt was himself convinced that Japanese, alien and citizen, were dangerous to American security. He, along with several members of his Cabinet and circle of advisers, persistently pushed for mass internment of the Hawaiian Japanese-Americans long after

the military had wisely rejected such a policy. And there was a kind of rationale for such a policy. If Japanese were a threat to security in California, where they represented fewer than 2 percent of the population, certainly in wartorn Hawaii, where they were more than a third of the population, they should have constituted a real menace. But it is one thing to incarcerate a tiny element of the population, as was done on the West Coast, and quite another to put away a sizable fraction of the whole. Apart from sheer size of the problem, relatively and absolutely, there was the question of the disruption that such a mass evacuation would cause in the local economy. Referring to Oahu alone, Lieutenant General Delos C. Emmons, the Army commander there, pointed out to the War Department in January 1942 that Japanese provided the bulk of the main island's skilled labor force and were indispensable unless replaced by an equivalent labor force from the mainland. In addition, the logistical problems of internment in the islands were so great that Emmons recommended that any evacuation and relocation be to the mainland.

At the Cabinet level, however, different views were held. On February 27, for example, Navy Secretary Knox, the most vocal Japanophobe in the Cabinet, suggested rounding up all the Japanese on Oahu and putting them under Army guard on the neighboring island of Molokai, better known as a leper colony. Stimson concurred as to the danger, but insisted that if they were to be moved they be sent to the states. (The shipping situation, for all practical purposes, made this impossible.) The President, according to Stimson, clearly favored Knox's plan. The President and his Navy Secretary continued to press for this policy well into 1942, but eventually were forestalled by a strongly worded joint recommendation to the contrary signed by both Chief of Staff Marshall and Chief of Naval Operations Admiral Ernest J. King. In other words, real rather than imaginary military necessity governed in Hawaii. Although Hawaii was the first real theater of war, fewer than 2000 of the territory's 150,000 Japanese were ever deprived of their liberty.

16

THE POLITICS OF SACRIFICE ON THE AMERICAN HOME FRONT IN WORLD WAR II

MARK H. LEFF

In 1941, the United States embarked on its largest military struggle since the Civil War. By the end of World War II, 16 million men and women had served in the armed forces and 405,000 had given their lives in defeating the Axis powers. On the home front, Americans donated blood; recycled paper and scrap metal; planted "victory gardens" to help feed the nation; limited their purchases through rationing; and invested their savings in government "Liberty Bonds." Reinforced by government propaganda that emphasized the need for national sacrifice, Americans at home were urged to feel a sense of shared sacrifice and commitment with the men and women who risked their lives serving in the European and Pacific theaters.

In most wars, however, the initial *rage militaire* is not universal and wears thin as the military struggle lengthens. In this essay, Mark H. Leff challenges what he calls "the mystique of home front sacrifice" by focusing on two case studies: President Franklin Delano Roosevelt's unsuccessful attempt to limit wage and salary increases during the war and the advertising industry's more successful effort to profit from the production of wartime propaganda. Looking at the political meaning of sacrifice during World War II and focusing on the ways in which wartime cooperation was achieved, he finds that the theme of sacrifice had distinctly political overtones. Who sacrificed and how much, and whether sacrifices were equally borne by all segments of society, became questions argued out and resolved by the political process. Americans on the home front made many personal sacrifices, to be sure, but Leff demonstrates that there were limits to what could be achieved even in wartime and that the entire idea of sacrifice, meant to bind the country together, could generate controversy and division.

"The Politics of Sacrifice on the American Home Front in World War II." Journal of **American History**, *77 (1991), pp. 1296–1318. Copyright © 1991 by the Organization of American Historians. Reprinted by permission of the* Journal of American History.

War is hell. But for millions of Americans on the booming home front, World War II was also a hell of a war. Both then and today, the mystique of home front sacrifice suffused visions of that wartime experience. The politics set in motion by a peculiar blend of profits and patriotism, of sacrifice amid unprecedented prosperity, gave a distinctive cast to American wartime life.

In subsequent American civic mythology, the public-spirited wartime community of World War II holds a cherished place. It is nostalgically recalled as *our* "finest hour," when Americans freely sacrificed selfish desires, did without, went all out, and "pulled together" in common purpose and spirit with "only one thing on their minds—winning the war." The allure of this golden age of home front sacrifice is not merely retrospective. During World War II, Americans gloried in the feeling that they were participating in a noble and successful cause by making "sacrifices." In common parlance sacrifice did not require the suffering of terrible loss. It instead comprehended a range of activities—running the gamut from donating waste paper to donating lives—in which narrow, immediate self-interest was subordinated to the needs of the war effort.

Despite, or even because of, its variegated usage, *sacrifice* decisively shaped the discourse of wartime politics. But polychromatic concepts can raise unsettling questions. Most Americans conceded that they had not made any "*real* sacrifices," a freighted expression largely reserved for our boys at the front. While it was more apparent in the war years than it is in retrospect that not everyone was going all out, the consecration of sacrifice inspired declarations of willingness to shoulder new burdens. Admittedly no specific additional sacrifice jumped readily to mind, but Americans in public opinion polls pledged their support—at least in principle—to an imposing list of wartime activities and restrictions, including wage and price freezes, no-strike pledges, rationing, and higher taxes. Amid these affirmations of unstinting patriotism, one contemporary commentator on wartime morale explained that the war had "subordinated or shelved" the precious "aims and values of individual citizens and special groups," as Americans "generally respond whole-heartedly to a major demand made of them when its essential necessity to the winning of the war is made clear."

The mystique of unconditional sacrifice, forged in the war itself and celebrated in collective memory, has not fared well as an interpretive guide to wartime politics and mobilization. Even at the time, staffers of American mobilization agencies commonly despaired of the difficulties of transforming "willingness into action" and cracking "the shell of public apathy," given "desultory, half-hearted" citizen involvement and "reluctance to forego the ordinary pleasures and comforts of 'life as usual.'" Americans, they noted, were often able to compartmentalize their advocacy of the principle of sacrifice, to excuse failures of civic responsibility by claiming that their sacrifices would not really have helped the war anyway, that someone else was receiving favored treatment, or that some blockheaded bureaucrat was bungling the whole thing. In the quest for alibis, standards of proof could be conveniently low. "Each of us," a top mobilization official conceded, "is likely to be slightly more eager to hold down the other fellow's prices, wages or profits, and to raise the other fellow's taxes. . . . Each of us will be looking for the moat in the other fellow's eye." President Franklin D. Roosevelt himself, despite warnings from pollsters that his "scolding approach" toward the shortcomings of American sacrifice might only impede cooperation, voiced his disgust at "the whining demands of selfish pressure groups who seek to feather their nests while young Americans are dying."

As recent historians who expand upon this indictment remind us, what Americans called sacrifice often involved limits on substantial gains rather than the horrific deprivations and destruction suffered by the citizens of other belligerents. Such reassessments can lead to a Manichaean dialogue as to whether Americans on the home front in World War II were saints or sinners—a singularly unpromising question in which assessments of virtue depend on the assessors' original inclinations and selectively applied standards.

More productive challenges await: not to gauge the extent of American cooperation in the war effort, but to examine how that cooperation was achieved, to clarify the principles by which policy makers decided that certain groups would have to give up something or forgo gains for the good of the whole, and to understand how the ubiquitous ethos of wartime sacrifice set the terms of wartime political discourse, shaping the public actions and manipulatory strategies of potentially affected groups.

What were the boundaries of sacrifice in a global war that disrupted customary patterns of limited government? What could be required and of whom? Sacrifice was clearly a subject for negotiation across a broad range of issues encompassing both public and private choices. In public forums—in the speeches and press conferences of political leaders, in the public opinion polls commissioned by government departments, in the internal correspondence of mobilization officials—concern centered on what might be termed the calculus of political obligation. This article examines the public choices made there, the politics.

The wartime recasting of political obligation touched many facets of American political life, but this article focuses on two case studies. The first treats a celebrated but surprisingly insubstantial and ultimately abortive effort: Franklin Roosevelt's executive order capping all wartime salaries. This startling assault on the ethos of boundless individual achievement demonstrates both the apparently open-ended possibility for renegotiating symbolic values (was the ethic of sacrifice powerful enough to neutralize the American Dream?) and, in its quick and crushing repeal by Congress, the actual limits to the wartime revaluation of values. Interwoven in the seeming challenge to traditional marketplace values was a politics in which the level of comparative sacrifice—the degree of sacrifice relative to other groups—became a standard of justice.

The second case study offers a marked contrast: the successful merchandising of sacrifice through the formation of the War Advertising Council to coordinate a vast private advertising campaign supporting wartime programs and propaganda themes. The unique and consequential American arrangement whereby privately donated advertising carried the brunt of the domestic propaganda effort not only shows the adaptability of the imagery of sacrifice; it also raises provocative questions about the interplay of political forces in the United States that allowed certain groups to domesticate and delimit the meaning of sacrifice—to define it in terms that reinforced the validity of their own political interests and claims. What ultimately stands out in the calculus of home front obligation in World War II is a political process in which claimed sacrifices and contributions could be parlayed into political advantage or into efforts to shift war burdens to others. That process, which I have labeled the politics of sacrifice, established a dynamic that mobilizers and interest groups alike took into account. Since the process stands out most clearly in a comparative framework, I conclude by considering the starkly different political context of sacrifice in Great Britain.

Though sounding radical by current standards, President Roosevelt's salary limitation proposal emerged in stages throughout 1942, rather prosaically, as part of a coordinated effort to control inflationary pressures. In April FDR announced that price stabilization could only be effective if pursued on all fronts; thus he supplemented proposals for across-the-board price ceilings, wage controls, and rationing with a proposed 100 percent "super-tax" that would draw off any "excess" income over $25,000 ($50,000 for families) once the federal income tax had been paid. This income limitation proposal garnered popular approval as "a symbol of the idea of equality of sacrifice," but editorialists soon buried it as a "Rooseveltian pleasantry." Just as deadly was the congressional response: utter dismissal—one contemporary comparison was to "a burp in church, something to be overlooked and forgotten as quickly as possible." But in October Roosevelt used a broadly phrased authorization for price stabilization that he had just forced through Congress as the pretext for an executive order clamping an after-tax limit of $25,000 (equivalent to $200,000 in 1990 dollars) on all salaries. The order did not apply to total incomes or profits, partly because no interpretation of existing law sanctioned such use of independent executive action.

From today's vantage point, one can easily predict the ferocious response from some quarters to this apparently daring initiative. Labeling it a product of communistic philosophy and class hatred, attackers called it an un-American assault on free enterprise that threatened the production necessary for an effective war effort. When the 1942 elections the next month buoyed the congressional conservative bloc with substantial Republican gains, the salary ceiling was doomed, despite FDR's efforts to save it. In March 1943 most House Democrats joined the Republicans to repeal it by attaching a rider to a veto-proof debt limit bill; the bill then passed the Senate by a 74-to-3 vote. Less than six months after FDR released his executive order and before it had really gone into effect, salary limitation had been beaten back.

Why did the administration open itself to damagingly reproachful defenses of private property and free enterprise? Did the logic of sacrifice extend so quickly to the core of capitalism? A number of less extreme answers come to mind. Scape-goating campaigns against the abuses of "economic royalists" had long been a staple of Rooseveltian politics. In part, they can be traced to the president's patrician distaste for ostentatious wealth. Before the war, lessons embedded in the political culture about profiteering "merchants of death"—the unresolved public resentment over issues of sacrifice in World War I—spurred Roosevelt to proclaim that the "burdens of possible war" should be equalized to prevent "war millionaires" from enriching themselves from the sufferings of others. Once World War II began, Roosevelt's acute awareness of the privileged position of the United States also made him indignant at what he saw as selfish bickering and maneuvering for partisan or monetary gain at home. His sense of equitable and active war participation as a paramount moral obligation also shaped such politically divergent Rooseveltian

lost causes as his national war service "labor draft" proposal and his veto of a loophole-ridden tax bill as "not for the needy but for the greedy."

This ideological component had a firm practical political base. In 1940 and 1941, Roosevelt repeatedly fretted that the economic concessions needed to entice businesses into war contracts could clash with the public's antiprofiteering sentiments. His fears were well founded. Despite the bad press and the congressional criticism that FDR's proposals received, commentaries on the $25,000 salary order commonly assumed that the public would be receptive to limiting incomes. Public opinion polls, including surveys solicited by the administration itself, bore out those assumptions, registering majorities of more than two to one—and well above that among farmers and industrial workers—for a $25,000 ceiling.

The salary limitation proposal had one other attraction: its potential victims were few and far between. The proposed ceiling applied to *after*-tax salaries. Given unprecedentedly high wartime tax rates, a salary earner needed to receive at least $67,200 (well over half a million in 1990 dollars) to fall under its provisions—a fate confined to roughly one in fifty thousand Americans. It is no wonder that one congressman was unsure if the salary order applied to any of his constituents. Roosevelt must have been aware of the advantages of his order's delimited impact in narrowing the potential base of opposition and in sidestepping any truly systemic challenge to economics as usual. In 1941, when batting around the idea of applying a 99 1/2 percent tax rate to income above $100,000, he jokingly dismissed doubts by asking, "Why not? None of us is ever going to make $100,000 a year. How many people report on that much income?"

So why bother? The salary order would have had no significant direct effect either in slowing inflation or in narrowing the budget deficit. The key lies in the order's symbolic value, in the messages it was intended to send, particularly to the labor movement. As Nelson Lichtenstein reports in *Labor's War at Home,* leaders of the Congress of Industrial Organizations (CIO) and CIO-affiliated United Automobile Workers (UAW) in 1942 urged a $25,000 income limit. In March 1942 CIO leaders capitulated to corporate and government demands to extend factory schedules and thus speed production by relinquishing a major union objective and achievement: "premium pay" for weekend and holiday work. To forestall a revolt and to show that its weekend pay concession should not be read as a sign that it had gone soft, the UAW executive board simultaneously publicized a broad "Victory through Equality of Sacrifice Program" that included a call for a $25,000 limit on incomes. The logic was clear: By prescribing "what other groups in the nation should give up to correspond to labor's sacrifice," UAW leaders sought to anticipate and quiet rank-and-file resentment about shouldering a disproportionate share of the war's burdens.

FDR's ill-fated plan to impose a "super-tax" on individual incomes above $25,000 represented a direct response to the challenge from labor. In accounting for the income limitation proposal, the undersecretary of the treasury explained that it "clarified the whole situation as far as labor was concerned in the Detroit area." The secretary of the treasury himself, referring to the antiprofiteering proposals of other mobilization officials, put it less kindly: "These stupid asses . . . in order to satisfy labor . . . want to go after the rich people."

The stupid asses had a point. Fighting a losing battle against inflation in the first three-quarters of 1942, they felt it necessary to clamp down hard on wage increases. One analyst after another recognized that wage earners could most readily be swayed, not by a simple appeal to patriotism, but by a politics of comparative sacrifice in which others too could be shown as "sacrificing," rather than gaining at the wage earners' expense.

War sharpens and reframes domestic internal conflict by disrupting customary standards of comparison. Peacetime inequalities are often taken for granted as "neutral" results of an impersonal market. But in wartime these same inequalities could rank—and rankle—as inequities, both because of a common code of modern wartime societies that delegitimized "profiteering" from a collective effort in which

many would give their lives, and because a planned wartime economy lends an element of purpose to every economic exchange, making it easy to blame inequities on conscious government decisions or on lobbyists' maneuverings. It is not coincidental that the term "relative deprivation" was coined during World War II, for war forges a sense of common aspirations and responsibilities. That sense broadens the range of others that individuals and groups consider in gauging their position and demanding equal treatment. As John Kenneth Galbraith recollected, "no feature of World War II or more recent mobilization experience has been more striking than the scrutiny which each of the several economic groups brings to bear upon what the others are getting."

The importance of this comparative framework did not escape the Roosevelt administration. As early as 1940, "labor trouble" was very much on the president's mind. It is "a damn sight simpler," he explained, "for all of us to appeal to [worker] patriotism if we say we are using exactly the same principle for the owners of industry as we are with the workers in industry." In a closed-door meeting with his Business Advisory Council, Roosevelt urged a measure of restraint: "I can hold labor to the present level if I can say to them, 'You [industry] won't profiteer.'" The Treasury Department highlighted the strategy, noting that "if we are to expect all classes of society, including laborers and farmers, to accept the sacrifices of the emergency period and not to press for every possible dollar of advantage, they must be convinced that sacrifices are being distributed according to ability and that no one is making unreasonably large profits."

Such statements betokened no special insight; they merely mirrored the conventional wisdom. In public speeches and internal memoranda, Roosevelt's advisers highlighted this notion of contingent sacrifice. Americans, they noted, not only worried that more might be asked of them than of other groups but also demanded proof that their sacrifices would further the war effort and not fatten someone else's wallet. Field reports by the Office of War Information isolated such concerns as the critical barrier to mobilization. "Each group," the reports explained, "thinks the others are using the emergency to win selfish advantage. At the same time, each fears that it, alone, will be slighted." Interest group leaders in particular, the reports warned, simultaneously insisted "that there must be no favored group" while expecting "special recognition for their own particular interests." Each jockeyed "for the best bargaining position" and "tended to claim unequal sacrifices" as an excuse for postponing "the program most directly affecting his group." The final report of FDR's interdepartmental anti-inflation committee in April 1942 thus endorsed an income ceiling as a way of "dramatizing the equality of sacrifice implicit in the proposed over-all [price stabilization] program." The chairman of the National War Labor Board, speaking of the difficulty of gaining labor acquiescence to concessions on overtime pay, graphically made this point:

> If you say to the boys, "Why don't you make a sacrifice for your country?" they are going to say, "That is fine. I am making a sacrifice for my country, but I am not going to make it to increase the profits of General Motors." Well, that profit thing comes in all the time.

Union leaders made the most of such resentments, publishing the salaries of industry executives and punctuating their speeches with reminders that "if labor is going to make these sacrifices . . . then labor certainly ought to ask the industrialists . . . to make a contribution somewhat equivalent to that contribution that you and I as workers must make." Polls of union members showed that they shared this quid-pro-quo "fair share" mentality. As one survey of industrial workers concluded, they "are willing to work overtime, they are willing to give up the right to strike, they are ready to make sacrifices for the war effort—*if* the other fellow will do the same, *if* the bosses don't reap new profits out of all proportion." But if the government did not respond to "labor's discontent with what it feels is an inequality of sacrifice," an Office of War Information report cautioned in the summer of

1942, union leaders would continue to experience "difficulty in managing the discontent of the rank and file," and "restlessness may be expected to increase and to manifest itself as small slowdowns, delays and walk-outs."

In a wartime economy, other groups besides labor manifested this mind-set. If the anti-inflation effort was to succeed, everyone had to shoulder new burdens: price ceilings for farmers, frustrating shortages and rationing for newly flush consumers, ballooning tax bills for the millions of Americans of average income previously exempt from income tax. Getting each group to accept its burden was no easy trick; Roosevelt's budget director despaired of what he termed "you-go-first" arguments in which "each group tries to shift the sacrifices to others." Roosevelt himself openly recognized the politics of sacrifice. In a fireside chat he explained that some were perfectly willing to endorse his entire anti-inflation package "except the one point which steps on their individual toes," while others "seem very willing to approve self-denial—on the part of their neighbors." The Roosevelt administration thus sought some sensational demonstration to show each group that it did not face economically painful restrictions alone. A proposed ceiling on incomes was an attractive vehicle for this drama: The absolute limit demonstrated the urgency of the situation, but the targeting of a relatively small number of rich salaried corporate executives (rather than, say, profits) personalized the demanded sacrifices without really threatening production. It was, as the president of the National Farmers' Union reminded Roosevelt, "most important as a symbol and token."

Many union leaders embraced the salary limitation effort as a way to take full advantage of the politics of comparative sacrifice. They challenged employers to "match us in corresponding sacrifices," explaining that workers were "sore" not "because they are being asked to sacrifice" but "because they are being asked to tighten their belts when other people are outgrowing theirs because they are too damned small to go around their fat bellies." The articles and cartoons in union newspapers and pamphlets were no less hard-hitting. "What sacrifices are these fat cats making?" the *American Federationist* asked. "Will someone tell us, please?" One much-reprinted CIO cartoon depicted a "War Sacrifice Blood Bank." Two donors—"labor" and "farmer"—were laid out on hospital beds with their arms hooked up to a container labeled "war sacrifice." In the foreground were two typical capitalist caricatures, complete with top hats and bulging vests upon which were emblazoned "corporate profits" and "big incomes." As they casually waved off the idea of donating their blood, a no-nonsense Dr. FDR, with tubing in hand, pointed insistently to the empty beds. The cartoon was entitled "Labor Should Help Put These Fellows to Bed."

On this battleground of corporate salaries and profits, defenders of business were at a clear psychological disadvantage. Some gave it their best shot, however. The *New York World-Telegram* pulled its readers' heartstrings by reporting that a utility holding company magnate and his wife "closed four of their five homes, put eight cars in storage, reduced the number of their household servants from twenty-five to ten, and shut off all except two floors of the thirty-room pink colonial brick mansion at 1130 Fifth Avenue where they now live." "Millionaires," it concluded, "are on the skids." The *Wall Street Journal* ran an eight-part series called "The New Poor" about the prospective plight of illustrious corporate executives under salary limitation. The forecast included dwindling country club memberships, imperiled vacation homes, and the forced dismissal of faithful servants. Other newspapers interviewed prominent society women about the prospective damage to their clothing budgets.

Such articles were deliciously easy to parody (the National Farmers' Union sponsored a satirical essay contest on "How to Live on $25,000 a Year") and only played to the strength of salary limitation supporters. The issue itself, after all, was fundamentally symbolic; not only was the ceiling pegged at a stratospheric level but the salary order also specifically exempted investment income, the most important source of great wealth. Yet, to win cooperation with mobilization efforts, precisely measured equivalency—real "equality of sacrifice"—was scarcely the point. Merely targeting luxurious "excess income" promised to soothe resentments over new burdens and perceived inequalities.

The politics of sacrifice moved the explosive issue of salary limitation from the periphery to the center of political debate. Yet Congress overwhelmingly bucked public opinion polls to repeal Roosevelt's salary order in March 1943. One might be tempted to attribute the administration defeat to shady manipulations by the media or special interests, to the limited political clout of a divided union movement, or to the unrepresentativeness of Congress or the American party system. But the explanation for repeal proves more revealing of the peculiar dynamics of wartime politics. Of undeniable importance was public exasperation with war restrictions, shortages, government bureaucrats, and other tangible barriers to the much-deferred "good life"—an irritation intense enough to overwhelm pledges of allegiance to ever greater sacrifice. After the 1942 elections, this attitude fueled the rise to dominance of a congressional conservative coalition that pounced on salary limitation to attack executive power grabbing and the remnants of New Deal reform. But, just as critically, the public image of business sacrifice itself was changing by 1943, giving way to a vision of United States war aims that eased the removal of salary ceilings. When combined with public resentment at wartime government regulations, the rise of business in popular estimation signaled a growing privatization of aspirations as the war progressed.

The second case study, the formation of the War Advertising Council, illuminates and verifies this transition. Under the tutelage of this private organization, corporate executive targets of the call to sacrifice broadcast that call. Defensive recitations of "the truth about advertising" and attacks on the New Deal gave way to the merchandising of the industry's contributions to the war effort. This new politics of sacrifice, adopted with uncanny precision at the moment of Pearl Harbor, proved a brilliant strategic political shift, as advertisers seized the rhetoric and imagery of sacrifice to validate prewar goals of self-defense and expansion.

On the face of it, the saga of the War Advertising Council seems quite straightforward. According to a radio propaganda show sponsored by Wrigley's chewing gum in November 1945, it was a standard story of selfless sacrifice in which businessmen wholeheartedly lent their skills and high reputation to the war:

Narrator: There was advertising . . . winning a big place for itself in our national life . . . and there was American business . . . just as anxious as you were to use all its resources, all its knowledge and experience, to help win the war. . . .

Businessman: Then, our place in the effort is clear. We, who have by our advertising earned the confidence of the public, can use that advertising as a vehicle for the messages of the government to the people.

Voices: Right. That's the way to do it . . .

Businessman: . . . Now—let's prove we are worthy of the faith and trust given us. I say—ask the government to tell us *what* is needed—and *we'll* take the information to the public—*in our own way!*

Narrator: That's the way it happened,—that's how the War Advertising Council came into being.

Truth has never been the essence of the propagandist's skill. In fact, in 1941 Madison Avenue was running scared. Mobilization demands were increasingly allowing manufacturers to sell effortlessly whatever they produced, removing the main rationale for big advertising budgets. Advertising representatives were also painfully aware that their reputation had taken a beating in the depression decade. They found it very easy to spook themselves by compiling long lists of "anti-advertising New Dealers" who had attacked "the accuracy and truth of advertising," branded it an economic waste, or warned of its contribution to inflation. A "pessimistic miasma" descended on much of Madison Avenue at the prospect of such figures making do-or-die decisions on the fate of the advertising industry. As the "growing alarm"

indicated, the war itself posed special threats that advertising was "going to be throttled." Foremost among advertisers' concerns was the question of whether the government would consider advertising a legitimate business expense for the purpose of corporate taxes and war contracts.

On the eve of Pearl Harbor, advertising trade journals overflowed with evidence of a siege mentality. One warned that "advertising is threatened today as it has never been threatened before." Another concluded that "all of American industry is in a mental state like anticipating a trip to the dentist." Sounding the alarm on the "imminence of the danger to all," the president of the Association of National Advertisers called on the industry to create "a united front." Rallying to the call that "the common cause . . . is survival" (the pervasive martial imagery is all the more striking since the issue was not the nation's survival, but the industry's), the nation's two main advertising associations summoned a joint meeting of 630 advertising, industry, and national media executives for November 1941. In that meeting one speaker after another stridently denounced the unfair and uninformed attacks on the industry. An influential group of "moderate" voices at this meeting talked of advertising's potential social contributions in wartime. Those moderates brought in government speakers who took the edge off the meeting's belligerent mood by announcing their desire to work with advertisers in furthering the war effort. Yet even the moderates compared advertisers to "His Majesty's Loyal Opposition" and urged a commitment to winning "the war of business" by defending free enterprise and preparing "the Case for Advertising."

The result of the conference was thus mixed. A consensus supported the need for advertisers to present a common front and to defend the advertising industry and the virtues of free enterprise. Yet some advertising executives feared that "a concerted campaign to preach the gospel of advertising at this juncture would fall on deaf or unfriendly ears" and advised that one essential part of the case for advertising was to "actively cooperate in solving national problems." In the immediate aftermath of the conference, its key organizers began to plan a new "governing group of the new Advertising Council or whatever it is to be called" to make that case.

Then came Pearl Harbor. From a strategic point of view, it was a godsend, a ticket to respectability for a battered industry. As one advertising executive later recalled, "we were losing" but "we were saved by the bell." "Now advertising has a chance to redeem itself . . . to prove it has a right to exist," a leading advertising journal rejoiced. The war provided "the greatest, the most golden, the most challenging opportunity ever to face American advertising," adman Walter Weir proclaimed. "If we make advertising fight today, we'll never again have to defend its place in our economy." Government mobilization officials encouraged advertisers' urge to serve, portraying it as a patriotic duty (though Donald Nelson, the "production czar," rather menacingly added in an off-the-record meeting that advertisers might ultimately need to choose between closing down—in which case "your future chances of coming back are something less than doubtful"—or converting to war-related advertising, which would preserve skills and facilities for postwar survival).

Thus the advertising industry formed what became the War Advertising Council, a private organization—currently called the Ad Council—that has dominated American "public service" advertising every since. Composed of volunteer representatives from major advertising agencies, large corporate advertisers, and the media, the War Advertising Council worked with such government agencies as the Office of War Information to plot out public information campaigns. By the war's end, it had supervised well over a hundred campaigns, using donated space to push war bonds, blood drives, food conservation, labor recruitment, and other mobilization demands deemed worthy of advertising support—with a value in space and personnel estimated (by the advertisers themselves, admittedly no strangers to exaggeration) at over a billion dollars.

One would be ill advised to dismiss those donations as mere artifice and calculation. In urging advertisers to sponsor public service messages under the company name or to inject official war messages into their product pitches, the War Advertising Council drew upon strong strains of patriotism. Win-the-war appeals anchored the council's efforts to gain industry cooperation.

Patriotic exhortation was of course paired with reminders that "public service advertising is shrewd business," since hook-ins to the war enhanced the ad and the firm's reputation. Shrewdness here was all-important; clients with no consumer goods to sell or no need to use advertising to sell their goods faced the "evaporation" of buyer and dealer loyalty. Advertising strategies shifted accordingly. One disarming solicitation for advertising explained, "Advertisers have but one thought in mind: post war 'prestige.' Not just 'prestige,'— but 'dollars and cents prestige,' the kind that will reflect itself in actual sales in the future." But how to maintain brand visibility without clashing with the wartime ethic of sacrifice and without creating unfulfillable product demands? Combining the company name with public service messages offered an answer, providing "momentum" to secure future sales and influence.

In the advertising industry, as in other sectors of American life, patriotism and public relations, sacrifice and self-interest intertwined. As one board member of the War Advertising Council put it, "Not for one minute is it necessary to say to an advertiser that he should try to win the war with his copy for the sake of winning the war." Instead, the advertiser was urged "that he can best serve his own selfish interests" by sensitivity to public demands, including the demand for information on how to contribute to the war. The War Advertising Council, its leaders repeatedly boasted, had combined "sensible idealism with the profit motive" in a show of social responsibility "which brings rich returns to those who act on it." That promise was an enduring part of the ethos of the Ad Council. As its president explained in 1947, "True, you are casting your bread upon the waters—but it will return to you well buttered."

With advertisers' show of sacrifice, the feared government barriers to the growth of the advertising industry crumbled. Soon advertisers could display an honor roll of glowing commendations, emanating from Franklin Roosevelt on down, of the inspiring example advertisers had set in their support of the war effort. In May 1942 the Treasury Department, reliant on the War Advertising Council and private donations to promote its war bond campaigns, granted Madison Avenue what one trade journal later called "advertising's Magna Charta under the tax laws." This ruling's generous interpretation of necessary and legitimate business expenses allowed full deduction of advertising costs from taxable incomes, even when firms had next to nothing to sell to ordinary consumers. With high excess-profits tax rates, that meant that the government was footing more than 80 percent of some companies' advertising bills. Especially at these cut rates, goodwill advertising directed toward post-war sales, the continued allegiance of distributors, employee productivity, or political aims became a highly attractive investment.

Thus the predicted wartime freefall in advertising budgets never took place. Even in the face of vanished consumer markets and supply shortages, expenditures on advertising—especially advertising in nationwide media—rose substantially, much to the relief of the industry itself. Favorable government decisions allowing certain advertising expenses to be factored into war contract prices and protecting advertised brands by including advertising in regulators' calculation of maximum allowable prices only bolstered the industry's assurance that the once-feared government was "friendly," "cooperative," and "helpful." "The important thing," admen exulted, "is that people *do* give us credit for doing the job." The council predicted all along that its show of sacrifice would reverse the antiprofiteering and anti-advertising attitudes that the industry had faced before Pearl Harbor, and the war indeed sharply raised the prestige of advertisers in particular and business in general.

One would be well advised to take with a grain of salt any inferences (some tastefully "planted"

by the council in the trade and general press) of War Advertising Council credit for this shift. Broader economic and political trends virtually assured a rise in business prestige even as the war began. As a leading pollster who contributed to the wartime boom in industrial public relations proclaimed in February 1942, the "dramatic theme" of the American production miracle "calls forth the deepest and sincerest praise the people can bestow," so that "out of this war should and can come renewed faith in individual enterprise and a lasting acclaim of the men who run the economic machine." Given the extent to which the government actually underwrote this expansion, this arrogation of credit to business (so much in contrast to the declining public stock of union leaders, whose involvement in strikes allowed them to be cast in that most unforgivable of roles: subverters of war production) was a tribute to careful and effective wartime public relations. John Blum and others have pointed to the administration's failure to forge a clear sense of the public purposes for which Americans were fighting and sacrificing, which left a vacuum that would be filled by private desires and conservative trends. Advertisers, newly legitimized by their "sacrifices" and empowered by their role as the chief messengers bearing government propaganda messages to the public, could thus press their own vision of war aims. As Frank Fox vividly demonstrates in his study of war advertisers, their depiction of American war aims in terms of an "American Way of Life" that encompassed abundant consumption and an absence of labor conflict reinforced other factors that cemented the postwar reputation and influence of "free enterprise" and the advertisers who celebrated it.

The contrast to the humiliation of Roosevelt's salary limitation order is instructive. In a political discourse in which the war came to be interpreted as a precursor of abundance and a protector of a harmonious "Americanism," associations with rampant New Deal reformism and a class-tinged rhetoric of conflict could be deadly. Charges that salary limitation undermined economic incentive or smacked of communism and a capitulation to unions thus hit home. Despite the popularity of Roosevelt's executive order, the ideological legitimacy of the arguments against it allowed congressmen to repeal a still-popular measure without fear of effective political retribution. The limited and discredited union influence on public opinion only clinched the defeat of salary limitation. Though workers might seek evidence that their sacrifices were matched by management's, their power to extract this equivalency through the political process had diminished.

The importance of this broader context for the politics of sacrifice emerges clearly in the contrast between American developments and home front politics in Great Britain. One could make a persuasive logical case that a country under fire, as Britain was then, does not have the luxury of the "you first" mentality or the political positioning associated with the politics of sacrifice in the United States. In terms of sacrifice, after all, Britons made a virtue out of a necessity, while Americans could afford to make a necessity out of a virtue. Though British casualties and disruptions of life as usual paled beside those of such combatants as the Soviet Union and Germany, the war's toll on Britain's home front—the Victory coffee made of ground acorns, the scarcity of everything from soap to saucepans, "the dull dismal drudgery" of everyday life, on top of the bombings that killed sixty-one thousand civilians, damaged one-third of the nation's homes, and forced mass evacuations of London—stands in emphatic contrast to American conditions. Throughout the war, many Britons defined their essential strength as a people by these mutual sacrifices; the mind-set was expressed in Prime Minister Winston S. Churchill's pronouncement that "I have nothing to offer but blood, toil, tears and sweat." The characteristic understatement and humor in British propaganda, which seemingly took for granted an indomitable British spirit of sacrifice amid menacing peril, differs markedly from the tone of American propaganda, full of bluster, high emotion, guilt over the greater sacrifices of soldiers, and other techniques appropriate to a country virtually compelled to fight the war "on imagination alone."

Given the lesser sense of urgency in the United States (which was geographically, economically, and even psychologically an ocean away from the battlefront), it is no wonder—the argument could continue—that Americans found political maneuvering room to manipulate images of sacrifice and to bargain over mobilization demands.

That line of reasoning is consistent, but it is wrong. A more careful comparison between Britain and the United States shatters the assumption that only the United States experienced political jockeying, while casting a revealing light on the contrasting balances of forces in the two countries. One fact critical to understanding the British home front is that Churchill felt compelled to make concessions to attach the minority Labour party—which, though few would have predicted its end-of-the-war landslide victory, was clearly on the rise—to his governing coalition. The implications of that situation for the politics of sacrifice were profound. Labour forces seized the initiative in the all-important battle that advertisers waged so well in the United States: sculpting the political agenda by defining the purposes for which people were sacrificing. While Americans fought for the "American way of life," the British spoke of a "people's war" for a postwar world offering expanded social programs, security, and equity.

A significant effect of the British "people's war" mentality is that the phrase "equality of sacrifice," which was at the core of arguments for salary limitation in the United States, cropped up more commonly in British debates, particularly in the speeches of the Labour party members. The effective use of comparative sacrifice themes emerges clearly in the debate in late May and June 1940 over the new coalition government's imposition of a 100 percent tax rate on corporate excess profits.

As a pure economic proposition, confiscatory tax rates make little sense, since they minimize incentive to produce while maximizing the temptation to avoid tax. But as with Roosevelt's salary ceiling proposal, the law's rationale was political, rather than financial. Early in the war, alarming reports recorded "a feeling among certain sections of the public that 'everything is not fair and equal and that therefore our sacrifices are not worth while'"; such sentiments placed a premium on dramatizing the equitable distribution of wartime burdens. Commenting ruefully on public sensitivity to what even he considered "unseemly" business profiteering, a leading Tory mobilization official worried that the public's willingness to "accept hardship," so essential to the successful prosecution of the war, would be undermined by the "social grievance" that "the only reason of it is to line the pockets of some individual." Fearing low worker morale, many warned of an "outburst of industrial unrest" if domestic problems were ignored. If people were compelled to "suffer these reductions in their standards of living, they must be convinced that they are doing it" with a goal of economic democracy that could justify their sacrifices.

These concerns reached a fever pitch in May 1940, on the eve of the Dunkirk evacuation. Recognizing the desperate need for Labour party help in reallocating labor to weapons production, the newly appointed prime minister Churchill had enlisted Ernest Bevin, Britain's top union leader, as his minister of labor. Bevin almost immediately received an unprecedented parliamentary authorization to direct workers to war employment. But he subordinated compulsion to a "grand design . . . to carry the assent of 'labour.'" The excess-profits tax fit neatly into this strategy. By seeming to confirm that "wealth as well as labour" was being placed "at the service of the nation," the levy on all profits in excess of 6 percent of capital was deemed "a most wholesome clearing of the air . . . to make labour throw itself heart and soul into the war effort." It thus facilitated a political "compromise": Labour party legitimization of sometimes unpalatable mobilization measures, paired with enhanced Labour influence in guiding mobilization and shaping home front goals.

The long-standing class consciousness of British workers posed a dual threat: the social and economic threat of a work force inclined to define its interest as separate from the government's and the focused political threat of the Labour party, which could vent workers' grievances. This challenge helps explain the British concern with social service schemes, such as the Beveridge report, that "in a sense, sanctified the nation's wartime sacrifices" by catering to aspirations for a postwar society in which a certain "equality of sacrifice" would continue. The "rhetoric of association between war sacrifice and peace-time reward" bolstered efforts to stave off class resentments and buck up public morale. Richard M. Titmuss went so far as to generalize from this British experience that the demands of mass cooperation, participation, and sacrifice in modern total wars necessitate social policy actions to reduce inequalities.

The pinched wartime and immediate postwar expansion of the American welfare state presents an obvious exception to this "Titmuss thesis," an exception that impels greater attention to differing levels of "sacrifice" and to the contrasting political contexts of British and American war aims. Yet these differences should not obscure intriguing parallels in the symbolic and strategic elements of the politics of sacrifice. These parallel strategic considerations emerge, for example, in the report of a Labour party M.P. and former coal miners' union president on a June 1940 miners' conference. The miners' representatives had pledged themselves to sacrifice for the war effort. But they demanded a 100 percent excess-profits tax as an essential counterpart to that commitment to assure that their efforts would not redound to the mineowners' profit. "In the interests of the nation we have asked the miners to give everything for the nation, and they will do so," he declared, "but if it goes out from this House that we are giving the mineowners more profits, that will undermine anything that we are doing."

The close correspondence to American arguments for income limitation is unmistakable. There is one telling distinction, however: Such arguments won in Britain and lost in the United States. Members of Parliament fell over themselves in endorsing the principle of taxing away all excess profits and of subordinating profits to patriotism. Amendments to soften the effects of the 100 percent rate through administrative adjustments and postwar credits were challenged and temporarily withdrawn, for fear of compromising the intended message of universal sacrifice. (The adjustments and credits were reinserted in succeeding laws while leaving the "principle" of a 100 percent rate intact—underlining the tax's symbolic function.) The results shocked some American conservatives. The financial editor of the *New York Sun* found it "difficult for many Americans to understand how Britain can expect anyone to make the tremendous extra productive effort required by war without some stimulus other than the vague one that it is necessary to save the country."

A similar difference in political context is apparent in British advertising. The British and American cases are not strictly comparable, partly because government restrictions and shortages of newsprint forced drastic cutbacks in advertising space in Britain. The government became Britain's largest advertiser, paying for its own ads; filtering government propaganda messages through private business sponsors seemed dubious indeed in the context of a "people's war" ("I shouldn't need to be told what I am fighting for . . . by a group of individuals who by so doing hope to line their pockets," one scandalized Briton observed in explaining why American advertising "would not succeed over here"). Much more than admen in the United States, British advertisers felt besieged. Their ranks depleted by the war's impact on this "most depressed of industries," British advertisers at times found themselves locked out of positions of government influence and reduced to the status of "social 'unfortunates'" for whom the mere mention of their occupation might "rais[e] a frown or arous[e] an exclamation of piteous surprise." Characterized as "vested interests" from a profit-obsessed "bad old world" and faced with pressure from Parliament and government offices to curb wasteful advertising, they looked longingly at the cozy relations with government secured by their prospering American counterparts. Feeling desperate, aggrieved, and unappreciated, British advertisers combined limited

efforts to gain goodwill through public service campaigns with a dogged commitment to "carry on" with ads that maintained trade names and protected postwar markets. Yet such efforts betrayed a defensive, even apologetic, mindset. Advertising that exploited associations with the war without serving a clear war information function might well be "open to criticism" as "a public scandal." The trade journal of the British gas industry, for example, conceded that "advertising which has no higher motive than to raise the prestige of the industry it serves certainly cannot justify its existence in time of war," since this would constitute an "unwarranted waste of money, labour, and raw materials, all treasonable offences."

American advertisers would have found such use of the term "treasonable" impolitic and unnecessary. They recognized the delicacy of the task of manipulating images of sacrifice and war contributions. They operated, however, in an environment where the "miracle" of production and promised consumption could take center stage, whereas in Britain the scene was set by special demands for coalitional concessions to Labour party forces and back-to-the-wall displays of solidarity to avert chaos and defeat. Hence, in the United States, the interest of the "free enterprise system" and the "American way of life" increasingly pushed aside demands for "equality of sacrifice" and a "people's war." American advertisers were in a better position to master the politics of sacrifice.

The mystique of home front sacrifice did indeed permeate American life and politics in World War II. But changes in the vocabulary of political obligation did not imply automatic or open-ended commitment to the exercise of civic responsibility. The central role of sacrifice in wartime political discourse might have threatened "free enterprise" values, as the push for "equality of sacrifice" through income limitation seemed to suggest. But in the struggle over the meaning of sacrifice, at least as judged from the foregoing case studies, ascendant political forces were positioned to curb its subversive potential and channel it in more established political directions, so that much of the political topography could survive in recognizable form. Sacrifice proved symbolically malleable. It could justify mobilization programs or policy positions, revitalize deep-rooted political and economic values, mask privileged status or shield it from political challenge, or project war aims that helped reshape the contours of American political culture. The long-term consequences of this manipulation of symbolic content were not negligible; the privatizing of the wartime propaganda apparatus and war aims through the advertising industry, for example, resonated in the postwar consumer culture long after the war's end.

Recognition of the politics of sacrifice penetrates the surface of American home front conflict. Further studies—both comparative and domestic in focus—are needed to trace the shifting and contested meanings of sacrifice over the course of the war and to pinpoint the specific appeals used to solicit citizen cooperation in such intrusive mobilization programs as rationing, the mass income tax, or wage and price freezes. Broader comprehension of the political meanings of home front sacrifice should sharpen the historical definition of the American sense of obligation to community and nation, and of the standards of equity required to activate that civic responsibility. But the course of American economic mobilization, and the allocation of its blessings and burdens, depended less on underlying conceptions of civic responsibility than on continuing negotiation and manipulation. On the home front as on the battlefront, victory came not only to the tactically sophisticated, but to those with power and vital positions that allowed them to determine the arena of conflict. In the home front war, the politics of sacrifice prevailed.

17

REBELS WITHOUT A CAUSE: TOWARDS AN UNDERSTANDING OF ANXIOUS YOUTH IN POSTWAR AMERICA

NILS KRISTIAN BOGEN

Almost every aspect of life in post–World War II America was touched by the geopolitical and ideological contest between the United States and the Soviet Union. Beginning during World War II, the Cold War entered the public domain with Winston Churchill's "Iron Curtain" speech of 1946. That speech, which warned Americans of the imminent threat that Soviet Communism posed to the "free world," joined with Harry Truman's Cold War policies to create an atmosphere of tension and misunderstanding in Soviet–American relations lasting until the present day.

It was from this atmosphere of profound distrust between the Soviet Union and the United States that the phenomenon known as "McCarthyism" rose to dominate American media, popular culture, and politics in the 1950s. McCarthy, a little-known senator from Wisconsin until his anti-Communist campaign placed him in the public spotlight, used the power of congressional inquiry to intimidate and harass political enemies and liberal intellectuals alike. Employing deceit, innuendo, falsification, and badgering, McCarthy fueled a climate of fear and paranoia throughout the country that made all but the most innocuous forms of collective activity appear potentially subversive and unpatriotic.

In this essay, Nils Kristian Bogen explores the impact of the Cold War and McCarthyism on the American youth culture of the 1950s. Bogen finds that unlike their predecessors of the 1930s, who looked beyond the hardships of the Depression to the prospect of community involvement and the defeat of fascism, post–World War II American youths were caught in a web of anxiety about their place in the postwar world and forced by the pressures of McCarthyism to retreat from potentially "subversive" public activities. Other writers have attributed the "conformity" of the postwar years to a mass desire to attain material prosperity. But Bogen argues that the anxiety brought about by the Cold War and McCarthyism were the true sources of the apolitical and consumption-oriented youth culture of the 1950s.

"Rebels Without a Cause: Towards an Understanding of Anxious Youth in Postwar America." Studies in Popular Culture, XII:2 (1989), pp. 1–19. *Reprinted by permission of* Studies in Popular Culture.

"We are people of this generation, bred in at least modest comfort, housed now in universities, looking uncomfortably to the world we inherit." These are the opening lines of *The Port Huron Statement,* authored by 59 young radicals at the Students for a Democratic Society's national convention in Port Huron, Michigan, June 11–15, 1962. The document was not only to become a manifesto for the New Left in the early sixties and thereby founding the basis for much of the mass student protest in the decade to come. Equally important, *The Port Huron Statement* also suggests a way to understand post–World War II youth culture in the late forties and fifties. In spite of widespread material comfort in the post-war era, the authors argue, society was penetrated by events "too troubling to dismiss." The image of American virtue seemed to them to tarnish, and "when the hypocrisy of American ideals was discovered, . . . [they] began to sense that what [they] had originally seen as the American Golden Age was actually the decline of an era." Looking back on the 1950s as an age of anxiety, the authors of *The Port Huron Statement* concluded that:

> America is without community impulse, . . . The apathy here is first, *subjective* [*sic*]—the felt powerlessness of ordinary people, the resignation before the enormity of events. But subjective apathy is encouraged by the *objective* [*sic*] American situation—the actual structural separation of people from power. The very isolation of the individual—from power and community and ability to aspire—means the rise of a democracy without publics.

The intensely felt anxiety and powerlessness, however, contradicts our understanding of the era. The authors of *The Port Huron Statement* obviously had in mind the interaction between culture and politics in the 1950s, a period in which the most powerful political movement was the rise of McCarthyism and anti-communism. Yet, while many historians of the era diligently record and deplore the excesses of McCarthy, they also assume that it had little effect on the

lives of ordinary people. For example, William O'Neill, in his book *Coming Apart: An Informal History of American Life in the Sixties,* actually claims that the anxiety of the fifties was just something felt by a cult of alienated artists and beats when observing that "materialism and conformity prevailed everywhere, it was said, though *few outside the intellectual community seemed to mind*" [emphasis added]. Eric Goldman, in one of the most widely read accounts of the era, expresses similar ideas when saying that "the intellectuals satirized and gloomed and warned, *and the general public did not listen*" [emphasis added].

A similar understanding prevails among intellectuals today observing the effect of McCarthyism on college campuses and among those who study youth. Some, such as Allan Bloom in his recent bestseller, *The Closing of the American Mind,* argue that McCarthyism in major universities "had no effect whatsoever on curriculum or appointments. The range of thought and speech that took place within them was unaffected . . . . Professors were not fired, and they taught what they pleased in their classrooms." Others, such as Helen Horowitz, in her thorough study of college life, observe that in the postwar years the campuses were very much dominated by World War II veterans. These men who came to campus under the G.I. Bill were different with regard to age, marital status, experience, and, most important of all, intention, and thus represented a "no-nonsense approach to higher education [that] gave little room for nonconformity." These men set the tone on campus in the postwar years, Horowitz proclaims, and "wealth and conservatism returned to campus." William Graebner sums up what has been the general understanding of youth culture when he argues that:

> despite anxieties, postwar youth remained remarkably and intensely optimistic. They were convinced that every problem had its solution and that progress—political, social, and personal—depended on what they thought and did.

Given this historical understanding of the period, there is no way we can comprehend *The Port Huron Statement*. Indeed, what seems to be the dominant popular perception of the 1950s is of it largely as being a safe and fun era. Assuming that the anxieties were basically an intellectual concern, no one has closely investigated what the implications of a cold war climate in American society were to youth. One reason why historians such as Horowitz and Graebner do not fully give us a satisfactory understanding of youth, is the *way* youth has been studied. What is called for is a more thorough look at the specific social and political setting of youth culture, providing an in-depth study of how these relations change over time. This study is a modest beginning towards that goal. It explores the institutional changes that took place in youth culture from the 1930s to the 1950s at two Minnesota high schools and at the University of Minnesota. This is not a random selection. Whereas most previous studies on youth have been based on primary sources such as student newspapers and yearbooks, this article's findings are based on a major social science study on student interests and degree of public involvement which was undertaken by the University of Minnesota in the early 1930s and again in the late 1940s.

The latter study took special care to include the same areas of inquiry that also were investigated in 1933. When the two were compared, the 1948 study concluded that there was a "general decrease in participation in both on- and off-campus activities. . . ." Although there was an increased amount of time and money spent on social activities oriented towards leisure in 1948 as compared to 1933, "many students were dissatisfied with the social life they had at the university." It is important to be aware that the study defined "social activity" as being "dating, dancing, and card playing." What we witness is that students were drawn towards a more privatized life. Thus as early as 1948 students began to withdraw from social life. The investigators also found that the students in 1948 were less happy about this aspect of life than the students of 1933

had been. Furthermore, the researchers seemed to look back on the 30s with a sort of nostalgia, suggesting that social life was more rewarding in the past. This essay will show that the finding of these two studies on student life are so different because of the political context of the time. In the depression years, the politics of reform engaged young people in a commitment to change their society through communal and public institutions at the high school and college level. But in the postwar period the politics of McCarthyism and the Cold War served to undercut the public life of students, leaving them with a sense of a privatized but alienated affluence.

In order to understand the changes in the experiences of adolescents that took place after World War II in Minnesota as well as the nation as a whole, we need to recognize the social basis for this culture. Historians have always recognized certain institutional forces at work in this process. The American commitment to education is one such key pillar, and the way schools interpret the society in which their students live is important for young people's understanding of it. Education in the U.S.A. has been viewed as a fundamental part of the democratization process and indeed as part of democracy itself.

After World War II education as a social basis for youth was also intimately linked with the rise of an unprecedented affluence. For the first time in history a whole generation had access to material prosperity. In spite of an uneven redistribution of this wealth, millions of Americans were far better off than they had ever before been and, although a considerable number of university students in the 1950s came from this upper income group, higher education was now also something that extended to lower-income groups.

This commitment to education and, eventually, the promise of an affluent society enabled more and more children to escape from the workforce. Not until the 1920s, as Paula Fass has shown in her extensive study of that era, do we see in schools and colleges a separate youth culture. Films, books, periodicals, radio, and, eventually, television were instrumental in that process. By the 1950s, adolescents were an important new consumer group representing a tremendous economic potential to the corporate industry. By 1959 it was estimated that American youth had somewhere between $9.5 and 11 billion to spend annually. A look at the time clearly shows these forces at work. Middle-class children participated in the "freewheelin' and easygoing" lifestyle of the fifties apparently without giving it any second thoughts at all. Seemingly, they had the leisure, the money, and a market more than ready to serve them.

Far from all aspects of this different youth culture were well received by the peers. The outflow of a series of sometimes bizarre activities in the 1950s, the so-called fads, serves as a good example. On May 19, 1952, the *Minnesota Daily* reported about the University of Minnisota's first panty raid in which a thousand sweatshirt clad male students raided the co-ed dormitories and sorority houses. University officials were deeply shocked and disturbed by the event and immediately expelled several of those thought to have been the leaders and put others on probation. Hostile reactions to incidents such as this one appeared even in the *Minnesota Daily*'s Monday magazine, the *Ivory Tower*. Under the title "The New Morality of the 'Cool Generation'," one commentator delivered a frontal attack on teenagers' behavior, morals, and attitudes, qualities which he claimed had deteriorated rapidly during recent years. And he concluded: "That something has happened there can be no doubt. What it is is hard to say. Maybe it is the times, the uncertainty."

In response to accusations such as this one, one student confessed that he had "seldom met any of Mr. Reeder's Cool Generation who was not a scared kid underneath his coolness." Another claimed that it appeared as if the students were exhibiting "the signs of the times; too much money, too much leisure, too much emphasis on 'growing up', too much fear of the future." At the same time an editor of a high school newspaper urged his fellow students "to rebuild the moral standards [they had] lost!"

Selfishness, irresponsibility, and loss of concern for their fellow men he stated as reasons for this loss. A Minneapolis high school principal began his address to the graduating class of 1951 in this way: "Today we face an age as drastic, as perilous and uncertain as any age this country of ours has faced since its founding. Our civilization, our democratic way of life is being threatened." A writer in a 1952 Minnesota high school yearbook was worried about the onset of the Atomic Age. The ending of the book provides a good example as it leaves off in the following philosophic mood: "What does the Atomic Age have in store for me? . . . Receiving this 1952 *Tiger* makes me wonder what our life's calling will be in this Era of the Atom." That this fear was something widespread is supported by the fact that as early as March 1946, 33% of those questioned in a public opinion poll nurtured fear of a possible "war with Russia, civil war [or] world war."

To adult observers of the time, this anxiety was a fundamentally new quality in youth culture, something radically different from the past. Constantly they asked what had happened. That it was something of great concern to students and university administration is shown by the fact that the administration at the University of Minnesota in 1948 undertook a major investigation of the student body to find out the interests and activities among the students and their participation in public life. A 10-per-cent stratified sample of the student body totaling 4629 students was given a four-page questionnaire concerning their participation in various activities, both on and off campus, organized and unorganized. The investigators carefully selected students who would be representative of the larger student body with respect to age, veteran status, marital status, race, and religion. In order to ensure a high return percentage, a stamped, addressed return envelope was enclosed, and four postal reminders were sent out at about one-week intervals in addition to telephone reminders by staff members from the office of the Dean of Students. The data were processed and analyzed by the Bureau of Institutional Research using modern IBM equipment.

Combined, these efforts ensured the high return percentage of 92.5, but equally important is its testimony of the weight the administration put on this investigation, which consequently allows us to put great store in the effort.

The report's main conclusion was that the students' interests and activities in the 1950s were very diverse, but there was a general decrease in participation in on-campus organized activities. What is also very clear is that the study shows that there was a sharp decline in public activity from 1933 to 1948, e.g., lecture attendance, participation in theater and concert activities, numerous civic organizations, and politics in general. Paralleling this decline was the increase in more privatized activities such as dating, dancing, and radio listening. In fact the 1948 study, when assessing the distribution of student activities, stated that "there is a very sharp decline in frequency beyond one activity, . . . the typical student does not participate in organized activities to any appreciable extent." Neither did it seem as if the students desired any further participation. "Apparently," the study assumed, "most of the students who were polled did not desire further participation in offcampus activities. Only 8 per cent of the men and 3 per cent of the women in the sample gave responses indicating a desire to join such organizations." The diversity of participation in organized campus activities showed a similar trend. As the study observed, "even the most popular, organized activity was participated in by fewer than one third of the total group." In leisure-time activities oriented towards public life the trend was also "toward a lower percentage of participation in [most] activities." Accompanying this decrease was a greater intensity of participation in those leisure activities students did participate in, a trend that seems to strengthen the tendency towards a more privatized form of activity among students in the late 1940s.

Somehow this finding seems quite startling. How could youth culture in the heart of the depression seem to provide a richer and more meaningful existence for young people than in the midst of affluence? This may at first glance seem strange when we know that the gross national product dropped from $104.4 billion in 1929 to $56.0 billion in 1933. During that same period of time personal income fell from $85.9 billion to $47.0 billion. In order to comprehend this apparent change, we need to investigate how youth related to social institutions in the pre–World War II culture. The 1933 study undertaken by the administration at the University of Minnesota does acknowledge that "the situation described probably represented the worst period of the depression from the standpoint of college students." Consequently many students experienced a shortage of means to participate as actively as they would have wished. The study observes, however, that "only two per cent stated that their non-participation was because of lack of interest in social activities." This finding is at variance with the tendency found in the 1948 study that in postwar society, students were basically dissatisfied with the quality of social life and tended to withdraw from it. In the 1930s, however,

> students [would] avail themselves of cultural opportunities if they [were] accessible and inexpensive. Excellent concerts [had] recently been offered on the campus at nominal prices and the free University gallery [had] been established. Each of these the students [had] attended in large numbers.

As Dean Williamson, the investigator in charge of the 1933 study, summed up when comparing the participation in group activities: "The general trend may be summarized in these terms: the 1933 students were more active than were the 1948 group."

Certainly one reason why students could look optimistically on the times was the fact that funding for education was not dramatically affected by the economic downturn. As D. Tyack and E. Hansot point out in an article on public schooling in the 1930s, it "remained remarkably stable in funding and continued its long-term trend of institutional expansion." Contrary to all other public institutions, education in the 1930s continued almost without interruption its general 20th century trend of expansion, and if we look at the numbers of high school graduates, we see a steady increase throughout the thirties. We also see in the 1930s a more vibrant communal and social life among students. Commenting on the magnitude of clubs and organizations, the Assistant Principal at a Minnesota high school says in a 1930 yearbook: "Through the sponsorship of the social life of the school, each student is given an opportunity to enjoy and cultivate the social graces necessary to the 'worthy use of leisure'." That same yearbook is a remarkable example of the gay and happy tone that had been so characteristic of the previous decade of prosperity: Pictures, fancy collages, and "jazzy" letters are merged to produce an optimistic entity. This positive air endured for a few more years, during which students had both the time and energy to put a lot of work into their yearbooks.

Tensions between youth and adults, as in the 20s and 50s, did of course exist. Moviegoing may serve as one such example of what could cause controversy in high schools. Amidst this timeless generational conflict, however, students seemed surprisingly estranged from the fact that America was in the midst of a depression. At high schools remarkable efforts were put into all kinds of extracurricular activities such as theater plays, Homecoming, Ice Carnivals, and Senior and Junior proms. One high school principal optimistically claimed in 1931 that "the future is before us" and "soon it will be sunlight." This "new freedom" is reflected on college campuses and in popular culture. One example was the increase in what by the 1960s Americans would call "lifestyle" ads in college newspapers during this period of time. In the *Minnesota Daily*, this could be seen in the sharp increase in use of ads on clothes, cigarettes, and leisure activities, and that weekly columns, such as *Minnesota Daily*'s "The Clothes Line" (on women's clothes), started to appear.

The media also played an important role in young people's lives as well as in their parents'. High school students formed radio clubs. The ad space spent on "radio shows" in college newspapers was formidable; one typical example would be Robert Burns' Panatela Program on WCCO radio station titled: "For Young Men . . . and Men with Young Ideas." Similarly, if we threw a glance at a copy of the *Minnesota Daily* one day, we might see the "Socially Speaking" column announcing that "pledging . . . Open Houses . . . and Romances Animate Social Life."

Yet, unlike the 1950s, this youth culture coexisted with the political and civic realities of the time. By the mid-thirties a distinct politicization was taking place, and it did not only focus on the problems caused by the Depression. Although the importance of a good education in order to "succeed" in a society suffering from a shortage of jobs and stiff competition was stressed, there is also a concern towards the larger questions of keeping peace in the world and what role America should play in that process. The new European situation that was emerging in the mid-thirties raised a serious concern among many American students. In October 1930 the *Minnesota Daily* briefly mentioned that "[a] Fascist leader had written a book called *My Fight* in which he foresees his Fatherland playing the part of world conqueror." The newspaper offered strong criticism of the ideas expressed in the book. However, not until the mid-thirties did the issue again resurface. In late 1934 the same newspaper reported that an antifascist rally had been held at the University of Minnesota. Indeed, from that time on antiwar protest seemed to have been a concern among students. In early 1935 more than 100 colleges throughout the country voted on a set of identical questions concerning war and peace and what stand America should take in relation to the increasing threat of war in Europe.

Another significant example of students' involvement in Minnesota in the mid-thirties was whether or not to take the Oxford pledge. It was hoped then that the number taking the pledge would disclose how much support the pacifist idea had among college youth. Yet this was not just rhetoric. In fact, it linked students to the larger public world of politics carried by adults. The peace "strikes," a characteristic of the politicized campus in the 30s, are a good example.

April 27, 1938, was proclaimed official "Student Peace Day" by Minnesota Governor Elmer A. Benson, and the campus newspaper reported that more than 40 organizations on campus would back that year's strike against governments of the world making plans for war. The increased interest for world affairs among students can also be seen by the fact that the university newspaper initiated a large front page column titled "Late News Flashes," which contained news from the international scene. This also was something that extended to high schools. As one commentator put it, youth programs in the thirties, such as the Civilian Conservation Corps (CCC) and National Youth Administration (NYA):

> provided opportunities toward which young people could direct their energies and make some contribution to society. The mid-thirties saw college and high school kids . . . demand control over school activities. They joined organizations to protest war, poverty, and school policy. On April 13, 1934, twenty-five thousand participated in a national student strike against war. Two years later, three hundred and fifty thousand college students followed suit and joined a walkout.

Editorials in high school papers commented on the threat of war in Europe and one newspaper saw the American society endangered by the same fascism and totalitarianism that threatened Europe. The editor urged American youth to distance themselves from those already under "the Fascist, Nazi, and Communistic symbols."

After the U.S.A. entered World War II, the political activity intensified. In 1943 a Minneapolis high school named their yearbook of that year *World Democracy* and dedicated it to the "People's March of the United Nations and to South High School's contribution to the War Effort." The whole book reflected a serious devotion on the students' behalf to make their contribution to the war effort. All clubs and organizations at the school centered their activities around the war. On could find headings such as: "Blue Triangle Organization Centers All Activities Around War, School Projects" and "Christian Fellowship Club Offers Daily Prayer

for Success of the United Nations." The presentation of faculty members was headed "Officers—'On the March'" and the graduate students were listed as "Soldiers—'On the March'."

At this point it is also possible to get perspective on the two studies of student attitudes. The 1933 study and our findings in student newspapers and yearbooks of the 1930s and early 1940s show us that students were involved in and concerned with what was going on in the world and their own lives and showed a willingness to try to do something about it. They lived in a world filled with just as much danger and anxiety as anything to be found in the 1950s. Yet, as the study of students in the 1950s showed, after the war students no longer were in control of their own lives, and their energies and anxieties were merely free-floating without focus or intent.

In 1953 the *Minnesota Daily* editor rhetorically asked: "Why have we been classified as the 'silent generation'?" In his answer, the editor pointed out that "our beliefs and principles are only notions—habits that we have been told are good. And we are silent because the foundations for our beliefs are shoddy and we haven't learned or don't take the time to dig any deeper." He calls for the educational institutions to assume responsibility when he says that it is "time our educators took this talk about the 'silent generation' to heart, especially at the high school and junior college level. Our first job is to learn to think and reason intelligently for ourselves."

Similarly, in an article submitted to the *Minnesota Daily* the same year, the author expressed his concern about the collapse of idealism when he claimed that the students were left in an intellectual void which lacked "an anchor of concrete values," and that students tried to fill this void with a middle-of-the-road decency. And he went on to state what we have been taught to see as only an intellectual concern of the 1950s when he remarks that students:

> face the world more realistically and less hopefully than their predecessors. . . . Students know the truth of the cliché that there will come a time when the world will be theirs to cope with. They

know this, but, *unlike younger generations before them,* they are not particularly anxious for that time to come [emphasis added]. They have no panaceas up their sleeve, which might explain why "they are nowhere near the rostrum." The mood is one of quiet pessimism, tempered perhaps, by a faith in their capacity to fill the void. . . . Meanwhile, [the student] attempts to live out his college days as if nothing is wrong out there. He dates, crams before tests, chews gum, smokes (too much, probably), drinks a bit, boos the referee and awaits his degree—and he listens in relative silence, while an older, careworn and draftproof generation continues to speculate on what the young folks are coming to.

What was it that caused this change? It was a question asked by investigators in school administrations at the time, but they had no explanation for this; they only observed the change taking place. However, when one looks at student newspapers, one explanation for the difference between the two eras lies in the realm of politics, namely the impact of McCarthyism. On numerous occasions, college newspapers warned students against dangerous ideas, the willingness to scrap freedoms when they apply to "undesirable" minorities, and the willingness to insist that students be "forced" at college level into an "acceptable" mode. In early April 1953 the *Minnesota Daily* ran a student poll about communist activities on campus. As many as 91.4 per cent of the student body reported that they did not know of any communist activities at the University of Minnesota and looked upon such accusations as unfounded. Yet in the same year E.G. Williamson published his study, the *Minnesota Daily* reported that "Redscare" was infiltrating campus, and numerous organizations, which in one way or another represented minorities or opinions that were not "mainstream," faded away out of fear of being persecuted. People were afraid to be seen in the wrong company.

The students' concern was real. A look into the directories of student organizations during these years shows that the *Minnesota Daily*'s suspicions were correct. In 1949–50 fourteen organizations were listed under "Political and Social

Action" organizations, and all were active. In 1951 two pacifist and peace clubs, "Student Fellowship of Reconciliation" and "United World Federalist," disappeared. The year after they were followed by the "Marxian Socialist Club." In 1953 NAACP and the "League for Democratic Socialism" faded away. In 1954 two student government organizations, "All-Campus Party" and "All-Residence Party," vanished together with "Young Progressives of America." What is significant here is that not only did the redscare appear to strip the campus of organizations with socialist or communist sympathies, it also forced many middle-of-the-road organizations off the university. Few others than mainstream clubs such as the "University Republican Club" and "Young Democratic Farmer Labor Club" survived the McCarthy era. The 1953–54 directory listed as many as seventeen organizations, but reported six to be "not active." For the next academic year, 1954–55, the number had decreased to ten. These findings suggest that McCarthyism had far-reaching effects for college students. Not only did it discourage public activity of students there, but it heightened the drive towards seeking fulfillment in the private realm.

Given this climate, many college students also observed that they were not allowed to participate in the decisionmaking of the university. There are strong indications that students in the 1930s to a much greater extent had participated in the formulation of university policies. A leaflet prepared by The University of Minnesota News Service in the mid-thirties pointed out that "students participate in forming and carrying out campus policies" and it specifically mentioned the *All-University Council* whose purpose was "to supervise and coordinate all student activities; to stimulate intelligent thinking upon college problems; to encourage closer cooperation between students and university authorities, and to represent the entire student body in matters affecting students interest." The lack of such opportunities in the postwar era seemed to be the essence of the critique of the university role in the 1950s raised by then Assistant Professor Mulford Q. Sibley at the Dept. of Pol. Science.

He said, in 1959, that he did not believe the university's role as "in loco parentis" had been healthy. The paternalistic tradition of university should be broken down and the students given more responsibility through student government. The Big Brother tactics would only create apathy and conformity.

Furthermore, there were side effects. Student newspapers focused on three main problems among the young that did not exist in the 1930s. Thus, one high school newspaper reported on teen age drinking as a "dangerous problem among high school students." A little later the same year, the same newspaper refers to dropouts as a problem: "Boredom, inability to cooperate, laziness, and poor attitudes in general— these are the real reasons for the disturbing rate of high school drop outs." A third area of major concern focused on juvenile delinquency. The steady increase in crimes among the young since 1941 received great public attention during the fifties also through mass media and popular culture. For example, more than sixty films were produced with juvenile delinquency as their topic, "Rebel Without a Cause" (1955) being perhaps the most famous one.

Juvenile delinquency was also an issue in Minnesota high school newspapers. Under the heading "Who Makes a Delinquent?" one newspaper stressed every youth's option not to become a juvenile delinquent. Only "the young person himself can choose what kind of a person he will be. . . . Those who become delinquent can only blame themselves." Another newspaper protested the tremendous publicity juvenile delinquency received and claimed that it did not tell the true story about the American teenager since only 5% of the total number of teenagers were delinquents.

One response from high school administrations was the introduction of "dress codes" to try to cope with some of these problems, a step which reflected the seriousness these changes in youth culture were met with by the authorities. The code at one Minnesota high school explicitly stated that the boys were required "to wear belts, button their shirts and refrain from wearing an Elvis Presley style haircut." The idea was that if the students dressed properly, they would also behave well. The school reported that there had been an improvement in dressing habits. With regard to behavior, a slight improvement had been noticed, but "such changes will come gradually." Another Minnesota high school newspaper reported on a "Teen Code" that had been drawn up through cooperation between the Youth Conservation Commission and the Governor's Advisory Council on Children and Youth. This Code was actually mailed to every PTA president, school superintendent, and student council president throughout Minnesota. That the dress code explicitly forbade an "Elvis Presley haircut" was hardly a surprise. This controversial singer rapidly became the personification of not only the immoral rock'n'roll phenomenon, but, more important, also the symbol of a whole generation led astray. The *Minnesota Daily* editor in 1956, contrary to many adults, did not believe that Elvis' "bumps and grinds" would lower the morale. That would be to put too little faith in the youth. "Presley," he concluded, "will not be a very enduring phenomenon. But rock and roll may last a little longer."

In the wake of young people's experience after World War II, it should be clear that what the authors of *The Port Huron Statement* saw in 1962 was not something that occurred in a vacuum. In the mid-thirties, large numbers of young people had felt responsibility when fascism was on the rise in the world and actively engaged to fight it. In spite of the hardships of the 1930s, American society at the time provided the young with a communal spirit and a sense of involvement. By the 1950s, in a society haunted by the Cold War, this ability seemed to have disappeared as authorities discouraged any community involvement and youth culture took a much more privatized form. The combined effect of these events created a backdrop for the student anxiety as witnessed in the 1950s. With this in mind the larger question that the Port Huron radicals asked should by now make more sense: "Some would have us believe that Americans feel contentment amidst prosperity—but might it not better be called a glaze above deeply felt anxieties about their role in the new world?" Thus, the information revealed in this article should also help us reach a new understanding of *The Port Huron Statement* itself. It is hard to make sense of this manifesto's ideas and its impact on the New Left and the broader spectrum of the sixties' culture without understanding its true origins in the previous decade.

Indeed, the 1950s was not, as many have assumed, an era of "golden youth." Contrary to what historians of the postwar era as well as specialists concerning themselves with youth culture have so far assumed, alienation was something that extended far beyond a limited group of people such as artists, beats, or intellectuals. As we have seen from these two major social science studies at the University of Minnesota, college life after the war did not represent a return to the happy, involved life of the 1920s and 30s. On the contrary, as this study suggests, young people were part of a generation cut off from its roots of public life as witnessed in the prewar youth culture and suffered from an alienation that differed sharply from the 1930s. Instead, a consumer culture had taken its place that, until the early sixties, prevented the fears and anxieties of youth from surfacing in social movements dedicated to political and social change.

18

THE DRIVE-IN CULTURE OF CONTEMPORARY AMERICA

KENNETH T. JACKSON

Nothing has so transformed the landscape and architecture of America as the automobile. At the beginning of the twentieth century the automobile was a plaything of the rich, but by the end of World War II a majority of Americans owned automobiles, and the proportion has grown ever since. As more and more Americans purchased cars in the postwar decades, and as an increasing proportion of the nation's manufactured goods was transported by highway instead of rail, entirely new kinds of industries emerged to service an increasingly motorized society.

In this essay, Kenneth T. Jackson documents the tremendous impact of the automobile and truck on contemporary America. From the interstate highway system inaugurated during the Eisenhower administration to such innovations as shopping centers, motels, and service stations, "automobility" has done much to turn America into a service society. But, Jackson suggests, this 30-year trend may be coming to an end. A countertrend has recently emerged, he tells us, in which central cities are increasingly being revitalized as living and shopping spaces, while the corporate consolidation of the gasoline, motel, and retail sales industries has led to the closing of independent service stations and many other artifacts of the early automobile age. If he is correct, the next decades may usher in yet another phase in America's constantly changing architectural landscape.

The postwar years brought unprecedented prosperity to the United States, as color televisions, stereo systems, frost-free freezers, electric blenders, and automatic garbage disposals became basic equipment in the middle-class American home. But the best symbol of individual success and identity was a sleek, air-conditioned, high-powered, personal statement on wheels. Between 1950 and 1980, when the American population increased by 50 percent, the number of their automobiles increased by 200 percent. In high school the most important rite of passage came to be the earning of a driver's license and the freedom to press an accelerator to the floor. Educational administrators across the country had to make parking space for hundreds of student vehicles. A car became one's identity, and the important question was: "What does he drive?" Not only teenagers, but also millions of older persons, literally defined themselves in terms of the number, cost, style, and horsepower of their vehicles. "Escape," thinks a character in a novel by Joyce Carol Oates. "As long as he had his own car he was an American and could not die."

Unfortunately, Americans did die, often behind the wheel. On September 9, 1899, as he was stepping off a streetcar at 74th Street and Central Park West in New York, Henry H. Bliss was struck and killed by a motor vehicle, thus becoming the first fatality in the long war between flesh and steel. Thereafter, the carnage increased almost annually until Americans were sustaining about 50,000 traffic deaths and about 2 million nonfatal injuries per year. Automobility proved to be far more deadly than war for the United States. It was as if a Pearl Harbor attack took place on the highways every two weeks, with crashes becoming so commonplace that an entire industry sprang up to provide medical, legal, and insurance services for the victims.

The environmental cost was almost as high as the human toll. In 1984 the 159 million cars, trucks, and buses on the nation's roads were guzzling millions of barrels of oil every day, causing traffic jams that shattered nerves and clogged the cities they were supposed to open up, and turn-

ing much of the countryside to pavement. Not surprisingly, when gasoline shortages created long lines at the pumps in 1974 and 1979, behavioral scientists noted that many people experienced anger, depression, frustration, and insecurity, as well as a formidable sense of loss.

Such reactions were possible because the automobile and the suburb have combined to create a drive-in culture that is part of the daily experience of most Americans. Because of unemployment and war, per capita motor-vehicle ownership was stable (at about 30 million vehicles) between 1930 and 1948, and as late as 1950 (when registrations had jumped to 49 million) an astonishing 41 percent of all Americans families and a majority of working-class families still did not own a car. Postwar prosperity and rising real wages, however, made possible vastly higher market penetration, and by 1984 there were about seventy motor vehicles for every one hundred citizens, and more cars than either households or workers. Schaeffer and Sclar have argued that high auto ownership is the result of real economic needs rather than some "love affair" with private transportation. Moreover, the American people have proven to be no more prone to motor vehicle purchases than the citizens of other lands. After World War II, the Europeans and the Japanese began to catch up, and by 1980 both had achieved the same level of automobile ownership that the United States had reached in 1950. In automotive technology, American dominance slipped away in the postwar years as German, Swedish, and Japanese engineers pioneered the development of diesel engines, front-wheel drives, disc brakes, fuel-injection, and rotary engines.

Although it is not accurate to speak of a uniquely American love affair with the automobile, and although John B. Rae claimed too much when he wrote in 1971 that "modern suburbia is a creature of the automobile and could not exist without it," the motor vehicle has fundamentally restructured the pattern of everyday life in the United States. As a young man, Lewis Mumford advised his countrymen to "forget the damned motor car and build cities for lovers and friends."

As it was, of course, the nation followed a different pattern. Writing in the *American Builder* in 1929, the critic Willard Morgan noted that the building of drive-in structures to serve a motor-driven population had ushered in "a completely new architectural form."

THE INTERSTATE HIGHWAY

The most popular exhibit at the New York World's Fair in 1939 was General Motors' "Futurama." Looking twenty-five years ahead, it offered a "magic Aladdin-like flight through time and space." Fair-goers stood in hour-long lines, waiting to travel on a moving sidewalk above a huge model created by designer Norman Bel Geddes. Miniature superhighways with 50,000 automated cars wove past model farms en route to model cities. Five million persons peered eventually at such novelties as elevated freeways, expressway traffic moving at 100 miles per hour, and "modern and efficient city planning—breathtaking architecture—each city block a complete unit in itself (with) broad, one-way thoroughfares—space, sunshine, light, and air." The message of "Futurama" was as impressive as its millions of model parts: "The job of building the future is one which will demand our best energies, our most fruitful imagination; and that with it will come greater opportunities for all."

The promise of a national system of impressive roadways attracted a diverse group of lobbyists, including the Automobile Manufacturers Association, state-highway administrators, motorbus operators, the American Trucking Association, and even the American Parking Association—for the more cars on the road, the more cars would be parked at the end of the journey. Truck companies, for example, promoted legislation to spend state gasoline taxes on highways, rather than on schools, hospitals, welfare, or public transit. In 1943 these groups came together as the American Road Builders Association, with General Motors as the largest contributor, to form a lobbying enterprise second only to that of the munitions industry. By the mid-1950s, it had become one of the most broad-based of all pressure groups, consisting of the oil, rubber, asphalt, and construction industries; the car dealers and renters; the trucking and bus concerns; the banks and advertising agencies that depended upon the companies involved; and the labor unions. On the local level, professional real-estate groups and home-builders associations joined the movement in the hope that highways would cause a spurt in housing turnover and a jump in prices. They envisaged no mere widening of existing roads, but the creation of an entirely new superhighway system and the initiation of the largest peacetime construction project in history.

The highway lobby inaugurated a comprehensive public relations program in 1953 by sponsoring a national essay contest on the need for better roads. The winner of the $25,000 grand prize was Robert Moses, the greatest builder the world has yet known and a passionate advocate of the urban expressway. The title of his work was "How to Plan and Pay for Better Highways." As his biographer Robert A. Caro has noted, Moses was "the world's most vocal, effective and prestigious apologist for the automobile," and he did more than any other single urban official to encourage more hesitant officials to launch major road-building efforts in their cities.

The Cold War provided an additional stimulus to the campaign for more elaborate expressways. In 1951 the *Bulletin of the Atomic Scientists* devoted an entire issue to "Defense through Decentralization." Their argument was simple. To avoid national destruction in a nuclear attack, the United States should disperse existing large cities into smaller settlements. The ideal model was a depopulated urban core surrounded by satellite cities and low-density suburbs.

Sensitive to mounting political pressure, President Dwight Eisenhower appointed a committee in 1954 to "study" the nation's highway requirements. Its conclusions were foregone, in part because the chairman was Lucius D. Clay, a member of the board of directors of General Motors. The committee considered no alternative to a massive highway system, and it suggested a major redirection of national policy to benefit the car and the truck. The Interstate Highway Act became law in 1956, when Congress provided for a 41,000-mile (eventually expanded to a 42,500-mile) system, with the federal government paying 90 percent of the cost. President Eisenhower gave four reasons for signing the measure: current highways were unsafe; cars too often became snarled in traffic jams; poor roads saddled business with high costs for transportation; and modern highways were needed because "in case of atomic attack on our key cities, the road net must permit quick evacuation of target areas." Not a single word was said about the impact of highways on cities and suburbs, although the concrete thoroughfares and the thirty-five-ton tractor-trailers which used them encouraged the continued outward movement of industries toward the beltways and interchanges. Moreover, the interstate system helped continue the downward spiral of public transportation and virtually guaranteed that future urban growth would perpetuate a centerless sprawl. Soon after the bill was passed by the Senate, Lewis Mumford wrote sadly: "When the American people, through their Congress, voted a little while ago for a $26 billion highway program, the most charitable thing to assume is that they hadn't the faintest notion of what they were doing."

Once begun, the Interstate Highway System of the United States became a concrete colossus that grew bigger with every passing year. The secret of its success lay in the principle of non-divertibility of highway revenues collected from gasoline taxes. The Highway Trust Fund, as it was called, was to be held separately from general taxes. Although no less a personage than Winston Churchill called the idea of a non-divertible road fund "nonsense," "absurd," and "an outrage upon . . . common sense," the trust fund had powerful friends in the United States, and it easily swept all opposition before it. Unlike European governments, Washington used taxes to support the highway infrastructure while refusing assistance to railroads. According to Senator Gaylord Nelson of Wisconsin, 75 percent of government expenditures for transportation in the United States in the postwar generation went for highways as opposed to 1 percent for urban mass transit.

The inevitable result of the bias in American transport funding, a bias that existed for a generation before the Interstate Highway program was initiated, is that the United States now has the world's best road system and very nearly its worst public-transit offerings. Los Angeles, in particular, provides the nation's most dramatic example of urban sprawl tailored to the mobility of the automobile. Its vast, amorphous conglomeration of housing tracts, shopping centers, industrial parks, freeways, and independent towns blend into each other in a seamless fabric of concrete and asphalt, and nothing over the years has succeeded in gluing this automobile-oriented civilization into any kind of cohesion—save that of individual routine. Los Angeles's basic shape comes from three factors, all of which long preceded the freeway system. The first was cheap land (in the 1920s rather than 1970s) and the desire for single-family houses. In 1950, for example, nearly two-thirds of all the dwelling units in the Los Angeles area were fully detached, a much higher percentage than in Chicago (28 percent), New York City (20 percent), or Philadelphia (15 percent), and its residential density was the lowest of major cities. The second was the dispersed location of its oil fields and refineries, which led to the creation of industrial suburbs like Whittier and Fullerton and of residential suburbs like La Habra, which housed oil workers and their families. The third was its once excellent mass-transit system, which at its peak included more than 1,100 miles of track and constituted the largest electric interurban railway in the world.

The Pacific Electric Company collapsed in the 1920s, however, and since that time Los Angeles has been more dependent upon the private automobile than other large American cities. Beginning in 1942, the Los Angeles Chamber of Commerce, the automoblie club, and elected officials met regularly to plan for a region-wide expressway network. They succeeded, and southern California's fabled 715 miles of freeways now constitute a grid that channels virtually all traffic and sets many communal boundaries. They are the primary form of transportation for most residents, who seem to regard time spent in their cars as more pleasurable than time walking to, waiting for, or riding on the bus. More than a third of the Los Angeles area is consumed by highways, parking lots, and interchanges, and in the downtown section this proportion rises to two-thirds. Not surprisingly, efforts to restore the region's public transportation to excellence have thus far failed. In 1976, for example, the state of California attempted to discourage single-passenger automobiles by reserving one lane in each direction on the Santa Monica Freeway for express buses and car pools. An emotional explosion ensued that dominated radio talk shows and television news, and Los Angeles's so-called "diamond lanes" were soon abolished.

More recently, southern California has followed the growing national enthusiasm for rail transit, and Los Angeles broke ground in 1984 for an 18-mile, $3.3 billion subway that will cut underneath the densely built, heavily trafficked Wilshire Boulevard corridor, cut through Hollywood, and end up in the residential San Fernando Valley. The underground will hopefully be the centerpiece of an eventual 160-mile network, second in size in the United States only to New York City's.

THE GARAGE

The drive-in structure that is closest to the hearts, bodies, and cars of the American family is the garage. It is the link between the home and the outside world. The word is French, meaning storage space, but its transformation into a multipurpose enclosure internally integrated with the dwelling is distinctively American.

In the streetcar era, curbs had been unbroken and driveways were almost unknown. A family wealthy enough to have a horse and carriage would have stored such possessions either in a public livery stable or in a private structure at the rear of the property. The owners of the first automobiles were usually sufficiently affluent to maintain a private stable. The first cars, there-

fore, which were open to the elements, often found lodging in a corner of the stable, side by side with the carriages they were soon to replace. These early accommodations for the automobile were often provided with gasoline tanks, for filling stations at the time were few and far between. This and the fact that cars often caught fire were good and sufficient reasons to keep the motor vehicles away from the family.

After World War I, house plans of the expensive variety began to include garages, and by the mid-1920s driveways were commonplace and garages had become important selling points. The popular 1928 *Home Builders* pattern book offered designs for fifty garages in wood, Tudor, and brick varieties. In affluent sections, such large and efficiently planned structures included housing above for the family chauffeur. In less pretentious neighborhoods, the small, single-purpose garages were scarcely larger than the vehicles themselves, and they were simply portable and prefabricated structures, similar to those in Quebec today, that were camouflaged with greenery and trellises. As one architect complained in 1924: "The majority of owners are really ashamed of their garages and really endeavor to keep them from view," and he implored his readers to build a garage "that may be worthy of standing alongside your house." Although there was a tendency to move garages closer to the house, they typically remained at the rear of the property before 1925, often with access via an alley which ran parallel to the street. The car was still thought of as something similar to a horse—dependable and important, but not something that one needed to be close to in the evening.

By 1935, however, the garage was beginning to merge into the house itself, and in 1937 the *Architectural Record* noted that "the garage has become a very essential part of the residence." The tendency accelerated after World War II, as alleys went the way of the horsedrawn wagon, as property widths more often exceeded fifty feet, and as the car became not only a status symbol, but almost a member of the family, to be cared for and sheltered. The introduction of a canopied and unenclosed structure called a "car port" represented an inexpensive solution to the problem, particularly in mild climates, but in the 1950s the enclosed garage was back in favor and a necessity even in a tract house. Easy access to the automobile became a key aspect of residential design, and not only for the well-to-do. By the 1960s garages often occupied about 400 square feet (about one-third that of the house itself) and usually contained space for two automobiles and a variety of lawn and wood-working tools. Offering direct access to the house (a conveniently placed door usually led directly into the kitchen), the garage had become an integrated part of the dwelling, and it dominated the front facades of new houses. In California garages and driveways were often so prominent that the house could almost be described as accessory to the garage. Few people, however, went to the extremes common in England, where the automobile was often so precious that living rooms were often converted to garages.

THE MOTEL

As the United States became a rubber-tire civilization, a new kind of roadside architecture was created to convey an instantly recognizable image to the fast-moving traveler. Criticized as tasteless, cheap, forgettable, and flimsy by most commentators, drive-in structures did attract the attention of some talented architects, most notably Los Angeles's Richard Neutra. For him, the automobile symbolized modernity, and its design paralleled his own ideals of precision and efficiency. This correlation between the structure and the car began to be celebrated in the late 1960s and 1970s when architects Robert Venturi, Denise Scott Brown, and Steven Izenour developed such concepts as "architecture as symbol" and the "architecture of communication." Their book, *Learning from Las Vegas*, was instrumental in encouraging a shift in taste from general condemnation to appreciation of the commercial strip and especially of the huge and garish signs which were easily recognized by passing motorists.

A ubiquitous example of the drive-in culture is the motel. In the middle of the nineteenth century, every city, every county seat, every aspiring mining town, every wide place in the road with aspirations to larger size, had to have a hotel. Whether such structures were grand palaces on the order of Boston's Tremont House or New York's Fifth Avenue Hotel, or whether they were jerry-built shacks, they were typically located at the center of the business district, at the focal point of community activities. To a considerable extent, the hotel was the place for informal social interaction and business, and the very heart and soul of the city.

Between 1910 and 1920, however, increasing numbers of traveling motorists created a market for overnight accommodation along the highways. The first tourists simply camped wherever they chose along the road. By 1924, several thousand municipal campgrounds were opened which offered cold water spigots and outdoor privies. Next came the "cabin camps," which consisted of tiny, white clapboard cottages arranged in a semicircle and often set in a grove of trees. Initially called "tourist courts," these establishments were cheap, convenient, and informal, and by 1926 there were an estimated two thousand of them, mostly in the West and in Florida.

Soon after clean linens and comfortable rooms became available along the nation's highways, it became apparent that overnight travelers were not the only, or even the largest, pool of customers. Convenience and privacy were especially appealing to couples seeking a romantic retreat. A well-publicized Southern Methodist University study in 1935 reported that 75 percent of Dallas area motel business consisted of one man and one woman remaining for only a short stay. Whatever the motivation of patrons, the success of the new-style hotels prompted Sinclair Lewis to predict in 1920:

Somewhere in these states there is a young man who is going to become rich. He is going to start a chain of small, clean, pleasant hotels, standardized and nationally advertised, along every important motor route in the country. He is not going to waste money on glit and onyx, but he is going to have agreeable clerks, good coffee, endurable mattresses and good lighting.

It was not until 1952 that Kemmons Wilson and Wallace E. Johnson opened their first "Holiday Inn" on Summer Avenue in Memphis. But long before that, in 1926, a San Luis Obispo, California, proprietor had coined a new word, "motel," to describe an establishment that allowed a guest to park his car just outside his room. New terminology did not immediately erase the unsavory image of the roadside establishments, however. In 1940 FBI Director J. Edgar Hoover declared that most motels were assignation camps and hideouts for criminals. Perhaps he was thinking of Bonnie and Clyde, who had a brief encounter with the law at the Red Crown Cabin Camp near Platte City, Missouri, one evening in July of 1933. Many of Hoover's "dens of vice" were once decent places that, unable to keep up, turned to the "hot pillow trade." Some Texas cabins, said the FBI director, were rented as many as sixteen times a night, while establishments elsewhere did business by the hour, with "a knock on the door when the hour was up."

Motels began to thrive after World War II, when the typical establishment was larger and more expensive than the earlier cabins. Major chains set standards for prices, services, and respectability that the traveling public could depend on. As early as 1948, there were 26,000 self-styled motels in the United States. Hard-won respectability attracted more middle-class families, and by 1960 there were 60,000 such places, a figure that doubled again by 1972. By that time an old hotel was closing somewhere in downtown America every thirty hours. And somewhere in suburban America, a plastic and glass Shangri La was rising to take its place.

Typical of the inner-city hotels was the Heritage in Detroit. The big bands once played on its roof, and aspiring socialites enjoyed crepethin pancakes. In 1975 a disillusioned former employee gestured futilely, "It's dying; the whole place is dying," as the famed hotel closed its doors. By 1984 about fifty historic establishments in downtown areas, such as the Peabody in Memphis, the Mayflower in Washington, the Galvez in Houston, the Menger in San Antonio, and the Biltmore in Providence were reopening with antique-filled rooms and oak-paneled bars. But the trend remained with the standard, two-story motel.

THE DRIVE-IN THEATER

The downtown movie theaters and old vaudeville houses faced a similar challenge from the automobile. In 1933 Richard M. Hollinshead set up a 16-mm projector in front of his garage in Riverton, New Jersey, and then settled down to watch a movie. Recognizing a nation addicted to the motorcar when he saw one, Hollinshead and Willis Smith opened the world's first drive-in movie in a forty-car parking lot in Camden on June 6, 1933. Hollinshead profited only slightly from his brainchild, however, because in 1938 the United States Supreme Court refused to hear his appeal against Loew's Theaters, thus accepting the argument that the drive-in movie was not a patentable item. The idea never caught on in Europe, but by 1958 more than four thousand outdoor screens dotted the American landscape. Because drive-ins offered bargain-basement prices and double or triple bills, the theaters tended to favor movies that were either second-run or second-rate. Horror films and teenage romance were the order of the night, as *Beach Blanket Bingo* or *Invasion of the Body Snatchers* typified the offerings. Pundits often commented that there was a better show in the cars than on the screen.

In the 1960s and 1970s the drive-in movie began to slip in popularity. Rising fuel costs and a season that lasted only six months contributed to the problem, but skyrocketing land values were the main factor. When drive-ins were originally opened, they were typically out in the hinterlands. When subdivisions and shopping malls came closer, the drive-ins could not match the potential returns from other forms of investments. According to the National Association of

Theater Owners, only 2,935 open-air theaters still operated in the United States in 1983, even though the total number of commercial movie screens in the nation, 18,772, was at a 35-year high. The increase was picked up not by the downtown and the neighborhood theaters, but by new multi-screen cinemas in shopping centers. Realizing that the large parking lots of indoor malls were relatively empty in the evening, shopping center moguls came to regard theaters as an important part of a successful retailing mix.

THE GASOLINE SERVICE STATION

The purchase of gasoline in the United States has thus far passed through five distinct epochs. The first stage was clearly the worst for the motorist, who had to buy fuel by the bucketful at a livery stable, repair shop, or dry goods store. Occasionally, vendors sold gasoline from small tank cars which they pushed up and down the streets. In any event, the automobile owner had to pour gasoline from a bucket through a funnel into his tank. The entire procedure was inefficient, smelly, wasteful, and occasionally dangerous.

The second stage began about 1905, when C. H. Laessig of St. Louis equipped a hot-water heater with a glass gauge and a garden hose and turned the whole thing on its end. With this simple maneuver, he invented an easy way to transfer gasoline from a storage tank to an automobile without using a bucket. Later in the same year, Sylvanus F. Bowser invented a gasoline pump which automatically measured the outflow. The entire assembly was labeled a "filling station." At this stage, which lasted until about 1920, such an apparatus consisted of a single pump outside a retail store which was primarily engaged in other businesses and which provided precious few services for the motorist. Many were located on the edge of town for safety and to be near the bulk stations; those few stations in the heart of the city did not even afford the luxury of off-street parking.

Between 1920 and 1950, service stations entered into a third phase and became, as a group, one of the most widespread kinds of commercial buildings in the United States. Providing under one roof all the functions of gasoline distribution and normal automotive maintenance, these full-service structures were often built in the form of little colonial houses, Greek Temples, Chinese pagodas, and Art Deco palaces. Many were local landmarks and a source of community pride. One cartoonist in the 1920s mocked such structures with a drawing in which a newcomer to town confused the gas station with the state capitol. Grandiose at the time, many of them molder today—deserted, forlorn structures with weeds growing in the concrete where gasoline pumps once stood. Their bays stand empty and silent, rendered that way by changing economics, changing styles, and changing consumer preferences.

After 1935 the gasoline station evolved again, this time into a more homogeneous entity that was standardized across the entire country and that reflected the mass-marketing techniques of billion-dollar oil companies. Some of the more familiar designs were innovative or memorable, such as the drumlike Mobil station by New York architect Frederick Frost, which featured a dramatically curving facade while conveying the corporate identity. Another popular service station style was the Texaco design of Walter Dorwin Teague—a smooth white exterior with elegant trim and the familiar red star and bold red lettering. Whatever the product or design, the stations tended to be operated by a single entrepreneur and represented an important part of small business in American life.

The fifth stage of gasoline-station development began in the 1970s, with the slow demise of the traditional service-station businessman. New gasoline outlets were of two types. The first was the super station, often owned and operated by the oil companies themselves. Most featured a combination of self-service and full-service pumping consoles, as well as fully equipped "car care centers." Service areas were separated from the pumping sections so that the two functions would not interfere with each other. Mechanics never broke off work to sell gas.

The more pervasive second type might be termed the "mini-mart station." The operators of such establishments have now gone full circle since the early twentieth century. Typically, they know nothing about automobiles and expect the customers themselves to pump the gasoline. Thus, "the man who wears the star" has given way to the teenager who sells six-packs, bags of ice, and pre-prepared sandwiches.

THE SHOPPING CENTER

Large-scale retailing, long associated with central business districts, began moving away from the urban cores between the world wars. The first experiments to capture the growing suburban retail markets were made by major department stores in New York and Chicago in the 1920s, with Robert E. Wood, Sears's vice president in charge of factories and retail stores, as the leader of the movement. A student of population trends, Wood decided in 1925 that motor-vehicle registrations had outstripped the parking space available in metropolitan cores, and he insisted that Sears's new "A" stores (their other retail outlets were much smaller) be located in low-density areas which would offer the advantages of lower rentals and yet, because of the automobile, be within reach of potential customers. With the exception of Sears's flagship store on State Street in Chicago (which was itself closed in 1983), Woods's dictum of ample free parking was rigorously followed throughout the United States. Early examples of the formula were the Pico Boulevard store in Los Angeles and the Crosstown store in Memphis. A revolution in retailing followed. Writing in the *American Builder* in 1929, the critic Willard Morgan found it natural that traffic congestion at the center would drive thousands of prospective customers to turn instead to suburban marketing centers.

Another threat to the primacy of the central business district was the "string street" or "shopping strip," which emerged in the 1920s and which were designed to serve vehicular rather than pedestrian traffic. These bypass roads encouraged city dwellers with cars to patronize businesses on the outskirts of town. Short parades of shops could already have been found near the streetcar and rapid transit stops, but, as has been noted, these new retailing thoroughfares generally radiated out from the city business district toward low-density, residential areas, functionally dominating the urban street system. They were the prototypes for the familiar highway strips of the 1980s which stretch far into the countryside.

Sears's big stores were initially isolated from other stores, while the retail establishments of highway strips were rarely unified into a coordinated whole. The multiple-store shopping center with free, off-street parking represented the ultimate retail adaptation to the requirements of automobility. Although the *Guinness Book of World Records* lists the Roland Park Shopping Center (1896) as the world's first shopping center, the first of the modern variety was Country Club Plaza in Kansas City. It was the effort of a single entrepreneur, Jesse Clyde Nichols, who put together a concentration of retail stores and used leasing policy to determine the composition of stores in the concentration. By doing that, Nichols created the idea of the planned regional shopping center.

Begun in 1923 in a Spanish-Moorish style with red tile roofs and little towers—its Giralda Tower is actually a replica of the original in Seville—Country Club Plaza featured waterfalls, fountains, flowers, tree-lined walks, and expensive landscaping. As the first automobile-oriented shopping center, it offered extensive parking lots behind ornamented brick walls. Most buildings were two stories high, with the second-floor offices typically occupied by physicians, dentists, and attorneys, whose presence would help stimulate a constant flow of well-heeled visitors. An enormous commercial success, Country Club Plaza stood in organic harmony with the prairie surroundings, and it soon became the hub of Kansas City's business and cultural activities.

Nichols's Country Club Plaza generated considerable favorable publicity after it became fully operational in 1925, and by the mid-1930s the concept of the planned shopping center, as a concentration of a number of businesses under one management and with convenient parking facilities, was well known and was recognized as the best method of serving the growing market of drive-in customers. But the Great Depression and World War II had a chilling effect on private construction, and as late as 1946 there were only eight shopping centers in the entire United States. They included Upper Darby Center in West Philadelphia (1927); Suburban Square in Ardmore, Pennsylvania (1928); Highland Park Shopping Village outside Dallas (1931); River Oaks in Houston (1937); Hampton Village in St. Louis (1941); Colony in Toledo (1944); Shirlington in Arlington, Virginia (1944); and Belleview Square in Seattle (1946). Importantly, however, they provided many of the amenities that shoppers would take for granted half a century later. In 1931, for example, Highland Park Village outside Dallas offered department, drug, and food stores, as well as banks, a theater, beauty and barber shops, offices, studios, and parking for seven hundred cars. The Spanish architecture was uniform throughout, and the rental charge included a maintenance fee to insure that the property was adequately cared for during the term of the lease.

The first major planned retail shopping center in the world went up in Raleigh, North Carolina, in 1949, the brainchild of Homer Hoyt, a well-known author and demographer best known for his sector model of urban growth. Thereafter, the shopping-center idea caught on rapidly in the United States and less rapidly in Canada, where the first shopping center—Dixie Plaza near Toronto—did not open until 1954. The most successful early examples, such as Poplar Plaza in Memphis, offered at least thirty small retailers, one large department store, and parking for five hundred or more cars. By 1984 the nation's 20,000 large shopping centers accounted for almost two-thirds of all retail trade, and even in relatively centralized cities like New York, Boston, and San Francisco downtown merchants adapted to the suburban shift. Easy facilities for parking gave such collections of stores decisive advantages over central city establishments.

The concept of the enclosed, climate-controlled mall, first introduced at the Southdale Shopping Center near Minneapolis in 1956, added to the suburban advantage. A few of the indoor malls, such as the mammoth Midtown Plaza in Rochester, New York, were located downtown, but more typical were Paramus Park and Bergen Mall in New Jersey; Woodfield Mall in Schaumburg outside Chicago; King's Plaza and Cross County outside Gotham; and Raleigh Mall in Memphis—all of which were located on outlying highways and all of which attracted shoppers from trading areas of a hundred square miles and more. Edward J. Bartolo, Sr., a self-made millionaire and workaholic, operated from a base in Youngstown, Ohio, to become the most prominent mall developer in the United States, but large insurance companies, especially the Equitable Life Assurance Society, increasingly sought high yields as shopping-center landlords.

During the 1970s, a new phenomenon—the super regional mall—added a more elaborate twist to suburban shopping. Prototypical of the new breed was Tyson's Corner, on the Washington Beltway in Fairfax County, Virginia. Anchored by Bloomingdale's, it did over $165 million in business in 1983 and provided employment to more than 14,000 persons. Even larger was Long Island's Roosevelt Field, a 180-store, 2.2 million square foot mega-mall that attracted 275,000 visitors a week and did $230 million in business in 1980. Most elaborate of all was Houston's Galleria, a world-famed setting for 240 prestigious boutiques, a quartet of cinemas, 26 restaurants, an olympic-sized ice-skating pavilion, and two luxury hotels. There were few windows in these mausoleums of merchandising, and clocks were rarely seen—just as in gambling casinos.

Boosters of such mega-malls argue that they are taking the place of the old central business districts and becoming the identifiable collecting points for the rootless families of the newer areas. As weekend and afternoon attractions, they have a special lure for teenagers, who often go there on shopping dates or to see the opposite sex. As one official noted in 1971: "These malls are now their street corners. The new shopping centers have killed the little merchant, closed most movies, and are now supplanting the older shopping centers in the suburbs." They are also especially attractive to mothers with young children and to the elderly, many of whom visit regularly to get out of the house without having to worry about crime or inclement weather.

In reality, even the largest malls are almost the opposite of downtown areas because they are self-contained and because they impose a uniformity of tastes and interests. They cater exclusively to middle-class tastes and contain no unsavory bars or pornography shops, no threatening-looking characters, no litter, no rain, and no excessive heat or cold. As Anthony Zube-Jackson has noted, their emphasis on cleanliness and safety is symptomatic of a very lopsided view of urban culture.

Despite their blandness, the shopping malls and the drive-in culture of which they are a part have clearly eclipsed the traditional central business districts, and in many medium-sized cities the last of the downtown department stores has already closed. The drive-in blight that killed them, like the Dutch Elm disease that ravaged Eastern towns in years past, has played hopscotch from one town to another, bringing down institutions that had once appeared invincible. The targets of this scourge, however, were not trees, but businesses, specifically the once-mighty department stores that anchored many a Main Street.

The most famous retailing victim of the drive-in culture thus far has been the stately J. L. Hudson Company of Detroit. It was a simple fact that all roads in the Motor City led to Hudson's. Featuring tall chandeliers, wood-paneled corridors, and brass-buttoned doormen, the 25-story, full-square-block emporium at its height ranked with Macy's in New York and Marshall Field in Chicago as one of the country's three largest stores. After 1950, however, the once-proud store was choked by its own branches, all of them in outlying shopping centers. As soon as Hudson's opened Northland, its biggest suburban outlet and one of the earliest in the nation,

sales downtown began to fall. They declined from a peak in 1953 of $153 million to $45 million in 1981. Finally, in 1981, the downtown landmark closed its doors for good. Hudson's was a victim of the product that made Detroit: the car.

In a Christmastime obituary for Detroit's most famous retailer, a WWJ radio commentator maintained that white flight to the suburbs, hastened by the Motor City's 1967 race riot, helped deal Hudson's a mortal blow. Actually, the 91-year-old store was killed by the free parking, easy accessibility, and controlled environment of the mega-malls.

By the 1960s, the primary rival to the shopping center as the locus of brief, informal communication and interaction had become the highway strip, with its flashing neon signs and tacky automobile showrooms. Especially in medium-sized cities, the vitality after dark is concentrated in the shopping malls or along the highway, not along Main Street.

THE HOUSE TRAILER AND MOBILE HOME

The phenomenon of a nation on wheels is perhaps best symbolized by the uniquely American development of the mobile home. "Trailers are here to stay," predicted the writer Howard O'Brien in 1936. Although in its infancy at that time, the mobile-home industry has flourished in the United States. The house trailer itself came into existence in the teens of this century as an individually designed variation on a truck or a car, and it began to be produced commercially in the 1920s. Originally, trailers were designed to travel, and they were used primarily for vacation purposes. During the Great Depression of the 1930s, however, many people, especially salesmen, entertainers, construction workers, and farm laborers, were forced into a nomadic way of life as they searched for work, any work. They found that these temporary trailers on rubber tires provided the necessary shelter while also meeting their economic and migratory requirements. Meanwhile, Wally Byam and other designers were streamlining the mobile home into the classic tear-drop form made famous by Airstream.

During World War II, the United States government got into the act by purchasing tens of thousands of trailers for war workers and by forbidding their sale to the general public. By 1943 the National Housing Agency alone owned 35,000 of the aluminum boxes, and more than 60 percent of the nation's 200,000 mobile homes were in defense areas. The government also built prefabricated homes without wheels near weapons factories. The ticky-tacky quality of these prefabricated shanty towns gave prefabs a lingering bad image, which remained after the war, when trailers found a growing market among migratory farm workers and military personnel, both of whom had to move frequently.

Not until the mid-1950s did the term "mobile home" begin to refer to a place where respectable people could marry, mature, and die. By then it was less a "mobile" than a "manufactured" home. No longer a trailer, it became a modern industrialized residence with almost all the accoutrements of a normal house. By the late 1950s, widths were increased to ten feet, the Federal Housing Administration (FHA) began to recognize the mobile home as a type of housing suitable for mortgage insurance, and the maturities on sales contracts were increased from three to five years.

In the 1960s, twelve-foot widths were introduced, and then fourteen, and manufacturers began to add fireplaces, skylights, and cathedral ceilings. In 1967 two trailers were attached side by side to form the first "double wide."

These new dimensions allowed for a greater variety of room arrangement and became particularly attractive to retired persons with fixed incomes. They also made the homes less mobile. By 1979 even the single-width "trailer" could be seventeen feet wide (by about sixty feet long), and according to the Manufactured Housing Institute, fewer than 2 percent were ever being moved from their original site. Partly as a result of this increasing permanence, individual communities and the courts began to define the structures as real property and thus subject to real-estate taxes rather than as motor vehicles subject only to license fees.

Although it continued to be popularly perceived as a shabby substitute for "stick" housing (a derogatory word used to describe the ordinary American balloon-frame dwelling), the residence on wheels reflected American values and industrial practices. Built with easily machined and processed materials, such as sheet metal and plastic, it represented a total consumer package, complete with interior furnishings, carpets, and appliances. More importantly, it provided a suburban type alternative to the inner-city housing that would otherwise have been available to blue-collar workers, newly married couples, and retired persons. After 1965 the production of factory-made housing (the term preferred by the industry) rarely fell below 200,000 per year, and in Florida, Wyoming, and Montana they typically accounted for more than a quarter of all new housing units. By 1979 manufactured housing was a $3.1 billion industry, and the nation counted more than ten million mobile-home dwellers. These figures exclude the "motor homes" made popular by Winnebago in the 1970s, the modular homes that are built on a floor system like a conventional house, and the prefabricated houses for which parts are built in a factory and shipped in sections to be assembled on the site.

A DRIVE-IN SOCIETY

Drive-in motels, drive-in movies, and drive-in shopping facilities were only a few of the many new institutions that followed in the exhaust of the internal-combustion engine. By 1984 mom-and-pop grocery stores had given way almost everywhere to supermarkets, most banks had drive-in windows, and a few funeral homes were making it possible for mourners to view the deceased, sign the register, and pay their respects without emerging from their cars. Odessa Community College in Texas even opened a drive-through registration window.

Particularly pervasive were fast-food franchises, which not only decimated the family-style restaurants but cut deeply into grocery store sales. In 1915 James G. Huneker, a raconteur whose tales of early twentieth-century American life were compiled as *New Cosmopolis,* complained of the infusion of cheap, quick-fire "food hells," and of the replacement of relaxed dining with "canned music and automatic lunch taverns." With the automobile came the notion of "grabbing" something to eat. The first drive-in restaurant, Royce Hailey's Pig Stand, opened in Dallas in 1921, and later in the decade, the first fast-food franchise, "White Tower," decided that families touring in motorcars needed convenient meals along the way. The places had to look clean, so they were painted white. They had to be familiar, so a minimal menu was standardized at every outlet. To catch the eye, they were built like little castles, replete with fake ramparts and turrets. And to forestall any problem with a land lease, the little white castles were built to be moveable.

The biggest restaurant operation of all began in 1954, when Ray A. Kroc, a Chicago area milk-shake-machine salesman, joined forces with Richard and Maurice McDonald, the owner of a fast-food emporium in San Bernardino, California. In 1955 the first of Mr. Kroc's "McDonald's" outlets was opened in Des Plaines, a Chicago suburb long famous as the site of an annual Methodist encampment. The second and third, both in California, opened later in 1955. Within five years, there were 228 golden arches drive-ins selling hamburgers for 15 cents, french fries for 10 cents, and milkshakes for 20 cents. In 1961 Kroc bought out the McDonald brothers, and in the next twenty years this son of an unsuccessful realtor whose family came from Bohemia built an empire of 7,500 outlets and amassed a family fortune in excess of $500 million. Appropriately headquartered in suburban Oak Brook, Illinois, the McDonald's enterprise is based on free parking and drive-in access, and its methods have been copied by dozens of imitators. Late in 1984, on an interstate highway north of Minneapolis, McDonald's began construction of the most complete drive-in complex in the world. To be called McStop, it will feature a

motel, gas station, convenience store, and, of course, a McDonald's restaurant.

Even church pews occasionally were replaced by the automobile. In early 1955, in suburban Garden Grove, California, the Reverend Robert Schuller, a member of the Reformed Church in America, began his ministry on a shoestring. With no sanctuary and virtually no money, he rented the Orange Drive-In movie theater on Sunday mornings and delivered his sermons while standing on top of the concession stand. The parishioners listened through speakers available at each parking space. What began as a necessity became a virtue when Schuller began attracting communicants who were more comfortable and receptive in their vehicles than in a pew. Word of the experiment—"Worship as you are . . . In the family car"—spread, the congregation grew, and in 1956 Schuller constructed a modest edifice for indoor services and administrative needs. But the Drive-in Church, as it was then called, continued to offer religious inspiration for automobile-bound parishioners, and in succeeding sanctuaries facilities were always included for those who did not want a "walk-in" church. By 1969 he had six thousand members in his church, and architect Richard Neutra had designed a huge, star-shaped "Tower of Power," situated appropriately on twenty-two acres just past Disneyland on the Santa Ana Freeway. It looked like and was called "a shopping center for Jesus Christ."

In 1980 a "Crystal Cathedral" was dedicated on the grounds. Designed by Philip Johnson, the $26 million structure is one of the most impressive and gargantuan religious buildings on earth. More than 125 feet high and 415 feet wide, its interior is a stunning cavern without columns, clad in over 10,000 panes of transparent glass. Yet the drive-in feature remains. Instead of separate services for his indoor and outdoor followers, Schuller broadcasts his message over the radio from an indoor/outdoor pulpit. At the beginning of each session, two 90-foot glass walls swing open so that the minister can be seen by drive-in worshippers. Traditionalists come inside the 3,000-seat "Crystal Cathedral," while those who remain in the "pews from Detroit" are directed to the announcement: "If you have a car radio, please turn to 540 on your dial for this service. If you do not have a radio, please park by the amplifiers in the back row." The appeal has been enormously successful. By 1984 Schuller's Garden Grove Community Church claimed to be the largest walk-in, drive-in church in the world. Its Sunday broadcasts were viewed by an estimated one million Californians and commanded the nation's highest ratings for religious programming.

THE CENTERLESS CITY

More than anyplace else, California became the symbol of the postwar suburban culture. It pioneered the booms in sports cars, foreign cars, vans, and motor homes, and by 1984 its 26 million citizens owned almost 19 million motor vehicles and had access to the world's most extensive freeway system. The result has been a new type of centerless city, best exemplified by once sleepy and out-of-the-way Orange County, just south and east of Los Angeles. After Walt Disney came down from Hollywood, bought out the ranchers, and opened Disneyland in 1955, Orange County began to evolve from a rural backwater into a suburb and then into a collection of medium and small towns. It had never had a true urban focus, in large part because its oil-producing sections each spawned independent suburban centers, none of which was particularly dominant over the others. The tradition continued when the area became a subdivider's dream in the 1960s and 1970s. By 1980 there were 26 Orange County cities, none with more than 225,000 residents. Like the begats of the Book of Genesis, they merged and multiplied into a huge agglomeration of two million people with its own Census Bureau metropolitan area designation—Anaheim, Santa Ana, Garden Grove. Unlike the traditional American metropolitan region, however, Orange County lacked a commutation focus, a place that could obviously be accepted as the center of local life. Instead, the experience of a local resident was typical: "I

live in Garden Grove, work in Irvine, shop in Santa Ana, go to the dentist in Anaheim, my husband works in Long Beach, and I used to be the president of the League of Women Voters in Fullerton."

A centerless city also developed in Santa Clara County, which lies forty-five miles south of San Francisco and which is best known as the home of "Silicon Valley." Stretching from Palo Alto on the north to the garlic and lettuce fields of Gilroy to the south, Santa Clara County has the world's most extensive concentration of electronics concerns. In 1940, however, it was best known for prunes and apricots, and it was not until after World War II that its largest city, San Jose, also became the nation's largest suburb. With fewer than 70,000 residents in 1940, San Jose exploded to 636,000 by 1980, superseding San Francisco as the region's largest municipality. As the automobile-based circulation system matured, the county's spacious orchards were easily developed, and bulldozers uprooted fruit trees for shopping centers and streets. Home builders, encouraged by a San Jose city government that annexed new territory at a rapid pace and borrowed heavily to build new utilities and schools on the fringes of town, moved farther and farther into the rural outskirts. Dozens of semiconductor and aerospace companies expanded and built plants there. In time, this brought twice-daily ordeals of bumper-to-bumper traffic on congested freeways. The driving time of some six-mile commutes lengthened to forty-five minutes, and the hills grew hazy behind the smog. As Santa Clara County became a national symbol of the excesses of uncontrolled growth, its residents began to fear that the high-technology superstars were generating jobs and taxes, but that the jobs attracted more people, and the taxes failed to cover the costs of new roads, schools, sewers, and expanded police and fire departments.

The numbers were larger in California, but the pattern was the same on the edges of every American city, from Buffalo Grove and Schaumburg near Chicago, to Germantown and Collierville near Memphis, to Creve Couer and Ladue near St. Louis. And perhaps more important than the growing number of people living outside of city boundaries was the sheer physical sprawl of metropolitan areas. Between 1950 and 1970, the urbanized area of Washington, D.C., grew from 181 to 523 square miles, of Miami from 116 to 429, while in the larger megalopolises of New York, Chicago, and Los Angeles, the region of settlement was measured in the thousands of square miles.

THE DECENTRALIZATION OF FACTORIES AND OFFICES

The deconcentration of post–World War II American cities was not simply a matter of split-level homes and neighborhood schools. It involved almost every facet of national life, from manufacturing to shopping to professional services. Most importantly, it involved the location of the workplace, and the erosion of the concept of suburb as a place from which wage-earners commuted daily to jobs in the center. So far had the trend progressed by 1970 that in nine of the fifteen largest metropolitan areas suburbs were the principle sources of employment, and in some cities, like San Francisco, almost three-fourths of all work trips were by people who neither lived nor worked in the core city. In Wilmington, Delaware, 66 percent of area jobs in 1940 were in the core city; by 1970, the figure had fallen below one quarter. And despite the fact that Manhattan contained the world's highest concentration of office space and business activity, in 1970, about 78 percent of the residents in the New York suburbs also worked in the suburbs. Many outlying communities thus achieved a kind of autonomy from the older downtown areas. A new "Americanism" even entered the language—"beltway"—to describe the broad expressways that encircled every important city by 1975 and that attracted employers of every description.

Manufacturing is now among the most dispersed of non-residential activities. As the proportion of industrial jobs in the United States work force fell from 29 percent to 23 percent of the total in the 1970s, those manufacturing enterprises that survived often relocated either to the suburbs or to the lower-cost South and West. Even tertiary industries, which do not utilize assembly-line processes and which require less flat space than larger factories, have adapted to the internal-combustion engine with peripheral sites. As early as 1963, industrial employment in the United States was more than half suburban based, and by 1981, about two-thirds of all manufacturing activity took place in the "industrial parks" and new physical plants of the suburbs. The transition has been especially hard on older workshop cities, where venerable factories are abandoned as employers are lured outward by the promise of open land, easy access to interstate highways, and federal investment tax credits. Between 1970 and 1980, for example, Philadelphia lost 140,000 jobs, many of them with the closing down or moving away of such Quaker City mainstays as Philco-Ford, Cuneo Eastern Press, Midvale Heppenstall Steel, Bayuk Cigar, Eaton and Cooper Industries' Plumb Tool Division, and the Container Corporation.

Office functions, once thought to be securely anchored to the streets of big cities, have followed the suburban trend. In the nineteenth century, businesses tried to keep all their operations under one centralized roof. It was the most efficient way to run a company when the mails were slow and uncertain and communication among employees was limited to the distance that a human voice could carry. More recently, the economics of real estate and a revolution in communications have changed these circumstances, and many companies are now balkanizing their accounting departments, data-processing divisions, and billing departments. Just as insurance companies, branch banks, regional sales staffs, and doctors offices have reduced their costs and presumably increased their accessibility by moving to suburban locations, so also have back-office functions been splitting away from front offices and moving away from central business districts.

Corporate headquarters relocations have been particularly well-publicized. Although the publishing firm of Doubleday and Company moved to quiet Garden City on Long Island in 1910 and Reader's Digest shifted to Pleasantville, New York, in Westchester County in 1936, the overall trend of corporate movement was toward central business districts until about 1950. The outward trend began in earnest in 1954, when the General Foods Corporation moved its home office from midtown Manhattan to a spacious, low-slung campus surrounded by acres of trees and free parking in suburban White Plains. The exodus reached a peak between 1955 and 1980, when, arguing, "It's an altogether more pleasant way of life for all," more than fifty corporations, including such giants as International Business Machines, Gulf Oil, Texaco, Union Carbide, General Telephone, American Cyanamid, Xerox, Pepsico, U.S. Tobacco, Cheeseborough Ponds, Nestlé, American Can, Singer, Champion International, and Olin, abandoned their headquarters in New York City.

Because Manhattan remained the dominant center of the nation's corporate and financial life, most companies simply moved within the region to more bucolic surroundings, principally in one of three small areas: a strip of central Westchester County from the Hudson River past White Plains to the Connecticut border, the downtown of Stamford and adjacent Greenwich in Fairfield County, Connecticut, and a narrow slice through the heartland of Morris and Somerset counties in New Jersey. All three areas built more than 16 million square feet of office space between 1972 and 1985, or more than exists in all but a handful of American cities.

The trend was particularly strong toward Connecticut, where executives could have the benefit of Gotham's business and cultural advantages without the bother of New York State's income taxes. In 1960 when the first urban renewal plans were drawn up for downtown Stamford, no consideration was given to building any commercial office space there. In the next three decades, however, while the original proposals were delayed by community resistance, Stamford's urban-renewal plans were redrawn to reflect changes in corporate attitudes toward relocating out of Gotham and into more comfort-

able suburban locations. For Stamford the delay was beneficial. When companies began their Manhattan exodus, Stamford had available space downtown. By 1984 Fairfield County was the third leading corporate headquarters site in the United States, after only New York City and Chicago.

Several studies have pointed out that the most important variable in determining the direction of a corporate shift was the location of the home and country club of the chief executive officer of the particular company. In fact, top officers were often the only ones to benefit from the suburban shifts. When A & W Beverages made the move from Manhattan to White Plains early in 1984, the company lost its entire support staff in the transition and had to spend a small fortune on severance costs. "Some of these people had been with us for many years, so we had to ask ourselves what we should do with loyal and good workers who will no longer have a job," said Craig Honeycutt, director of personnel for A & W, about the employees who quit rather than commute from Manhattan, Brooklyn, or New Jersey to White Plains.

Because the construction of suburban office headquarters tends to be expensive, the purpose of most such moves is to improve employee morale and productivity as much as to reduce costs. To this end, a company typically hires a well-known architect to design a rustic complex on the model of a college campus or a self-contained village. Free parking and easy access to interstate highways presumably make possible a longer work day, while stone piazzas, landscaped gardens, impressive sculpture, and splashing water fountains, as well as gymnasiums, showers, and saunas presumably make possible a more relaxed one. Company-owned cafeterias replace the downtown restaurants, shopping districts, and even noontime concerts of the city centers. To some employees the result is "close to perfect." Others find the campus environment boring and bemoan that "the main thing of interest out here is what's new in the gift shop."

Corporate relocation in the postwar period has been overwhelmingly a city-to-suburb phenomenon rather than a regional shift. The move of Gulf Oil to Houston and of American Airlines to Dallas, both from New York, were exceptions to this general rule. Only occasionally have large firms shifted both from a city to a suburb and from one region to another. The Johns-Manville Company, which transferred in the 1970s from a Manhattan office tower to a sleek and gleaming spaceship-style structure in the midst of a 10,000-acre ranch in the foothills of the Rocky Mountains, is a clear exception. Perhaps coincidentally the Johns-Manville Corporation was saved from bankruptcy in 1982 only by the intervention of a court.

Since World War II, the American people have experienced a transformation of the man-made environment around them. Commercial, residential, and industrial structures have been redesigned to fit the needs of the motorist rather than the pedestrian. Garish signs, large parking lots, one-way streets, drive-in windows, and throw-away fast-food buildings—all associated with the world of suburbia—have replaced the slower-paced, neighborhood-oriented institutions of an earlier generation. Some observers of the automobile revolution have argued that the car has created a new and better urban environment and that the change in spatial scale, based upon swift transportation, has formed a new kind of organic entity, speeding up personal communication and rendering obsolete the older urban settings. Lewis Mumford, writing from his small-town retreat in Amenia, New York, has emphatically disagreed. His prize-winning book, *The City in History*, was a celebration of the medieval community and an excoriation of "the formless urban exudation" that he saw American cities becoming. He noted that the automobile megalopolis was not a final stage in city development but an anticity which "annihilates the city whenever it collides with it."

The most damning indictment of private transportation remains, however, the 1958 work of the acid-tongued John Keats, *The Insolent Chariots*. He forcefully argued, as have others since that time, that highway engineers were wrong in constantly calling for more lanes of concrete to accommodate yet more lines of automobiles. Instead, Keats's position was that motorcars actually created the demand for more highways, which in turn increased the need for more vehicles, and so on ad infinitum. More ominously, he surmised, public expenditures for the automobile culture diverted funds from mass transit and needed social services.

The automobile lobby swept everything and everybody before it, however, and it was not until the first oil boycott of 1973 that Americans would seriously ponder the full implications of their drive-in culture. Especially in the 1950s, expressways represented progress and modernity, and mayors and public officials stumbled over themselves in seeking federal largesse for more and wider roads. Only a few people realized that high-speed roads accelerated deconcentration, displaced inner-city residents, contributed to the decay of central business districts, and hastened the deterioration of existing transportation systems. As Raymond Tucker, mayor of St. Louis and former president of the American Municipal Association, put it, "The plain fact of the matter is that we just cannot build enough lanes of highways to move all of our people by private automobile and create enough parking space to store the cars without completely paving over our cities and removing all of the . . . economic, social, and cultural establishments that the people were trying to reach in the first place."

Because structures built to accommodate the demands of the automobile are likely to have an ephemeral life, it is a mistake for cities to duplicate suburban conditions. In 1973 a RAND study of St. Louis suggested as an alternative strategy that the city become "one of many large suburban centers of economic and residential life" rather than try to revive traditional central city functions. Such advice is for those who study statistics rather than cities. Too late, municipal leaders will realize that a slavish duplication of suburbia destroys the urban fabric that makes cities interesting. Memphis's Union Avenue, once a grand boulevard lined with the homes of the well-to-do, has recently fallen victim to the drive-in culture. In 1979 one of the last surviving land-marks, an elegant stone mansion, was leveled to make room for yet another fast-food outlet. Within three years, the plastic-and-glass hamburger emporium was bankrupt, but the scar on Union Avenue remained.

There are some signs that the halcyon days of the drive-in culture and automobile are behind us. More than one hundred thousand gasoline stations, or about one-third of the American total, have been eliminated in the last decade. Empty tourist courts and boarded-up motels are reminders that the fast pace of change can make commercial structures obsolete within a quarter-century of their erection. Even that suburban bellweather, the shopping center, which revolu-tionized merchandising after World War II, has come to seem small and out-of-date as newer covered malls attract both the trendy and the family trade. Some older centers have been recycled as bowling alleys or industrial buildings, and some have been remodeled to appeal to larger tenants and better-heeled customers. But others stand forlorn and boarded up. Similarly, the characteristic fast-food emporiums of the 1950s, with uniformed "car hops" who took orders at the automobile window, are now relics of the past. One of the survivors, Delores Drive-In, which opened in Beverly Hills in 1946, was recently proposed as an historic landmark, a sure sign that the species is in danger.

19

THE PAUL ROBESON–JACKIE ROBINSON SAGA: A POLITICAL COLLISION

RONALD A. SMITH

In the immediate post–World War II years, American public culture was dominated by the Cold War. Often bordering on hysteria, anti-Communist sentiment reached fever pitch in the United States during the late 1940s, as the Soviet Union successfully tested the hydrogen bomb, China fell to Mao Zedong's Communist army, and rumors of Soviet spy networks proliferated throughout America. It was in this atmosphere of international distrust and domestic anxiety that the House Un-American Activities Committee began its search for evidence of "Communist" infiltration of American organizations and institutions. Focusing on organizations and individuals critical of various aspects of American society, the House committee effectively used the national media to convince the public that lawful dissent was tantamount to treason. Showing little regard for constitutional protections of individual liberties, the Committee called scores of Americans before its hearings to ferret out "Communists" in all walks of life.

One of the most dramatic appearances before the House committee was that of Jackie Robinson in the spring of 1949. Called before the committee to neutralize Paul Robeson's recent denunciation of American race relations, the hearings brought the man who had desegregated baseball before it to testify against one of America's foremost black actors. As Ronald A. Smith argues in this essay, the Robeson–Robinson saga was part of a larger debate within African-American society over the most effective means to bring about racial integregation. Although both men agreed about the need to end segregation, Robeson took a less accommodative and more critical view of American race relations. In an atmosphere of mounting anti-Communist hysteria, Robeson's brief remark comparing American and Soviet attitudes toward blacks was enough to have him condemned by the House Committee and branded as an internal threat to American society. In the years following the committee hearing, Jackie Robinson's moderate path led him to prosperity and public acclaim, while Paul Robeson never recovered from the financial and public loss caused by the House hearings.

"The Paul Robeson–Jackie Robinson Saga: A Political Collision." Journal of Sport History, *6 (1979), pp. 5–27. Reprinted by permission of the* Journal of Sport History *and the author.*

Time: October 21, 1947, nearly two years before the collision

Locale: Washington, D.C., U.S. House of Representatives

Scene: Hearings of the House Un-American Activities Committee Regarding the Communist Infiltration of the Motion Picture Industry

Main Performers: Congressman Richard M. Nixon (R), California
Actor Adolphe Menjou

———

Nixon: (Questioning his Committee's subpoenaed guest) Other than belonging to a communist-front organization, do you, Mr. Menjou, have tests which you would apply which would indicate to you that people acted like communists?

Menjou: Well, I think attending any meetings at which Mr. Paul Robeson appeared and applauding or listening to his Communist songs in America. . . .

∘∘∘∘∘∘∘

Time: One and one-half years later, April 19, 1949

Locale: Paris, France

Scene: World Congress of the Partisans of Peace

Main Performer: Singer, actor, and ex-athlete Paul Robeson

Robeson: (Standing tall and addressing the Congress) It is unthinkable that American Negroes would go to war on behalf of those who have oppressed us for generations against a country [the USSR] which in one generation has raised our people to the full dignity of mankind.

∘∘∘∘∘∘∘

Time: Three months later, July 18, 1949

Locale: Washington, D.C., U.S. House of Representatives

Scene: Hearings of the House Un-American Activities Committee Regarding Communist Infiltration of Minority Groups

Main Performers: Congressman Morgan Moulder (D), Missouri
Professional baseball player Jackie Robinson

———

Moulder: Mr. Robinson, this hearing regarding communist infiltration of minority groups is being conducted to give an opportunity to you and others to combat the idea Paul Robeson has given by his statements.

Robinson: Thank you, Congressman Moulder, for this opportunity. Paul Robeson's statement in Paris to the effect that American Negroes would refuse to fight in any war against Russia . . . sounds very silly to me. . . . I've got too much invested for my wife and child and myself in the future of this country . . . to throw it away because of a siren song sung in bass.

Moulder: I think you have rendered a great service to your country and to your people and we are proud of you and congratulate you upon being the great success that you are in this great country of ours.

∘∘∘∘∘∘∘

Two Afro-American performing heroes, Paul Robeson and Jackie Robinson, collided politically during the turbulent anti-communist days of the early Cold War era. The House Un-American Activities Committee erected a stage for star athletic performer Jackie Robinson, the twentieth century desegregator of professional baseball. At the same time it attempted to construct the political gallows for ex-athletic great and premier singer and actor Paul Robeson, who was praising the Soviet Union's race relations as he fought for the rights of blacks in America. The political collision of two black heroes tells us much about the nature of American society and of the place of sport and the performing arts during the precipitous years of the communist-hunting post–World War II era. For symbolic reasons, Jackie Robinson was asked by government officials to help obliterate Paul Robeson's leadership role among Americans. So successful were Robinson and others that for a generation Paul Robeson remained for most Americans a non-person.

It is ironic that Paul Robeson (1898–1976), who had been involved himself in the desegregation of professional baseball, should have the desegregator, Jackie Robinson (1919–1972), play an important role in Robeson's departure from the public forum. Robeson, who was over fifty years old when the confrontation occurred, was a product of the latter nineteenth and early twentieth centuries. The fact that Robeson's early life and career took place in the depths of Jim Crowism in America may help explain why he developed certain racial and political positions perceived as radical and became a target for Robinson and others in the desegregation movement of the Cold War Years.

ROBESON AND JIM CROW

Paul Robeson was born the same decade that baseball, then the unquestioned national pastime, rid itself of all blacks playing the professional game. At about the same time, the League of American Wheelmen, a key amateur bicycle association, inserted a whites-only clause in its constitution; John L. Sullivan, the first great American boxing champion, refused to fight blacks; and the newly formed Jockey Club of New York began to restrict the licensing of black jockeys. Two years before the birth of Robeson, the historic 1896 Supreme Court *Plessy* v. *Ferguson* "separate but equal" decision judicially sanctioned the segregation of blacks from whites. This was followed during Robeson's first year by Supreme Court decisions to uphold literacy tests and poll-tax qualifications for voting, policies devised to keep the Negro out of politics. Justice Henry Brown rationalized these decisions when he wrote in the *Plessy* decision: "If one race be inferior to the other socially, the Constitution of the United States cannot put them on the same plane. . . ." It would have been natural for blacks born at the time to be socialized in believing that they were inferior. Even the evolutionary theory of natural selection, struggle for existence, and survival of the fittest indicated to many Americans that blacks were placed low on the evolutionary ladder.

The belief in the racial inferiority of blacks at the time of Robeson's birth influenced the racial question in at least two important ways. First, Jim Crow laws multiplied greatly so that in the leisure domain, recreational facilities such as swimming pools, playgrounds, and public parks were segregated, though almost never equally. Especially in the South, laws mandated separate entrances, ticket windows, and seating arrangements and created such curiosities as an Oklahoma ban on blacks and whites fishing together in the same boat and a Birmingham, Alabama, ordinance prohibiting racially mixed play at dominoes or checkers. Second, the hue and cry of voices proclaiming racial superiority of whites affected the way blacks thought of themselves. Increasingly, Negro leaders and masses turned toward an accommodation with the Jim Crow system rather than protest against it. The dominant Negro leader of the turn-of-the-century America, Booker T. Washington, led the way toward accommodation with the whites. In his famous Atlanta Compromise speech in 1895, Washington held up his hands, fingers outstretched, to a mixed crowd of blacks and whites, and proclaimed that "in all things that are purely social we can be as separate as the fingers. . . ." Washington believed that it was more valuable for blacks to prove their worth by their own productivity than to demand either political or social rights.

If most blacks became accommodated to the unjust system, some, such as W. E. B. Du Bois, the historian and social critic, attacked racial prejudice where they found it. Du Bois criticized Booker T. Washington's views arguing that they represented "in Negro thought the old attitude of adjustment and submission . . . [which] practically accepts the alleged inferiority of the Negro races." Du Bois called for "work, culture, liberty,—all these we need, not singly but together, not successively but together, each growing and aiding each, and all striving toward that vaster ideal that swims before the Negro people, the ideal of human brotherhood, gained through the unifying ideal of Race. . . ." Said Du Bois: "All that makes life worth living—Liberty, Justice, and Right, [should not be] marked 'For White People Only.'"

Paul Robeson was raised with beliefs more in sympathy with Du Bois than with Washington. From an early time, his preacher-father, a former runaway slave, ingrained in the boy a sense of pride and worth as a black man. He soon found that in mental and physical qualities he was superior to most whites. As one of only three blacks graduating from his high school in Somerville, New Jersey, Robeson scholastically headed his class of 250 students. He was a skilled debator in his high school, was a soloist of the glee club, acted in the drama club, and excelled in several sports. During his senior year he achieved the highest score on a statewide examination for a scholarship to attend Rutgers College. From that day on, he later recalled, "Equality might be denied but I *knew* I was not inferior."

ROBESON AND ROBINSON IN THE 1920S AND 1930S

Indeed, Robeson was not inferior physically or mentally, and he showed remarkable abilities during his college years and after. He was an all-American football player at Rutgers in 1917 and 1918, and was called the greatest defensive end of all time by Walter Camp, the so-called father of American football. Robeson won twelve varsity letters in football, basketball, baseball, and track and field. He led his class academically and was elected to Phi Beta Kappa in his junior year. After college, he played professional football on the first championship team of what today is the National Football League. He took a law degree at Columbia University, before becoming a Shakespearean actor and a world renowned singer. Yet, by the 1960s and 1970s, he had become, for most, a forgotten man. While Jackie Robinson was generally recognized for desegregating professional baseball, Robeson was not widely remembered even among blacks.

Jackie Robinson was born on a share-cropper farm in Cairo, Georgia, in 1919, the year Babe Ruth was sold to the New York Yankees and the Black Sox scandal took place. The same year saw Jack Dempsey winning the heavyweight boxing championship and immediately announcing that he would pay "no attention to Negro challengers." Both Robeson and Robinson grew up in a Jim Crow society in which social and legal separation was readily apparent.

While Jackie Robinson moved to southern California with his mother and older brothers and sisters in 1920, Paul Robeson attended Columbia Law School. On weekends, he traveled to Ohio and played football with another black, Fritz Pollard, on the championship Akron Pros. Later, as he was completing his law degree, he competed for the Milwaukee Badgers in the fledgling National Football League. Upon graduation from Columbia, the American Bar Association denied him membership, and he suffered other severe limitations on his chosen profession. He soon withdrew from law practice and launched an acting and singing career. The summer before his last term at Columbia Law School, he had toured Great Britain singing and acting in a play titled *Voodoo.* By the mid-1920s, Robeson starred in Eugene O'Neill's plays, *The Emperor Jones* and *All God's Chillun Got Wings.* Robeson portrayed a black man who married a white woman in *All God's Chillun.* Reaction to his involvement in a racially mixed drama in Jim Crow America included hate mail and threats to both Robeson and playwright O'Neill from the Ku Klux Klan and individuals with equally harsh racist feelings. Favorable audience reaction and reviews, however, brought Robeson recognition among both whites and blacks. He gained further public recognition from musical concerts featuring his rich voice singing Negro spirituals.

Robeson spent increasing periods of time in Europe and England in the 1920s and 1930s. Especially in London he found less racial hatred and greater personal freedom than in America. Becoming more politically aware as areas of the world moved toward fascism during the 1930s, Robeson began to question the imperialistic policies of European nations and America toward colonial Africa, of fascist Italy toward Ethiopia, and of Nazi Germany toward the Spanish Civil War. By the mid-to-late 1930s, Robeson took the side of those who favored freedom for blacks in Africa. He campaigned for the Republican cause against totalitarian Franco in Spain, and deeply opposed fascism in Italy and especially in Germany. In Nazi Germany in 1934, on his way to Russia to confer with a film director, Robeson was threatened and racially abused by German storm troopers near Berlin.

In Moscow, Robeson was greatly impressed with the Russian people and what he considered their lack of racial prejudice. He wrote: "I, the son of a slave, walk this earth in complete dignity." From that point on, Robeson continued his praise of the Soviet Union while speaking out against fascist thought wherever he found it. He found much to criticize in America. Two decades later he would testify before the House of Representatives Committee on Un-American Activities, stating:

> I would say in Russia I felt for the first time a full human being, and no colored prejudice like in Mississippi and no colored prejudice like in Washington and it was the first time I felt like a human being, where I did not feel the pressure of color as I feel in this committee today.

In September, 1939, Paul Robeson returned to live in the United States after spending most of the previous twelve years abroad. This was the same month that Jackie Robinson began attending college at UCLA after first going to Pasadena Junior College. Unlike Robeson, who attended Rutgers as the only black on campus and the first to participate in athletics, Robinson had as a teammate on the football squad the Negro Kenny Washington, possibly the most outstanding football player in America that year. Like Robeson, Robinson lettered in each of four sports, football, basketball, baseball, and track and field. Besides being an outstanding back in football, he led his team in scoring in basketball and won the Pacific Coast title in the broad jump. In baseball, he played shortstop while displaying exceptional speed and daring on the base paths.

During the time Robinson starred in athletics at UCLA, Robeson was attaining new heights of popularity as a singer and actor. When the United States entered World War II as an ally of the Soviet Union, little was said about Robeson's praise of life in the Soviet Union—most saw him as a strong opponent of fascism. He helped con-

duct war bond drives as he continued to sing Russian folk songs and speak out for black rights everywhere. Like a number of civil rights leaders, he saw World War II as having a positive effect in breaking down Jim Crow laws and customs. Robeson even had a part in the attempt to desegregate professional baseball in the midst of the war.

WORLD WAR II AND ROBESON'S INVOLVEMENT IN BASEBALL DESEGREGATION

Segregation existed in professional baseball during World War II as it had for more than a half-century when it had first drawn the color line. It seemed hypocritical to Robeson and others that America would fight to end the myth of Aryan supremacy in Germany while the nation preserved its own myth of racial supremacy at home. A movement to end baseball segregation began soon after Pearl Harbor. It is not surprising that the American Communist Party took a lead in the agitation for integrating baseball and in accepting any role Paul Robeson would play in it.

The American Communist Party organ, the *Daily Worker,* had called for breaking the color line in the 1930s, but in early 1942 its sports editor, Lester Rodney, began attacking the Commissioner of Baseball, Kenesaw Mountain Landis, for not eliminating Jim Crowism in America's most visible sport. After the great black pitcher Satchel Paige and his Kansas City Monarchs defeated a group of Major Leaguers, who were in military service and headed by pitcher Dizzy Dean, Rodney wrote contemptuously:

> Can you read, Judge Landis? . . . The Stars could get only two hits off Satchel Paige in seven innings of trying. Why does your silence keep him and other Negro stars from taking their rightful place in our national pastime at a time when we are at war and Negro and white are fighting and dying together to end Hitlerism?

The *Daily Worker* quoted Jimmy Dykes, manager of the Chicago White Sox, as saying to

Jackie Robinson, the young Negro shortstop: "I'd love to have you on my team and so would all the other big league managers. But it's not up to us. Get after Landis." To a similar statement, Commissioner Landis replied that if any managers "want to sign one, or 25 Negro players, it is all right with me. That is the business of the managers and the club owners." Arguing against the entry of blacks in baseball was Larry McPhail, president of the Brooklyn Dodgers. He stated that the lack of Negroes in organized baseball "is not due to racial discrimination," but rather that "Negro baseball leagues might be wrecked if the major leagues raid these clubs and grab a few outstanding players." This argument of ruining black baseball by desegregating white baseball was likely more economically than altruistically derived, for Major League owners profited from the existence of Negro teams which rented their parks.

Pressure to change baseball's six decades of segregation continued to be exerted during the first summer of America's entry into World War II. There was one report of a heated discussion of club owners over blacks in baseball at the time of the Major League All-Star game and of the meeting transcripts being ordered destroyed. That same summer the president of the Pittsburgh Pirates announced that blacks would be given tryouts for his team. There is, however, no evidence that blacks of the stature of Josh Gibson, a catcher, or Sammy Bankhead, an outfielder, of the nearby Homestead Grays Negro team—or any other—were given the opportunity. Thirty-five-year-old Satchel Paige, the best known and highest paid black player of the times, indicated that he would only come into white baseball if it were on a team of all blacks because the racial tension in both the South and the North would be too high if a white team were desegregated. A writer from Los Angeles mocked the scene: "Let the Negro have his name in the casualty lists of Pearl Harbor or Bataan or Midway. But, for heavensakes, let's keep his name out of the boxscores." Indeed, the old argument of possible race riots, as had occurred after the Jack Johnson–Jim Jeffries Great White Hope

fight of 1910, was still brought up in discussions of desegregation in American sport.

Agitation continued into 1943, eventually involving Paul Robeson. A resolution was introduced in the New York State legislature protesting the unwritten ban against blacks in baseball, and Brooklyn's communist councilman, Peter V. Cocchione, introduced a resolution calling for desegregation of baseball. The Negro Publishers Association became involved and requested Commissioner Landis to discuss the question of blacks in organized baseball at the annual meeting of Major League teams. The Commissioner agreed, and for the first time in its history professional baseball officially examined the desegregation issue in its December meeting. Eight black newspapermen and Paul Robeson attended the meeting. Robeson's presence dominated the session.

Robeson was one of three blacks to address the club owners. He was introduced by Landis who said that he had brought Robeson to the meeting "because you all know him. You all know that he is a great man in public life, a great American." Robeson told the owners: "I come here as an American and former athlete. I come because I feel this problem deeply." He expressed his belief that the time had come for baseball to change its attitude toward the Negro and told them he had become the first black actor to play in Shakespeare's Othello on Broadway less than two months before. He declared that if he could be a black in an otherwise all-white play, then a Negro in a white cast should no longer be incredible to baseball owners. Robeson said that though he understood the owners' fears of racial disturbance if baseball were desegregated, "my football experience showed me such fears are groundless." When he finished, the owners gave him what a black writer called a "rousing ovation," but the owners neither questioned Robeson nor the other two speakers. Landis did reiterate a previous statement that "each club is entirely free to employ Negro players to any extent it pleases and the matter is solely for each club's decision without any restrictions whatsoever."

One club owner, Philip K. Wrigley of the Chicago Cubs, did not believe that the middle of World War II was the time to hire blacks in baseball, but said that he would consider hiring a scout to pursue a talent search for future Negro players. Wrigley showed his understanding of baseball when he observed that the sport was not progressive and only accepted something new after everyone else had already adopted it. "Baseball hesitates to break a custom," Wrigley told a Chicago delegation for baseball integration in late 1943, "whether it is using Negro players or removing the traditional sleeve out of uniforms." Whether baseball was conservative or not, there was great social pressure to keep the "National Pastime" free of blacks. The problem of bringing blacks into baseball was enormous when one considers that in the midst of World War II, both the American and National League teams from St. Louis prevented black spectators from purchasing tickets for any section of their stadiums except the bleachers. Allowing blacks to sit in the grandstand seemed minute compared to allowing them to play on the field. To this sentiment Robeson countered that the temper of the Negro had changed, that the Negro was fighting "a world-wide war for the right of people to be free, and he will resist any attempt to keep him tied down to a reactionary status quo."

ROBINSON DESEGREGATES BASEBALL

Blacks did not break the color barrier in baseball during World War II, but there is little doubt that the war was a catalyst in bringing about black entry into both professional baseball (closed to Negroes since the 1880s) and professional football (closed to Negroes since 1933). Near the close of the war, the *New York Times* editorialized: "If we are willing to let Negroes as soldiers fight wars on our team, we should not ask questions about color in the great American game." Economic and political pressure as well as moral pressure was being exerted. In Boston, city councilman Isadore Munchnick threatened to cancel Sunday permits to the Boston Red Sox

and the Boston Braves Major League teams unless both clubs agreed to end discrimination against Negroes. Munchnick agreed to withdraw his motion after the Boston clubs verbally assented to give equal opportunity to blacks. In mid-April, Jackie Robinson and two others were given "tryouts" by the Red Sox although all three blacks agreed that there was no intent by the Boston team to sign any of them. After the tryouts, one of the three, Sam Jethroe, told black sportswriter Wendell Smith of the *Pittsburgh Courier:* "We'll hear from the Red Sox like we'll hear from Adolph Hitler." The Secretary of the Negro National League said the tryouts in Boston were a travesty, "the most humiliating experience Negro baseball has yet suffered from white organized baseball." Jackie Robinson was more circumspect. "We can consider ourselves pioneers," commented Robinson. "Even if they don't accept us, we are doing our part and, if possible, making the way easier for those who follow. Some day some Negro player will get a break. We want to help make that day a reality."

Pressure to desegregate baseball was occurring elsewhere, mostly in the state of New York. Vito Marcantonio, the only U.S. Congressman of the left wing American Labor Party, asked the Interstate Commerce Committee to hold a hearing on discrimination in baseball. He also conferred with the New York baseball clubs asking them to break the color line. One club owner, Branch Rickey of the Brooklyn Dodgers, voluntarily gave a tryout to two Negroes. The tryout of these well-travelled Negroes, Terris McDuffie (thirty-six years old) and Dave Thomas (thirty-nine years old), could not be seen as highly promising for blacks as neither had had a good record in the Negro league the previous year. McDuffie had a losing record as a pitcher, and Thomas batted only .248 in 1944. It appeared that voluntary tryouts such as Rickey's might become mandatory in the near future. The New York state Fair Employment Practices Bill had recently passed and had forbidden discrimination in employment on the basis of race, color, or creed. If this were applied to baseball, it might be shown that baseball owners in New York City had not given equal opportunity to blacks. Larry McPhail, by then owner of the New York Yankees, rhetorically asked to "name me the colored players today who have the qualifications for a career in the major leagues, or in the minors, for that matter!" The same day Jackie Robinson opened the season at shortstop for the Kansas City Monarchs of the Negro American League. Several months later and just two days before Japan surrendered ending World War II, Branch Rickey was appointed by Mayor LaGuardia of New York City to a Committee of Ten which was established to study racial discrimination in baseball. The little publicized Committee of Ten worked rapidly and concluded in November of 1945 with two special points. The report emphasized that no racial differences in baseball skill existed between blacks and whites and that action, not silence, was needed to end sixty years of segregation. "The time is never ripe for social reform," the report stressed; the Major Leagues must act soon.

Branch Rickey had already begun to act by quietly beginning his quest to find the right player to break the discrimination policy. He had done this before the LaGuardia Committee of Ten had been announced. Using subterfuge to accomplish his desegregation plan, Rickey announced in the spring of 1945 the formation of a six-team, black baseball league including his own team, the Brooklyn Brown Dodgers. The Brown Dodgers were used as a front to cover his talent search—a quest which determined that Jackie Robinson should be the first black to enter organized baseball in the twentieth century. Robinson had been chosen because he was an outstanding athlete, and it was done with the knowledge that his highly competitive nature would make him stand up and fight for his rights as an individual. Robinson had stood up against racism as a young boy, during his college career, and while he was in military service during World War II. While stationed at a Southern military camp, Robinson was court-martialed and later acquitted for challenging the Jim Crow tradition which dictated that blacks should sit in the rear of a military bus.

While Jackie Robinson endured the torture of desegregating organized baseball, Paul Robeson entered the post–World War II era criticizing American racial policies and praising those of the socialistic Soviet Union. Robeson had noted during the war the influence that he believed would be brought on the United States' racial policies from abroad. "We in America," Robeson said, "criticize many nations. We know that international conscience has great influence in spite of wars. One important part of the solution of the Negro problem here will be the pressure of other countries on America from the outside." These were prophetic remarks in light of the effect of the Cold War politics on breaking down America's Jim Crow policies in the 1950s and 1960s. After World War II, Robeson was much involved in that external influence, probably giving it more visible support than any other black American. His outspoken stance for black rights and his pro-communist ideology created a furor wherever he went as America turned to a hate-Russia campaign in the post-war era.

Jackie Robinson, unlike Robeson, was restrained from certain actions for the first several years in the Brooklyn Dodger organization as Branch Rickey believed that his venture in race relations would fail if Robinson reacted outwardly to racial slurs. Robinson gave his assurance that he would not retaliate against insults from players nor complain to umpires; he promised not to make public endorsements, write newspaper or magazine articles, frequent night spots, or accept social invitations from whites or blacks. He was also warned by heavyweight boxing champion Joe Louis, who himself had been cautioned, not to get cocky so that whites might call him an "uppity nigger." During his first year with the Dodgers he received death threats against himself and his family while he stoically took verbal abuse, the worst from manager Ben Chapman and his Philadelphia Phillies. A challenge by the St. Louis Cardinals to boycott the Brooklyn Dodgers if Robinson played was cut short by league president Ford Frick who warned the Cardinals that those who took part would be suspended, and Frick added bluntly: "I don't care if it wrecks the National League for five years." Later, the Cardinals Enos Slaughter and Joe Garagiola spiked Robinson—maliciously, Robinson believed. Nevertheless, he became Rookie of the Year and helped Brooklyn reach the World Series. Thus, Robinson came into the Major Leagues under rules created to make him more acceptable to whites, something Robeson would not have done at that time in his life.

As Jackie Robinson attempted to make his impact in baseball with his base hits and effective fielding, Paul Robeson plowed forth on his own crusade. The day after Robinson made his first Major League base hit, Robeson's scheduled concert appearance in Peoria, Illinois, was unanimously banned by the city council. Not long after that incident, the Albany, New York, Board of Education withdrew permission previously granted to Robeson for a concert in its school auditorium. Said a board member: "The color of Paul Robeson's skin has nothing to do with this case, but the color of his ideologies has." Retorted Robeson: "Whether I am a communist or a communist sympathizer is irrelevant. The question is whether American citizens, regardless of their political beliefs or sympathies, may enjoy their constitutional rights." The Albany case was eventually taken to the New York Supreme Court, which granted Robeson the right to sing in the Albany school. Robeson gave his concert, and that same day Jackie Robinson revealed hate letters written to him threatening his life if he did not quit baseball.

THE ROBESON–ROBINSON POLITICAL CONFRONTATION

It was in context of Robinson's desegregation of baseball under white terms and Robeson's stand for human rights under free political terms that a collision arose between Robinson and Robeson. The catalyst was the House Un-American Activities Committee (HUAC) of the United States Congress. In the late 1930s, HUAC had been established principally to investigate fascist and communist activities. It became an inquisitorial committee which ferreted out political

deviants for public exposure and ridicule. Organizations and individuals which HUAC considered heretical were singled out to be destroy-ed or at least immobilized. Extended hearings were conducted in which accused and accusers were questioned at length. One historian has written that the accused would leave HUAC hearings "with a mark of Cain," while the accuser would depart "the tribunal with a halo of potential market value." Another has concluded that HUAC's "endless harassment of individuals for disagreeable opinions and actions has created anxiety, revulsion, indignation, [and] outrage. . . ."

Paul Robeson was one HUAC's targets. He had been chastised previously by HUAC, but in 1949 the Committee, representing American fear of and hysteria over the Cold War political left, attacked Robeson violently. This vendetta came as a result of a comment made by Robeson at the World Congress of Partisans held in Paris, France on April 20, 1949. Robeson, along with W. E. B. Du Bois, directed the American delegation to the communist-led meeting. Both men spoke to the 1800 delegates from about sixty nations, and both condemned America's international actions. It was Robeson, however, whose rhetoric drew the attention of the American press and the ire of governmental officials. One of Robeson's unwritten statements caught the ear of the press:

> It is unthinkable that American Negroes would go to war on behalf of those who have oppressed us for generations against a country [the Soviet Union] which in one generation has raised our people to the full dignity of mankind.

The next day the nation's newspapers reported Robeson's remarks indicating that blacks would never fight against the Soviet Union. As one Negro leader, Lester B. Granger, commented: "A nation-wide 9-day sensation was manufactured." Most black leaders were quick to castigate Robeson for his Paris speech. "We American Negroes," declared Max Yergan, a black who had once led the Council of African Affairs with Robeson, "can be deeply grateful Mr. Paul

Robeson did not speak for us in Paris a few days ago." Exclaimed Walter White, head of the National Association for the Advancement of Colored People: "We will not shirk equal responsibilities. . . . We will meet the responsibilities imposed upon all America." Robeson is "an ingrate" chided Dr. Channing Tobias, a member of the NAACP board of directors. Wrote Mary McLeod Bethune, President of the National Council of Negro Women: "I am chagrined at his presumption. . . . I think he has missed his cue and has entered the stage during the wrong scene." Edgar G. Brown, Director of the National Negro Council, went further by calling Robeson's speech communist propaganda while quoting Stephen Decatur's "In peace and war— my country, right or wrong." To all of this a black columnist stated that "we all know that our professional leaders had to say officially that Paul does not speak for Negroes as a group." He then criticized others for joining the bandwagon which he believed was essentially saying, "Deed, Boss, that bad old Paul ain't speaking for me and you know I'll fight for democracy, if I ain't been lynched first."

Newspapers intended for a Negro audience were almost as unequivocal in their stands against Robeson as were white newspapers and black leaders, and their immediate reaction to Robeson's Paris statement clearly showed that Robeson did not speak for all American blacks, probably not even most blacks. The *Pittsburgh Courier* editorialized that Robeson's declaration that blacks would never fight the Soviets was a "pathetic statement." The *Chicago Defender* snapped "Nuts to Mr. Robeson," and the less hostile *Philadelphia Afro-American* stressed that "Robeson does not speak for us and millions of other colored people." Some black columnists, though, sided with Robeson. This was only natural, for at the time Robeson spoke in Paris, lynchings were still prevalent in the South while anti-lynching bills before Congress died; Jim Crow conditions existed in the nation's capital; segregation continued in the military; and the Ku Klux Klan persisted in America. One writer, while condemning Robeson's "fat-headed" statement about fighting the Soviets, nevertheless com-

mented that the "racial consciousness of Americans sorely needs to be stirred up." Another believed that the "fear of Russia and of communism, as well as outside criticism of the United States, have been the Negro's greatest benefactor in recent years." Few took the stance of Robeson's friend, W. E. B. Du Bois, who praised Robeson and condemned the "sheep-like disposition, inevitably born of slavery" which Negroes showed in following white leadership.

Most reaction by both blacks and whites was hostile to Robeson, but there was an uneasy feeling exposed in the American press that there was some truth to what Robeson was saying. Would blacks fight for America in a war against the Soviet Union? In a sample of whites in several Northern cities, over 50 percent questioned Negroes' loyalty to America. Members of HUAC, who had used Robeson previously as a favorite target, believed that they could attack the problem positively and leftist Paul Robeson negatively at the same time. They would conduct a hearing on the communist infiltration of minority groups and invite prominent blacks to testify about Negro loyalty and Robeson's disloyalty. Invited to testify before HUAC, among others, were Lester Granger, National Urban League head; Dr. Charles S. Johnson, President of Fisk College; Thomas W. Young, Negro publisher; and Clarence Clark, a disabled Negro veteran of World War II. Of greatest importance because of his popular stature as desegregator of America's "National Pastime," was the invitation sent to Jackie Robinson. Chairman of HUAC, John S. Wood of Georgia, telegrammed Robinson asking him to testify before his Committee "to give the lie" to statements by Paul Robeson.

By 1949, Jackie Robinson was probably the best known black in America with the possible exception of Joe Louis and Paul Robeson. At the time of the HUAC hearings on communist infiltration of minority groups, Robinson was leading the National League in batting with a .360 average and was also the top vote getter in the annual all-star balloting in his league. It was not unexpected that HUAC would ask a black of Robinson's public exposure to testify against another prominent black. According to Alvin

Stokes, a black investigator for HUAC, the Committee felt it was necessary to get someone of the popular stature of Robinson to discredit Robeson.

The decision to speak out against Robeson was not an easy one for Robinson. He recounted his dilemma. If he testified he might merely be the black pawn in a white man's game which pitted one black against another, and he might be considered a "traitor" to his own people. If he did not testify he feared that Robeson's statement might discredit all blacks in the eyes of whites. At that time, Robinson had faith that whites would ultimately render justice to blacks. He chose to testify before HUAC. With advice from Branch Rickey and Lester Granger, Robinson prepared a statement which he delivered before HUAC on July 18, 1949.

Seated before the Committee, Robinson testified, rather naively but with good effect, that baseball was "as far removed from politics as anybody can possibly imagine." Referring to Robeson's statement which he had been called upon by HUAC "to combat," Robinson said:

> I can't speak for any 15,000,000 people any more than any other one person can, but I know that I've got too much invested for my wife and child and myself in the future of this country, and I and other Americans of many races and faiths have too much invested in our country's welfare, for any of us to throw it away because of a siren song sung in bass.

Robinson continued:

> But that doesn't mean that we're going to stop fighting race discrimination in this country until we've got it licked. It means that we're going to fight it all the harder because our stake in the future is so big. We can win our fight without the Communists and we don't want their help.

With those strong words he closed his testimony. Earlier in his statements he had qualified his harsh remarks by stating that Robeson should have a "right to his personal views, and if he wants to sound silly when he expresses them in public, that is his business and not mine."

Acknowledging that Robeson was "still a famous ex-athlete and a great singer and actor," Robinson said that "Negroes were stirred up long before there was a Communist party and they'll stay stirred up long after the party has disappeared—unless Jim Crow has disappeared by then as well." Robinson saw progress, though slow, in black rights, pointing out that there were only seven blacks out of 400 Major League players and that only three of the sixteen Major League teams were desegregated. "We're going to keep on making progress," Robinson told the probers, "until we go the rest of the way in wiping Jim Crow out of American sports."

Robinson's testimony against Robeson was predictably praised by HUAC, which for the first time that year allowed motion and still photographers free access in the room during Robinson's testimony. The Committee obviously knew the publicity value of a sports performer well-known to Americans. Major newspapers emphasized the anti-Robeson comments of Robinson while giving little space to the pro–civil rights statements of the all-star second baseman. Newspaper accounts accomplished HUAC's objective of discrediting Robeson's Paris statement. Headlines of "ROBESON SILLY, JACKIE ROBINSON TELLS RED QUIZ" and "DODGER STAR RAPS ROBESON 'SIREN SONG'" appeared in leading Chicago and Philadelphia newspapers. The *New York Times* editorialized: "Jackie Robinson scored four hits and no errors" testifying before HUAC, while the *Washington Post* editor praised Robinson and denigrated Robeson for his "insulting libels."

Opinions expressed by blacks were not as consistent. First, some blacks were suspicious of HUAC, questioning why it had never thoroughly investigated the Ku Klux Klan or any other American fascist group. They also distrusted HUAC because its committee chair had been held by Southern racists of the likes of Martin Dies (Texas) and John Rankin (Mississippi). Commented one black writer: "How come your committee can investigate everything from Reds to second basemen, and can't investigate the Ku Klux Klan?" Second, one of their own black heroes Paul Robeson, even though tainted, was being attacked by the white establishment. However questionable were some of Robeson's beliefs, he was one of their own. While major white newspapers were cheering Robinson for for castigating Robeson, black papers were generally cheering Robinson for advocating black civil rights and criticizing HUAC'S investigation for dividing blacks against each other. "LYNCHERS OUR CHIEF ENEMY JACKIE TELLS 'RED' PROBERS" headlined the *Philadelphia Afro-American.* One of its writers claimed that the hearings were a "witchhunt." Meanwhile a Pittsburgh writer asserted that Robinson had been a "stooge" for HUAC and had put Negroes on the defensive, hamstringing the civil rights movement. Others, too, criticized Robinson. A woman from the west coast chided Robinson claiming that "the habit of 'bad mouthing' is a slavery trait and should have been outgrown ere this time." An angry individual from Boston wrote that "Paul Robeson was fighting for his people's rights when Jackie Robinson was in knee pants." If HUAC had been successful in creating a negative climate around Robeson's name, it had also created division among blacks over two of their heroes.

A POSTSCRIPT TO THE ROBESON–ROBINSON SAGA

The Robeson-Robinson confrontation added to the mounting pressure in America to cleanse itself of any sympathy for the Soviet Union. Robeson soon began his rapid decline to near oblivion. A Robeson concert in Peekskill, New York, later in the summer of 1949 brought about a united effort by several military veterans groups to stop it. Concert-goers were prevented from attending the first concert attempt, and after it was given a week later, a riot resulted with hundreds injured, numerous autos and buses wrecked, and crosses burned as if it were a Ku Klux Klan rally. Concert managers soon refused to book him, and his recordings were often taken out of record shops. There was even a move by Rutgers University alumni to remove his name from the college rolls. *The American Sports*

Annual deleted Robeson's name from its list of football all-American selections for the years 1917 and 1918. The Federal Bureau of Investigation continually harassed Robeson, and the Secretary of State, John Foster Dulles, had his passport cancelled—two methods used by the federal government to deny Robeson personal freedom and economic independence. The vicious attacks upon Robeson were part of the hysteria created out of the Cold War ideology of the post–World War II era. It was the same hysteria which gave rise to the demagogic character of Joseph McCarthy, who as Senator used character assassination involving the issue of communism in his rise to prominence around 1950.

By the mid-1950s, the anti-communist excesses diminished considerably. Though HUAC was still active, the Senate's censuring of McCarthy helped to control the most outrageous charges of communism in America. Robeson was still effectively blacklisted in America, however, and the denial of a passport for almost a decade placed him in a difficult economic position. He, like the Communist Party which had been legislated out of existence, was successfully silenced. But the question of equal political and social rights for blacks, for which Robeson had been active for a generation, was beginning to come to a head. The landmark Supreme Court decision of 1954, *Brown* v. *Board of Education,* overturned the earlier "separate but equal" decision. Other court actions and federal legislation soon brought resistance and physical confrontation as America faced the proposition of equal rights for all its citizens regardless of race.

Jackie Robinson increasingly spoke out for black rights and, like Robeson before him, was classified by some as an "uppity nigger." Unlike Robeson, Robinson kept his remarks within a more conservative framework. When Robinson announced publicly after the 1956 baseball season that he was retiring from baseball, he wrote:

> I don't regret any part of these last 10 years. There's no reason why I should. Because of baseball I met a man like Branch Rickey and was given the opportunity to break the major-league

color line. Because of baseball, I was able to speak on behalf of Negro Americans before the House Un-American Activities Committee and rebuke Paul Robeson for saying most of us Negroes would not fight for our country in a war against Russia.

Robinson soon joined the National Association for the Advancement of Colored People, and he contributed effectively as a fund raiser. A decade later he withdrew as a protest against its inflexible and conservative nature. Yet Robinson actively campaigned in the 1960 presidential election for Richard Nixon. Nixon had no strong civil rights record, and he had, like Senator Joe McCarthy, used character assassination and the communist issue to promote his popularity. Robinson eventually became disillusioned with Nixon. He also became more pessimistic about the status of American race relations.

Although Jackie Robinson never became reconciled to the beliefs of Paul Robeson, he saw something more positive in Robeson shortly before his own death. Writing in his autobiography published in 1972, titled *I Never Had It Made*, Robinson stated that he never regretted his statements about Robeson made two decades before. "But," Robinson wrote:

I have grown wiser and closer to painful truths about America's destructiveness. And I do have increased respect for Paul Robeson who, over a span of that twenty years, sacrificed himself, his career, and the wealth and comfort he once enjoyed because, I believe, he was sincerely trying to help his people.

When Jackie Robinson died on October 24, 1972, his place in history was almost assured. Paul Robeson died on January 23, 1976. Because he had tied the black rights movement in America to what he considered was a positive Soviet racial policy, he had become a political leper and was in almost total eclipse in the 1950s and 1960s. There was, indeed, a curtain of silence surrounding him. By the 1970s, and especially after his death, a growing number of individuals began to see greatness in Robeson. Even

politicians, who often fear to speak out on controversial individuals and issues, began to speak of Robeson's historic concern for humanity. One of the outspoken was Congressman Andrew Young, a black who later became Ambassador to the United Nations under President Jimmy Carter. He wrote:

Paul Robeson was the hero of my youth. . . . I can never forget the strength of conviction that helped strengthen our backs and set our feet in the path of self-liberation as a people. Paul loved people of all colors and of many nations. He loved justice, freedom, and compassion. He had no tolerance for injustice, oppression, or tyranny. Few men in their lifetime bequeath a legacy to the living.

If both Paul Robeson and Jackie Robinson, as performers, were on the cutting edge of racial reform in America, it appears that they were approaching change from different directions. Robeson wanted reform on his own terms, not necessarily those of white society. Robinson was more willing to compromise with white society for a time to accomplish positive racial goals and his own advancement. Robeson was more idealistic and unyielding, and because of it he was politically, economically, and socially alienated from the greater American society. Robinson was more realistic and pragmatic, and he fared far better socially and financially than did Robeson. What was common to both Robeson and Robinson was that they were both black performers, one an ex-athlete and an actor and singer and the other solely an athlete, who in their own ways fought for equal rights for blacks. Robinson's position as desegregator of professional baseball seems assured. Robeson's status as a crusader for black rights everywhere seems likely to rise with time. If "men will judge men by their souls and not by their skins," as W. E. B. Du Bois advocated in the early twentieth century, it appears that both Paul Robeson and Jackie Robinson, despite their acknowledged differences, will be judged not only as athletic and performing champions but as leaders in race relations as well.

20

THE VIETNAM WAR, THE LIBERALS, AND THE OVERTHROW OF *LBJ*

ALLEN J. MATUSOW

The Vietnam War dominated much of American life in the decade between 1964 and 1974. With an active draft supplying the bulk of the quarter of a million American troops and advisers fighting in Vietnam, three presidents—Kennedy, Johnson, and Nixon—sought to project American military power into Southeast Asia in an effort to "contain communism."

Between 1954—when the United States assumed the role of supporter of the corrupt but anti-Communist South Vietnamese regime—and the early 1960s, American involvement in Vietnam was limited to small numbers of military and civilian advisers. But beginning in 1962, when President John F. Kennedy created the Green Berets, a special counterinsurgency force, American involvement in the region took the path of escalation. Slowly at first, but with increasing speed after the mid-1960s, the American military presence grew until daily reports from the war zone dominated the nightly television news.

As the war continued, with little evidence of success or purpose, growing numbers of Americans began to question the propriety of the war. At the same time, students and other Americans, including many church leaders, organized the most effective antiwar movement in American history. By the late 1960s, antiwar protest took on epic proportions as tens of thousands of Americans—men and women, young and old alike—demonstrated across the country to end the war and bring American troops home.

One of the Vietnam War's more famous casualties was President Lyndon Johnson. In the arrogance of his belief that he could convert the peasants of Vietnam into his image of upwardly mobile American farmers, Johnson escalated U.S. involvement on an unprecedented scale. Mindless of local conditions and the history of the Vietnamese people, Johnson and his advisers committed billions of dollars to a war that many military analysts agreed could not be won. As Allen J. Matusow shows in this essay, Johnson's arrogance cost him the support of American liberals and ultimately the presidency itself.

From The Unraveling of America *by Allen J. Matusow (New York: Harper & Row, 1984), pp. 376–394. Copyright © 1984 by Allen J. Matusow. Reprinted by permission of HarperCollins Publishers.*

In April 1965, three months after Lyndon Johnson made his decision to bomb North Vietnam, Democratic Senator Wayne Morse of Oregon predicted that Johnson's war policy would send him "out of office the most discredited President in the history of the nation." Given the popularity of both the war and the president at the time, Morse's prophecy seemed absurd on its face. But, as Vietnam dragged on month after month, it did indeed become an acid eroding Johnson's political base, until in the end it destroyed his presidency. The first constituency to be alienated by Vietnam—and the most dangerous opponent of Johnson's war policy— proved to be the liberal intellectuals.

At first glance the split between the president and the intellectuals seemed surprising. He was, after all, attempting to govern in the liberal tradition not only in his conduct of domestic policy but in foreign affairs as well. They must hate him, he came to believe, not really for anything he did but because of who he was—a crude Texas cowboy without a Harvard degree. What he failed to understand was that his liberalism and theirs—apparently so similar in 1964— thereafter rapidly diverged, his remaining rooted in the ideas of the 1950s, theirs moving far beyond.

The root of the difficulty was the breakup of the Cold War consensus. In the 1950s, of course, liberal intellectuals typically had embraced the Cold War as a holy crusade, becoming in the process staunch defenders of the American way of life. Even after Sputnik in 1957, when the intellectuals began denouncing the nation for its materialism and complacency, they did so primarily to goad the people into greater sacrifice for the struggle against world Communism. The first sign of restlessness began to appear around 1960. That was the year, for example, when Norman Podhoretz, a New York intellectual who had been a dutiful Cold War liberal but now felt the old ideas going stale, "going dead," became editor of the influential magazine *Commentary*. Daring to open his early issues to dissident voices, he discovered among the intellectuals who wrote for his magazine and read it "a hunger for something new and something radical." Radicalism was hardly the term to describe the outlook of the intellectuals in the Kennedy era, but they were more open to novelty, more willing to acknowledge the flaws in American society, than they had been for years. In 1963, when Kennedy and Kruschchev moved toward détente following the Cuban missile crisis, the international tension that for so long had sustained the Cold War mentality began to dissipate, the old obsession to bore. Liberal intellectuals supported Johnson's 1964 presidential campaign because they believed he shared not only their renewed commitment to social justice but their growing willingness to reach an accommodation with the Russians.

Strains in Johnson's relations with the liberals first appeared in February 1965 when Johnson launched his air war over North Vietnam. Immediately the *New Republic,* a leading journal of liberal opinion, and the Americans for Democratic Action (ADA), the leading liberal organization, condemned the bombing and called for a negotiated settlement. Johnson was perplexed by the criticism since he correctly believed that he was merely applying in Vietnam the doctrine of containment so recently espoused by the liberals themselves. He did not grasp that that doctrine had suddenly fallen from fashion. Among the prominent liberal intellectuals who attempted to account for the shifting views of their community were Hans Morgenthau, an academic specialist in foreign affairs, member of the ADA board, and an early and formidable war critic; Reinhold Niebuhr, the renowned theologian and a founder of ADA, ailing but still influential; Arthur Schlesinger, Jr., a historian, former White House aide of Kennedy and Johnson, half-hearted defender of the war in 1965, but a leading foe by 1966; John Kenneth Galbraith, the Harvard economist, Kennedy's ambassador to India, and in 1967 the ADA chairman; Richard Goodwin, a precocious speech writer for Johnson till September 1965, and a war critic by the following spring; and Richard Rovere, the prestigious political correspondent of *The New Yorker,* a late but important convert to the dove side of the war argument.

The liberal intellectuals did not apologize for their past support of the Cold War. So long as Communist parties everywhere had subordinated themselves to the malign purposes of the Soviet Union, every Communist gain threatened American security. But times had changed, the liberals said. The Communist world was now "polycentric" (many-centered), a situation resulting from the Sino-Soviet split and the emergence of conflicting national aspirations among Communist states. Wrote Schlesinger, "Communism is no longer a unified, coordinated, centralized conspiracy." According to Rovere, since Tito's break with Stalin in 1948, the U.S. should have known that "international Communism" was a myth, "that national interest was more powerful than ideology, and that while we might on occasion find it advisable to resist the outward thrust of certain Communist nations, it made absolutely no sense to have a foreign policy directed against an alliance that did not exist." In short, it was no longer necessary to oppose every Communist initiative on every part of the globe.

With the exception of Morgenthau, who favored recognizing spheres of influence, these intellectuals continued to advocate containing China. But they denied that the war in Vietnam followed logically from this policy. Secretary of State Dean Rusk's opinion to the contrary, China was not the enemy here. The war in South Vietnam, they argued, was primarily a civil war, pitting indigenous revolutionaries against the corrupt and repressive regime in Saigon. If the Communists won, Vietnam might well become a bulwark against the spread of Chinese influence in the region. As a practical matter, the U.S. could not win. Escalation on the ground in the South could easily be offset by the enemy and would do nothing to remedy the defects of the Saigon government. Bombing the North would merely strengthen the enemy's will to fight. If Johnson proceeded on the course of escalation,

he would destroy the country he was trying to save or else provoke war with China.

The war, the liberals said, was not a result of American imperialism but a mistake of policy deriving from obsolete assumptions about international Communism. Unfortunately, it was a mistake not easily remedied. Liberals rejected unilateral withdrawal on the grounds that it would mean abandonment of America's friends in the South, a blow to U.S. prestige, and maybe even the rise at home of a new Joe McCarthy to exploit the frustrations attending defeat. The liberal solution was a negotiated settlement—the middle course, they called it. Stop the foolish bombing in the North, since Hanoi demanded it as a precondition for negotiations. Convince Ho Chi Minh that the U.S. could not be dislodged by force. Offer the Vietcong a seat at the conference table and a role in the postwar political life of South Vietnam. It was possible, of course, that negotiations would fail. In that event, said Galbraith, "We must be prepared to defend for the time being the limited areas that are now secure." Indeed, on close inspection, it turned out that the liberals were waist deep in the Big Muddy along with LBJ and were no more certain than he of getting back to shore. The difference was that they thought the war was all a big mistake, and he was there on principle.

As opposition to the war among the intellectuals mounted, so did their impatience with the administration's response to the great racial and urban crisis that was tearing the country apart. As they never would have done during the American celebration that had characterized the heydey of the Cold War, liberals were now earnestly discussing the menace of corporate monopoly, redistribution of income, and a Marshall Plan for the cities. In its January 1967 issue *Commentary* ran both a long article by Theodore Draper attacking Johnson's foreign policy for its "willingness to use and abuse naked military power" and an essay by the Keynesian economist Robert Lekachman summarizing the case of many liberal intellectuals against the president's domestic policies. Lekachman wrote:

Possibly Mr. Johnson went just about as far as a conservative politician in a conservative, racist country could have gone. The Great Society has distributed the nation's income even less equally than it was distributed before 1960. It has enlarged the prestige and influence of the business community. It has lost its token bouts with racism and poverty. The Great Society, never a giant step beyond the New Deal which was President Johnson's youthful inspiration, has ground to a halt far short of a massive attack on urban blight, far short of the full integration of Negroes into American society, and far short of a genuine assault upon poverty and deprivation.

Where liberal intellectuals led, liberal politicians usually followed. But politicians skeptical of the war in Vietnam initially hesitated to tangle with a president to whom most were bound by ties of party loyalty and whose vindictive character was legend. In 1965 even senators held their tongues, excepting of course Oregon's Wayne Morse and Alaska's Ernest Gruening, the lone opponents of the 1964 Gulf of Tonkin Resolution. Among those who privately worried but publicly acquiesced in Johnson's war policy were Senators Mike Mansfield, George McGovern, Frank Church, Joseph Clark, Eugene McCarthy, and J. William Fulbright. Fulbright was the pivotal figure. If he moved into the open against Johnson, the rest would follow.

A senator from the ex-Confederate state of Arkansas, Fulbright was a gentleman of inherited wealth, excellent education, and illiberal record on matters of race and social reform. But for more than twenty years, on matters of foreign policy, Fulbright had been the leading spokesman in Congress for the views of the liberal community. Though he had had his share of arguments with presidents, he was by nature a contemplative rather than a combative man, a Senate club member who played by the rules. Fulbright's early opinions on Vietnam were hardly heretical. In March 1964, in a wide-ranging speech attacking Cold War mythology, he paused over Vietnam long enough to make a few hawkish observations. The allies were too weak militarily to obtain "the independence of a non-Communist South Vietnam" through negotiations, he said. The only "realistic options" were to hasten the buildup of the regime in the South or to expand the war, "either by the direct commitment of large numbers of American troops or by equipping the South Vietnamese Army to attack North Vietnamese territory." In August 1964 Fulbright sponsored the Gulf of Tonkin Resolution, which gave Johnson authority to expand the war.

For reasons unknown, Fulbright had second thoughts about escalation once it actually began. Publicly in the spring of 1965 he backed Johnson's policy, though he called for a temporary bombing halt to induce Hanoi to negotiate. Privately, he warned his old friend in the White House against waging war on North Vietnam and tempted him with the vision of a Communist Vietnam hostile to China. Johnson seemed bored by Fulbright's conversation. Fulbright gave a Senate speech in June that both criticized the bombing and praised Johnson's statesmanship. In July Johnson began the massive infusion of ground troops into South Vietnam.

Fulbright's first real attack on the Johnson administration was occasioned not by Vietnam but by policy in the Dominican Republic. In April 1965 Johnson sent U.S. troops into the midst of a developing civil war, ostensibly to protect Americans but really to prevent a possible Communist takeover. Fulbright brooded over this intervention, held secret hearings on it, and finally in September delivered a powerful Senate speech attacking the administration's conduct as ruthless and lacking in candor. The president promptly ended all pretense of consulting the chairman of the Foreign Relations Committee and cut him socially.

As Fulbright edged toward open rebellion on the issue of the war, so did the other Senate doves, almost all of whom were liberal Democrats. This was probably one reason why Johnson halted the bombing of North Vietnam on Christmas Eve, 1965, and launched a well-advertised peace offensive allegedly to persuade

Hanoi to negotiate. The State Department moved closer to Hanoi's conditions for negotiations in early January, and both sides scaled down ground action in South Vietnam. Diplomats in several capitals worked to bring the wary antagonists together. But on January 24, 1966, Johnson hinted to a group of congressional leaders that he might soon resume the bombing. Two days later fifteen senators, all of them liberal Democrats, sent a letter to Johnson urging him to continue the pause. Fulbright and Mansfield did not sign but were on record with similar views. On January 29, Johnson ordered the air attack to recommence. The episode convinced many liberals that Johnson's talk about peace masked his private determination to win total military victory.

In February 1966 Fulbright held televised hearings on the war. The scholar-diplomat George Kennan and the retired general James Gavin argued the case against it on grounds of American self-interest. Dean Rusk and General Maxwell Taylor parried the thrusts of liberal committee members now openly critical of Johnson's policy. Neither side drew blood in debate, but by helping legitimize dissent, the Fulbright hearings were a net loss for Johnson. Fulbright, meantime, was reading, talking to experts, and rethinking first principles. In the spring of 1966 he took to the lecture platform to hurl thunderbolts at orthodoxy. Revised and published as a book later in the year, Fulbright's lectures were a critique of American foreign policy far more advanced than any yet produced by the liberal academicians.

"Gradually but unmistakably America is showing signs of that arrogance of power which has afflicted, weakened, and in some cases destroyed great nations in the past," Fulbright said. Harnessing her might to a crusading ideology, America had overextended herself abroad and was neglecting vital tasks at home. Americans meant well overseas, Fulbright conceded, but they often did more harm than good, especially in the Third World. A conservative people, Americans supported necessary social revolutions in traditional societies only if they were peaceful,

that is, in "our own shining image." To violent revolutions, which "seem to promise greater and faster results," Americans reacted with automatic hostility or panic. Fulbright was hardly an apologist for revolutions, but neither would he oppose them, even if they were led by Communists. Fulbright dared to find much that was praiseworthy in Castro's Cuba and even extended sympathy to the aims of the Chinese revolutionaries, whose regime he would recognize de facto. In Vietnam, he said, the U.S. had blundered into a war against Communism in the only country in the world "which won freedom from colonial rule under communist leadership." Fulbright favored a negotiated settlement that would provide self-determination for South Vietnam through the mechanism of a referendum.

President Johnson had expected his main trouble to come from hawks who wanted to escalate faster than he did. Stung by the sweeping attacks of Fulbright and other doves, he resorted to a scoundrel's last refuge. Before a friendly audience of Democratic politicians in Chicago mid-May 1966, Johnson defended the war as a patriotic effort to secure lasting peace by punishing aggression and then said, "There will be some 'Nervous Nellies' and some who will become frustrated and bothered and break ranks under the strain, and some will turn on their leaders, and on their country, and on our own fighting men. . . . But I have not the slightest doubt that the courage and the dedication and the good sense of the wise American people will ultimately prevail." The attack failed to silence the critics. The majority of the people still backed the war, but not with the passion aroused by wars of the past. Fulbright continued to assault the premises of American foreign policy and, indirectly, the president who was acting on them. Confronted with irreconcilable views of world politics, members of the liberal public in ever-increasing numbers deserted the president and sided with the senator.

To make matters worse for Johnson, he faced a personal as well as an intellectual challenge to his party leadership. When Robert Kennedy emerged from mourning in early 1964, he discovered a remarkable fact. Despite his squeaky voice, diffident public manner, private shyness, and reputation as a ruthless backroom operator, he was the sole beneficiary of his brother's political estate. In him resided the hopes of millions who believed the myth of Camelot and longed for a Kennedy restoration. Robert Kennedy believed the myth himself and shared the longing. Lyndon Johnson, however, despised Kennedy personally and made himself the great obstacle to the younger man's ambitions. After Johnson denied him the vice-presidential nomination in 1964, Kennedy repaired to New York, where he successfully ran for the Senate. Soon there grew up around him what the political columnists called the Kennedy party—Kennedy loyalists still in the bureaucracy, some senators, New Frontiersman out of favor, and lesser politicians, lawyers, and professors scattered around the country. Most of the Kennedy loyalists were liberals, but by no means all liberals were Kennedy loyalists. Robert Kennedy, after all, had been an ally of Joe McCarthy, an advocate of wiretapping, too zealous a pursuer of the Teamster chief Jimmy Hoffa, and a frequent offender of liberal sensibilities. But liberals unhappy with Johnson needed a popular leader, and Kennedy needed to broaden his party base. The one issue guaranteed to bring them together was Vietnam.

The issue posed problems for Kennedy. As a Cabinet officer, he had been an enthusiastic student of guerrilla warfare and a strong supporter of his brother's counterinsurgency program in South Vietnam. When Johnson escalated in 1965, Kennedy questioned less the attempt to rescue South Vietnam by force of arms than the tendency to subordinate political to military considerations in fighting the war. Speaking at the graduation ceremony of the International Police Academy in July, he said, "I think the history of the last 20 years demonstrates beyond doubt that our approach to revolutionary war must be political—political first, political last, political always." To avoid offending Johnson, he excised from his prepared text the view that "victory in a revolu-

tionary war is won not by escalation but by de-escalation." Kennedy waited one whole year after escalation before putting real distance between his position and Johnson's. It bothered Kennedy that, when Fulbright asked Rusk during the television hearings of February 1966 to state the options other than "surrender or annihilation" that he was offering the Vietcong, Rusk had replied, "They do have an alternative of quitting, of stopping being an agent of Hanoi and receiving men and arms from the North." The war could go on forever if this was the American requirement for peace. So Kennedy decided to propose another option. On February 19, 1966, he became the first senator to suggest a negotiated settlement that would give the Vietcong "a share of power and responsibility"—in what he did not say. Assuming he meant the government of Vietnam, the administration dismissed the idea contemptuously. Kennedy's proposal, said Vice President Humphrey, would be like putting "a fox in the chicken coop" or "an arsonist in a fire department." Kennedy spent the next week clarifying and qualifying, and though he retreated some, he was clearly moving toward the peace wing of his party.

Strange things were happening to Bobby Kennedy. Perhaps prolonged grief deepened his social sympathies, perhaps he was trying in his own life to vindicate his brother's legend—or outdo it. Whatever the cause, Kennedy plunged into the currents of change that were swirling through America in the mid-1960s, currents that were altering the perspective of liberalism and passing Johnson by. Kennedy opened a running dialogue with students, made a friend of Tom Hayden, felt the yearnings of the poor and the black for power and dignity, and took unnecessary political risks. Blood donations for the Vietcong? Burial for a Communist war hero in Arlington Cemetery? Why not? he asked. Kennedy went to South Africa in mid-1966 to aid the opponents of apartheid. He attacked administration witnesses at Senate hearings in August for unresponsiveness to the poor. He flew to California to stand with Cesar Chavez in his fight to unionize the grape pickers. A man who risked his life scaling mountains and defying tropical storms on the Amazon, Kennedy was becoming an existentialist in politics, defining himself in action and moving where his heart told him to go.

As Kennedy and Johnson edged closer toward political combat, their personal relations worsened. In February 1967 *Newsweek* erroneously reported that Kennedy had brought back from a recent trip to Paris a peace feeler from Hanoi. The story enraged Johnson, who, believing it was planted by Kennedy, called him to the White House for a tongue lashing. According to *Time*'s colorful account, Johnson told Kennedy, "If you keep talking like this, you won't have a political future in this country within six months," warned him that "the blood of American boys will be on your hands," and concluded, "I never want to see you again." Uncowed, Kennedy called Johnson an s.o.b and told him, "I don't have to sit here and take that —." Whether Kennedy really used vulgarity was a matter of some dispute, but there was no doubt that the gist of the conversation had been accurately reported. Less than a month later (March 2, 1967) Kennedy gave a major Senate speech calling for a halt to the bombing and a compromise settlement through negotiations. A few party malcontents, especially in the liberal wing, permitted themselves a small hope that maybe the crown prince of the Democratic party would claim his inheritance sooner than expected.

In the summer of 1967 gloom descended on the camp of the liberals. In August Johnson sent 45,000 more troops to Vietnam and asked for higher taxes to finance the war. And, though Defense Secretary Robert McNamara himself voiced public criticism of the bombing, day after day the bombs continued to fall. Liberals who had once viewed it merely as politically stupid watched in horror as the carnage mounted and now pronounced the war morally wrong as well. Meanwhile domestic insurrectionaries were gutting great American cities, the War on Poverty was bogging down, and the long-awaited white backlash finally arrived. Among those surrender-

ing to despair that summer was Senator Fulbright. Speaking to the American Bar Association in August, he said, "How can we commend democratic social reform to Latin America when Newark, Detroit, and Milwaukee are providing explosive evidence of our own inadequate efforts at democratic social reform? How can we commend the free enterprise system to Asians and Africans when in our own country it has produced vast, chaotic, noisy, dangerous and dirty urban complexes while poisoning the very air and land and water?" Fulbright called the war "unnecessary and immoral" and blamed it for aggravating grave domestic problems. The country "sickens for lack of moral leadership," he said, and only the idealistic young may save us from the "false and dangerous dream of an imperial destiny."

Fulbright's charges about the damage done at home by the war were confirmed in the autumn. Driven by hatred of the war, new left students began acting out their guerrilla fantasies, and major campuses were threatened by chaos. No less disturbing to liberals was the fever of discontent rising in intellectual circles. Some of the nation's most brilliant writers and artists were concluding, as had their counterparts in France during the Algerian war, that they now had no choice but to resist the state.

From the beginning a minority of the nation's intellectual elite—call them radicals—saw the war as more than a blunder in judgment. Most of these radicals had life histories punctuated by episodes of dissent but had stayed aloof from politics during the Cold War. Vietnam brought them back to political awareness and gave focus to their inchoate alienation. To people like the novelists Norman Mailer and Mary McCarthy, the critics Susan Sontag and Dwight Macdonald, *New York Review of Books* editor Robert Silvers, the linguist Noam Chomsky, the anarchist writer Paul Goodman, and the poet Robert Lowell, America appeared to be in the hands of a technological elite that was debauching the American landscape and lusting after world dominion. Morally revolted by the imperial war against the peasants of Vietnam, the radicals found traditional politics insufficient to express their opposition. The war was a matter of conscience, and good men would act accordingly.

Their first impulse was to avoid complicity with the crime. Thus when Johnson invited a group of writers and artists to participate in a White House Festival of the Arts in June 1965, Robert Lowell refused to come. Scion of a distinguished American family, perhaps the best of living American poets, and a draft resister in World War II, Lowell sent a letter to the president, saying, "Every serious artist knows that he cannot enjoy public celebration without making subtle public commitments. . . . We are in danger of imperceptibly becoming an explosive and suddenly chauvinistic nation, and we may even be drifting on our way to the last nuclear ruin. . . . At this anguished, delicate and perhaps determining moment, I feel I am serving you and our country best by not taking part." Robert Silvers took the lead in circulating a statement in support of his friend Lowell and in two days attracted the signatures of twenty of the nation's most prominent writers and artists, among them Hannah Arendt, Lillian Hellman, Alfred Kazin, Dwight Macdonald, Bernard Malamud, Mary McCarthy, William Styron, and Robert Penn Warren. Johnson was so angry at "these people," these "sonsofbitches" that he almost canceled the festival.

By 1967 the radicals were obsessed by the war and frustrated by their impotence to affect its course. The government was unmoved by protest, the people were uninformed and apathetic, and American technology was tearing Vietnam apart. What, then, was their responsibility? Noam Chomsky explored this problem in February 1967 in the *New York Review*, which had become the favorite journal of the radicals. By virtue of their training and leisure, intellectuals had a greater responsibility than ordinary citizens for the actions of the state, Chomsky said. It was their special responsibility "to speak the truth and expose lies." But the "free-floating intellectual" who had performed this function in the past was being replaced by the "scholar-expert" who lied for the government or con-

structed "value-free technologies" to keep the existing social order functioning smoothly. Chomsky not only enjoined the intellectuals once again "to seek the truth lying behind the veil of distortion"; he concluded by quoting an essay written twenty years before by Dwight Macdonald, an essay that implied that in time of crisis exposing lies might not be enough. "Only those who are willing to resist authority themselves when it conflicts too intolerably with their personal moral code," Macdonald had written, "only they have the right to condemn." Chomsky's article was immediately recognized as an important intellectual event. Along with the radical students, radical intellectuals were moving "from protest to resistance."

The move toward resistance accelerated through 1967. Chomsky announced in the *New York Review* that for the second consecutive year he was withholding half his income taxes to protest the war. Paul Goodman invited federal prosecution by acknowledging his efforts to aid and abet draft resistance. Mary McCarthy, back form a trip to Vietnam, said that "to be in the town jail, as Thoreau knew, can relieve any sense of imaginary imprisonment." On the cover of its issue of August 24, 1967, the *New York Review* put a diagram of a Molotov cocktail, while inside Andrew Kopkind, in the midst of dismissing Martin Luther King for having failed to make a revolution, wrote, "Morality, like politics, starts at the barrel of a gun." (Some intellectuals never forgave the *New York Review* for that one.) On October 12, 1967, the *New York Review* published a statement signed by 121 intellectuals and entitled "A Call to Resist Illegitimate Authority." The statement denounced the war on legal and moral grounds and pledged the signers to raise funds "to organize draft resistance unions, to supply legal defense and bail, to support families and otherwise aid resistance to the war in whatever ways may seem appropriate.

A few days later Stop the Draft Week began. This was an event whose possibilities excited radical intellectuals as well as radical students. Paul Goodman kicked the week off with a speech at the State Department before an audience of big business executives. "You are the military industrial of the United States, the most dangerous body of men at the present in the world," Goodman declaimed. On Friday, October 20, 1967, Lowell and Mailer spoke on the steps of the Justice Department prior to the efforts of the Reverend William Sloane Coffin to deliver to the government draft cards collected from draft resisters across the country earlier in the week. (This occasion provided evidence for later federal charges of criminal conspiracy against Coffin, Dr. Benjamin Spock, and three other antiwar activists.) Saturday began with speeches at the Lincoln Memorial ("remorseless, amplified harangues for peace," Lowell called them), and then the march across the bridge toward the Pentagon. Lowell, Mailer, and Macdonald, described by Mailer as "America's best poet? and best novelist??, and best critic???," walked to the battle together. Lowell wrote of the marchers that they were

> . . . *like green Union recruits*
> *for the first Bull Run, sped by*
>   *photographers,*
> *the notables, the girls . . . fear, glory, chaos,*
> *rout . . .*
> *our green army staggered out on the*
>   *miles-long green fields,*
> *met by the other army, the Martian, the ape,*
>   *the hero,*
> *his new-fangled rifle, his green new steel*
>   *helmet.*

At the Pentagon Mailer was arrested, much to his satisfaction, but Lowell and Macdonald failed of their object. Noam Chomsky, also present, had not intended to participate in civil disobedience, feeling its purpose in this occasion too vague to make a point. Swept up by the events of the day, Chomsky found himself at the very walls of the fortress, making a speech. When a line of soldiers began marching toward him, he spontaneously sat down. Chomsky spent the night in jail with Mailer.

In his brilliant book *The Armies of the Night*, Mailer probed for the meaning of these apocalyptic events. For him the siege of the Pentagon was a rite of passage for the student rebels, for the intellectuals, for himself. The few hundred fearful youths who sat on the Pentagon steps till dawn on Sunday were a "refrain from all the great American rites of passage when men and women manacled themselves to a lost and painful principle and survived a day, a night, a week, a month, a year." The battle at the Pentagon was a pale rite of passage, he thought, compared to that of the immigrants packed in steerage, Rogers and Clark, the Americans "at Sutter's Mill, at Gettysburg, the Alamo, the Klondike, the Argonne, Normandy, Pusan." But it was a true rite of passage nonetheless, the survivors having been reborn and rededicated to great purpose. On departing from jail Sunday morning, Mailer felt as Christians must "when they spoke of Christ within them." For Mailer and many other radical intellectuals, American institutions seemed so illegitimate that a moral man could find redemption only in resisting them. As for the liberals, they could only wonder what would happen to America if Lyndon Johnson was not stopped.

Signs of a liberal revolt against Johnson's renomination were plentiful in the fall of 1967. Reform Democrats in New York, the liberal California Democratic Council, party factions in Minnesota, Michigan, Wisconsin, and elsewhere were preparing to oppose him. In late September the ADA national board implicitly came out against him by promising to back the candidate who offered "the best prospect for a settlement of the Vietnam conflict." The *New Republic* explicitly rejected his candidacy in an editorial that same week. And Allard Lowenstein, thirty-eight-year-old liberal activist and ADA vice-chairman, opened an office in Washington and began organizing a movement on campuses, in the peace movement, and among dissident Democratic politicians to "dump Johnson."

Lowenstein wanted Robert Kennedy to be his candidate. And the existentialist Bobby was tempted. Kennedy worried about the frustration building up in the antiwar movement and had himself come to view the war as morally repugnant. "We're killing South Vietnamese, we're killing women, we're killing innocent people because we don't want to have the war fought on American soil, or because they're 12,000 miles away and they might get 11,000 miles away," he said on *Face the Nation* late in November 1967. But Bobby the professional hated losing, and in his view he could not defeat Johnson in a fight for the nomination, and neither could anybody else. On that same TV program he stated flatly that he would not be a candidate. If he were, he said, "it would immediately become a personality struggle," and the real issues would be obscured. Asked about some other Democrat, such as Senator Eugene McCarthy of Minnesota, taking on the president, Kennedy replied, "There could be a healthy element in that." He would endorse neither Johnson nor McCarthy but support whoever was the eventual party nominee.

Eugene McCarthy had become convinced that someone would have to raise the issue of the war in the party primaries in 1968. When Kennedy and other leading doves rejected Lowenstein's pleas to be the candidate, McCarthy agreed to run. Explaining his purpose at a press conference on November 30, 1967, he said, "There is growing evidence of a deepening moral crisis in America—discontent and frustration and a disposition to take extralegal if not illegal actions to manifest protest. I am hopeful that this challenge . . . may alleviate at least in some degree this sense of political helplessness and restore to many people a belief in the processes of American politics and of American government." In other words, McCarthy was offering his candidacy as an alternative to radicalism.

Only an unusual politician would undertake what no one else would dare. In truth McCarthy, who had spent eight months of his youth as a novice in a Benedictine monastery, was in the political world but not of it. He was a senator bored by the Senate, an office seeker who distained intrigue and self-advertisement, a profes-

sional who valued honor more than influence. In recent years he had seemed more interested in Thomistic theology and writing poetry than in the business of government. His career, it appeared, would not fulfill its early promise. But the political crisis in the United States in late 1967 provided McCarthy with an opportunity perfectly suited to his self-conception. Like his hero Thomas More, he would play the martyr in a historic confrontation between conscience and power.

McCarthy's candidacy prospered beyond anyone's expectation, even his own. Though Johnson's rating on the Gallup poll was only 41 percent in November, the professionals were mesmerized by the cliché that no president could be denied renomination by his own party. The war was the biggest cause of Johnson's unpopularity. Hawks and doves disagreed on how best to end the war but otherwise had much in common: both disliked the war, wanted its early termination, and tended to blame Lyndon Johnson for dragging it on. It was the public's declining confidence in Johnson's ability to conclude the war that made him vulnerable to McCarthy's candidacy.

What little confidence still existed in the president's war leadership was shattered on January 31, 1968, when the Vietnamese Communists launched a massive attack in the midst of a truce called for the Tet holiday. Sixty-seven thousand enemy troops invaded more than one hundred of South Vietnam's cities and towns. The allies recaptured most urban areas after a few days and inflicted huge casualties on the attackers. But the Tet Offensive had astounded military men by its scope and daring. It showed that no place in South Vietnam was secure, not even the American embassy, whose walls had been breached in the first hours of the attack. And it temporarily derailed the pacification program in the countryside by drawing allied troops into the cities. Coming after recent administration assurances that the war was being won, the Tet Offensive dealt Johnson's credibility its crowning blow. When he and the U.S. commander in

Vietnam, General William Westmoreland, issued victory statements after the offensive ended, few took them seriously, though militarily they were right. The chief political casualty of the Tet Offensive, therefore, was Lyndon Johnson.

In the six weeks after Tet, such pillars of establishment opinion as Walter Cronkite, *Newsweek,* the *Wall Street Journal,* and NBC News gave way and called for de-escalation. High officials in the government finally dared express their private doubts about the war to the president. The Gallup poll reported a seismic shift in public opinion: in February self-described hawks had outnumbered doves 60 percent to 24 percent; in March it was hawks 41 percent, doves 42 percent. And on March 10, two days before the New Hampshire primary, the *New York Times* set off waves of national anxiety by reporting a secret request from the generals to the president for 206,000 more troops for the war.

Meanwhile, in New Hampshire, the first primary state, McCarthy was proving an eccentric candidate. A lazy campaigner, he often did not return phone calls, would not court potential contributors, and avoided local politicians. His manner on the stump was uninspired, and even his references to the war were low-key. (McCarthy opposed unilateral withdrawal and advocated a negotiated settlement.) But McCarthy had an insight denied to his detractors: he mattered less in this campaign than the movement he represented. At the climax of the campaign there were so many student volunteers in the tiny state (3,000, or one for every 25 Democratic voters) that McCarthy's lieutenants begged potential workers to stay home. Scrubbed and shaven, the students ran a canvassing operation that was the envy of the professionals. Even McCarthy's peculiar style proved to be an asset. At a time when the country was fed up with politicians, shrill voices, and the hard sell, there was something reassuring in McCarthy's unhurried, dignified manner. He did not frighten people. He seemed safe.

Governor John W. King, one of the inept managers of Johnson's write-in campaign in New Hampshire, said in the beginning that McCarthy would get 5 percent of the vote. McCarthy himself predicted 30 percent. On March 12, 1968, 49 percent of New Hampshire's Democratic voters wrote in the name of the president of the United States, and 42 percent marked their ballots for a senator of whom days before few had heard. Poll data showed that more McCarthy voters in New Hampshire were hawks than doves. McCarthy's remarkable showing, then, was not a victory for peace, merely proof that Lyndon Johnson, who could neither pacify the ghetto, speak the plain truth, lick inflation, nor above all end the war, was a mighty unpopular president indeed.

McCarthy had done more than demonstrate Johnson's vulnerability. As he had hoped, his candidacy drained off some of the discontent flowing into illegal protest. Thousands of students who might otherwise have joined SDS got "clean for Gene." Intellectuals who had flirted with resistance a few months before became the senator's avid fans. McCarthy's traveling companion through much of New Hampshire was Robert Lowell—a symbolic relationship whose significance was probably lost on neither of these famous poets.

It had been a hard winter for Robert Kennedy. He realized after the Tet Offensive that his refusal to run had been a mistake. Throughout February 1968, while McCarthy's New Hampshire campaign was getting started, Kennedy and his advisers wrestled again with the problem of his candidacy. Kennedy was ready to go early in March and set in motion machinery for a campaign. But still he found reason to delay a public announcement. By the time he declared on March 16, 1968, the results of the New Hampshire primary had already electrified the country. Much of the constituency that would have been his now belonged to McCarthy. Lyndon Johnson, however, took Kennedy's candidacy more seriously than McCarthy's. He knew, even if the students did not, that Kennedy was the one man in the party who might beat him.

McCarthy refused to set aside for Kennedy and moved on to the Wisconsin primary, whose date was April 2. Early in March the president's men in Wisconsin had been confident of victory. But McCarthy arrived with more students, money, and prestige than he had had in New Hampshire, and by mid-month the Johnson managers knew their man was in trouble. On March 28 Postmaster Larry O'Brien, an old political pro, returned from a look around the state to tell Johnson that his cause there was hopeless.

While the political storms raged around them, Johnson and his advisers were deep into a momentous review of war policy. General Earl Wheeler, chairman of the Joint Chiefs of Staff, had blundered in late February when he privately requested 206,000 additional troops for Vietnam. Since General Westmoreland was in no danger of being overrun, there was never much chance that Johnson would dispatch massive reinforcements. The tax money to pay for escalation was not there, and neither was the political support. Wheeler's request had one unintended result. By asking so much, it forced policy makers to resolve the basic ambiguity that had characterized America's policy since 1965. Militarily, Johnson had been seeking victory over the Vietcong. Diplomatically, he paid lip service to a negotiated settlement, which implied compromise. Since his generals were in effect telling him that they needed more troops than he could furnish to win, Johnson had no choice now except to opt for negotiation. Accounts differ on how Johnson reached this conclusion in March 1968. But in the end those of his advisers urging some steps in the direction of de-escalation prevailed. On March 31 Johnson went on television to announce that he was stopping the bombing over most of North Vietnam and would end it entirely if Hanoi demonstrated comparable restraint. Johnson called on the North Vietnamese to respond to his partial bombing halt by accepting his invitation to negotiate. A few days later they did so.

Johnson announced another decision in this speech. For some time he had been dropping hints among friends and advisers that he might not run in 1968. Only at the last minute did he determine not to make his 1968 State of the Union Message the occasion for announcing his retirement. But his mood seemed to change after that, and he took steps to organize a re-election campaign. Even after the ambush in New Hampshire, Johnson authorized Larry O'Brien to meet with cabinet officers and give them marching orders for the political battle ahead.

Though most Johnson intimates believed he would run, he had compelling reasons not to. Exhausted, haunted by fear of another heart attack, bitter at the vilification he had suffered, the man had had enough. "The only difference between the [John F.] Kennedy assassination and mine," he said in this period, "is that I am alive and it has been more tortuous." There were other reasons too. Politically he faced a Congress opposed to his programs, a public that had lost confidence in his leadership, a defeat at the hands of McCarthy in the Wisconsin primary, and an uncertain contest with Robert Kennedy. On the diplomatic front, he wished to take a step toward peace, which his opponents, domestic and foreign, would probably dismiss as insincere if he remained a potential candidate. In his speech of March 31, Johnson spoke of "division in the American house" and declared his intention to keep the presidency above partisanship in this election year. "Accordingly," he told a stunned nation, "I shall not seek, and I will not accept, the nomination of my party for another term as your President." The liberals, with an assist from the peace movement, the attackers of Tet, and war-weariness, had dumped Johnson.

21

"RONALD REAGAN"—THE MOVIE

MICHAEL ROGIN

The 1980 election represented an abrupt turn toward conservatism in American political life. The election of Ronald Reagan as the fortieth president capped a campaign on the part of New Right conservatives, begun in the years immediately following World War II, to capture the White House. Frustrated by the defeat of their presidential candidate, Barry Goldwater, in the 1964 election and ill-served by the Watergate scandal of the Nixon administration in the 1970s, conservatives viewed Reagan's election as the final triumph of an agenda that had been more than 30 years in the making.

But who was this new president who had promised to dismantle the American welfare state? Reagan had not come from a traditional political background. In fact, though he had served two terms as governor of California, his true vocation was as an actor. From World War II until the early 1960s, Reagan played in dozens of movies and television programs, usually portraying traditional masculine and patriotic characters. As Michael Rogin suggests, it was his acting out of these roles more than any political platform or ideology that defined Ronald Reagan. The key to understanding both the man and his remarkable political success during the 1980s, Rogin suggests, is in appreciating the unconscious blurring of the real and make-believe worlds that Reagan accomplished with such seeming effortlessness.

While Rogin focuses on the cultural and psychological appeal of Ronald Reagan, other writers have pointed to the unraveling of post–World War II liberalism as the true reason for the conservative triumph in 1980. Viewed from this perspective of long-range cultural and political change, Reagan may have been simply the right man with the right appearance and the right message at the right time.

The year is 1940; Stalin and Hitler have signed their pact, and Europe is at war. Saboteurs are operating inside America as well, blowing up bridges and trains. The House Un-American Activities Committee, investigating sabotage and sedition, subpoenas Joe Garvey, the chairman of the Society of Loyal Naturalized Americans. Speaking with a foreign accent, Garvey insists that the purpose of his organization is simply to preserve American neutrality and keep the country out of war. When asked by HUAC's chairman if labor racketeering, unlawful assembly and sabotage are the activities of loyal Americans, Garvey responds that such accusations are "capitalistic" lies.

In truth, however, Garvey heads a ring of foreign spies. One of Garvey's saboteurs has been killed in a train wreck, and the Secret Service has sent a secret agent to impersonate him. To test the agent's identity, Garvey's toughs masquerade as policemen and knock him around; they accuse him of being a Wobbly and a Red. Satisfied that the secret agent really is one of them, an anti-American subversive, Garvey's men take him to their boss.

America has invented a miraculous secret weapon that paralyzes electric currents at their source. The inertia projector, as it is called, stops and destroys anything that moves. It will, according to newspaper reports, "make America invincible in war, and therefore be the greatest force for peace ever invented." When Garvey and another foreign spy fly off with the plans for the weapon, the secret agent follows. He turns the inertia projector on the spy plane; it stops in mid-air, catches fire and plummets to the ground.

Murder in the Air—the name of the movie I have been describing—is a minor incident in the 1940s politicization of Hollywood. It would remain forgotten, as it has until now, if the man who played the secret agent, Brass Bancroft, were not Ronald Reagan. The attack on subversion; the merger of Communism and fascism; the flippancy about matters of life and death, peace and war; the obsession with intelligence agents as the means to national security; and, most strikingly, the existence of an airborne defensive

superweapon that will make America invulnerable—all these look forward beyond World War II to the "Star Wars" militarization of space and the Reagan presidency. Believing that there has never been a time in history "when there wasn't a defense against some kind of threat," President Reagan ignored his own scientific consultants and normal bureaucratic processes to write out in longhand the paragraphs of his March 1983 speech advocating a ballistic missile defense system that "holds the promise of changing the course of history." "The Strategic Defense Initiative has been labeled 'Star Wars,'" the President said two years later. "But it isn't about war. It is about peace. . . . If you will pardon my stealing a film line—the force is with us." Are we now being ruled by the fantasies of a 1940s countersubversive B movie?

This essay investigates the making of Ronald Reagan in 1940s Hollywood. The Presidential character, we shall see, was produced from the convergence of two sets of substitutions that generated cold war countersubversion in the 1940s and that underlie its 1980s revival—the political replacement of Nazism by Communism, from which the national security state was born; and the psychological shift from an embodied self to its simulacrum on film. Reagan, I suggest, found out who he was from the characters he played on film. By responding to type-casting that either attracted or repelled him, by making active efforts to obtain certain roles and to escape from others, Reagan gradually merged his on- and off-screen identities. The confusion between life and film produced "Ronald Reagan," the image that has fixed our gaze. In deliberate imitation of the Reagan process, this essay explores that confusion between life and film to bring the making of this President into view.

I

"Movies Are Forever," was the theme of the 1981 Academy Awards. President Ronald Reagan, the first actor elevated to the Presidency, was scheduled to welcome the Academy from the White House. "Film is forever," the President was to tell the Academy. "It is the motion picture that tells us not only how we look and sound but—more important[ly]—how we feel." Hollywood movies, Reagan was suggesting, mirror back to us the feelings we see on the screen as if they were our own. As if to confirm the President's faith in the power of film, John W. Hinckley, Jr., imitating the plot of *Taxi Driver*, deliberately shot the President on the day of the Academy Awards.

Millions of Americans experienced the assassination attempt by watching it over and over again on TV. The power of the image to confirm the shooting also allowed Reagan to speak to the Academy the next night as if it had never happened. The television audience watching their screens saw a Hollywood audience watching another screen. One audience saw the other applaud a taped image of a healthy Reagan, while the real President lay in a hospital bed. Reagan was President because of film, hospitalized because of film and present as image because of film. The shooting climaxed film's ingestion of reality. In doing so it culminated, in an uncanny way, Reagan's personal project: the creation of a disembodied self that, by rising above real inner conflicts, would reflect back to the President and all the rest of us not only how he looked and sounded but—more importantly—how he felt and who he was.

The Hollywood movie in its classic years—the late 1930s through the 1950s, the years of Reagan's Hollywood career—was at once overdone and improbable and yet continuous with ordinary life. Hollywood films relaxed mundane constraints, not to obliterate daily life, but to allow its daydreams to take over. The stories and the methods of these movies broke down the conventional boundaries between fantasy and reality, heroes and ordinary people. Early cinema, whether in Eisenstein's social mode or in German expressionism's psychological mode (both fathered by D. W. Griffith), was self-conscious about its technique. It called attention to the filmmaker and his instruments, to the camera eye and the film cut. By contrast, "the Hollywood aim was," in Kevin Brownlow's words, "to perfect

technique and thus render it imperceptible." The Hollywood movie blended the storyteller with the narrative and disguised the artfulness of film cuts. Dialogue and the moving camera made movies seem mimetic of quotidian reality. By hiding technique, film naturalized the fantasy nature of its content. Hollywood naturalism, in which depth of focus gave the illusion of ordinary three dimensionality, kept viewers on the surface of the image. The audience knew they were at a motion picture theater, but were not led to ask whether what they were seeing was real. Classic Hollywood films encouraged confusion between "daydreams," as Martha Wolfenstein and Nathan Leites call these films, and daily life. Movies functioned as arenas for role-playing. They may not have done so for everyone in the mass audience, but they were the place where one role-player, who was to become President of the United States, discovered his identity.

"It has taken me many years to get used to seeing myself as others see me," Reagan wrote in his autobiography. "Very few of us ever see ourselves except as we look directly at ourselves in a mirror. Thus we don't know how we look from behind, from the side, walking, standing, moving normally through a room. It is quite a jolt." But the actor, Reagan says, learns to see himself from the outside in, as seen by others, not from the inside out. He gives up the "mental picture" of the character he plays as separate from himself. He becomes at once the viewer of the object and the object seen.

Movies use the mirror image again and again as a double of the self, and in particular as a split of the ideal self from its dark reflection. But the self that sees itself from all angles fragments and disappears into its image. The mirror, which points to a self outside of itself, is replaced by the screen, which obliterates the difference between the self and its reflection by absorbing the self into itself. Thus, as Nancy Reagan assures us, "there are not two Ronald Reagans." In her words, "[cynics] look in back of a statement of what the man really means. But it takes people a while to realize that with Ronnie you don't have to look in back of anything." She is describing a man whose most celebrated spontaneous moments—"Where do we find such men?" about the American D-Day dead; "I am paying for this microphone, Mr. Green," during the 1980 New Hampshire primary debate—are not only preserved and projected on film, but also turn out to be old lines from movies.

When in 1967 Governor Reagan refused to visit a mental hospital to see the effects of his cuts in state aid, a psychiatrist suggested that he was under strain. "If I get on that couch, it will be to take a nap," Reagan responded. He seems to have fulfilled Freud's lament that Americans lack an unconscious. Reagan does not seem to register, even in a return of the repressed, the real consequences of his wishes and his politics. He appears insulated not simply from external reality but from internal demons as well. Unlike earlier countersubversives, who also divided the world between the forces of good and an evil empire and traced all troubles at home and abroad to a conspiratorial center, Reagan does not seem possessed. As many commentators have noted, he combines political punitiveness with personal charm, right-wing principle and political salesmanship. Like a radio announcer or talk show host (he was both), he presents political events of his own making as if he were somehow not responsible for them. He promotes not the producer self who makes things happen, but the celebrity self who shows them off.

Robert Dallek has explained this disjunction between the form and content of Reagan's politics by invoking the twentieth-century shift from idols of production to idols of consumption. The hero of production was a hard-working figure, admired for his achievements. The idol of consumption is a celebrity; his (or her) appeal comes from looks, not action. The idol of production made durable goods. The idol of consumption is a salesman of the sold object. The former idol, like Reagan's rhetoric, acted on the supply side. The latter, like Reagan's tax cut, stimulates demand. The one flourishes in a manufacturing, the other in a service and information economy. The idol of production rose on its merits; the idol of consumption rises through good fortune, from

being in the right place at the right time. He is the chosen, not the chooser, the product, not the producer. He inhabits "a world of dependency," Leo Lowenthal writes in his classic study of the heroes of popular biography, "in which the average man is never alone and never wants to be alone." The President who urges a return to a time before Americans were "robbed of their independence" plays the values of production but does not live them, for he was formed as an idol of consumption.

The idol of production was inner-directed, aggressive and driven. A self-controlled ego, divided between duty and desire, he had a superego and an id. The celebrity pleases others; intimate before the mass audience, he plays privacy in public. Neither a repressed interior nor an intractable reality exercise claims over the celebrity, for he exists only in the eye of the beholder. Since he replaces reality with fantasy, his pleasure and reality principles do not collide. Freed from the reproaches of either conscience or the unconscious, he preserves a reassuring serenity.

Although idols of consumption increasingly displace idols of production in mass culture, other recent political leaders still evoke hard work and self-denial. No president before Reagan has come so completely from the world of entertainment and leisure. Since people are not images, however, neither Reagan nor any other human being is produced as a pure idol of consumption. The category represents an ideal type, an aspiration. Consumption idols respond in part to economic and social imperatives, but for Reagan the personal and the political converged on the movie screen.

The desire to have one's identity scripted on film is not unmotivated. Movies, we shall see, allowed Reagan to disown and enact aggression at one and the same time. Called to violence in his films, Reagan acted it in offhand and derealized forms. His roles taught the actor how to insulate himself from experiencing aggression as his own. He played characters who buried anger in wisecracks, suffered from external attack and employed violence in self-defense. The actor was directed to show the emotional effects of violence only when he was its victim. Otherwise, watching himself play one of the boys on screen, Reagan observed a figure with no distinctive, individuating, inwardly pointing signs. Buried, disturbing feelings, if there were any, dissolved in the reassurance that "Ronald Reagan" was like everyone else.

Reagan's detachment marks an important departure in the history of American political demonology. Puritans, for example, deliberately twinned themselves with their American Indian enemies, for "savages" were signs of man's fallen nature within. Subsequent countersubversives, on the other hand, crusading against aliens or blacks, denied the identity between themselves and their shadow sides. Their frenzy nevertheless revealed the connections their ideology tried to hide. Repressive politics in these traditional forms of countersubversion invite the analyst to psychoanalyze repression. But Reagan's affability, by insulating him from the subversive, seems to exclude the investigator as well. As Joel Kovel writes in distinguishing racial domination from racist avoidance: "The dominative racist, when threatened by the black, resorts to direct violence; the aversive racist, in the same situation turns away and walls himself off." Asked at the Great Wall of China if he would like a great wall of his own, President Reagan responded, "Around the White House." The joke points beyond the President's desire for physical safety to his wish for insulation. If traditional countersubversives consciously or unconsciously doubled themselves by means of their political demons, Reagan aspired to a self in which, to recall Nancy Reagan's words, there would not be two Ronald Reagans. There would not be two Reagans because the disowned, subversive part would have been lopped off. That wish for an amputated self was granted in Hollywood.

II

Ronald Reagan's entry into the movies was marked by an uncanny slippage between life and film. Other aspiring stars were rebaptized in Hollywood, receiving stage names to replace their own. Reagan had been baptized Ronald, his mother's choice, but he was always called by the nickname his father gave him, Dutch. Dutch Reagan came to Hollywood and proposed Ronald Reagan as his stage name. "Ronald Reagan, Ronald Reagan," repeated the head man, and the others around the table said it after him. "I like it," the boss decided, and gave Ronald Reagan back his own name. "That's my boy," Reagan's mother cried when she saw him in his first movie, *Love is on the Air* (1937). "That's the way he is at home. He's no Robert Taylor. He's just himself." Reagan was playing the role he'd left behind to come to Hollywood, that of a popular sports announcer. His real radio station had fired him under sponsor pressure and then rehired him; his movie station followed suit. In life, sports reporter Reagan invented play-by-play baseball games from minimal, ticker-tape reports. He embroidered on the sports events for his listeners. Movies audiences could confirm Reagan's filmed-on-the-spot reporting because the events they watched with him were staged.

More slippage occurred when Reagan met Jane Wyman on the set of another of his early movies, *Brother Rat* (1938). He dated her in the movie, married her in life; the studio then cast them as husband and wife in *An Angel from Texas* (1940), and Warner Brothers and Louella Parsons publicized their romance and happy marriage. "The Reagans' home life is probably just like yours, or yours, or yours," the studio quoted Reagan as saying. "Mr. Norm is my alias," the actor wrote in a 1940s movie magazine, presenting himself as the average American. Asked what the electorate saw in him on the eve of his 1980 victory, Reagan replied, "I think maybe they see themselves and that I'm one of them." On camera even when he was off-screen, Reagan seemed in the 1940s, as in the 1980s, to have nothing to hide, no self tucked away from public inspections.

It is a long way, nevertheless, from the 1940s to the 1980s, from a B-movie actor to President of the United States. *Murder in the Air*, even as it seems to collapse that distance, exposes it.

Ronald Reagan as Brass Bancroft, the secret agent, is too brash, too aggressive, too hard-edged. He does not convey reassurance and he is not a convincing actor. Distorted facial expressions and wooden gestures mar Reagan's performance in *Love is on the Air* as well. He does less indicating in *Murder in the Air,* but though he approaches a naturalistic performance, his cockiness is still exaggerated. Nothing seems to touch him. To acquire Presidential stature, Reagan had to combine the images of independence and dependence, power and loss, aggression and receptivity. He could not simply be seen to do damage to others; he had to appear to have damage done to him. He had to learn to be seen not simply as the man who sent American boys to die in Lebanon but, as in the film clip shown at the 1984 Republican convention, as the mourner identified with those who stand beside their coffins.

Reagan's persona as a B-movie crime fighter climaxed in a World War II film, *Desperate Journey* (1942). The movie perfectly exemplifies Béla Balázs' characterization of the American World War II films "in which the bloodiest catastrophe in world history is portrayed like an amusing, raw-humored manly adventure." Although Reagan, as Johnny Hammond, is trapped behind enemy lines for most of the movie, the war has no internal impact upon him. In the climatic scene of mass destruction, Reagan, Errol Flynn and Arthur Kennedy steal a German plane and Reagan, swiveling a machine gun in the bubble of the nose, mows down row after row of Germans as they rush to stop the aircraft from taking off. The slaughter is both horrifying and painless because the Germans have been portrayed as buffoons throughout the film. No one really gets hurt in *Desperate Journey,* since by not taking war seriously, the film turns war into a movie.

But the rugged individualists Reagan played in such films, even as organization men, were not protective, reassuring figures. Although Brass Bancroft is knocked out and left to drown during his adventures, both he and Johnny Hammond remain emotionally untouched by what they have been through. Since these characters communicate so little feeling, the viewer does not feel cared for by them. For Reagan to gain Presidential stature, he had to acquire a visibly vulnerable, objectified self to stand in for the self missing in action. To become a successful idol of consumption, he had to move beyond the rugged individualistic American past with which he wished to be identified. He did so by reconnecting through his film roles to his childhood experience of dependence and, by finding a cinematic substitute for that dependence, positioned himself to play freedom.

Warner Brothers was quick to spot the dependent side. The studio allowed him to win in B-movies, but made him lose in the feature. Reagan was Bette Davis' playboy boyfriend in *Dark Victory* (1939). He is mostly drunk on screen, and is never seen without a glass in his hand. Davis is aggressive, Reagan is passive. She begins the movie as his girl and turns to him in her refusal to face both her imminent death and her love for the fatherly doctor who operated (unsuccessfully) on her. Davis is a wired cigarette-smoking projectile, a spoiled, independent young woman. Her apotheosis is to turn into a good girl/wife and to die. Although the film is all too clear about what it wants from women, Reagan is not the beneficiary of Davis' surrender. Glass in hand, he relinquishes Davis to George Brent (Dr. Steele). Reagan hated playing that scene and refused to do so in the effeminate manner called for by the director. But although his performance is stilted, Reagan's character is not unsympathetic. *Dark Victory* foreshadowed a future in which Reagan could acquire heroic stature not simply by playing the tough guy, but by first enacting and then shedding his playboy persona.

Worried that he would be stuck in B movies, Reagan introduced Warner Brothers to the idea of a film about Knute Rockne. Reagan had played football all through his youth; he got his first radio job by simulating the end of a game his college had won in the last twenty seconds by using "the old Rockne special." Though Reagan missed his block in the actual game, he made it in his radio reconstruction. For the Knute Rockne movie, however, Reagan aspired higher than his college position on the line. He suggested Pat O'Brien for Rockne and himself for the legendary Notre Dame halfback, George Gipp. The studio cast O'Brien willingly, but did not think Reagan looked like a football player. He only got the part, with O'Brien's help, after ten other actors failed screen tests and after he showed the studio pictures of himself in his college football uniform. A journeyman actor like Reagan normally had little to say about his parts, but Reagan initiated *Knute Rockne* because he wanted to play the Gipper. It is his favorite role, and, as President, he invokes it again and again.

The Gipper is a small part; Reagan is on screen for barely fifteen minutes. "I would give my right arm for a halfback who could run, pass and kick," says Rockne, and he trips over the Gipper's feet. Reagan plays a rangy, good-looking, wise-cracking young man who scores a touchdown on his first run from scrimmage and makes long gains rushing or passing in game after game. But the football star is also an enigma. "I don't like people to get too close to me," on the field or off, he tells Rockne's wife. That admission comes in a moment of self-revelation when, in Rockne's absence and with his wife as mediatrix, the father-son love between the coach and his star is declared. As if the insulated, male American hero cannot survive that self-revelation, the Gipper immediately gets a sore throat, Rockne send him to the hospital and he dies of viral pneumonia.

But, as every American now knows, the Gipper lives on as an inspiration for Notre Dame and the country. Stricken by phlebitis years after Gipp's death, Rockne also faces defeatism on his team. He is wheeled to the annual Army–Notre Dame game in a wheelchair; at halftime with his players beaten and behind, Rockne repeats the Gipper's dying words. "Someday when the team is in trouble," Gipp has told Rockne, "tell them to win one for the Gipper." The inspired team members leap up and rush out onto the field. "That's for you, Gipp!" says the player who scores the first of many touchdowns that bring victory to Notre Dame.

At the 1981 Notre Dame commencement, in his first public appearance after he was shot, President Reagan insisted that the movie line, "Win one for the Gipper!" not be spoken "in a humorous vein." "Do it for the Gipper," Reagan told the U.S. Olympic team in the summer of 1984. "Win those races for the Gipper!" was how Reagan urged crowds to vote the straight Republican ticket during the fall campaign. But the Gipper (as played by Reagan) was dead when these words were spoken in the movie. If you elect Republicans, Reagan told the crowds, "wherever I am, I'll know about it, and it'll make me happy." The President spoke as if playing the Gipper, he were witness to his own death and ascension. After his defeat at the 1976 Republican convention, Reagan quoted lines he'd memorized as a child: "Lay me down and bleed a while. Though I am wounded, I am not slain. I shall rise and fight again." Slain as George Gipp, Reagan rose to fight again, to invoke the spirit of the dead hero into whom he had dissolved.

Knute Rockne doubles the theme of regenerative sacrifice by having Rockne reenact Gipp's martyrdom. The coach risks his life to attend the football game when he has phlebitis, speaks the Gipper's line from a wheelchair with a blanket over his legs and dies in a plane crash soon after. A priest tells the mourners at Rockne's funeral, "The spirit of Knute Rockne is reborn in the youth of today." "It's like seeing a younger son I never knew I had," Reagan jokes when he watches reruns of *Knute Rockne*. The sacrifice of that son first knit the team and then the country together. But whereas Gipp's sacrifice brought down the film father, Knute Rockne, it gave birth to the actor father, now President, Ronald Reagan.

The sacrifice of Reagan/Gipp broke down the boundary between not only son and father, Gipp and Rockne, but also the boundary between human body and body politic. In his speech to the joint session of Congress after he was shot, Reagan shifted from his own recovery to his economic recovery program for the nation. He identified the healing of his body with his program to restore health to America. The President was employing a very old symbolism, one that conflates the body of a leader with the body of his realm, and derives both body mortal and body politic from the body of Christ. As if anticipating the attempted assassination, Gipp's death had merged the mortal body with the corpus mysticum. The Gipper's sacrifice was mediated through film, however, and not religious ceremony, pointing to the shift in the locus of sacred value from the Church to Hollywood. Reagan could claim to embody the nation, exploiting the boundary confusion between the President's body and the body politic because he had risen from the confusion between life and film.

Knute Rockne inverted Reagan's familial past, replacing an unreliable, dependent father with an idealized strong one, and transforming forbidden anger at the historical father into the film son's sacrifice. That self-sacrifice was Reagan's gift to his real father, just as Reagan's need to deny the conflicts in his personal history attracted him to the idealized father in Rockne. Idealization buried anger, and though the idealized father was also sacrificed, *Knute Rockne* left no room for the aggression that fed the young Reagan's sacrificial desire. The film in which Reagan actually reinhabited his past in order to emancipate himself from it is *King's Row*, the movie that made him a star, that he places at the center of his autobiography and that he has singled out as the film with the deepest personal significance for his life.

III

> My face was blue from screaming, my bottom was red from whacking, and my father claimed afterward that he was white when he said shakily, "For such a little bit of a fat Dutchman, he makes a hell of a lot of noise. . . . " "I think he's perfectly wonderful," said my mother weakly. "Ronald Wilson Reagan."

Blue face, red bottom, white father: "I have been particularly fond of the colors that were exhibited," announces the author, wrapping himself at birth in the American flag. We are on the first page of Ronald Reagan's autobiography, *Where's the Rest of Me?* "In those early days I

was living the whole life of Reagan," he continues. "It was not until thirty years later that I found that part of my existence was missing."

The missing part of Reagan's existence was his legs, and he lost them in *King's Row*. Some might find that loss troublesome, but it was the making of the actor's career. In his words, "I took the part of Drake McHugh, the gay young blade who cast a swathe among the ladies." Reagan romanced the town surgeon's daughter. When a railroad accident knocked him unconscious, the "sadistic doctor" took his revenge. He "amputated both my legs at the hips." Reagan woke in a hospital bed to speak the line that made him a star: "Where's the rest of me?"

Those five words, Reagan reports, presented him with the most challenging acting problem of his career. He had to become a legless man, or the line would not carry conviction.

> I rehearsed the scene before mirrors, in the corners of the studio, while driving home, in the men's room at restaurants, before selected friends. At night I would wake up staring at the ceiling and automatically mutter the lines before I went back to sleep. I consulted physicians and psychologists; I even talked to people who were so disabled, trying to brew in myself the cauldron of emotions a man must feel who wakes up one sunny morning to find half of himself gone.

When at last Reagan climbed into bed to shoot the scene, "in some weird way, I felt that something horrible had happened to my body." Trying "to reach for where my legs should be," and twisting in panic, Reagan delivered in a single take the finest shot of his career. "The reason was that I had put myself, as best I could, in the body of another fellow." But Drake McHugh was not simply "another fellow," for Reagan made a discovery about himself (that he was only "half a man," that "part of my existence was missing") in *King's Row*. Why should the body of a legless man have possessed Reagan so personally?

Reagan begins *Where's the Rest of Me?* with his birth, switches to his rebirth in *King's Row* and then returns to his father. Jack Reagan was a shoe salesman. "He loved shoes. He sold them as a clerk . . . and spent many hours analyzing the bones of the foot." But Jack Reagan failed as a shoe salesman, and his son remembers at age eleven coming upon his father "flat on his back on the front porch, . . . his arms spread out as if he were crucified," passed out from drink. Jack Reagan was an alcoholic. He had lost "another bout with the dark demon of the bottle," and the son had to overcome "the sharp odor of whiskey" to drag his father into the house. Jack Reagan "never lost the conviction that the individual must stand on his own feet," but he could not do so himself. He survived the Depression by distributing relief checks for the WPA.

Like many another self-made man, this son who celebrates the family had first to escape his own. How, if your father is a failed shoe salesman, do you avoid stepping into his shoes? *King's Row* provided the answer: by cutting off your legs. The Christian loses himself as body to find himself as spirit. Reagan was born again in Hollywood by relinquishing "part of myself" in *King's Row.*

King's Row is set, a sign announces at the beginning of the film, in "A good clean town—A good town to live in, a good place to raise your children," like Tampico, Illinois, where Reagan was born, or Dixon, where he grew up. But the American family in *King's Row* turns out to consist of sadistic fathers, demonic mothers and daughters whose dangerous sexual desires place young men in jeopardy. Parris Mitchell (Robert Cummings) is drawn (in the Tower family) into maternal insanity, implied father–daughter incest (explicit in the book), and the power of the father (Claude Rains) who kills his daughter and himself. Drake McHugh confronts (in the Gordon family) a monstrous mother (Judith Anderson), a sexually sadistic father and the loss of his legs. *King's Row* is an American Gothic melodrama. Although it sides with good, it is fascinated by evil. It illustrates the shift from the wise-cracking surface of 1930s Hollywood movies to 1940s psychological nightmares (and its director, Sam Wood, would become obsessed with the dangers of Communist influence in Hollywood in the years after World War II).

Reagan underscores the connection between *King's Row* and his own youth. He calls the film

"a slightly sordid but moving yarn about antics in a small town, something I had more than a slight acquaintance with"; then he describes the movie's "accident in the railroad yards" in which a moving train that is supposed to be stationary costs Drake McHugh his legs. A few pages later Reagan reports an escapade in which his brother and he crawled under a train stopped at the town station, getting to the other side just before the train pulled out. The notion of "antics" allows Reagan to place himself within the movie by shutting out its horror, his form of acknowledgment by denial. Still, the Towers and Gordons are hardly replicas of the Reagans. In spite of the family's poverty, the father's alcoholism and the several moves from one small town and shoe salesman's job to another, Reagan remembers a happy childhood. That must be part of the truth; yet the son who, influenced by his mother, "could feel no resentment against" his passed-out father is dissociated from his feelings. *King's Row* supplied a target for Reagan's anger by relocating it outside himself. It provided the negative family from which Reagan had cut himself off. The movie reunited him to his problematic history in order, by amputation, to free him from it.

In her psychological study of the President, Betty Glad addresses the anger young Reagan was not allowed to feel; similarly, Robert Dallek emphasizes Reagan's fear of helplessness. Dallek locates the President's political hostility to dependence in his need to separate himself from his dependent father. Such a need would illuminate Reagan's resistance to playing the alcoholic role in *Dark Victory*. But the "dark demon" of alcohol pointed not just to Jack Reagan's helplessness, but to the son's in the face of his father. *King's Row* not only gave Reagan a target for anger, but also allowed him to reexperience and conquer his helplessness.

Drake McHugh feels defeated after his legs are cut off until he discovers who to blame. "Where did Doctor Gordon think I lived, in my legs?" Drake scoffs when he learns that the doctor amputates his legs not to save his life but to turn him into "a lifelong cripple." Drake's anger at Gordon frees him from self-pity, and he and his wife go on to make their fortune in real estate. At the film's end they move into one of the new houses in a suburb outside King's Row. The two films that made Reagan a star supplied him with an idealized authority to sacrifice and a sadistic authority to overcome. Jack Reagan died between the filmings of *Knute Rockne* and *King's Row*. Freed from the gothic small town, Reagan would reinhabit, as fantasy life for millions, an ideal version of the American past.

Filmed amputation did not emancipate Reagan from his father, however. It made Drake McHugh helpless, cared for by a maternal woman as Nelle Reagan had cared for Jack. That may have constituted a happy ending in film and childhood fantasy, but it came at the price of manhood. Drake has had sexual romance with Randy Monaghan, his working-class Irish girl-friend, before he loses his money and his legs. Drake's poverty, which sends him to the railway station job, brings him closer to Reagan's child-hood. But when Drake marries Randy, as both the book and the movie make explicit, he has lost his sexuality. *King's Row* freed Reagan from his father by placing him under female power.

Reagan still inhabits *King's Row*. He made it the center of his autobiography, he watched it again and again with Jane Wyman and their guests, he watches it with Nancy Reagan and he chose its music as the fanfare for his 1980 inauguration. But the *King's Row* solution created a problem, Reagan says in his autobiography, that plagued him for the remainder of his Hollywood career.

"An actor spends half his waking hours in fantasy," Reagan wrote. "If he is only an actor, I feel, he is much like I was in *King's Row*, only half a man." No line better speaks to an actor's condition, wrote Reagan, than "Where's the rest of me?" That is why he left Hollywood. As an actor Reagan had lost his "freedom." He was "a semi-automaton, 'creating' a character another had written." Deciding to "find the rest of me . . . I came out of the monastery of movies into the world." Warner Brothers would not let Reagan play the traditional hero on the screen. The studio deprived him of the idealized self he wanted to enact and gave him parts that exposed his weakness instead. Reagan shifted from film to

reality in order to cast reality in terms of make-believe, stand up for America in another Hollywood drama and end Communist influence in the movies.

IV

Reagan was in the army when *King's Row* appeared. Stationed in Hollywood, he made training, morale and re-enlistment movies for soldiers, defense workers and the public. Although never close to combat, Reagan did participate, he reports, in "one of the better-kept secrets of the war, ranking up with the atom bomb project." "Everyone who has ever seen a picture based on World War II," writes Reagan, will recognize the briefing in which he played a role. To prepare pilots to bomb Tokyo, Hollywood special effects men built a complete miniature of the city. They "intercut their movies of the model with real scenes taken from flights over Tokyo," thereby creating a series of movies that enacted bombing runs. Reagan narrated the films, and each one concluded "when my voice said, 'Bombs away.'" Reagan's account of his wartime service slips from the Manhattan project to the moving picture theater, from real war to a mock-up of war. To make himself a participant, Reagan breaks down the distinction between real bombs and simulated bombing runs. As a result, none of the explosives in his account, from the bombs he narrates to the atom bomb, fall on real targets. When Reagan told crowds in his first campaign for governor that he served as an adjutant at an Air Force base, he did not mention that it was in the film community.

As if to compensate for taking care of Reagan during the war, Hollywood cast him in a series of postwar films that placed him in the wrong kind of danger. Before *King's Row,* Reagan had played the young Custer in *Santa Fe Trail* (1940) and, in *International Squadron* (1941), a carefree RAF pilot who atones for his costly nonchalance by dying on a heroic mission. These roles, which came from his success as the Gipper, joined heroism to sacrifice. But *King's Row* type-cast the actor as a figure vulnerable not in combat but in romantic entanglements. The characters

Reagan played after the war were invaded by illness and by women.

Reagan wanted a big-budget western for his first postwar film. The studio cast him instead in the black-and-white *Stallion Road* (1947). The movie "opened the door to finding another part of me," writes Reagan. He brought the horse he rode in the movie, changed its name to Tarbaby (its name in *Stallion Road*) and, imitating the character he portrayed, acquired a horse ranch. But Reagan does not play a western hero in the film. He is a veterinarian who develops a serum that saves cattle from an anthrax epidemic, but then catches the disease himself. Given up for dead, he is nursed back to health by Alexis Smith. In *Night Unto Night* (1949), the Reagan character has epilepsy. He has lost the will to live and plans suicide, but is saved by Viveca Linfors' love. In *The Hasty Heart* (1950), Richard Todd plays a soldier dying of a fatal disease and Reagan is reduced to feigning illness in order to remain at Todd's side. Todd won an Academy Award nomination. As Grover Cleveland Alexander in *The Winning Team* (1952), his last Warner Brothers film, Reagan makes a comeback from epilepsy. In *Tennessee's Partner* (1955), Reagan's penultimate Hollywood movie, he plays an unworldly cowboy, humiliated by a woman, who dies saving the life of his best friend.

Reagan did not always sicken or die in his postwar films, but women invariably gave him trouble. Romantic comedies like *That Hagen Girl* (1947), *Louisa* (1950), *Bedtime for Bonzo* (1951) and *She's Working Her Way Through College* (1952), with their erratic women and emasculated leading man, exemplify domestic anxieties on the postwar Hollywood screen. The films also, to recall the President's words, tell us something not simply about how Reagan looked to the casting directors but about how he felt as well. Resenting accusations that he "never got the girl" in his movies, Reagan once listed all the girls he got. "I always got the girl," he insisted, but as he knew at the time, the issue was not *whether* he got the girl but *how*. His list included girls he got by losing his legs, by nearly dying of epilepsy and anthrax, and by undergoing other forms of humiliation. He got the girl by being

dependent. Reagan did not like making these movies and left Warner Brothers because of them. He found the roles particularly disturbing because they mirrored his private life.

Soon after he caught anthrax in *Stallion Road*, Reagan came down with viral pneumonia. That disease, which killed George Gipp, almost killed him. Jane Wyman was several months pregnant and, under the strain from Reagan's illness, she gave premature birth to a stillborn baby. The next year, 1948, she filed for divorce. "I was notified that I was going to be a bachelor again," Reagan writes. "I came home from England and broke my leg in a half a dozen places." Reagan wanted domesticity, but Wyman preferred a more glamorous life. She "couldn't stand," she complained, "to watch that damn *King's Row* one more time." Wyman's career was rising, while Reagan's was in decline. When she won an Academy Award for her role in *Johnny Belinda*, Reagan quipped, "I think I'll name *Johnny Belinda* as the co-respondent." Their separate careers, as Reagan saw it, had taken his wife from him. Reagan's career diverged from Wyman's, however, not because they both made movies—and this is the reason other than watching *King's Row* she gave for leaving him—but because he was turning from movies to anti-Communist politics.

In 1946, five years after Drake McHugh asked, "Where's the rest of me?" Reagan recalls that "under different circumstances than make-believe, I had to ask myself the same question." He answered it by leading the fight against "the Communist plan . . . to take over the motion picture business." "We had a weekly audience of about 500,000 souls. Takeover of this enormous plant and its gradual transformation into a Communist grist mill was a grandiose idea. It would have been a magnificent coup for our enemies." Reagan, as he tells it, recovered his legs in the struggle to prevent a Communist takeover of Hollywood.

"Russ Imperialism Seen By Veteran," ran the headline over a 1950 story in the *Los Angeles Times*. "A former captain of the Army Air Force," as the story identified him, "Reagan portrayed the screen as the great purveyor of information about the American way of life[. He] said it was this that Red Russia cannot match, so it tried to take over. When it failed, he said, it tried various schemes to ruin the industry. 'The Russians sent their first team, their ace string, here to take us over,' he said. 'We were up against hard-core organizers.'"

The fantasy of Communists taking over Hollywood was delusional, the stuff of a Hollywood movie. But two factors gave credence to this delusion and made it continuous with mundane life. The first was the presence of significant numbers of Communists in the motion picture business in the 1930s and '40s. They had little influence on movie content, but they were not imaginary. The second was the widely shared belief in their conspiratorial power. Reagan, a supporter of FDR, had joined with the Communists in popular-front organizations; when he turned against them, he remained a New Deal liberal. He was a founder and national board member of Americans for Democratic Action, a supporter of Harry Truman and Hubert Humphrey. Reagan's cold war liberalism did not make him soft on Communism, however. It rather testified to universal hysteria. The actor was forced neither to see his fear of subversion as one perception among many nor to repress acceptable political alternatives; his was the only legitimate point of view. Reagan's demonology was not marginal, a sign of personal disturbance. It was the norm.

Reagan's enlightenment about Communism in postwar Hollywood defines the founding moment of the politics in which we now live. As President, Reagan brought with him to Washington other men who had participated in intelligence work during World War II and then shifted to the fight against Communism. There was a romance of World War II in 1940s America that was denied to countries on whose soil the war was fought. President Reagan has revived that romance, filtered it through Hollywood and frozen it at the moment when Nazis turned into Communists (in theory, of course, for real ones went to work for American intelligence). Reagan learned that Communists were "monsters," he told Bob Scheer in 1980, "when they were trying

to take over Hollywood." He learned then what he still believes, that "the Soviet Union was the mother lode, the center, which controlled subversives around the world."

Hollywood anti-Communism, as Reagan understood it, restored his independence by freeing him from make-believe. But Communist influence was not the only fantasy Reagan took with him from the movies; he took the fantasy of independence as well. Reagan wore a gun during his postwar battle with the Communists in order to protect himself from red reprisals. As he put it, "I mounted the holstered gun religiously every morning and took it off last thing at night." Pioneer heroism and Indian war had moved from American history into Hollywood fantasy. "We are for the free enterprise system," Reagan told the Los Angeles Rotary Club in 1948. "We have fought our little Red brothers all along the line." Reagan meant Communists, but his phrase evoked American Indians. Shifting from one red enemy to another, Reagan brought frontier individualism back into history again.

Reagan is fond of quoting Sterling Hayden's testimony before HUAC that the Communists were taking over Hollywood until "we ran into a one-man battalion named Ronnie Reagan." But the man alone in Hollywood was actually a victim of corporate, countersubversive cooperation. HUAC, the motion picture industry, the unions and private agencies like the American Legion all worked together, blacklisting those who refused to name names. As President of the Screen Actors' Guild (SAG), the one-man battalion joined a surveillance network that imitated the enemy it was designed to destroy.

Reagan was drawn to SAG, he wrote in his autobiography, because it was an avenue to the stars. When he walked into the union board room, he "saw it crowded with the famous men of the business. I knew that I was beginning to find the rest of me." The statement unwittingly replaces the legs that rooted him to his failed father by the support of famous men. Reagan rejected the Left, he told Tom Hayden, when he discovered that it operated through secret caucuses in large, popular-front organizations. He had given the same testimony before HUAC decades earlier. Reagan had innocently lent his name to a charitable cause, he told the Committee, only to find out that the Communists were using him. The discovery that he was being "spoon-fed and steered" transferred him from innocent victim to one-man battalion.

But Reagan prefers playing the one-man battalion to living it. "He simply looks to someone to tell him what to do," says his former campaign manager John Sears. "He can be guided." Reagan agrees. When former press spokesman Larry Speakes stepped in front of him to ward off a reporter's question about the reappointment of Anne Burford, the President quipped, "My guardian says I can't talk." Asked on another occasion if he thought of Michael Deaver, his closest aide, as a son, Reagan replied, "Gee, I always thought of him more as a father figure." Reagan has found the support his father had, but did not give him.

That process climaxed during the Hollywood inquisition. Refusing to be manipulated as a front for the Communists, Reagan fronted instead for the powerful men in Hollywood who led the fight against Communist influence. He found the rest of him playing a one-man battalion and hiding the rest of himself, which guided that battalion behind the scenes. Replacing the personal with the political, Reagan helped orchestrate a blacklist whose existence he denied.

"There was no blacklist in Hollywood. The blacklist in Hollywood, if there was one, was provided by the Communists," Reagan told Bob Scheer in 1980. But as President of SAG from 1947 to 1952, and member (and President for one year) of the Motion Picture Industry Council, Reagan enforced the blacklist. He supported a provision in the Guild constitution barring Communists from membership. He told the actress Gail Sondergaard, after she took the Fifth Amendment before HUAC, that the union opposed a blacklist. "On the other hand, if any actor by his actions outside of union activities has so offended public opinion that he has made himself unemployable at the box office, the Guild cannot and would not force any employer to hire him." Reagan refused to defend Sondergaard because she would not become an informer. But

he met with repentant ex-radicals to help them cooperate with HUAC, name names, rehabilitate themselves and continue to work in the movies.

When he joined the fight against Communism, Reagan put the Reds in Drake McHugh's place, for they became the sacrificial victims. By casting Communists from the body politic, Reagan directed his violence away from authority and outside the family circle. But, whereas he presented the shift from Drake McHugh to anti-Communism as a restoration of his legs, he actually acquired institutional support to substitute for his family of origin. Reagan displaced his dependence on others—those ruled by the monstrous "mother lode"—and punished them for his desire.

V

Anti-Communism gave Reagan an explanation for and an alternative to his declining Hollywood career. It also, he tells us, supplied him with a new wife. Reagan met Nancy Davis when, as SAG President, he established that she was not the Nancy Davis on a list of Communist sympathizers. "That's the girl I've decided to marry," Drake McHugh says of the surgeon's daughter. But the surgeon cuts off his legs, and he ends up with a working-class woman instead. Reagan learned on his first date with Nancy that her father "was one of the world's truly great surgeons"; the actor was on crutches because he had broken his leg. Reagan lost Bette Davis in *Dark Victory* to a neurological surgeon old enough to be her father. He married the daughter of a neurological surgeon, a woman who, unlike Jane Wyman, would subordinate her career to his. "My life began when I got married. My life began with Ronnie," says Nancy Reagan. "If Ronnie were a shoe salesman, I'd be out selling shoes."

Reagan had once been, as he put it, "a near-hopeless hemophiliac liberal. I bled for 'causes': I had voted Democratic, following my father, in every election." He left behind Jack Reagan's politics when he married Loyal Davis' daughter, and adopted the punitive, right-wing politics of the surgeon. Backed by the Movie Corporation of America (MCA), Reagan hosted the GE Television Theater in the 1950s and, like Drake McHugh, made his fortune in real estate. Together, his new politics, his new wealth and his new family made him whole. The autobiography ends with Clark Gable's reminder, "The most important thing a man can know is that, when he approaches his own door, someone on the other side is listening for the sound of his footsteps." The actor has his legs back; his concluding sentence is, "I have found the rest of me."

Bodily metaphors and the language of doctors and patients run through the Reagan Presidency. The President presented himself as the healing body after he was shot, shifting from the doctors who had improved his health to his own plan to restore health to the economy. He has also compared "cutting back on the runaway growth of government" to "performing surgery on a patient to save his life." Being a lame duck would not hinder his efforts to cut government spending, Reagan told his cabinet secretaries at their first meeting after his reelection. "I'll put a cast on that lame leg, and that will make it a heck of a kicking leg." To prove independence, not so easy in a corporate world, the President acquires power over others, and punishes those dependent on him. Reagan has successfully merged aggressor and victim, surgeon and patient, Dr. Gordon and Drake McHugh.

Reagan did not slay his father and rise above him. Rather, by identifying with his father's wound and his mother's denial, he inherited both the father's need for support and the mother's cheerful blindness to internal trouble. Reagan's first marriage and his postwar roles had called attention to his dependency needs without gratifying them. His new marriage and new politics provided upward mobility based neither on the rugged independence of the self-made hero nor on ties to an actual past, but on corporate and domestic support. Fearful that dependence exposed the self to aggression, Reagan did not relinquish the desire for care; he instead found caretakers he could trust. The President was silent in response to a reporter's question on arms control until he repeated aloud his wife's whisper, "Doing all we can." Reagan has realized

the dream of the American male—to be taken care of in the name of independence, to be supported while playing the man in charge.

VI

The Communists failed to capture Hollywood, according to Reagan, but they initiated a series of costly studio strikes that caused the decline of Hollywood as entertainment capital of the world. Reagan does not regret that decline for himself, he implies, for he became whole only when he stopped making movies. The autobiography's final chapters comprise an elegy for Hollywood, suggesting that Reagan rescued that world by transferring it to Washington. And his final movies form a bridge from the actor to the President.

Reagan left Warner Brothers so he could choose his own roles. He wanted to make westerns, and his first post–Warner Brothers film was *The Last Outpost* (1951). While fighting Communists off-screen, he fought American Indians in front of the camera. Just as Truman supporters thought the Communist threat should unite Democrats and Republicans, so the Apache danger in *The Last Outpost* united Union and Confederate soldiers. Reagan starred in several other westerns in the early '50s; he also made a cold war parable, *Storm Warning* (1951), in which the Ku Klux Klan stands in for the Communist Party. But, though we think of Reagan as a movie cowboy, he apparently does not want to be seen shooting anyone. Reagan mimed a cowboy firing his six-shooters after American planes shot down Libyan jets in 1981, but he did so in front of his aides—not the television cameras.

Reagan's movies played with hidden identity from the beginning (*Accidents Will Happen* [1938] and *Murder in the Air* [1940]) to the end (*Cattle Queen of Montana* [1954] and *Prisoner of War* [1954]) of his career. He portrayed characters who joined criminal of subversive organizations in order to expose them, allowing the innocent actor to participate in forbidden activities. Although the theme of identity confusion was appropriate for an actor who found his identity through film, the process threatened to raise doubts about who Reagan actually was. He came to rest in his final Hollywood movie, *Hellcats of the Navy* (1957), the film that successfully turned Dr. Gordon into Drake McHugh. I shall end where I began, with a World War II film.

Reagan plays Casey Abbott, a submarine commander accused of making military decisions for personal motives. *Hellcats* opens with frogmen leaving the sub to bring back Japanese mines. Abbott submerges his vessel to escape a Japanese destroyer, thereby abandoning one frogman who has not yet returned to the sub. The frogman was romancing Abbott's former girlfriend, and the ship's lieutenant, Don Landon, thinks that is why the captain left him behind to die. Nurse Helen Blair, the woman in question, is played by Nancy Reagan.

Abbott won't risk the sub to save his rival. He risks it instead to chart a path through the underwater mines. The ship is sunk, and although Abbott and Landon survive, sixty men, riddled with bullets or trapped below, die. Landon accuses his captain of endangering the sub for personal glory. But it is Landon, not Abbott, the film tells us, who confuses personal needs with military necessity.

Abbott is trapped in a twisted cable outside the sub in the movie's climactic scene. A Japanese destroyer is approaching, and Landon must decide whether to submerge the vessel. The men on the ship are your responsibility, Abbott tells Landon, advocating his own death. Like Abbott before him, Landon must be mature enough to sacrifice a rival, not for reasons of personal hostility but for national security. Miraculously, however, when the ship surfaces Abbott is still alive. He has freed himself at the last minute form the cable. Although the conscious mind knows that Abbott survived by not submerging with the ship, the imagery suggests death and resurrection.

Abbott had broken off his romance with Helen to protect her from the risks of war. But she never stopped loving him, remaining loyal in the face of suspicion that he deliberately killed the man who took his place. By reenacting his rival's sacrifice, Abbott frees himself from the charge of bad motive; he is now united with the men who died under his command. Since Abbott is above suspicion, he can have a personal life. At the movie's end he and Helen prepare to wed. Reagan's final Hollywood movie, mixing life and film in the end, supplied him with the perfect marriage of military and familial authority. It is not the commander-in-chief who is contaminated by bad motives, says the film, but subordinates (Landon the junior officer, Rogin the critic) who can't accept his authority.

The Nancy Reagan film shown at the 1984 Republican convention cut from shots of her among children and drug abusers to a scene from *Hellcats of the Navy*. Nancy Reagan, who cried real tears while filming that scene, repeats her faith in the commander as he leaves on his climactic voyage. In cutting from life to the movie, the Republican National Committee may seem to have exposed the manufactured nature of its real-life image of the President's wife. But another film event suggests that the media men deliberately dissolved the boundary between life and image to offer us the reassurance of film. The President reelected in 1984 does not promote the telescreen as an instrument of surveillance and personal invasion on which Big Brother is watching you. Instead he offers freedom from public and private anxieties by allowing you to watch Big Brother. When Nancy Reagan spoke at the convention following the film of her life, Ronald Reagan watched her on television from their hotel suite. "Make it one more for the Gipper," she urged, and the mass television audience (including him) saw her tiny figure turn with arms raised, in support of an enormous image on the screen behind her, larger than life. On camera in the hotel room, the image watched itself wave back, forming the truncated head and shoulders of her husband, the President of the United States.